MW01253044

# The Questioning Child

Questioning others is one of the most powerful methods that children use to learn about the world. How does questioning develop? How is it socialized? And how can questioning be leveraged to support learning and education? In this volume, some of the world's leading experts are brought together to explore critical issues in the development of questioning. By collecting interdisciplinary and international perspectives from psychology and education, *The Questioning Child* presents research from a variety of distinct methodological and theoretical backgrounds. It synthesizes current knowledge on the role of question-asking in cognitive development and charts a path forward for researchers and educators to understand the pivotal function that questioning plays in child development and education.

**Lucas Payne Butler** is Assistant Professor of Human Development at the University of Maryland, College Park. His work focuses on how children leverage their understanding of the social world in order to guide learning from evidence, and how children learn to evaluate others' empirical claims.

**Samuel Ronfard** is Assistant Professor of Psychology at the University of Toronto Mississauga. His work explores how children learn about, come to believe in, and come to understand ideas and concepts that defy their everyday experiences and their intuitive theories about how the world works.

**Kathleen H. Corriveau** is Associate Professor of Applied Human Development at Boston University, and Director of the Social Learning Lab. Her research focuses on social and cognitive development in childhood, with a specific focus on how children decide what people and what information are trustworthy sources.

# Tables

# Figures

# Contents

To Caroline, Chandler, Elena, Jacob, Julian, and Nicolas – our own questioning children

# CAMBRIDGE
## UNIVERSITY PRESS

University Printing House, Cambridge CB2 8BS, United Kingdom

One Liberty Plaza, 20th Floor, New York, NY 10006, USA

477 Williamstown Road, Port Melbourne, VIC 3207, Australia

314–321, 3rd Floor, Plot 3, Splendor Forum, Jasola District Centre,
New Delhi – 110025, India

79 Anson Road, #06–04/06, Singapore 079906

Cambridge University Press is part of the University of Cambridge.

It furthers the University's mission by disseminating knowledge in the pursuit of
education, learning, and research at the highest international levels of excellence.

www.cambridge.org
Information on this title: www.cambridge.org/9781108428910
DOI: 10.1017/9781108553803

© Cambridge University Press 2020

First published 2020

Printed in the United Kingdom by TJ International Ltd. Padstow Cornwall

*A catalogue record for this publication is available from the British Library.*

ISBN 978-1-108-42891-0 Hardback

Cambridge University Press has no responsibility for the persistence or accuracy of
URLs for external or third-party internet websites referred to in this publication
and does not guarantee that any content on such websites is, or will remain,
accurate or appropriate.

# The Questioning Child

*Insights from Psychology and Education*

*Edited by*

## Lucas Payne Butler
*University of Maryland*

## Samuel Ronfard
*University of Toronto*

## Kathleen H. Corriveau
*Boston University*

CAMBRIDGE
UNIVERSITY PRESS

# Contributors

MAUREEN CALLANAN, University of California, Santa Cruz

PETER CARRUTHERS, University of Maryland, College Park

CLAUDIA CASTAÑEDA, University of California, Santa Cruz

MARY GAUVAIN, University of California, Riverside

ROBERTA MICHNICK GOLINKOFF, University of Delaware

PAUL L. HARRIS, Harvard University

TONE KRISTINE HERMANSEN, The Norwegian Center for Child Behavioral Development

KATHY HIRSH-PASEK, Temple University, Brookings Institute

JENNIFER JIPSON, California Polytechnic State University, San Luis Obispo

ANGELA JONES, Max Planck Institute for Human Development, Berlin

DEANNA KUHN, Columbia University

KELSEY LUCCA, University of Washington

CANDICE M. MILLS, University of Texas at Dallas

ANAHID S. MODREK, University of California, Los Angeles

CAROLINE MORANO, University of Delaware

ROBERT L. MUNROE, Pitzer College

DAVE NEALE, University of Delaware

ANGELA NYHOUT, University of Toronto

JONATHAN OSBORNE, Stanford University

EMILY REIGH, Stanford University

MEREDITH L. ROWE, Harvard University

AZZURRA RUGGERI, Max Planck Institute for Human Development, Berlin, and School of Education, Technical University of Munich

WILLIAM A. SANDOVAL, University of California, Los Angeles

KAITLIN R. SANDS, University of Texas at Dallas

GRACIELA SOLIS, Loyola University Chicago

NORA SWABODA, Max Planck Institute for Human Development, Berlin

BRIAN N. VERDINE, University of Delaware

CAREN M. WALKER, University of California, San Diego

HENRY M. WELLMAN, University of Michigan

IMAC MARIA ZAMBRANA, The Norewegian Center for Child Behavioral Development, and University of Oslo

# 1 Questions about Questions
## Framing the Key Issues

*Lucas Payne Butler, Samuel Ronfard, Kathleen H. Corriveau*

How do children make sense of the world around them? One theoretical approach emphasizes how children actively construct an evolving understanding of the world as they interact with it in the course of everyday life. Like "little scientists," children independently track patterns and regularities in their environment, make inferences on the basis of those patterns, and test out and revise hypotheses as they accumulate relevant evidence. Another theoretical approach emphasizes how children learn by paying attention to others, as well as from direct instruction. This approach emphasizes children's dependence on information they receive from other people. Despite the complementary nature of these two approaches, research steeped in each tradition often operates independently from the other. Some research has focused on how children acquire information through first-hand observation and experimentation (e.g., Carey & Gelman, 1991; Gopnik & Schulz, 2007; Weisberg et al., 2015). Other research has focused on children's sensitivity to the types of individuals who are good sources of information (see Harris, 2012; Harris et al., 2018). In both learning approaches, children's use of questions is critical: Questions complement children's independent first-hand investigations of the world, and questions redirect instruction and modify the input they receive from individuals. Further, questioning may provide a conduit for the socialization of information-seeking. That is, the ways in which peers, parents, and educators ask and answer questions may play a critical role in shaping children's approach to searching for and making use of information as they go about constructing a conceptual understanding of the world. These two complementary uses of questioning, as well as the potential ways in which they are socialized and shaped by the environment, highlight the importance of understanding the role of questioning in learning and development, both for researchers aiming to generate a broad understanding of how children develop as well as for parents and educators who accompany children in that development. And yet, relative

1

to other aspects of children's inquiry, research on children's questions has been relatively sparse.

Research on question-asking behaviors has been conducted across a number of disciplines, most notably in psychology and education. Research in psychology has focused on the role of domain-general cognitive abilities and on the role of prior knowledge as constraints on children's question-asking behaviors, and has gathered information about the development of question-asking from infancy to elementary school. Research in education has examined how the ability to formulate questions and use them to guide inquiry can be taught to students, as well as how the development of this skill impacts various aspects of students' learning, from reading comprehension to their ability to engage in scientific inquiry. However, despite obvious synergies between these different approaches to investigating questioning in learning and development, rarely has research across these disciplines been brought together. This diversity of perspectives makes this volume unique insofar as many of these researchers might not otherwise appear alongside one another. Our goal in editing this volume was to bring together an interdisciplinary and international group of experts in psychology and education, representing a variety of distinct methodological and theoretical backgrounds. The inclusion of diverse perspectives allows for a broader synthesis than would otherwise be possible, and results in a volume wherein researchers and educators from diverse backgrounds can gain new knowledge and develop a fuller, interdisciplinary understanding of how questions play a pivotal role in child development and education. Ultimately, this volume synthesizes the current knowledge on the role of question-asking in cognitive development and learning, with the hope that it will stimulate interdisciplinary dialogue, galvanize interest, and stimulate collaboration and further research on the topic of questioning in development.

Taken together, the chapters in this volume answer three broad questions. First, **where do questions come from, and how do children engage in questioning across development?** There are several key issues here. One encompasses when and how questions begin in development, including whether they are initially rooted in affective or noncognitive attitudes or whether they are metacognitive from the outset, and what the relation is between nonverbal gestures and later verbal questions. Further issues include how questioning changes as children develop both in their social cognitive capacities and their conceptual representations, as well as how questioning relates to, facilitates, and is shaped by a developing understanding of evidence and inquiry.

Second, **to what extent is a questioning stance universal, and in what ways is this stance socialized?** Essentially, our key overarching concern here is how environment and culture influence the development of questioning. This includes issues such as how the nature and mode of questioning may vary across contexts and cultures, how different experiences with the ways in which adults both pose and respond to questions may shape the child's own process of inquiry, and how different educational environments may foster the growth of questions. This also includes important issues surrounding how we view practices in non-Western cultures, and on how this should inform our understanding of what constitutes questioning and inquiry in different cultures.

Third, **what role does questioning play in learning more broadly, in both formal and informal learning environments?** Here, our key goal is to map out the ways in which questioning can impact learning. This includes exploring how questions both from and to the child can facilitate an ongoing, interactive exchange of information, how this can foster learning in a variety of ways, and how educational environments and practices can best facilitate questioning and inquiry.

In addressing these questions, the volume is divided into three primary sections. The first section provides an overview of several theoretical approaches to thinking about and researching questioning, its development, and its effects on learning. **Carruthers** (Chapter 2) presents a theoretical account of how questioning might "get off the ground" early in development, through what he describes as nonverbal questioning attitudes, or a general questioning stance. **Harris** (Chapter 3), meanwhile, focuses on the importance of metacognition in questioning. How is it that children come to be aware of their own uncertainty, how do they express that uncertainty, and how does that affect their inquiry and learning? **Wellman** (Chapter 4) proposes that questioning is driven by two complementary drives: to understand and to learn. He then reviews the evidence that, from very early in development, questioning is driven by and towards both goals. Finally, **Callanan, Solis, Castañeda, and Jipson** (Chapter 5) discuss cross-cultural differences in questioning in development, focusing on how best to frame, investigate, and interpret evidence for these differences.

The second section chronicles the development of question-asking in childhood as well as how this development is influenced by children's cognitive development. Children's questioning behavior has been seen as an important source through which they interact with social others to gather information. The authors of this section highlight the various nonverbal and verbal strategies associated with children's information-seeking behavior, as well as individual differences in children's behavior based on cognitive, social, and environmental factors. Specifically, the first few chapters in this section explore the development of children's information-seeking behavior. **Lucca** (Chapter 6) outlines how a questioning stance develops and is present in children's nonverbal pointing prior to the child's first expressive language. **Jones, Swaboda, and Ruggeri** (Chapter 7), and **Mills and Sands** (Chapter 8), highlight how verbal questioning develops through early childhood and elementary school as a strategy to constrain the possible conclusions drawn from evidence. **Neale, Morano, Verdine, Golinkoff, and Hirsh-Pasek** (Chapter 9) demonstrate that not only are children's questions useful for constraining inferences, but they also highlight the limits of children's understanding of a particular categorical boundary – in their case, understanding of shape. Finally, **Gauvain and Munroe** (Chapter 10) describe children's question-asking behavior (and lack of questioning) across four diverse societies, highlighting the need for considering questions as one of multiple possible strategies children use to gain information about the world.

The third section explores how questions posed *to* children influence their inquiry, learning, and reasoning. This section also draws explicit connections to classroom and educational practice. **Zambrana, Hermansen, and Rowe** (Chapter 11) explore how mothers' use of questions impacts both children's learning and their language development, presenting both an in-depth review of the literature addressing this issue, as well as showcasing a new study building on this prior work. **Kuhn, Modrek, and Sandoval** (Chapter 12) focus on the importance of questioning later in childhood, emphasizing the continued relevance of questioning throughout children's formal education, and discussing ways in which educational environments can foster questioning, inquiry, and argument. **Walker and Nyhout** (Chapter 13) discuss how "wh-questions" directed to children shape their reasoning and identify benefits and pitfalls of three question prompts: requests for explanations (why?), requests for additional explanations (why else?), and counterfactuals (what if?). **Osborne and Reigh** (Chapter 14) explore what makes a good question, presenting a novel epistemic framework for classifying questions, and discussing how this framework could be put to use in the classroom in order to facilitate high-quality questioning.

Finally, in a closing chapter (Chapter 15), we return to the key questions posed above. For each question, we synthesize the ways in which the contributed chapters address it, as well as considering new and important concerns that have arisen over the course of the volume. We conclude by charting a path forward for the field as a whole, laying out an agenda for the coming years of research along several dimensions. The current state of the field as laid out in this volume presents exciting opportunities for deepening our understanding of the role of questioning in development. But it also presents a number of theoretical, methodological, and practical challenges that researchers will need to grapple with. We hope that the path we pose for the future of investigations into the questioning child will guide scientists working in this important area of research, and help generate potential tools for addressing important societal issues in the coming years.

## References

Carey, S., and Gelman, R. (eds.) (1991). *The epigenesis of mind: Essays in biology and cognition*. Hillsdale, NJ: Erlbaum.

Gopnik, A., and Schulz, L. (eds.) (2007). *Causal learning: Psychology, philosophy, and computation*. New York, NY: Oxford University Press.

Harris, P. L. (2012).*Trusting what you're told: How children learn from others*. Cambridge, MA: Harvard University Press.

Harris, P. L., Koenig, M. A., Corriveau, K. H., and Jaswal, V. K. (2018). Cognitive foundations of learning from testimony. *Annual Review of Psychology*, *69*, 251–73. https://doi.org/10.1146/annurev-psych-122216-011710

Weisberg, D. S., Hirsh-Pasek, K., Golinkoff, R. M., Kittredge, A. K., and Klahr, D. (2015). Guided play: Principles and practices. *Current Directions in Psychological Science*, *25*, 177–82. https://doi.org/10.1177%2F0963721416645512

# 2 Questions in Development

*Peter Carruthers*

## Introduction: Questioning Attitudes

Everyone will likely acknowledge that attitudes such as *curiosity* and *interest* are vitally important for learning, and that young children ask so many questions because they are intensely curious and interested in the world around them. But the nature of these questioning attitudes themselves is poorly understood. Indeed, many have a mistaken view of them – or so I will claim. In consequence, many are led to give mistaken accounts of the cognitive processes that underlie children's asking and answering of questions, too. This matters, both for our understanding of childhood development generally and for designing interventions that are intended to help children learn.

This chapter has two main goals. One is to offer a fresh set of conceptual resources for those wanting to understand childhood development – specifically, the likely existence from infancy of a set of first-order, non-metacognitive, questioning attitudes. The second is to suggest that the early question-asking and question-answering behavior of infants and toddlers is best understood as expressive of such attitudes, rather than providing evidence of early metacognition.

(Metacognition is defined as cognition that is *about* cognition, or "thinking about thinking," and the term is generally restricted to cases where one thinks about one's own thoughts, rather than the thoughts of other people; see Flavell, 1979; Nelson & Narens, 1990; Dunlosky & Metcalfe, 2009.)

People can ask questions for instrumental reasons ("Where are the car keys?"), but often they are just curious ("Why do birds sing?"). And almost all philosophers and cognitive scientists who have written on the topic of curiosity have addressed it in metacognitive terms – as involving a desire for knowledge or true belief, or as an intrinsic motivation to learn, or something of the sort. (See Foley, 1987; Goldman, 1999; and

Williamson, 2000, among philosophers; and see Litman, 2005; Gruber et al., 2014; Blanchard et al., 2015; and Kidd & Hayden, 2015, among psychologists.) Even Loewenstein's (1994) well-known "information gap" theory of curiosity, which *sounds* as if it might not require metacognition, is actually framed in metacognitive terms. Curiosity is said to arise from "a discrepancy between what one knows and what one wishes to know" (p. 93).

The main problem with metacognitive accounts of curiosity, however, is that they make it hard to understand how animals other than ourselves can be curious. For if any such account is correct, only animals with the concept of knowledge – or something sufficiently close – can be curious. This is because curiosity is said to be *wanting to know* (or *wanting true belief*, or *wanting to learn*, or something similar), and you can only want what you have some conception of (Delton & Sell, 2014). This consideration has motivated a small set of philosophers – just three, to my knowledge – to propose that curiosity should instead be understood as a first-order attitude to a question (Whitcomb, 2010; Friedman, 2013; Carruthers, 2018).

In a previous piece (Carruthers, 2018), I have developed and defended such a view at length. Indeed, I argued that questioning attitudes constitute basic and sui generis forms of affective state, while arguing that such states are widespread throughout the animal kingdom. Curiosity is one instance of a questioning attitude. Others are manifested in instrumental and exploratory search, as well as in mere attentional search (that is to say, where the emotion of *interest* is directed toward something) and memory search. Note, however, that I actually remain neutral on the question whether the set of questioning attitudes is a plurality or a singleton. The answer depends on difficult and hard-to-resolve issues concerning the individuation of emotions as psychological kinds. Referring to them in the plural is for convenience only.

In my view, questioning attitudes are desire-like or emotion-like states, but states that take questions rather than propositions as contents. A cat that is curious about the identity of a novel object is motivated to explore the object by a state whose content is *what that is*. Curiosity is satisfied – and the question is answered – when the animal acquires a belief of the form *that is an F*. Likewise, a monkey that is interested in a conflict between two males in the troupe is motivated to attend to the fight by a state with the content *who will win*. And interest is satisfied when the animal observes the outcome, coming to believe a proposition of the type *monkey X won*. Moreover, just as other emotions motivate adaptive forms of action directly, without requiring planning or executive selection (fear motivates running, anger motivates attacking, and so on), so too do questioning attitudes. They directly activate exploratory or investigative behavior of various sorts.

Note that on the proposed account, questioning attitudes are first-order states with first-order (potentially quite simple) contents. The only concepts that an animal needs to have are ones like *what*, *where*, *when*, and *who*, together with concepts for kinds and for individuals. (Of course, these might only qualify as "proto-concepts" if one places especially stringent demands on concept-possession, as many philosophers do; see Bermúdez, 2003, and Carruthers, 2009, for contrasting views on this topic.) Such attitudes are caused by (salient instances of) ignorance without representing ignorance (i.e., without the organism being aware of its own ignorance as such). And their functional role is to directly motivate forms of action that have been sculpted by evolution and individual learning to issue in the acquisition of the relevant kinds of information. (Compare the way in which the role of fear is to directly motivate forms of escape or avoidance behavior.) A curious animal might approach the thing, look at it, sniff it, lick it, and so on.

I propose that questioning attitudes are among the foundational components of human and animal minds. They are possessed by all mammals, and likely by most vertebrates. Indeed, they may even be possessed by navigating-while-foraging insects like bees. In fact, any animal that needs to acquire targeted information – as opposed to just hoovering up information through some sort of random walk through the environment – is likely to have motivational states that embed questions as contents, which can serve to direct its search.

Note that if this is correct, then one can expect that the questioning attitudes might play an especially important role in human development, given the importance of cultural learning (and information acquisition generally) in human life. Note, too, that no fundamental evolutionary change would need to be postulated in order to account for the extraordinary levels of curiosity found among humans. One can suppose that what happened in the hominin lineage was just a ramping up of the *sensitivity* of the questioning-attitude systems held in common with other animals. No new structures would need to have been added.

I will be assuming in what follows that human infants are successful mind readers, and are capable of attributing at least a limited range of mental states to other people. This is partly because I believe this view to be adequately supported by the evidence, as I have argued elsewhere (Carruthers, 2013, 2016). But it is also because I aim to show that even if the conceptual resources necessary for attributing states of knowledge and ignorance to oneself are fully available (employed in attributing such states to others), it is nevertheless more plausible to interpret the interrogative behavior of infants and toddlers as manifesting first-order questioning attitudes, rather than metacognitive awareness of their own states (which is what many in the field assume).

The present project is thus part of a larger agenda, and is motivated, in part, by a broader set of considerations. The agenda is to oppose neo-Cartesian accounts of our knowledge of mental states. Many still assume that knowledge of one's own mental states is somehow primary, with knowledge of the mental states of other people emerging later (in both phylogeny and ontogeny), dependent on one's awareness of one's own mental life (Goldman, 2006). I have argued, in contrast (Carruthers, 2011), that the reverse is true: awareness of the mental states of other people emerges first in ontogeny, and is likely to be an adaptation that evolved to undergird human, ape, or primate social life (depending on the distribution of these capacities across primates, which is still a matter of controversy). Self-knowledge, on the other hand, results from turning one's mind-reading abilities on oneself, and relies mostly on a range of indirect (and only partly reliable) attribution-heuristics and sensorily-accessible cues (such as one's own feelings, one's own visual and auditory imagery, and observation of one's own behavior).

Neo-Cartesian assumptions continue to underpin a number of research programs in psychology. One such program, as we will see, concerns the nature and explanation of young children's interrogative behavior, which is thought to manifest metacognitive awareness of the child's own ignorance. I will argue, in contrast, that it is better explained in terms of a set of first-order questioning attitudes. But our focus will be on infants and toddlers specifically (up to the age of about two). Once children become capable of metacognitive awareness, no doubt their interrogative behavior will not only become more flexible and sophisticated, but may well sometimes reflect metacognitive knowledge of their own ignorance. I will return to this point in the section below entitled Beyond Two.

### Questions in Infancy

The present section will focus on infants in the first year of life. It will argue that the existence of the assumed questioning attitudes is at least consistent with what we know about human children of this age. Drawing on the same perspective, it will also propose a novel hypothesis for future exploration, concerning question-based mind reading in infants.

For more than thirty years, researchers have employed *expectancy-violation* paradigms to explore human infants' "core knowledge" of the world around them (Baillargeon et al., 1985; Spelke & Kinzler, 2007). When an infant has had her expectations violated she will look longer at the object or event than when the latter was expected. Seen in the light of the proposed questioning attitudes, such behavior manifests questions directed at the environment, such as the question *how that happened*. And indeed, infants don't just passively attend to expectancy-violating objects or events, but they preferentially learn from them, and if given the opportunity they will explore them in ways related to the nature of the initial expectation (Stahl & Feigenson, 2015). A ten-month-old infant shown an object apparently passing through a solid wall, for example, will try banging it on a surface when later given an opportunity to handle the object (seemingly asking whether it is solid); whereas the same infant shown an object that seems to remain in the air without support will thereafter repeatedly drop it (as if inquiring whether it can float).

Note that it was initially the same expectancy-violation method that was used to explore the mind-reading abilities of infants and toddlers in the first eighteen months of life, too (Woodward, 1998; Onishi & Baillargeon, 2005; Baillargeon et al., 2010). But similar findings have now been confirmed using a wide variety of different methods. These include anticipatory looking (Southgate et al., 2007), active helping (Buttelmann et al., 2009), mirror-neuron activation (Southgate & Vernetti, 2014), and more.

Even if it is true (as I believe, and as I propose to assume) that core mind-reading abilities are innately channeled, and emerge with little or no learning early in development, it doesn't follow, of course, that attributions of curiosity or interest are among the components of that core system. The fact that infants are capable of having questioning attitudes themselves from early stages of development doesn't imply that they are capable of attributing such attitudes to others. It may well be that the behavioral cues that indicate the presence of such states need to be learned, and/or that concepts for the relevant attitudes need to be constructed out of others. For example, curiosity might come to be understood as a *desire to know* something – incorrectly, in my view, since I claim that curiosity is a first-order desire-like questioning attitude, not a metacognitive one that embeds the concept KNOW within its content. Young children might thus need to build a conception of curiosity over time out of the concepts of desire and knowledge (or want and think).

(Note that the metacognitive conception of curiosity does appear to be part of our commonsense folk-psychology, at any rate. For it – or something like it – has been endorsed by nearly everyone who has written on the topic, as we saw earlier. So it isn't implausible that children might construct just such a conception over the course of the first few years of life.)

On current evidence it seems likely that concepts such as WANT and THINK would be among the core components of an innately channeled mind-reading system. And a reasonable working assumption would be that infants can (given appropriate evidence) attribute to others as the embedded contents of such concepts any proposition that they themselves can think. Thus, an infant who can think a thought like *the ball is in the box*, and who sees the ball placed inside the box in the presence of another agent, may form a belief with the content *he thinks that the ball is in the box*. In contrast, if an infant as yet lacks the concept IDENTITY, then she will be incapable of forming a belief with the content *he thinks that Peter is the firefighter*.

What is an infant to think, however, on seeing another agent look into the box, when the infant herself is ignorant of the contents of the box? In order to explain such cases, Kovács (2016) postulates the existence of what she calls "empty belief files." Supposing that belief-attributions normally possess the structure {AGENT THINKS: PROPOSITION}, she suggests that in such cases the infant will form a belief whose content has the structure {AGENT THINKS: —}, where the content-slot in the belief-attribution is left empty. This is possible, of course, but quite unnatural. And it would leave one floundering to explain how an incomplete belief-attribution of this sort could give rise to determinate expectations – for example, an expectation that the agent should be capable of reporting on the contents of the box to another person. Indeed, notice that if the content-slot of the belief-file is left truly empty, then there is nothing even to indicate that the person's belief concerns the box or its contents.

If infants are capable of questioning attitudes like curiosity, however, then they can think thoughts that embed questions as well as propositions as contents. And in that case there should be nothing to stand in the way of attributing such a content to another person. On seeing the person look into the box, for example, an infant might form a belief whose content has the structure {AGENT THINKS: WHAT IS IN THE BOX}, where what is embedded in the belief-attribution is not a proposition but a question. This would be an entirely natural attribution to make, since on seeing the adult look into the box, the infant herself is likely to be at least mildly curious what is in the box. (And notice that the content of her curiosity is then the very same as the content of the belief attributed to the agent.) This proposal seemingly avoids all the difficulties that attend the notion of empty belief-files. In particular, if the agent knows what is in the box, then she should able to tell other people what is in it.

One wrinkle in this suggestion, however, is that in English (and most other languages, I believe) one cannot attribute belief in a question. One can say, "John *knows* what is in the box," but not, "John *thinks* what is in the box," nor, "John *believes* what is in the box." Why this should be so is itself an interesting question. It may have something to do with the central role of knowledge-reports in information-transmission (and thus question-answering), whereas belief-reports are more commonly employed in psychological explanation. But in any case, there seems no reason to expect that there should be similar restrictions on what prelinguistic infants can think. Indeed, when children acquire language, it takes them a few years to sort out the difference in semantics between "think" and "know" (Dudley et al., 2015; Dudley, 2018). So it makes sense that their initial concept THINKS might incorporate aspects of each; and in particular, that it might permit completion by an embedded question. Note that this would enable infants to represent and draw inferences from cases where someone has a false belief about the contents of the box (even when the infant herself is ignorant of the truth) – for example, where the box the agent was seen looking into has been switched for another while the agent was absent.

This issue is an empirical one, of course (even if the innately channeled nature of core mind-reading abilities is taken for granted). My point here is that once we accept that infants are capable of entertaining questions as the contents of their own thoughts (when curious about something or interested in something, for example), then this opens up the possibility that they might be capable of attributing questions to others as the content of a THINKS-attitude. At the very least, the idea seems worthy of investigation by developmental psychologists alongside (and in competition with) the notion of empty belief-files.

### Interrogative Behavior

Let me now turn to the interrogative behavior of infants and toddlers, focusing initially on the former. A number of experimenters have shown that by the age of twelve months, infants use gestures and vocalizations in a variety of different ways. One is to provide information intended to benefit those who are ignorant (Liszkowski et al., 2007, 2008). But another is to *request* information from caregivers (Southgate et al., 2010; Begus & Southgate, 2012; Kovács et al., 2014). And from that point onwards, development of questioning behavior is quite swift. Thus Chouinard (2007) shows from a longitudinal discourse-analysis that by two years of age well-formed verbal questions constitute a large proportion of the speech of young children when interacting with a caregiver. Furthermore, at the initial stages of development one might expect that question-asking would be an indiscriminate strategy, but would rapidly begin to interact with the output of the mind-reading system, enabling children to identify whom best to direct questions toward. (That is, who knows or is ignorant; who is the most reliable informant; who is a member of one's own social group and is thus the most relevant informant; and so on.) And this, too, appears to be the case (Mills et al., 2010; Harris, 2012; Begus et al., 2016).

Given the standard metacognitive construal of curiosity, the interrogative behavior of infants and toddlers can be interpreted as manifesting both *awareness* of their own ignorance and a corresponding desire to *acquire knowledge*. And this is just the interpretation that is often given in the empirical literature. The child is assumed to ask her question because she realizes she is *ignorant* of the answer, and *wants to know* it (Balcomb & Gerken, 2008; Mills et al., 2010; Goupil et al., 2016). But this interpretation is by no means mandatory. We could view the child's interrogative behavior as an expression of a (non-metacognitive) questioning attitude instead. The child can be said to ask what the box contains, for example, because she is curious what the box contains, not because she wants to know what the box contains. In such cases the child's curiosity can be caused by her ignorance of the contents of the box, given its salience in the current context, without her being aware of her ignorance as such (i.e., in the absence of metacognition).

Suppose that curiosity is an affective attitude to a question. Then we can suppose that curiosity, like other affective attitudes such as fear and anger, is apt to motivate directly (without any need for executive decision-making) forms of action that are designed to alleviate the affective state in question (i.e., to extinguish curiosity). Consider how this works in the case of fear and anger. Fear motivates forms of escape or defensive behavior that are likely to render one safe; anger motivates forms of aggression that are likely to deter or punish those who have harmed one; and so on for other affective attitudes. And note, too, that the behavior in question is motivated *directly*, independently of one's beliefs. On meeting an aggressive-looking black bear in the forest, for example, and feeling fear, one will likely experience an urge to run away, even though one knows full well that the best strategy is to make oneself look as large as possible while making a lot of noise. Likewise, on becoming angry with a colleague at a meeting one may experience an urge to make a cutting remark, even though one knows it would be counterproductive to do so. Still, even given the general assumption that curiosity should directly cause forms of behavior that are likely to remove (i.e., satisfy) one's curiosity, one might wonder *how*, exactly, curiosity comes to cause the kinds of interrogative behavior that we observe in infants.

One possibility is that the connection is innate, and is part of the hyper-social endowment characteristic of all normal humans. That is, states of curiosity in humans might be directly wired (or "innately channeled") to issue in behavior such as pointing at the unfamiliar object while looking quizzically toward an adult carer, just as curiosity in a cat seems to be directly wired to cause it to approach an unfamiliar object, sniff it, walk around it while looking at it closely, and so on. There is evidence that infants need to *learn* that pointing to an object reliably elicits information from a caregiver, however, in a way that other sorts of gesturing or joint-attention behaviors don't. Thus Lucca & Wilbourn (2016) show that at 18 months, but not at 12 months, infants understand the information-eliciting nature of their own pointing gestures.

Another possibility, however, is that infants' interrogative behavior might be shaped through normal processes of affective, reward-based learning. What follows is a sketch of how that story might go. When an infant is curious about or interested in something, she will attend to it, and will engage in behavior that is easily interpreted by surrounding mind readers (generally the child's caregivers) as manifesting just such attitudes. She may turn her head toward the source of an unusual sound, for example, or look intently at and/or reach toward an unfamiliar object; or she may exhibit a surprised facial expression when something unexpected happens; and so on. In such circumstances, the infant's caregivers will often provide information that satisfies or partially satisfies the attitude, and which is thus experienced as rewarding – by naming the source of the sound or the unfamiliar object, for example, or by explaining the event that has just happened (Kishimoto et al., 2007; Wu & Gros-Louis, 2014). One might expect that infants would rapidly learn that by drawing a caregiver's attention to the object of curiosity or interest, they can generally secure just such a reward. And hence we see the emergence of behavior that is readily interpreted by adults as interrogative. Note that on this account the infant doesn't have to be aware of her own ignorance in order to engage in interrogative behavior. She just has to be curious, and to have learned a set of social behaviors that are apt to satisfy her curiosity.

Consistent with this account, we know that curiosity-satisfaction *is* directly rewarding in animals (and hence presumably in human infants likewise). In an experimental paradigm that has now been used with both monkeys and pigeons, animals will opt to give up between 20 and 30 percent of their eventual food-reward in order to learn whether that reward is, or is not, coming (Bromberg-Martin & Hikosaka, 2009; Gipson et al., 2009). Animals will choose an option that reliably signals whether or not a food-reward is coming a few seconds later, even though this choice has no impact on the likelihood of the reward, and even though the animal knows that selecting the informative option will reduce the size of the eventual reward, if it comes. (Compare how one might pay a premium to learn whether or not one has won a lottery of some sort via express mail rather than regular mail.) Moreover, we know that the reward-systems in the brains of monkeys respond positively to the prospect of the informative option independently of their responses to the prospect of the food itself, with distinct neural signatures discernible in the orbitofrontal cortex (Blanchard et al., 2015).

Suppose that the hypothesis outlined here is correct, that infants and toddlers learn to engage in interrogative behavior via adult feedback and affective learning. Then we can predict that rates of question-asking among two-year-olds will depend not just on trait-curiosity (insofar as this can be independently measured) but also on earlier adult responsiveness to signs of curiosity in the child (Begus & Southgate, 2018). Children who are frequently rewarded for behavior that is interpreted by adults as expressing curiosity, interest, or puzzlement should acquire interrogative behavior more swiftly and robustly – via the provision of information that satisfies the desire-like states in question.

## Verbal Questions

How young children learn to ask *verbal* questions is a more complicated issue, one that is entangled with the development of linguistic ability more generally. This cannot be addressed here. However, it is worth noting a couple of features of the present account that suggest that learning the verbal question-form should be especially easy for a developing child. For one thing, the distinctive components of wh-questions ("what," "where," "when," and so on) express concepts that the language-learning child already possesses. This is because, by hypothesis, even infants have attitudes to questions such as *what* that thing is, *where* Mother is, *when* she *will return*, and so on. So the concepts will already be there for the linguistic wh-terms to be fast-mapped to (in the sense of Bloom, 2002).

Second, recall that questioning attitudes are attitudes whose content is a question, just as truth-directed attitudes like belief are attitudes whose content is a proposition. But linguistic questions, too, have questions as contents, just as assertions have propositions as contents. (However, the contents of linguistic questions may specify sets of possible *answers* – Karttunen, 1977 – rather than sets of possible *satisfiers*, which form the contents of the underlying attitudes.) One might expect, then, that the natural language question-form would be fast-mapped to the questioning attitudes it can be used to express, just as children readily grasp that the assertoric form can be used to express propositional attitudes like belief. And note, by the way, that no one would claim that children need to be aware of their own beliefs in order to assert them. Standard models of speech production start from a message to be communicated – in the case of assertion, normally a belief – not from any kind of metacognitive knowledge, such as awareness of one's own belief (Levelt, 1989). Nor too, I claim, should anyone think that children need to be aware of their own ignorance, or their own curiosity, in order to ask questions. Rather, ignorance (when made salient by the context) results in a state of curiosity with a question as its content, and curiosity directly motivates the behavior of *asking* a question with that content – behavior that has previously been found to be rewarding, since question-asking is apt to lead to responses that satisfy one's curiosity.

To illustrate some of the points made in this section, consider the work of Goupil et al. (2016). They presented twenty-month-old toddlers with memory-based choices ranging from easy to impossible. The children either observed, or did not observe, a toy being placed under one of two boxes. They then had to point to the correct box after a short or a long delay to be rewarded with the toy. The experimental group, however, were shown during a warm-up phase that they could turn to their caregivers for help before indicating their choices. These children were more likely to ask for help after a long delay (when their own memory was more likely to have faded) than after a short one; similarly, they were more likely to ask for help when they hadn't observed the hiding event (and so were ignorant of the toy's location) than when whey had. (Both groups of children *pointed* in all conditions when making their choices. But these were points that expressed a forced-choice guess or some degree of belief. These points were not themselves interrogative.)

The experimenters interpret these findings as demonstrating the children's metacognitive awareness of their own states of knowledge and ignorance. But given the existence of questioning attitudes, a better interpretation is available. In cases where the child knows and remembers the location of the toy, simple (first-order) practical reasoning is sufficient to explain the child's behavior. The child can reason: *To get the toy I need to point to where it is; the toy is in that box; so I'll point to that box.* Metacognitive awareness of the child's own belief isn't needed. Likewise, in cases where the child is ignorant of the toy's location, we can suppose that ignorance, in this context, will give rise to a desire-like questioning attitude with the content, *where the toy is.* Moreover, some of the children will have learned through the warm-up training that turning to their caregiver for help is an effective way of satisfying this attitude, and subsequently receiving the toy. (Only a subset of the infants in the experimental group ever asked for help, in fact, so it seems not all of them learned this.) Again, metacognitive awareness isn't needed.

Consider, in contrast, the explanatory burden that needs to be taken on if one insists that the behavior of the toddlers in these experiments manifests metacognitive awareness of their own ignorance. As Goupil et al. (2016) themselves note, similar behavior has been experimentally elicited from many species of animal, including invertebrates like honey bees (Perry & Barron, 2013). Almost all animals will act to secure information when ignorant; and likewise many species of animal will make choices that differ depending on their confidence in the outcome. Goupil and colleagues are sanguine in asserting that all such creatures are capable of metacognitive awareness. But for this to be true, creatures like bees must possess mental-state concepts such as KNOWS or BELIEVES. (To be aware of one's own ignorance, one needs to have the concept IGNORANT, or the concept DOESN´T KNOW.) And this means they must possess some idea of the causal structure of their own minds. This is possible, but seems quite unlikely. We should surely prefer simpler, less demanding, explanations if available. That is what I have attempted to provide in this section.

### Giving Positive Answers

Toddlers don't just ask questions, of course, they answer them. But as we noted above in the section entitled Verbal Questions, the issue of how children come to understand the significance of the verbal question-form is beyond the scope of the present discussion. Yet plausibly, toddlers (like adults) come to interpret verbal questions as manifesting the speaker's desire to know something (or better: as manifesting the desire to think something, since the likely conceptual primitive employed is an undifferentiated THINKS concept). Note that this is a metacognitive desire. And one might then wonder how it could rationally issue in a question-answering response unless the child's reasoning is mediated by a metacognitive premise. It might seem, that is, that the child's reasoning would have to take the form: *He wants to think whether P; I think P; so I can give him what he wants by saying that P.* If this is right, then question-answering behavior manifests metacognitive knowledge, specifically the knowledge that one knows (or has a belief about) the answer.

There is an alternative – weaker and more plausible – account of the rational basis of question-answering, however. This is that the toddler's reasoning would go: *He wants to think whether P; P; so I can give him what he wants by saying that P.* Since we are dealing at the moment only with positive answers to questions (negative answers will be considered below in the section entitled Giving Negative Answers), the child in such a case already has the knowledge that *P*. Moreover, it seems plausible that decoding the embedded content of the question asked – namely, *whether P* – should be sufficient to evoke this knowledge into an active state, making it available to guide a verbal response. If this is right, then the toddler just has to *have* a belief, not be *aware* that she has that belief. While the toddler needs to represent the goals and thoughts of the speaker, she doesn't need to represent her own thoughts in order to construct an appropriate reply.

I have argued, then, that we have no need to attribute to young children metacognitive awareness of their own thoughts in order to explain their capacity to provide (positive) answers to questions. But it might be objected that toddlers, like adults, will often answer a question with an assertion of the form "I think that P" (less commonly, of the form, "I know that P"; see Harris et al., 2017a). Since the thought they are expressing, here, is that they *think* or *believe* "P" to be the case, it might be said that such statements are evidence of metacognitive awareness. Since children's answers are often metacognitive in form, isn't the simplest conclusion that such answers reflect metacognitive thoughts about the child's own thoughts?

This line of argument is unconvincing, however, because most uses of "I think" are not really attributive, but formulaic. And this is true in adult speech to children as well as in the speech of children themselves (Shatz et al., 1983; Bloom et al., 1989; Diessel & Tomasello, 2001; Simons, 2007; Lewis et al., 2012). Prefacing a statement with "I think" serves to weaken it somewhat, but it doesn't usually change the topic. If one asserts, "There will be a storm this evening," then plainly the topic is the weather, and the message to be communicated concerns the likelihood of rain and/or wind (depending on the context). But if one says instead, "I think there will be a storm this evening," the topic is unchanged: one is still talking about the weather, but perhaps expressing less than complete confidence in one's prediction. The topic is not (as the form of the sentence might suggest) oneself and one's beliefs. The topic remains the weather, not one's own psychology. Even if the literal semantic content of the sentence makes reference to the speaker's beliefs, the message to be communicated doesn't. As a result, when children communicate answers to questions using an "I think . . ." sentence-form, one cannot presume that the message they are communicating concerns their beliefs, or that they are expressing a metacognitive thought. Indeed, one *shouldn't* presume this, given the prevalence of indirect uses of "I think" in speech generally.

It is possible that a child who responds to a question from an adult by saying, "I think the box is empty," and hears her own reply, *thereafter* comes to have metacognitive awareness that she believes the box to be empty. One reason for thinking this might be that young children are poor pragmatists (Westra, 2016). That is, hearing her own reply and extracting its literal semantic content rather than the intended message to be communicated, the child may *subsequently* arrive at a metacognitive belief. But if so, this is metacognition that is indirect, dependent on the child's mind-reading and interpretive abilities, rather than resulting from intro-spective awareness of her own beliefs. The process that initially generated the statement in question is most likely to have begun with the proposition *the box is empty* as the message to be communicated, with the modifier "I think" being added during the course of speech-production given its prevalence in ordinary discourse.

In fact, however, it is unlikely that young children interpret themselves to be describing their own psychological states when hearing themselves say something of the form "I think that P." For indirect assertion, merely modifying, uses of "think" are *so* prevalent in ordinary discourse that some linguists have claimed that children interpret "think" in general (whether in the first, second, or third person) as indirect by default, and only draw on the attributive (psychological) sense when the indirect interpretation is clearly implausible (Lewis et al., 2012; Hacquard, 2014; Dudley et al., 2015). So when the child hears herself say, "I think it is empty," she will likely discount the semantic contribution of "I think" and interpret herself (correctly) as asserting that the box is empty. Nevertheless, the end-state is likely to be the same. Since people generally only assert what they believe, the child may interpret her own assertion that the box is empty as a manifestation of the belief that the box is empty. But as already noted, this means that metacognitive awareness is the outcome of question-answering behavior (and depends on the child's own mind-reading abilities, directed at herself), not the starting point.

### Giving Negative Answers

I have argued that we need not – and should not – interpret young children's interrogative behavior as manifesting metacognitive awareness. Nor should we regard young children's positive answers to questions as displaying metacognitive awareness of their own beliefs, even when their answers take the form "I think that P" or "I believe that P." For such answers are generally just indirect assertions of the content *P*. Negative answers, however, might seem like another matter. For toddlers don't merely fail to answer, or answer irrelevantly, when they don't know the answer to a question (although they do sometimes do each of these things). On the contrary, they frequently respond by *saying* they don't know. This is a metacognitive statement, which can only bear a metacognitive interpretation. In contrast with "I think that P," which is often just an indirect way of asserting "P," "I don't know [whether P]" can only mean just that: that the speaker is ignorant of the answer. Since the message to be communicated is that one is ignorant, it would seem that it has to start from a metacognitive thought: it is because the child *believes* she is ignorant of the answer that she *says* she is ignorant of the answer.

When toddlers answer a question by saying, "I dunno," then, does this reflect (as it seems to) a prior metacognitive awareness of their own ignorance? It may subsequently cause such awareness, of course. Hearing and understanding their own answers, they may become aware of their own ignorance. For there is, as we have just noted, no other way in which the content of such an assertion can be understood. But do children possess such awareness at the outset, in formulating the message to be communicated? Do such metacognitive statements reflect prior metacognitive thoughts?

In addressing these questions, it will be helpful to note that there are close parallels between question-answering in general and the sorts of word/nonword decision tasks that have been widely used in psychology. In such tasks one is presented with a string of letters and required either to respond "Yes" if it is a word or "No" if it is a pseudo-word or impossible word. So a "Yes" response is warranted if one recognizes the stimulus as a word, whereas a "No" response reflects ignorance of (i.e., failure to recognize) a word. By parity of reasoning, then, one might think that people in these experiments would need to be metacognitively aware of their own ignorance of a word whenever they answer "No." But no one in the field would make such a claim.

For example, Dufau et al. (2012) use a leaky competitive accumulator model (LCA) to explain performance in these tasks, following Usher & McClelland (2001). Such models are widely employed in psychology, and are thought to be neurologically realistic, reflecting a gradual buildup of activity in the relevant neural populations. On such an account, then, evidence accumulates over time for a "Yes" answer (with some leakage). A "No" answer, in contrast, is determined by a fixed value minus the evidence for "Yes" (meaning that a "No" answer is the default), with the two answers competing with one another. In effect, then, if one isn't sufficiently inclined to answer "Yes" within some fixed time frame (fixed by one's goals or the task instructions – e.g., for accuracy versus speed or vice versa), then one answers "No" instead.

It is easy to see how this model can be extended to explain question-answering behavior in general. If a child is asked, "What is that thing called?" then evidence will accumulate in parallel for a number of possible names. If one of them exceeds threshold swiftly enough given the context, the child responds positively (e.g., by saying "cow"). But if no word makes it to threshold during that time, the child responds by saying,

"I dunno." In effect, the message to be communicated is not that one lacks knowledge as such (that would require metacognitive awareness), but rather that one doesn't have a positive answer. And then this same model can easily be extended to account for cases where the child is asked, "Do you *know* what that thing is called?" rather than being asked for the name directly. Exactly the same strategy can be followed: replying, "No" or "I dunno" if no name comes to mind.

There are significant differences between a "No" response in a word/ nonword task and an "I dunno" response to a question, of course. Most salient is that the contextually expanded content of one's answer in the former case is that the stimulus is not a word, whereas the only available content in the latter is that one is ignorant of the answer. The former answer is first-order whereas the latter answer has a metacognitive content. Nevertheless, essentially the same LCA process can underlie each. In word/nonword tasks people are instructed to respond "No" if they don't recognize the stimulus as a word. (Notice, however, that they *could* be instructed to say, "I don't recognize it," giving a semantically metacognitive answer instead. Arguably the process that would generate such an answer would remain exactly the same.) Presumably children learn that the appropriate way to respond to questions they can't answer is by saying, "I dunno" (or by shrugging their shoulders, or other behavior that can be interpreted as an expression of ignorance). This can be the direct output of an LCA process, only subsequently interpreted by the child (as well as the hearer) in metacognitive terms.

Consider, for contrast, what a metacognitive account of the production of an "I dunno" response would have to look like. Supposing that such utterances reflect the prior formation of a belief with the content, *I don't know*, what would be the cues that could give rise to such a belief? Only one serious contender is available: the cue would be one's *failure* to produce a positive verbal answer within some specified time. No one who studies metacognition thinks that people have direct introspective access to their memory systems or beliefs (Dunlosky & Metcalfe, 2009). Rather, people are reliant upon various kinds of indirect cue, such as feelings of fluency or disfluency, failure to produce an answer, and so forth. So, in effect, the cue for formation of a metacognitive belief is the very same as that postulated above to underlie production of the "I dunno" response directly – it is one's failure to produce a substantive answer. The latter direct account is therefore simpler and more parsimonious – especially since "I dunno" responses are so ubiquitous in early childhood discourse (Harris et al., 2017a).

One might wonder whether my proposed interpretation of children's "I dunno" responses is consistent with the main conclusions drawn by

Harris et al. (2017b) from their longitudinal discourse-analysis of the speech of three young children. They note that children generally use "I dunno" correctly, in circumstances where they are ignorant of some fact or answer to a question; and that when "know" is used in the second person it mostly figures in the context of a question or request for information ("Do you know?"). More generally, Harris and colleagues conclude that two-year-olds have a working conception of knowledge and ignorance that they make appropriate use of in the context of communication with an interlocutor. Note that the second-personal component of this conclusion is fully consistent with the assumption I adopted at the outset, that even infants possess core mind-reading abilities. The real question for us is whether Harris and colleagues are entitled to conclude that first-personal metacognition is also present.

It is worth noting up front that the children who participated in this study were somewhat older than the infants and toddlers we have been considering: they were in the third year of life. But more importantly, the findings are in any case consistent with the claim defended here, that children's use of "I dunno" doesn't reflect (but at best causes) a metacognitive belief in their own ignorance. The initial production of "I dunno" can still be formulaic, and can still be the default direct response in the LCA process that generates answers to a question (whether that question is explicitly asked by an interlocutor or is tacit in the context of the ongoing conversation).

## Beyond Two

My main focus in this chapter has been on the nature of curiosity and other questioning attitudes, and their role in the first two years of life. I have emphasized, especially, that questioning behavior during this time period can be understood as manifesting the influence of such attitudes, rather than as displaying any kind of metacognitive awareness. But it may be worth making a few speculative remarks about the years thereafter before we conclude.

Curiosity and interest remain what they are throughout the lifespan, of course – first-order affective attitudes. And they will continue to motivate forms of behavior – including verbal questions – that one has learned will satisfy those attitudes. Moreover, the motivation involved will be direct, without any need for metacognitive awareness. But the conditions that elicit curiosity and interest will greatly expand with learning, as will the range of the behaviors that are used to satisfy those attitudes. As the child's knowledge expands, this will provide an opportunity for new questions and new forms of curiosity to develop. And once a child learns that books can both stimulate and satisfy interest, for example, then reading can become intrinsically motivating.

How will questioning behavior interact with children's emerging meta-cognitive awareness and knowledge, which seem to develop gradually from the age of about three years (Lockl & Schneider, 2007; Ghetti et al., 2013; Lyons & Ghetti, 2013; Destan et al., 2014)? The result will surely be a new set of motives for asking questions. Knowing that you don't know something, but knowing that you *need* to know it to achieve a goal or solve a problem, will provide an instrumental motive for trying to find out – and in many cases that will mean asking a question. But this source of motivation is often a pale shadow of that provided by curiosity, especially when the goals in question are distal ones (like passing a test next week, or doing well in school). This is, of course, why teachers try to make their material interesting: to provide an intrinsic motivation to attend, and to provoke intrinsically motivated forms of questioning.

What matters most for learning, I suggest, is not merely the relevance of the knowledge in question to one's goals, but that the appraisal mechanisms that issue in emotions of curiosity and interest should be sensitive to that relevance. Although I am not aware of any direct evidence on the topic, my guess is that these appraisal mechanisms aren't easily influenced by one's metacognitive knowledge that one lacks knowledge or needs knowledge. If this is right, then the central goal for parents and educators should be to engage curiosity and sustain interest, not to equip children with a set of metacognitive abilities. The latter may help learning at the margins, especially when intrinsic motivation is lacking; and it may well become increasingly important as children progress through the school years. (Everyone has to learn *some* stuff that doesn't interest them!) But the questioning attitudes will surely remain central to successful learning throughout.

## Conclusion

Drawing on the work of Whitcomb (2010), Friedman (2013), and myself (Carruthers, 2018), I have suggested that among the building blocks of the human mind – available from early in infancy – are a set of questioning attitudes, encompassing curiosity, interest, and more. These are affective, desire-like, states that take questions rather than propositions as contents. As with other emotional states, they are caused by appraisal systems that are likely sensitive to existing knowledge, current goals, and standing values. They are activated by ignorance, in particular – especially ignorance made salient by features of the context (including one's current goals as well as background values). And also like other emotional states, they directly motivate adaptive forms of behavior – in this case, behavior that has been sculpted by evolution and individual learning to issue in answers to the embedded questions.

With the existence of such questioning attitudes accepted, a number of new lines of inquiry open up for developmental psychologists. One is whether infants can deploy the distinctive contents of these attitudes (questions) for other purposes, specifically for tracking the unknown beliefs of another agent (see Questions in Infancy). In addition to entertaining thoughts like *He thinks the toy is in the box*, might they also be capable of thoughts such as *He thinks what is in the box*, where the specific content of the person's belief is left unspecified (because unknown to the infant)?

Another possible line of inquiry is to see whether rates of interrogative behavior in infants and toddlers is a function of the frequency with which their questioning attitudes (as manifested in their surprise, puzzlement, evident curiosity, and so on) have been satisfied. For I have suggested that those behaviors will likely have been acquired, in part, through reward-based learning (see Interrogative Behavior).

Our discussion in the remaining sections, however, has turned especially on the fact that the questioning attitudes are hypothesized to be first order in nature. For they take first-order questions as contents. (This is only true for the most part, of course. One can be curious about someone's beliefs or goals as well, and in that case the question will have a second-order content such as *what he thinks* or *what he wants*.) Indeed, the content of such an attitude can be as simple as *what that is* or *where the toy is*. As a result, we can give explanations of the question-asking and question-answering behavior of infants and toddlers that are more parsimonious than standard metacognitive ones. At the very least, one might think that the burden of proof has now been shifted onto those wishing to give metacognitive interpretations of experimental results such as those reported by Goupil et al. (2016).

## References

Baillargeon, R., Spelke, E., and Wasserman, S. (1985). Object permanence in five-month-old infants. *Cognition*, *20*, 191–208. http://doi:10.1016/0010-0277(85)90008-3
Baillargeon, R., Scott, R., and He, Z. (2010). False-belief understanding in infants. *Trends in Cognitive Sciences*, *14*, 110–18. http://doi:10.1016/j.tics.2009.12.006
Balcomb, F., and Gerken, L. (2008). Three-year-old children can access their own memory to guide responses on a visual matching task. *Developmental Science*, *11*, 750–60. http://doi:10.1111/j.1467-7687.2008.00725.x
Begus, K., and Southgate, V. (2012). Infant pointing serves an interrogative function. *Developmental Science*, *15*, 611–17. http://doi:10.1111/j.1467-7687.2012.01160.x

(2018). Curious learners: How infants' motivation to learn shapes and is shaped by infants' interactions with the social world. In M. Saylor and P. Ganea (eds.), *Active Learning from Infancy to Childhood* (pp. 13–37). Cham, Switzerland: Springer. http://doi:10.1007/978-3-319-77182-3_2

Begus, K., Gliga, T., and Southgate, V. (2016). Infants' preferences for native speakers are associated with an expectation of information. *Proceedings of the National Academy of Sciences, 113*, 12397–402. http://doi:10.1073/pnas.1603261113

Bermúdez, J. (2003). *Thinking without Words*. Oxford: Oxford University Press.

Blanchard, T., Hayden, B., and Bromberg-Martin, E. (2015). Orbitofrontal cortex uses distinct codes for different choice attributes in decisions motivated by curiosity. *Neuron, 85*, 602–14. http://doi:10.1016/j.neuron.2014.12.050

Bloom, L., Rispoli, M., Gartner, B., and Hafitz, J. (1989). Acquisition of complementation. *Journal of Child Language, 16*, 101–20. http://doi:10.1017/s0305000900013465

Bloom, P. (2002). *How Children Learn the Meanings of Words*. Cambridge, MA: MIT Press.

Bromberg-Martin, E., and Hikosaka, O. (2009). Midbrain dopamine neurons signal preference for advance information about upcoming rewards. *Neuron, 63*, 119–26. http://doi:10.1016/j.neuron.2009.06.009

Buttelmann, D., Carpenter, M., and Tomasello, M. (2009). Eighteen-month-old infants show false belief understanding in an active helping paradigm. *Cognition, 112*, 337–42. http://doi:10.1016/j.cognition.2009.05.006

Carruthers, P. (2009). Invertebrate concepts confront the generality constraint (and win). In R. Lurz (ed.), *The Philosophy of Animal Minds* (pp. 89–107), New York: Cambridge University Press. http://doi:10.1017/cbo9780511819001.006

(2011). *The Opacity of Mind: An Integrative Theory of Self-Knowledge*. Oxford: Oxford University Press.

(2013). Mindreading in infancy. *Mind & Language, 28*, 141–72.

(2016). Two systems for mindreading? *Review of Philosophy and Psychology, 7*, 141–62. http://doi:10.1111/mila.12014

(2018). Basic questions. *Mind & Language, 33*, 130–47. http://doi:10.1111/mila.12167

Chouinard, M. (2007). Children's questions: A mechanism for cognitive development. *Monographs of the Society for Research in Child Development, 72*, no.1, 1–129.

Delton, A. and Sell, A. (2014). The co-evolution of concepts and motivation. *Current Directions in Psychological Science, 23*, 115–20. http://doi:10.1177/0963721414521631

Destan, N., Hembacher, E., Ghetti, S., and Roebers, C. (2014). Early metacognitive abilities: The interplay of monitoring and control processes in 5- to 7-year-old children. *Journal of Experimental Child Psychology, 126*, 213–28. http://doi:10.1016/j.jecp.2014.04.001

Diessel, H., and Tomasello, M. (2001). The acquisition of finite complement clauses in English: A corpus-based analysis. *Cognitive Linguistics, 12*, 97–141. http://doi:10.1515/cogl.12.2.97

Dudley, R. (2018). Young children's conception of knowledge. *Philosophy Compass*. Advance online publication. http://doi.org/10.1111/phc3.12494

Dudley, R., Orita, N., Hacquard, V., and Lidz, J. (2015). Three-year-olds' understanding of know and think. In F. Schwarz (ed.), *Experimental Perspectives on Presuppositions* (pp. 241–62), Cham, Switzerland: Springer. http://doi:10 .1007/978-3-319-07980-6_11

Dufau, S., Grainger, J., and Ziegler, J. (2012). How to say "no" to a nonword: A leaky competing accumulator model of lexical decision. *Journal of Experimental Psychology: Learning, Memory, and Cognition, 38*, 1117–28. http://doi:10.1037 /a0026948

Dunlosky, J., and Metcalfe, J. (2009). *Metacognition*. New York: Sage Publications.

Flavell, J. H. (1979). Metacognition and cognitive monitoring: A new area of cognitive-developmental inquiry. *American Psychologist, 34*, 906–11. https:// doi.org/10.1037/0003-066X.34.10.906

Foley, R. (1987). *The Theory of Epistemic Rationality*. Cambridge, MA: Harvard University Press.

Friedman, J. (2013). Question-directed attitudes. *Philosophical Perspectives, 27*, 145–74. http://doi:10.1111/phpe.12026

Ghetti, S., Hembacher, E., and Coughlin, C. (2013). Feeling uncertain and acting on it during the preschool years: A metacognitive approach. *Child Development Perspectives, 7*, 160–5. http://doi:10.1111/cdep.12035

Gipson, C. D., Alessandri, J. J., Miller, H. C., and Zentall, T. R. (2009). Preference for 50% reinforcement over 75% reinforcement by pigeons. *Learning & Behavior, 37*(4), 289–98.

Goldman, A. (1999). *Knowledge in a Social World*. Oxford: Oxford University Press.

(2006). *Simulating Minds*. Oxford: Oxford University Press.

Goupil, L., Romand-Monnier, M., and Kouider, S. (2016). Infants ask for help when they know they don't know. *Proceedings of the National Academy of Sciences, 113*, 3492–6. http://doi:10.1073/pnas.1515129113

Gruber, M., Gelman, B., and Ranganath, C. (2014). States of curiosity modulate hippocampus-dependent learning via the dopaminergic circuit. *Neuron, 84*, 486–96. http://doi:10.1016/j.neuron.2014.08.060

Hacquard, V. (2014). Bootstrapping attitudes. *Proceedings of SALT, 24*, 330–52. http://doi:10.3765/salt.v24i0.2434

Harris, P. L. (2012). *Trusting What You're Told: How Children Learn from Others*. Cambridge, MA: Harvard University Press.

Harris, P. L., Ronfard, S., and Bartz, D. (2017a). Young children's developing conception of knowledge and ignorance: Work in progress. *European Journal of Developmental Psychology, 14*, 221–32. http://doi:10.1080/17405629 .2016.1190267

Harris, P. L., Yang, B., and Cui, Y. (2017b). "I don't know": Children's early talk about knowledge. *Mind & Language, 32*, 283–307. http://doi:10.1111/mila .12143

Karttunen, L. (1977). Syntax and semantics of questions. *Linguistics and Philosophy, 1*, 3–44. http://doi:10.1007/978-94-009-9509-3_6

Kidd, C., and Hayden, B. (2015). The psychology and neuroscience of curiosity. *Neuron*, *88*, 449–60. http://doi:10.1016/j.neuron.2015.09.010

Kishimoto, T., Shizawa, Y., Yasuda, J., Hinobayashi, T., and Minami, T. (2007). Do pointing gestures by infants provoke comments from adults? *Infant Behavior & Development*, *30*, 562–7. http://doi:10.1016/j.infbeh.2007.04.001

Kovács, Á. (2016). Belief files in theory of mind reasoning. *Review of Philosophy and Psychology*, *7*, 509–27. http://doi:10.1007/s13164-015-0236-5

Kovács, Á., Tauzin, T., Téglás, E., Gergely, G., and Csibra, G. (2014). Pointing as epistemic request: 12-month-olds point to receive new information. *Infancy*, *19*, 543–57. http://doi:10.1111/infa.12060

Levelt, W. (1989). *Speaking: From Intention to Articulation*. Cambridge, MA: MIT Press.

Lewis, S., Hacquard, V., and Lidz, J. (2012). The semantics and pragmatics of belief reports in preschoolers. *Proceedings of SALT*, *22*, 247–67.

Liszkowski, U., Carpenter, M., and Tomasello, M. (2007). Pointing out new news, old news, and absent referents at 12 months of age. *Developmental Science*, *10*, F1–F7. http://doi:10.1111/j.1467-7687.2006.00552.x

(2008). Twelve-month-olds communicate helpfully and appropriately for knowledgeable and ignorant partners. *Cognition*, *108*, 732–9. http://doi:10.1016/j.cognition.2008.06.013

Litman, J. (2005). Curiosity and the pleasures of learning: Wanting and liking new information. *Cognition and Emotion*, *19*, 793–814. http://doi:10.1080/02699930541000101

Lockl, K., and Schneider, W. (2007). Knowledge about the mind: Links between theory of mind and later metamemory. *Child Development*, *78*, 148–167. http://doi:10.1111/j.1467-8624.2007.00990.x

Loewenstein, G. (1994). The psychology of curiosity: A review and reinterpretation. *Psychological Bulletin*, *116*, 75–98. http://doi:10.1037/0033-2909.116.1.75

Lucca, K., and Wilbourn, M. (2016). Communicating to learn: Infants' pointing gestures result in optimal learning. *Child Development*, *89*, 941–960. http://doi:10.1111/cdev.12707

Lyons, K., and Ghetti, S. (2013). I don't want to pick! Introspection on uncertainty supports early strategic behavior. *Child Development*, *84*, 726–736. http://doi:10.1111/cdev.12004

Mills, C., Legare, C., Bills, M., and Mejias, C. (2010). Preschoolers use questions as a tool to acquire knowledge from different sources. *Journal of Cognition and Development*, *11*, 533–560. http://doi:10.1080/15248372.2010.516419

Nelson, T. O., and Narens, L. (1990). Metamemory: A theoretical framework and new findings. In G. H. Bower (ed.), *The Psychology of Learning and Motivation* (pp. 125–73). New York: Academic Press.

Onishi, K., and Baillargeon, R. (2005). Do 15-month-olds understand false beliefs? *Science*, *308*, 255–258. http://doi:10.1126/science.1107621

Perry, C., and Barron, A. (2013). Honey bees selectively avoid difficult choices. *Proceedings of the National Academy of Sciences*, *110*, 19155–19159. http://doi:10.1073/pnas.1314571110

Shatz, M., Wellman, H., and Silber, S. (1983). The acquisition of mental verbs: A systematic investigation of the first reference to mental state. *Cognition, 14,* 301–321. http://doi:10.1016/0010-0277(83)90008-2

Simons, M. (2007). Observations on embedding verbs, evidentiality, and presup position. *Lingua, 117,* 1034–1056. http://doi:10.1016/j.lingua.2006.05.006

Southgate, V., and Vernetti, A. (2014). Belief-based action prediction in preverbal infants. *Cognition, 130,* 1–10. http://doi:10.1016/j.cognition.2013.08.008

Southgate, V., Senju, A., and Csibra, G. (2007). Action anticipation through attribution of false belief by 2-year-olds. *Psychological Science, 18,* 587–592. http://doi:10.1111/j.1467-9280.2007.01944.x

Southgate, V., van Maanen, C., and Csibra, G. (2010). Infant pointing: Communication to cooperate or communication to learn. *Child Development, 78,* 735–740. http://doi:10.1111/j.1467-8624.2007.01028.x

Spelke, E., and Kinzler, K. (2007). Core knowledge. *Developmental Science, 10,* 89–96. http://doi:10.1111/j.1467-7687.2007.00569.x

Stahl, A., and Feigenson, L. (2015). Observing the unexpected enhances infants' learning and exploration. *Science, 348,* 91–94. http://doi:10.1126/science .aaa3799

Usher, M., and McClelland, J. (2001). The time course of perceptual choice: The leaky, competing accumulator model. *Psychological Review, 108,* 550–592. http://doi:10.1037/0033-295x.108.3.550

Westra, E. (2016). Pragmatic development and false belief task. *Review of Philosophy and Psychology, 8,* 235–257. http://doi:10.1007/s13164-016-032 0-5

Whitcomb, D. (2010). Curiosity was framed. *Philosophy and Phenomenological Research, 81,* 664–87. http://doi:10.1111/j.1933-1592.2010.00394.x

Williamson, T. (2000). *Knowledge and Its Limits.* Oxford: Oxford University Press.

Woodward, A. (1998). Infants selectively encode the goal object of an actor's reach. *Cognition, 69,* 1–34. http://doi:10.1016/s0010-0277(98)00058-4

Wu, Z., and Gros-Louis, J. (2014). Caregivers provide more labeling responses to infants' pointing than to infants' object-directed vocalizations. *Journal of Child Language, 42,* 1–24. http://doi:10.1017/s0305000914000221

# 3    The Point, the Shrug, and the Question of Clarification

*Paul L. Harris*

In the course of the last century, research on children's questions sparked intermittently but did not lead to a sustained research program. I am optimistic that this is about to change. In earlier work, based largely on diary studies, the focus was primarily on the child and his or her motives for asking a question. The child's interlocutor was kept in the background. By contrast, current research has increasingly underlined the dialogic setting in which questions are asked and the nature of the replies that children might receive. In these more recent studies, questions are viewed as a way for children to gather information from other people and beyond that as an important component of children's emerging skill at maintaining a conversation. To explain my optimism about where we are headed, it is useful to look back at several earlier contributions and to underline the progress we have made in our conceptualization of children's question.

## Early Approaches

One of the earliest students of child psychology, James Sully, was intrigued by the extent to which young children, including his own son, broached existential questions, for example, "Who made God?" (Sully, 2000 [1896]). Sully was less interested in the capacity for asking questions than in the motive – the almost philosophical puzzlement – behind such questions.

Some thirty years later, Piaget's approach was similar in spirit, albeit more judgmental in practice (Piaget, 1926). He argued that children naively assume that most phenomena are designed for human purposes. Hence, when they ask a question about a given outcome or entity – for example, "Why can you see lightning better at night?" – their motive is to understand the particular human purpose that it serves. By implication, young children are not really prone to the metaphysical probing that intrigued Sully. Rather, they assume that the cosmos has been designed for human purposes and they simply want to know the function of particular items of cosmic furniture.

Criticizing Piaget's view, Nathan Isaacs claimed that he was misinterpreting children's thinking (Isaacs, 1930). He acknowledged that children are often puzzled and ask many why-questions but, he insisted, they are puzzled mainly when they encounter an outcome that they regard as unexpected or untoward. For example, when they ask why butter sinks into hot toast, they do so because chunks of matter do *not* ordinarily sink into a supporting surface. What they are seeking, therefore, is not some teleological explanation of this unexpected outcome in terms of human purposes – as implied by Piaget. Rather they are asking for the resolution of an anomalous departure from their past experience of everyday causality.

Despite the differences among these early theorists, they ultimately shared a similar perspective and methodology. They effectively looked past the various illustrative questions that they discuss in order to propose an underlying motivation for a gamut of questions – be it existential angst, a need to understand the purpose served by a given phenomenon, or puzzlement at an anomalous deviation. All three writers were also inclined to regard children's questions as the speech acts of quasi-autonomous individuals. Hence, they paid little attention to the dialogue in which the questions were embedded, the persons being asked, or the answers supplied. This meant that they did not portray children as participants in an ongoing conversation that might add to their existing knowledge or indeed help to shape their assumptions about how knowledge can be acquired. Admittedly, there are exceptions. Sully, for example, reported some sustained exchanges between one child and his parent. But, even in such instances, Sully's focus was one-sided – on the child's tenacity in pursuing a given issue rather than on the answers supplied by the parent or their potential role in provoking more questions by the child.

In the 1980s, Barbara Tizard and Martin Hughes moved decisively away from these early endeavors. Instead of collecting examples of interesting questions noted down by parents and companions, they made use of audio recording to collect a representative sample of questions (Tizard & Hughes, 1984). They were also more systematic in their choice of sample and setting – they made recordings of working and middle-class four-year-olds, recording the same children both at home and in preschool.

Three key findings emerged. First, Tizard and Hughes concluded that children's questions should not be viewed simply as manifestations of epistemic puzzlement. They are often embedded in a dialogue in which children can, in principle, gather information from a parent or teacher to allay their puzzlement. Thus, Tizard and Hughes emphasized a basic characteristic of questions that Sully, Piaget, and Isaacs tended to over-look or downplay. Questions can serve as a tool by which children gather information from other people. As such, they are likely to be an important engine for children's cognitive development, especially in those cultures where question-asking is encouraged. (For further discussion of cross-cultural variation in such encouragement, see Chapter 5 as well as Chapter 10.) The second feature of children's questions highlighted by Tizard and Hughes is the recurrence of what they call "passages of intellectual search." Children did not simply ask a single question about a given topic. They often asked a series of questions, building on the answers that they received in order to pursue further lines of inquiry. Such passages reinforced the conclusion that children use questions to enlarge their stock of information about the world. Finally, Tizard and Hughes found that the frequency with which children ask questions depends markedly on the social setting. Children asked more questions, and engaged in passages of intellectual search more often, when they were at home talking to a familiar caregiver rather than at preschool surrounded by peers.

Taken together, the recordings made by Tizard and Hughes (1984) helped to move away from the view of the child as a quasi-autonomous questioner. They successfully showed that questions thrive in particular social settings and that some exchanges amount to a sustained tutorial in which children can propose and refine their ideas. Still, as we shall see, subsequent research has also highlighted the heterogeneity of children's questions. Some are decidedly epistemic in orientation but others are not.

Chouinard (2007) took a closer look at children's questions in the home setting. Using the CHILDES database, she explored the variety of answers that children ranging from two to five years aim to elicit when they ask a question. In her approach, unlike that of Sully, Piaget, and Isaacs, there was no attempt to identify a single, governing principle underlying children's questions. Nor was there a focus on the sustained, curiosity-based dialogues highlighted so vividly by Tizard and Hughes. Instead, in a systematic survey of all the questions that children asked, Chouinard identified a heterogeneous set of motives. Many questions are indeed aimed at securing information. In fact, from the earliest observa-tions at two years of age, information-seeking questions form the majority of the questions that children ask. Some of those questions aim to secure relatively straightforward factual information whereas – from about thirty months – there are others that aim at securing explanatory information. However, children ask a variety of questions that are not information-seeking in any straightforward sense. They use questions to seek atten-tion, permission, help, or clarification from an interlocutor. In sum, even if we acknowledge – as Sully, Piaget, and Isaacs did not – that children can often learn a good deal about the world from asking questions, we should certainly not assume that such an epistemic motive is the only motive. Questions serve a variety of interpersonal functions – as discussed in more detail below in the context of questions of clarification.

In a follow-up study that included still younger children ranging from 1 to 5 years with a focus on two early age periods: 12–17 months and 18–23 months, Chouinard (2007) invited parents to keep a diary record of their children's question-asking. Given that many of the youngest children were not able to formulate their questions in words, parents were trained to keep a careful, descriptive record of their child's behavior and vocalizations, and to venture their interpretation of what the child intended to ask. For example, one child picked up an unfamiliar fruit – a kiwi – held it toward her parent with a puzzled expression on her face and said, "Uh?" The parent glossed this combination of action, expression, and vocalization as a question: "What's this?" As in the initial CHILDES-based study, the majority – but again not the entirety – of children's questions recorded in this follow-up study proved to be information-seeking questions and this held true even for the two groups of one-year-olds. Also, in line with the CHILDES-based study, younger children mainly asked for simple factual information. Explanation-seeking questions became more frequent – albeit still in the minority – from around thirty months, as expected from the first study.

This brief survey of past research shows that there is not one single, overarching epistemic motive that lies behind all of children's questions. Children ask questions with a range of motives, some prosaic and practical, some deeper and more reflective. The recognition that question-asking is a flexible and early-emerging tool for social interaction and social learning highlights the species-specific nature of that tool. There is no doubt that our primate cousins engage in social learning. For example, they imitate the use of tools by a conspecific with varying degrees of fidelity (Horner et al., 2006). Yet they do not gather information or seek clarification by asking questions. Even when they have learned to use a communication system, such as a keyboard of symbols – a system that could, in principle, be used to ask questions – they do not do so, despite the fact that they put the keyboard to other interpersonal uses by seeking help or requesting treats (Harris, 2012).

Below, I take a closer look at three intriguing aspects of children's early questions. First, given that even preverbal toddlers are often glossed by their caregivers as asking information-seeking questions, I ask whether that attribution is really warranted. Second, if toddlers and young children do ask information-seeking questions, apparently aimed at filling an epistemic gap, I ask whether they are able to monitor their own knowledge states, especially states of ignorance. Third, I turn to a distinctive, but neglected, motive for asking questions. Chouinard (2007) found that children sometimes ask questions not just to gather information about the world but also to clarify what an interlocutor has just said. A comprehensive account of early question-asking needs to incorporate children's ability to monitor not just their states of ignorance but also glitches in their ongoing comprehension of the conversation in which they are engaged.

## The Early Emergence of an Interrogative Stance

Granted that children appear to start asking questions at an early age, it is worth probing the basis for such questions in more detail. One possibility – especially in the second year of life – is that toddlers' questions are best seen as diffuse, expressive reactions to an encounter with an unfamiliar object or situation. For example, when the child described by Chouinard (2007) held up a kiwifruit and said "Uh?" she may have been simply expressing her curiosity about a novel object. By contrast, the parent's gloss – "What's this?" – attributes a more straightforwardly interrogative stance. It implies that the child did not know the name or function of the object and was asking her caregiver to supply pertinent information to fill that epistemic gap. Recent experimental research lends support to this richer interpretation. In particular, index finger pointing, which typically emerges toward the end of the first year, displays several question-like characteristics.

First, infants produce points more frequently when they interact with an informative or knowledgeable interlocutor rather than with someone who has recently proved uninformative or ignorant (Begus & Southgate, 2012; Kovács et al., 2014). Second, information that is received in the wake of pointing toward an object tends to be retained more accurately than information supplied in the wake of other signals of attention, such as looking toward or reaching for an object (Begus et al., 2014; Lucca & Wilbourn, 2016). By implication, pointing is accompanied by a preparedness to receive and encode information. Third, infants are more likely to display neural signs of cognitive readiness (i.e., theta activity) when they see that a hitherto informative interlocutor – as contrasted with a hitherto uninformative interlocutor – is about to interact with a novel object. Such differential neural activity is also shown when infants see someone they know to be a speaker of their language – as contrasted with a speaker of a foreign language – about to interact with a novel object (Begus et al., 2016). Fourth, caregivers are prone to view infant pointing as a request for information, especially linguistic information. Wu and Gros-Louis (2015) observed twelve-month-old infants during free play with their parents. When infants simply looked at an object and vocalized, parents were less likely to respond by labeling the object as compared to when infants pointed at the object. Overall, mothers tended to respond with more labels than did fathers but the bias to offer a label in response to an infant point was evident in both mothers and fathers.

These various findings are consistent with the idea that infants are capable of adopting a questioning stance, especially via a pointing gesture. In adopting that stance, they are prone to seek information from a potentially informative interlocutor via pointing, to manifest a neural signal associated with cognitive receptivity, and to retain input provided in the wake of a pointing gesture. In turn, caregivers are disposed to treat a pointing gesture as an interrogative act to which they respond informatively, especially by supplying object names. By implication, even in the absence of the ability to produce a well-formed verbal question targeting a specific piece of information such as the name, or function, or location of an object, infants possess the ability to produce question-like acts of communication and are treated as so doing. Such competence implies that key features of regular question-asking are available in infancy, i.e., ahead of children's eventual recourse to the verbal channel. These features are: (i) an ability to monitor for the existence of an epistemic gap – especially ignorance with respect to a novel object; and (ii) a disposition to signal that epistemic gap to an interlocutor. In the next section, I seek to document those two features in more detail.

### Monitoring and Expressing Ignorance

Chimpanzees and young children (aged 27–32 months) appropriately seek out more information when they are uncertain about the location of a hidden object. For example, both species proceed to search in a given tube if they have seen a desirable object inserted into it. By contrast, if they have not seen the insertion and face several tubes in which the object might be located, they are likely to adjust their posture – to bend their head or body – in order to peer inside each tube before searching in the tube where the desirable object can be seen; alternatively, they reject the uncertainty of obtaining a large reward and opt instead for a smaller reward in a known location (Call & Carpenter, 2001; Neldner et al., 2015). These results imply that chimpanzees and children are able to monitor their own cognitive states. They recognize when they are ignorant or uncertain and, in such cases, they seek more information or opt instead for more certain outcomes. Still, such uncertainty monitoring is not equivalent to an expression of ignorance if, by that, we mean a deliberate communicative act or gesture, aimed at a conspecific in order to signal ignorance or uncertainty.

Recent research has started to uncover when infants begin to produce such signals. Goupil et al. (2016) first sought to train a group of twenty-month-old infants to signal when they were uncertain. On training trials, an object was presented hidden inside one of two containers. When infants pointed to one of the containers, their caregivers did not respond. Instead, they waited for infants to turn to look at them and then pushed the correct container toward them. Thus, infants were effectively taught to seek help by looking at their caregiver when they could not be certain of the hidden object's location. A control group, by contrast, received no such training in help seeking.

Both groups then received test trials, which were either "possible" or "impossible." On possible trials, infants were able to watch a toy being hidden in one of two containers whereas on impossible trials, the hiding was done behind a curtain. Following either type of hiding, the two containers were covered with a screen for several seconds. Once uncovered, infants could point to one of the two containers and that particular container was pushed within the infant's reach.

When the trained infants needed help – i.e., when they were uncertain of the toy's location – they often signaled in an appropriate fashion. Thus, they were more likely to look toward their caregiver on impossible as compared to possible trials. Moreover, on possible trials, they were more likely to signal for help if the containers had been covered for a long delay, thereby making it harder for them to remember the correct container. Not surprisingly, given their well-calibrated help seeking, the trained infants did better at obtaining the hidden toy than the untrained group. The untrained infants also looked at their caregiver sometimes but not in the systematic fashion displayed by the trained infants. Thus, the untrained infants did not increase looks to their caregiver on impossible or long delay trials. By implication, training appears to have been needed for such looks to be produced in a deliberate fashion aimed at signaling uncertainty. Overall, these findings confirm that infants of around twenty months can be trained to signal ignorance. By implication, young children are capable not just of monitoring states of uncertainty and adjusting their search behavior accordingly, they are also capable of signaling that uncertainty to a caregiver. However, given that this was, by design, a training study, the findings provide no evidence that infants spontaneously signal their ignorance under appropriate circumstances.

In discussing the interrogative stance, we saw that young infants deploy index finger pointing as a nonverbal precursor for a verbal question. Is there an equivalent nonverbal gesture that infants might employ to express ignorance? An interesting candidate – the shrug – was first described and analyzed in some detail by Darwin (1872). He observes that this gesture can include several components – the lifting of the shoulders, the raising of the hands with the palms flipped outward, a tilt of the head, elevation of the eyebrows together with wrinkling of the forehead, and the mouth generally open. Interestingly, although he was a meticulous observer, Darwin acknowledges that it was only when he watched himself in the mirror that he realized that his eyebrows were raised and his mouth opened when he shrugged. He also notes that the gesture can vary by degrees – for example, in someone seated it might consist only of the "the mere turning outwards of the open hands with separated fingers" (Darwin, 1872, p. 265).

Speculating on the origins of the gesture, Darwin writes that he had never seen young English children shrug their shoulders but nevertheless goes on to recount a report that he had received concerning two young English girls, raised in England with an English nursemaid. Both girls, for a period before the age of eighteen months, produced the shrug gesture. Based on information supplied by the girls' father, Darwin proposes that the gesture may have been inherited via their French grandfather. At the same time, Darwin's subsequent remarks on the ubiquity of the shrug gesture in a wide range of cultures lead him to describe the shrug as "a gesture natural to mankind" – one that conveys a helpless or apologetic frame of mind.

Despite Darwin's fascinating observations, there has been little systematic research on the development of the shrug gesture. There is, however, tantalizing evidence from the case study of a single child. Acredolo and Goodwyn (1985) recorded the utterances and gestures of Kate, the firstborn child of professional parents, between the ages of nine and twenty-four months. At the age of fifteen months, Kate acquired what Acredolo and Goodwyn describe as an "I dunno" gesture. In line with Darwin's description, Kate raised her shoulders and lifted her hands up, with her palms flipped outward. At this point her spoken vocabulary was very limited (twenty-two words) although she did go on to produce the verbal phrase "I dunno" some two months later.

Kate produced some gestures autonomously – for example, to indicate a slide, she waved her hand downward. The "I dunno" gesture, by contrast, appears to have been acquired via imitation of an adult action. More specifically, Kate had observed her parents modeling the gesture in combination with a question such as: "Where's the ...?" Nevertheless, her production of the gesture went beyond faithful imitation of her parents because she spontaneously deployed it later in novel contexts. For example, at sixteen months, she watched a computer-generated graphics display of flower-like designs on a TV screen. The designs changed shape in time to music and then disappeared from the screen. Kate turned to her mother and produced her sign for a flower – a pretend sniffing action – together with a shrug. Acredolo and Goodwyn report that: "It was clear to the adults around her that she wanted to know where the flowers had gone" (1985, p. 48). From this point on, Kate often combined a shrug in a pivot-like fashion either with another gesture, as in the example of the flower designs just described, or with a word in her growing vocabulary of between approximately 50 and 100 words.

In a follow-up study, Acredolo and Goodwyn (1988) interviewed mothers of infants aged sixteen to eighteen months about their children's repertoire of gestures. A small proportion of the gestures that mothers described fell into the category of "replies" in response to a question and within this category, the shoulder shrug indicating "I don't know" was the most common gesture – with an average onset at the age of fourteen months. However, Acredolo and Goodwyn (1988) provide no further information about the number of toddlers who produced this particular gesture.

To study the emergence of the shrug gesture and its relationship to the production of verbal statements of ignorance, notably "I don't know," Bartz (2017) analyzed data from 64 children enrolled in a longitudinal study of early language development – the Language Development Project (Goldin-Meadow et al., 2014). The children's families were a representative sample of the U.S. population in terms of socioeconomic status and education. Starting at 14 months, children's speech with their caregivers was recorded on a regular basis at 4-month intervals. By 18 months, 12 of the 64 children (19 percent) had been observed to produce what coders judged to be a shrug or flip of the hands that expressed ignorance – typically in response to a question from a caregiver – and by 42 months, 48 of 64 (75 percent) had done so. Verbal statements of ignorance were slower to emerge. Thus, the utterance "I don't know" was almost completely absent at 18 months but its production increased sharply with age. By 42 months, 60 of the 64 children (94 percent) had been heard to say, "I don't know."

These findings suggest that many toddlers initially signal their ignorance nonverbally with verbal claims of ignorance emerging soon thereafter. Moreover, children produce that signal in the course of ongoing social interaction in the home – for example, when a caregiver asks a question that the child cannot answer. By implication, expressions of ignorance occur not just when toddlers encounter a practical dilemma and look toward an adult for help. They are also produced in the context of a dialogue – for example, in reply to a caregiver's question.

Bartz (2017) went on to examine this possibility in an experimental study. Children ranging from 16 to 37 months were shown a set of pictures and the experimenter invited them to name each of the entities depicted by asking: "What's that?" Some pictures were deliberately chosen because they would be easy for toddlers to name (e.g., a bird, a book, etc.) but others were chosen because they would be difficult to name (e.g., an unusual hardware tool). Not surprisingly, children made more naming errors when faced with the hard-to-name entities. However, beyond such naming errors, they also produced more filled speech pauses (e.g., "umm"), looked more often at a nearby adult (either the experimenter or their mother), asked a question (e.g., "What's that?"), or said, "I don't know." This differential pattern of responding with respect to hard- as compared to easy-to-name entities was found among younger infants (16 to 27 months) but was more systematic among older infants (28 to 37 months). By implication, beginning in the middle of the second year, toddlers increasingly monitor their own knowledge states and signal gaps in an appropriate fashion.

Further insight into young children's expressions of ignorance – as well as knowledge – can be obtained by looking more systematically at children's production of the mental state verb "know" in the context of everyday conversation. Early analyses of children's production of cognitive verbs adopted a relatively conservative stance by discarding "I don't know" utterances on the grounds that such utterances amount to little more than a conversational demurral (Shatz et al., 1983; Bartsch & Wellman, 1995). Harris et al. (2017b) opted for a more inclusive analysis by analyzing all children's utterances that included the verb "know," focusing on three children: Adam and Sarah, who spoke English, and Qiānqian, who spoke Mandarin. Roger Brown and his colleagues had recorded the utterances of Adam and Sarah at regular intervals in the context of a study of language acquisition (Brown, 1973). All recorded utterances produced by Adam and Sarah that included the mental verb "know" were analyzed from twenty-seven months (the age at which recordings had begun) to the age of thirty-six months. The utterances of Qiānqian (芊芊) had been recorded and transcribed from sixteen to thirty-nine months by her mother, a psycholinguist. All utterances produced by Qiānqian that included the mental verb *zhi1dao4* were analyzed. *Zhi1dao4* is an epistemic verb that is used in the context of factual knowledge.

An initial analysis showed that – for all three children – most of their references to "know" were spontaneous, rather than echoes of their interlocutor's prior utterance. Next, children's "know" utterances were examined to determine whether children referred only to themselves – as in "I don't know" – or also made references to other people. The majority of references were indeed to children's own states of knowledge or ignorance but they also referred to those of their interlocutor. Interestingly, all three children rarely referred to those of a third party, i.e., someone who was not part of the conversation.

Children used "know" utterances for three main pragmatic functions: (i) to affirm knowledge; (ii) to deny knowledge; and (iii) to ask a question about knowledge. But the frequency of these functions varied sharply depending on whom the child was talking about. Affirmations were produced with respect to both the self ("I know . . .") and the interlocutor ("You know . . ."). Denials, by contrast, were almost exclusively produced with respect to the self ("I don't know . . .") rather than the interlocutor ("You don't know . . ."). Finally, questions displayed the opposite asymmetry – they were never posed with respect to the self ("Do I know . . .?") but often posed with respect to the interlocutor ("Do you know . . .?"). To firmly establish the existence of this asymmetry, the utterances of a further eight English-speaking children from the CHILDES database were subsequently analyzed (Bartz, 2017; Harris et al., 2017a). Like Adam, Sarah, and Qiānqian, these children also restricted denials almost exclusively to utterances concerning the self rather than the interlocutor whereas they restricted questions almost exclusively to utterances concerning the interlocutor rather than the self.

How can this markedly asymmetric pattern be explained? Standard analyses of young children's theory of mind have emphasized the fact that, as a theory, it is neutral with respect to the person being conceptualized – the theory is applied with equal facility or difficulty to the self and to other people (Gopnik, 1993). Indeed a large body of findings, especially with respect to children's understanding of false belief, has pointed to a very similar timetable whether children are invited to conceptualize the beliefs of others or the beliefs of the self (Wellman et al., 2001).

However, against this routine assumption of theoretical neutrality with respect to different persons, a plausible interpretation of early talk about knowing is that children have some kind of privileged access to their own states of knowledge and ignorance (Harris, 2018). This would be consistent with the evidence described earlier suggesting that toddlers can monitor their cognitive states. On this view, when asked a question, children search their knowledge base and either retrieve the requested information or fail to do so. In the latter case, they register their ignorance and say: "I don't know." When told something that they already know, they are aware of their prior knowledge and they say so: "I know." Finally, possessing such awareness of their states of knowledge and ignorance, they do not pose questions about those states. Thus, children do not pose questions about their own knowledge to their interlocutors. For example, they did not ask: "Do I know …?"

What about children's monitoring of the knowledge or ignorance of other people, especially their interlocutor? A plausible answer is that lacking any such comparable privileged access into the cognitive states of other people, children come instead to rely on overt evidence and simple heuristics in assessing what others know or might know. For example, children are likely to encounter evidence of a broad asymmetry between what they themselves know and what others know. As a result, they may be led toward a deferential stance: to assume that, on many topics, others know more than they themselves know. Especially when children ask a question, their interlocutors are likely to supply evidence of knowing something that children do not. To illustrate with the help of an earlier example, when a toddler holds up an unfamiliar fruit and says "Uh" or points to it and says, "What's that?" he or she is likely to receive an informative answer: "That's a kiwi." More generally, whenever children's pointing gestures, interrogative vocalizations, and verbal questions are answered informatively, they will receive a tacit reminder that they know less than their interlocutor and that their own ignorance is no guide to what their interlocutor knows. Thus, by engaging in conversation, and especially by having their questions answered, children can come to realize that in many domains, knowledge is distributed unequally. Even if they do not know something and are aware of their ignorance, their interlocutor may be better informed. By implication, when children engage in conversation, they do not simply draw important, person-neutral lessons about the nature of mental states (Harris, 1996), as shown by the large body of findings demonstrating that deaf children make slow progress in conceptualization of belief (Peterson & Siegal, 2000). When they engage in conversation, they also have an opportunity to draw person-specific lessons – to realize that their own ignorance is a poor guide to what others know – so that questions about what their interlocutor knows are appropriate whereas denials of what their interlocutor knows are likely to be misplaced.

Admittedly, children will sometimes encounter the reverse asymmetry – situations in which they know what their interlocutor does not. Indeed, experimental evidence has shown that toddlers from eighteen months upward are alert to occasions when their interlocutor was absent and failed to observe where or how a desirable object might be retrieved. Under such circumstances, they spontaneously provide helpful information via pointing, vocalization, or a mimed demonstration (O'Neill, 1996; Knudsen & Liszkowski, 2012; Behne et al., 2014). Reflecting such asymmetrical knowledge, there will also be occasions when interlocutors pose genuine questions to children – inviting them to supply information that they, the interlocutors, lack even if the scope of those questions is likely to be relatively narrow. Thus, caregivers may ask toddlers questions about their preferences and feelings ("More milk?" "Does it hurt?"), their possessions ("Where's Teddy?" "Is that your cup?"), as well as episodes that occurred in their absence ("Where did Daddy go?" "Did you fall over?"). On these occasions, children can reasonably conclude that they know what their interlocutor does not and supply the missing information. However, these occasions will mostly pertain to the child's own subjective states and immediate umwelt.

Granted this pattern, it is likely that children will end up being circumspect with respect to what their interlocutors do not know. In general, and especially with respect to the type of common knowledge that is stored in semantic memory, children will be less informed than their interlocutors. Hence, when they do not know something it would make sense for them to ask information-seeking questions and it would also make sense for them not to assume and not to affirm that their interlocutor does not know something. As we have seen, toddlers do indeed display these two characteristics: they ask many information-seeking questions whereas they almost never aver their interlocutor's ignorance.

To what extent does this account attribute meta-awareness to young children and if so what is the scope of that meta-awareness? The language data just discussed do suggest that two-year-olds are aware of their own cognitive states. Thus, in their own case, they talk appropriately about what they know and also what they do not know. Carruthers (Chapter 2) is dubious about such a claim. He argues instead that existing experimental evidence shows that infants are capable of meta-awareness but primarily with respect to other people. The indices of self-awareness discussed hitherto can be better construed as the workings of a simpler accumulator model whereby, when insufficient evidence is accumulated to answer a question, children can communicate that lack by saying: "I don't know." On this view, it is not the case that children are aware of lacking an answer to the question. Rather, they simply lack enough evidence to supply an answer and that lack is sufficient to trigger the "I don't know" formula.

For the moment, two comments are worth noting. First, different techniques, including the violation-of-expectancy paradigm and the predictive looking paradigm seemed to provide persuasive evidence that infants can attribute ignorance, and arguably a false belief, to another agent. However, recent findings show less convergence (Dörrenberg et al., 2018; Kulke et al., 2018). For the time being then, caution is warranted in the attribution of metacognition about others to infants.

Second, it is hard to see how toddlers could come to adopt and produce the "I don't know" formula without some awareness of the mental state – notably ignorance – that is the setting for the production of that formula. Consider a couple of parallel cases. We might be tempted to propose that when toddlers say "Ouch!" we should beware of assuming that they have any awareness of the pain that they are experiencing. Instead, it could be argued children have acquired a formula – a formula that they have learned to utter when in a certain state of physical discomfort. Similarly, they might acquire a formula such as "Yuck" or "Yummy" when in particular gustatory states, or a formula such as "Scared" or "Mad" when in particular emotional states (c.f. Wellman et al., 1995). But in all of these cases, it is unclear how the unaware child could learn the circumstances in which it is appropriate to produce the relevant formula. For the time being then, I prefer to claim that children are aware of being in various mental states – affective as well as cognitive – and report them appropriately.

## Questions of Clarification

Recent experimental analysis has drawn attention to intriguing features of adult conversation that help it to proceed smoothly, especially in the context of question and answer sequences. First, across a diverse set of languages, the average temporal gap between the end of a speaker's question and the start of the respondent's answer is remarkably short – approximately 250 msec. – with some modest variation across languages (Stivers et al., 2009). Indeed, the gap is sufficiently short that some of the psychological processing undertaken by the respondent in formulating a reply almost certainly takes place as the question is being delivered. In other words, the processes of comprehension and production conducted by the respondent are likely to be partially concurrent.

Second, in the case of yes-no questions, respondents often take longer to initiate their answer if it is a negative, or some variant of a negative. A plausible explanation for this delay is that respondents effectively take longer to deliver a reply, which they presume to run counter to the reply expected by the questioner. By implication, respondents calculate prior to delivering their answer the reply that their interlocutor is anticipating.

Third, respondents appear to be sensitive to the obligation that faces them in the immediate wake of a question, namely, to offer a reply within a relatively brief interval. A tacit acknowledgment of that obligation is apparent in respondents' non-lexical vocalizations such as "umm" or "uh" – effectively signaling that a reply is on its way.

These various findings are consistent with the existence of what has been dubbed an interaction engine (Levinson, 2006) or conversation machine (Enfield, 2017): a distinctively human mental mechanism that is highly attuned to the temporal and social demands of everyday conversation, especially those that arise in the context of simple questions. At present, we do not know much about the development of this conversation engine in early childhood.

One possibility is that children are slowly inducted into the obligations that conversation imposes, especially on the recipient of a question. They might initially comprehend simple questions from a caregiver about their personal concerns – for example, "Do you want some more?" "Is that yours?" "Are you thirsty?" – but have less sensitivity to the obligation upon them to answer or to the temporal envelope within which their answer should be delivered (Stivers et al., 2018). Alternatively, children might, from the early stages of their language-learning career, operate with some generic assumptions about the turn taking that is routine in a great deal of conversation and especially prominent in question and answer sequences. On this view, even toddlers might recognize the cues signaling that their interlocutor has asked a question, and feel some pressure to supply an answer even if they do not routinely honor the kind of time constraints present in adult conversation. Below, I review a modest body of research suggesting that one key feature of the conversation machine is up and running among young children – including two- and three-year-olds – although it does not display the calibration observed among adults.

In the course of everyday adult conversation, listeners engage in online monitoring of their comprehension. When there is a glitch, they ask a question calling for some type of repair or clarification by the speaker. Sometimes, the listener's signal consists of a specific interrogative such as, "Who?" or "Where?" but sometimes it is a more generic signal such as "Huh?" or "What?" Among adults, repair sequences in which a listener asks for clarification following a glitch in understanding and the speaker provides that clarification – via a repetition, by speaking more slowly, or by adding clarification – are frequent in everyday conversation. For example, in a study of more than 2,000 listener-initiated repair sequences across 12 different languages, repair sequences occurred once every 84 seconds during informal conversation (Dingemanse et al., 2015). Apparently, in the course of adult conversation, comprehension problems are frequently signaled by listeners and frequently dealt with by speakers.

Do young children ask for clarifications when they have a comprehension problem? In principle, we might expect them to do so more often than adults because their comprehension processes are likely to be less efficient. On the other hand, a considerable body of research on the development of metacognition has implied that young children have quite limited insight into their own cognitive processes (Flavell, 1979). Indeed, Markman (1977) showed that elementary school children claimed to have understood a set of verbal instructions about an activity even though the instructions were riddled with gaps and obscurities. Studies of children's reading comprehension have reinforced this negative view by showing that children rarely query blatant inconsistencies in an expository text or narrative (Markman, 1979; Harris et al., 1981). Educational interventions in the context of reading highlight the assumption that children are not disposed to engage in active comprehension monitoring (Palincsar & Brown, 1984).

However, in these various studies of metacognition, children were rarely participating in the back and forth of ordinary conversation. Instead, they listened to a set of instructions or read a text. It was only afterwards that they were invited to say how far they had understood the materials they had been presented with. By contrast, the analyses of everyday conversation between adults described earlier show that comprehension glitches are signaled swiftly – typically in the turn immediately following the problematic utterance. By implication, repair signals are the output of online comprehension processes rather than of retrospective reflection. Accordingly, a more positive assessment of young children's comprehension-monitoring might emerge if we take a close look at how they react to comprehension glitches in the context of ongoing conversation – with either a caregiver of a peer. In particular, we can ask if they ply speakers with questions or clarification when they fail to understand.

Two survey studies immediately suggest a positive answer – even if they differ on the frequency with which children ask clarification questions. First, recall that Chouinard (2007) found that the majority of children's questions in the preschool period were information-seeking but a minority of their questions – approximately 9 percent – were questions of clarification, aimed at understanding what a speaker has just said. In a study of children aged four to eight years, Stivers et al. (2018) found that questions of clarification were actually more frequent than information-seeking questions among both four- to five-year-olds and six- to eight-year-olds. A plausible explanation for the discrepancy in frequency is that Chouinard (2007) focused on the questions that children put to a familiar adult caregiver whereas Stivers et al. (2018) focused on the questions that children put to their peers. Children are likely to think of an adult caregiver as better able to answer information-seeking questions than their peers; conversely, they may find their peers less easy to understand than a caregiver. Below, I review in more detail the emergence and development of clarification questions.

Ninio and Snow (1996) report that although very few children asked clarification questions of adults at fourteen months, about one-third did so at twenty months, and the majority did so at thirty months. Throughout this early period, clarification questions almost always consisted of "Huh?" "What?" or a (partial) repetition of the adult's utterance with a rising intonation. Gallagher (1981) reported similar findings in a study of nine children – mostly two-year-olds. Children produced clarification questions approximately every 8–9 minutes whereas their adult partners did so approximately every 3 minutes. Children mostly produced requests for repetition (e.g., "Huh?") or produced a (partial) repetition of their interlocutor's utterance with a rising intonation. Clarification questions targeting a specific element in the adult's utterance by means of a wh-question remained infrequent. Aviezer (2003) recorded conversations among trios of two- and three-year-olds. Approximately 5 percent of children's turns as speakers were questions of clarification with some indication of an increase with age. These children also asked for a repetition ("What?" or "Huh?") but sometimes asked more targeted questions. Most clarification questions received an appropriate response from the speaker. In summary, from approximately two years children ask simple questions of clarification. In particular, they request that an utterance be repeated or repeat it themselves with a rising interrogative intonation. Targeted questions of clarification also occur but are infrequent.

Spilton and Lee (1977) recorded the spontaneous conversations of pairs of four-year-olds engaged in play activity. They focused on so-called elaborative sequences in which an initial statement by one child led to a puzzled response by the other followed by subsequent attempts at clarification. In about two-thirds of these sequences, the initial statement was judged to be clear in meaning and articulation by adult coders, suggesting that listeners' failure to understand was often due to inattention. The remaining third were judged to be unclear in meaning – for example, the speaker used a pronoun whose referent was unclear. In approximately half of the elaborative sequences, the listener's immediate response was a question aimed at clarification. Children posed generic (e.g., "What?" or "Huh?") and specific (e.g., "Which one?" or "Where?") clarification questions with equal frequency but, as might be expected, specific questions were more effective in eliciting a clarification from the speaker.

Finally, Revelle et al. (1985) conducted a quasi-naturalistic experiment rather than a purely observational study. Three- and four-year-olds interacted with an adult who made a variety of requests. Some requests were deliberately problematic – the intended referent was ambiguous, or too many items were mentioned, or the request was not clearly articulated. Control requests were unproblematic but otherwise similar. As in the study by Spilton and Lee (1977), children responded to problems with questions of clarification – both generic ("What?" or "Huh?") and specific ("The rabbit?" "The big one or the little one?"). Moreover, they asked clarification questions more often for problematic as compared to unproblematic requests. This difference was clearer among four-year-olds but in part because three-year-olds were prone to ask clarification questions even after unambiguous requests.

Children also differentiated between feasible (e.g., "Bring me the cup") and impossible (e.g., "Bring me the refrigerator") requests. They responded to impossible requests with either a question (e.g., "How can I bring it?") or an assertion of difficulty (e.g., "I can't get one") – responses that they almost never gave to feasible requests. By implication, children monitored the adult's requests not just for problems in comprehension but also for their real-world feasibility. Children thought through the request and signaled a glitch ahead of any effort to comply.

In summary, clarifying questions that initiate the repair of a conversational glitch, rather than gather new information about the world, are surprisingly frequent in adult conversation. Indeed, as Enfield (2017) points out, the likelihood of a clarifying question being asked rises very steeply as a conversation proceeds. Ninety-five percent of repair initiations occur within about 4 minutes of the last one. Contrary to the implications of research in the metacognitive tradition, we have intriguing evidence that young children also monitor their comprehension. Like adults, they are prompt in seeking to resolve glitches by asking for clarification with either generic or specific questions. Indeed, questions of clarification appear to be an integral part of children's conversational development. They are evident at two years of age and throughout the preschool period.

## Conclusions

Several interlocking conclusions have emerged from this review. First, it is tempting to think of children's emerging ability to ask questions as the development of a predominantly verbal skill, but there is increasing evidence that an early interrogative stance antedates children's production of explicit, verbal questions. That interrogative stance is especially obvious when toddlers point at unfamiliar objects, sometimes – but not always – with an accompanying vocalization, such as "uh." In adopting that stance toddlers are receptive – as indexed by neural activity and by their enhanced memory – to the information that they elicit. Moreover, their caregivers are prone to supply information in the wake of pointing gestures. Importantly, even at this early, pre-conversational stage, toddlers gauge who is an informative and understandable respondent and who is not. By implication, the considerable sensitivity that preschool children display to the epistemic characteristics of potential informants (Harris, 2012, 2019) is already operating in this earlier phase. Indeed, it is plausible that, based on their experience of the responsiveness of key informants – especially primary caregivers – toddlers form a more generalized expectation about the extent to which the social circle in which they are growing up is or is not responsive to their bids for information.

Analysis of toddlers' signaling capacities – as indexed by their shrug gestures, their verbal disclaimers ("I don't know"), and by their broader production of utterances that include "know" – indicates that they monitor their ongoing states of uncertainty or ignorance. Indeed, such metacognitive awareness would seem to be a prerequisite for asking questions. Toddlers do not assume that others share their ignorance on many matters. When they do not know something, they seek information from other people or ask them what they know.

Finally, a neglected but interesting type of metacognitive awareness is evident in young children's efforts at fixing glitches and gaps in their comprehension. Children ask questions not just to learn about the world but also to ensure their comprehension of what they are told. Indeed, their online sensitivity to whether or not they have understood what an interlocutor has said is likely to impact their subsequent decisions about whom to ask for information.

## Acknowledgments

This work was motivated by a stimulating workshop funded by the Radcliffe Institute in 2016.

## References

Acredolo, L. P., and Goodwyn, S. W. (1985). Symbolic gesturing in language development: A case study. *Human Development, 28,* 40–9. http://doi:10.1159/000272934

(1988). Symbolic gesturing in normal infants. *Child Development, 59,* 450–66. http://doi:10.2307/1130324

Aviezer, O. (2003). Bedtime talk of three-year olds: Collaborative repair of miscommunication. *First Language, 23,* 117–39. http://doi:10.1177/0142723703023001006

Bartsch, K., and Wellman, H. M. (1995). *Children talk about the mind.* New York: Oxford University Press.

Bartz, D. T. (2017). Young children's meta-ignorance. PhD thesis. Cambridge, MA: Harvard University.

Begus, K., and Southgate, V. (2012). Infant pointing serves an interrogative function. *Developmental Science, 15*, 611–77. http://doi:10.1111/j.1467-7687.2012.01160.x

Begus, K., Gliga, T., and Southgate, V. (2014). Infants learn what they want to learn: Responding to infant pointing leads to superior learning. *PLOS ONE, 9*. http://doi.org/10.1371/journal.pone.0108817

(2016). Infants' preferences for native speakers are associated with an expectation of information. *PNAS, 113*, 12397–402. http://doi:10.1073/pnas.1603261113

Behne, T., Carpenter, M., and Tomasello, M. (2014). Young children create iconic gestures to inform others. *Developmental Psychology, 50*, 2049–60. http://doi:10.1037/a0037224

Brown, R. (1973). *A first language: The early stages*. Cambridge, MA: Harvard University Press.

Call, J., and Carpenter, M. (2001). Do apes and children know what they have seen? *Animal Cognition, 3*, 207–20. http://doi:10.1007/s100710100078

Chouinard, M. (2007). Children's questions: A mechanism for cognitive development. *Monographs of the Society for Research in Child Development*, serial no. 286, *72* (no. 1).

Darwin, C. (1872). *The expression of the emotions in man and animals*. London: Murray.

Dingemanse, M., Roberts, S. G., Baranova, J., et al. (2015). Universal principles in the repair of communication problems. *PLOS ONE, 10* (no. 9). http://doi.org/10.1371/journal.pone.0136100

Dörrenberg, S., Rakoczy, H., and Liszkowski, U. (2018). How (not) to measure infant theory of mind: Testing the replicability and validity of four non-verbal measures. *Cognitive Development*. http://doi:10.1016/j.cogdev.2018.01.001

Enfield, N. J. (2017). *How we talk*. New York: Basic Books.

Flavell, J. H. (1979). Metacognition and cognitive monitoring: A new area of cognitive-developmental inquiry. *American Psychologist, 34*, 906–11. http://doi:10.1037/0003-066x.34.10.906

Gallagher, T. M. (1981). Contingent query sequences within adult–child discourse. *Journal of Child Language, 8*, 51–62. http://doi:10.1017/s0305000900003007

Goldin-Meadow, S., Levine, S. C., Hedges, L. V., et al. (2014) New evidence about language and cognitive development based on a longitudinal study: Hypotheses for intervention. *American Psychologist, 69*, 588–99. http://doi:10.1037/a0036886

Gopnik, A. (1993). How we know our minds: The illusion of first-person knowledge of intentionality. *Behavioral and Brain Sciences, 16*, 1–14. http://doi:10.1017/s0140525x00028636

Goupil, L., Romand-Monnier, M., and Kouider, S. (2016). Infants ask for help when they don't know. *PNAS, 113*, 3492–6. http://doi:10.1073/pnas.151529113

Harris, P. L. (1996). Desires, beliefs and language. In P. Carruthers and P. K. Smith (eds.), *Theories of theories of mind* (pp. 200–20). Cambridge: Cambridge University Press. http://doi:10.1017/cbo9780511597985.014

(2012). *Trusting what you're told: How children learn from others*. Cambridge, MA: Belknap Press/Harvard University Press.

(2018). Revisiting privileged access. In J. Proust and M. Fortier (eds.), *Metacognitive diversity: An interdisciplinary approach* (pp. 83–96). Oxford: Oxford University Press. http://doi:10.1093/oso/9780198789710.003.0005

(2019). Infants want input. In V. Grover, P. Uccelli, M. L. Rowe, and E. Lieven (eds.), *Learning through language: Towards an educationally informed theory of language learning* (pp. 31–9). Cambridge: Cambridge University Press.

Harris, P. L., Kruithof, A., Meerum Terwogt, M., and Visser, T. (1981) Children's detection and awareness of textual anomaly. *Journal of Experimental Child Psychology*, *31*, 212–30. http://doi:10.1016/0022-0965(81)90013-8

Harris, P. L, Ronfard, S., and Bartz, D. T. (2017a) Young children's developing conception of knowledge and ignorance: Work in progress. *European Journal of Developmental Psychology*, *14*, 221–32. http://doi:10.1080/17405629.2016.1190267

Harris, P.L., Yang, B., and Cui, Y. (2017b). "I don't know": Children's early talk about knowledge. *Mind and Language*, *32*, 283–307.

Horner, V., Whiten, A., Flynn, E., and de Waal, F. M. (2006). Faithful replication of foraging techniques along cultural transmission chains by chimpanzees and children. *PNAS*, *103*, 13878–83. http://doi:10.1073/pnas.0606015103

Isaacs, N. (1930). Children's "why" questions. In S. Isaacs (ed.), *Intellectual growth in young children*. London: George Routledge & Sons.

Knudsen, B., and Liszkowski, U. (2012). Eighteen and 24-month-old infants correct others in anticipation of action mistakes. *Developmental Science*, *15*, 113–22. http://doi:10.1111/j.1467-7687.2011.01098.x

Kovács, A., Tauzin, T., Téglás, E., Gergely, G., and Csibra, G. (2014). Pointing as epistemic request: 12-month-olds point to receive new information. *Infancy*, *19*, 543–57. http://doi:10.1111/infa.12060

Kulke, L., Reiß, M., Krist, H., and Rakoczy, H. (2018). How robust are anticipatory looking measures of theory of mind? Replication attempts across the life span. *Cognitive Development*. http://doi: 10.1016/j.cogdev.2017.09.001

Levinson, S. C. (2006). On the human "interaction engine." In N. J. Enfield and S. C. Levinson (eds.), *Roots of human sociality* (pp. 39–69). Oxford: Berg.

Lucca, K., and Wilbourn, M. P. (2016). Communicating to learn: Infant's pointing gestures result in optimal learning. *Child Development*, *89*, 941–60. http://doi:10.1111/cdev.12707

Markman, E. M. (1977). Realizing that you don't understand: A preliminary investigation. *Child Development*, *48*, 986–92. http://doi:10.2307/1128350

(1979). Realizing that you don't understand: Elementary school children's awareness of inconsistencies. *Child Development*, *50*, 643–55. http://doi:10.2307/1128929

Neldner, K., Collier-Baker, E., and Nielsen, M. (2015). Chimpanzees (Pan troglodytes) and human children (Homo sapiens) know when they are ignorant about the location of food. *Animal Cognition*, *18*, 683–99. http://do i:10.1007/s10071-015-0836-6

Ninio, A., and Snow, C. E. (1996). *Pragmatic development*. Boulder, CO: Westview Press.

O'Neill, D. K. (1996). Two-year-old children's sensitivity to a parent's knowledge state when making requests. *Child Development*, *67*, 659–77. http://doi:10.2307/1131839

Palincsar, A. S., and Brown, A. L. (1984). Reciprocal teaching of comprehension-fostering and comprehension-monitoring activities. *Cognition and Instruction*, *1*, 117–75. http://doi:10.1207/s1532690xci0102_1

Peterson, C. C., and Siegal, M. (2000). Insights into theory of mind from deafness and autism. *Mind & Language*, *15*, 123–45. http://doi:10.1111/14 68-0017.00126

Piaget, J. (1926). *The language and thought of the child*. New York: Harcourt Brace.

Revelle, G. L., Wellman, H. M., and Karabenick, J. D. (1985). Comprehension monitoring in preschool children. *Child Development*, *56*, 654–63. http://do i:10.2307/1129755

Shatz, M., Wellman, H. M., and Silber, S. (1983). The acquisition of mental verbs: A systematic investigation of the first reference to mental state. *Cognition*, *14*, 301–21. http://doi:10.1016/0010-0277(83)90008-2

Spilton, D., and Lee, L. C. (1977). Some determinants of effective communication in four-year-olds. *Child Development*, *48*, 968–77. http://do i:10.2307/1128348

Stivers, T., Enfield, N. J., Brown, P., et al. (2009). Universals and turn-taking in conversation. *PNAS*, *106*, 10587–92. http://doi:10.1073/pnas.0903616106

Stivers, T., Sidnell, J., and Bergen, C. (2018). Children's responses to questions in peer interaction: A window into the ontogenesis of interactional competence. *Journal of Pragmatics*, *124*, 14–30. http://doi:10.1016/j .pragma.2017.11.013

Sully, J. (2000) [1896]. *Studies of childhood*. London: Free Association Books.

Tizard, B., and Hughes, M. (1984). *Young children learning*. London: Fontana.

Wellman, H. M., Harris, P. L., Banerjee, M., and Sinclair, A. (1995). Early understanding of emotion: Evidence from natural language. *Cognition and Emotion*, *9*, 117–49. http://doi:10.1080/02699939508409005

Wellman, H. M., Cross, D., and Watson, J. (2001). Meta-analysis of theory of mind: The truth about false belief. *Child Development*, *72*, 655–84. http://do i:10.1111/1467-8624.00304

Wu, Z., and Gros-Louis, J. (2015). Caregivers provide more labeling responses to infants' pointing than to infants' object-directed vocalizations. *Journal of Child Language*, *42*, 538–61. http://doi:10.1017/s0305000914000221

# 4     The Quest for Comprehension and Learning
## Children's Questions Drive Both

*Henry M. Wellman*

Two crucial human cognitive goals are to understand and to learn. Both goals often require active management, actively questing for knowledge. Children's questions, both purposeful and incidental, both verbal and nonverbal, do this. Questions start early in life, change in nature and influence, but powerfully impact cognitive development all along the way. Often, they do so as an antecedent and a consequence of children's investment in explanatory understanding. I use my research and the research of my collaborators to address these topics as well as describe several of the steps and processes whereby questions and explanations drive the development of children's comprehension and learning.

## Introduction

Social transmission of information is one of the key ways in which both children and adults interact with as well as learn about the world. Potentially, these interactions manifest crucial human cognitive goals: to understand and learn. Importantly, understanding and learning often require active questing for knowledge. Here is where questions play such an important role in children's development, as a way to facilitate, shape, and provoke information transmission via social-communicative exchanges.

"Trust in testimony" studies have emerged and exploded over the last fifteen years (beginning, more or less, with Koenig et al. (2004) and Sabbagh & Baldwin (2001)). It has always been clear that children learn from information provided by others. Otherwise how could they acquire their native languages, know that the earth is round, that mom likes tea but dad prefers coffee? That social-communicative learning takes place in childhood, and does so from an early age, essentially required no research demonstration. What did require research, however, was discovering that and how early in life children were judicious acquirers of information from others, appropriately trusting and learning from previously accurate informants over inaccurate ones, expert over naïve informants, truthful rather than deceptive informants, and more (Harris, 2012). Some of these "decisions" about whom to trust are not logical or explicit, or deliberate (Bascandziev & Harris, 2016). Here I explore a related but different and less-studied topic, and one where children's actions are demonstrably and increasingly explicit: the ways that children actively seek such socially provided information in order to (discriminately) learn from the answers they receive. That is, how they quest for information and, focally, do so via their questions.

All questions potentially elicit information and allow learning, questions about names, about facts, about uses, about permission, about preferences, and requests for explanations. In what follows, however, after some general information about children's question-asking and comprehension-seeking, I will preferentially focus on children's quest for explanatory understanding – why things happen. Explanatory understanding and learning prove to be extremely important for children in their quest to comprehend and learn about the world around them, both in their question-asking and their learning from the answers they receive.

## Questions Are Important to Children

Children begin to ask questions early in life. In two studies, one examining verbatim transcripts of parent–child conversations (from the CHILDES; MacWhinney & Snow, 1990) and the other a diary study where parents reported their child's questions, Chouinard (2007) found that young children asked about one question a minute when talking with their caregivers. Even children aged just one and two years did so. Early on children's questions can be largely nonverbal: an inquisitive point (Begus & Southgate, 2012), holding up an unfamiliar object, frowning and saying "huh" (Chouinard, 2007).

What are children asking about? In Chouinard's analyses, roughly 70 percent of even young children's question were information-seeking requests (with the remainder being requests for attention, help, permission, or completely unclear). Largely, young children asked questions of fact – e.g., names or locations of objects, animals, and people. For the youngest children, one- and young two-year-olds, this accounted for 90 percent or more of all their information-seeking questions. But by about two years or so children increasingly also asked for explanations not just facts; by 2.5 years Chouinard's child subjects were doing so for roughly 25 percent of their information-seeking questions, and by 3.5 years explanation-seeking occupied about 33 to 40 percent of children's information-seeking questions.

Hickling and Wellman (2001) focused more specifically on children's requests for explanations also examining transcripts of everyday conversation (also from the CHILDES) for children's naturally occurring causal questions and explanations using terms like *why*, *because*, *how*, and *so*. We analyzed almost 5,000 child utterances from extended parent–child conversations. On average, causal questions appeared early in these recorded transcripts, with why-questions being some of the earliest causal utterances that children produced. In longitudinal analyses, causal questions appeared earlier than causal statements (earliest appearance, M = 2 years 5 months vs. 2 years 8 months) and were produced more frequently than causal statements at age 2.5 years. In contrast, by ages three and four, these children gave explanations more often than they asked others to explain things to them, due to a steady increase in children's explanations with age while children's explanatory questions remained stable. Such data empirically underwrite anecdotal observation of an early period when children engage in intense explanation-seeking. Children are often asking, "Why, why, why?"

The data in these studies – by Chouinard (2007), Hickling and Wellman (2001), and others (e.g., Callanan & Oakes, 1992) – were overwhelmingly from advantaged, middle-class American homes. Homes where we can presume parents (often) encourage questions and respond encouragingly to them. This is an important limitation I'll return to later, but nonetheless it is clear that often questions are important to young children: they start asking questions early, ask them often, and, as we'll see, persistently.

## Comprehension and Learning

Of course, in asking these hundreds of questions young children could just be seeking attention, or exercising a language acquisition device, asking questions in order to learn appropriate question syntax. Early investigations of children's questions (see e.g., Brown, 1973) largely confined themselves to this linguistic focus: when and in what steps do children's questions become syntactically well-formed? Much research on young children's questions (e.g., Rowland & Pine, 2000) tackles their learning of the language of questions; that may be what children are tackling as well – acquiring and practicing how to use grammatically mature question-forms.

Still, children's information-seeking questions appeared to Chouinard to be legitimately seeking information. That's what allowed her to separate them into information-seeking questions versus others. And children's why-questions seemed to us to often be children's legitimate requests for explanations. But are they?

### Seeking Information

Question–answer exchanges include (a) asking a question (such as "what?" or "why?"), (b) getting a response (perhaps a name or an explanation), and (c) evaluating, processing, and potentially learning from the answer. The way in which children evaluate, process, and react to the responses they receive sheds key light on the nature of their questions to begin with. In particular, their reactions of satisfaction or dissatisfaction with the answers they receive can illuminate if their initial questions worked in the way they hoped, or not.

That is, assume that even young children tend to want information when they ask questions. If so, getting appropriate information in response to their questions (e.g., a name or fact to a "What's that?" question, an explanation to a "Why did that happen?" question) should be more satisfying than getting non-informative responses and answers. More specifically, if children get a non-informative response, they could reveal their relative dissatisfaction by disagreeing, re-asking the original question, or providing their own answer instead. If children get an informative response, they could reveal their satisfaction by agreeing or following up with a comment or question that incorporates that answer.

In an early study using this basic logic, Kemler Nelson et al. (2004) showed two- through four-year-olds unfamiliar objects. These objects often elicited ambiguous questions from children, such as, "What is it?" which could be requests for the object's name ("What's it called?") or its function ("What is it for?"). To half the children, the adult always gave the object's name, to the other half always its function. Children who initially got answers about function tended to ask no more questions at that point. But children who got names overwhelmingly tended to ask further questions, seeking the object's function – "What's it do?" "What's it for?" This was true of even the youngest children, two-year-olds. In other words, children seemed to want to know the objects' functions, leading them to be satisfied when they heard that, but leading them to be dissatisfied and to ask additional, clarifying questions when they got names instead.

Chouinard (2007) employed a similar method. In her natural conversational data (for four children in the CHILDES) she looked further at what she'd coded as children's information-seeking questions, which recall in her data were mostly questions of fact (along with a small minority of requests for explanations). She then looked at children's reactions to the answers they received, coded as informative or non-informative replies. She took as evidence of dissatisfaction – children not getting the type of answer they were seeking – instances when children repeated the same question multiple times in a row. This behavior was much more frequent following non-informative adult responses than following informative ones. Thus, when children persisted in their questioning (again, largely factual questions in those data) it seemed to be with the goal of obtaining information, rather than just to get attention or for their own enjoyment.

## Seeking Comprehension

Often, if not always, achieving understanding and learning require monitoring one's comprehension of the information involved and then either continuing as is *or* seeking additional clarity. When and how do children actively monitor their understanding and if they are being understood, and seek to clarify and correct potential misunderstandings? When and what strategies or attempts to receive further information do they employ, to be alert for and attempt to correct misunderstandings?

"Comprehension monitoring" was studied in an earlier literature with old preschoolers and elementary school children. Crucially, however, almost all of the research with preschool children focused on referential ambiguity, which occurs when a message has several ambiguous referents – e.g., "Look at the horse," when several horses are in view. Preschoolers generally did not react differently to ambiguous and unambiguous messages, simply choosing one of the potential referents, suggesting young children systematically fail to monitor their comprehension (e.g., Robinson & Robinson, 1977; Beal & Flavell, 1982). However, the overwhelming focus on ambiguity arguably led to an underestimate of preschoolers' monitoring. To clarify some of this, Revelle et al. (1985) gave preschool children several contrasting messages in natural-seeming situations and used children's contingent reactions to assess their comprehension monitoring and management. In the course of a play interaction within a room full of carefully composed objects, an adult interspersed the play episode with a series of requests, some of which were designed to be difficult for the child to understand or to execute. For example, in an *unintelligible* request the adult said "bring me the [yawn]" obscuring the referent's name; in an *impossible* request it was "bring me the refrigerator" for a real refrigerator that was clearly too big and heavy to move; in an *ambiguous* request it was "bring me the cup" when there were four cups side by side in the room. Children's responses to these requests were compared with their responses to control requests that were easy to comprehend and comply with (e.g., "bring me the ball" when there was one ball present).

Three-year-olds exhibited appropriate monitoring responses – for example, saying things like "what?" "this one?" or "can't hear" for some target messages more than control ones. In particular, they did so for unintelligible or impossible messages. Even so, three-year-olds systematically failed to monitor referential ambiguity. Four-year-olds displayed discriminative monitoring for all types of problems presented, but even for them referential ambiguity was especially difficult.

At the very least this older, prior research suggests that comprehension monitoring must have an earlier developmental emergence. Arguably, because of its ubiquity and importance it could have a very early appearance – for example, in children's communicative exchanges. Following this thinking, we examined the early development of very young children's ability to monitor and manage their understanding in two studies (Wellman et al., 2019): one tracking children and their parents in their everyday conversational exchanges; one where we experimentally controlled a natural-seeming situation to examine young children's reactions to, for example, correct naming of common objects (e.g., calling a shoe a shoe) and misnaming (calling a ball a shoe).

In this quasi-naturalistic study we demonstrated that very young children who have just attained their second birthdays detect communicative breakdowns of understanding and attempt to correct them. When children heard misnaming they responded appropriately more than 80 percent of the time. Appropriate responses often took the form of questions: "What?" "This one?" "A shoe?" And, of course, sometimes children just disagreed: "No." "A ball." In contrast they gave these sorts of reactions to correct naming about 4 percent of the time.

A judiciously discriminating response pattern also emerged if children heard appropriate or inappropriate requests – e.g., were asked to bring a ball versus bring a clock affixed high up on a wall. For appropriate requests children mostly complied; for inappropriate ones they again frequently questioned the speaker: "What?" "That one?" "The clock?" And, of course, sometimes just refused, by doing nothing or saying, "No."

Even very young children seek to monitor and repair comprehension breakdowns. They do so often, and focally, by asking questions to better determine what the speaker actually meant.

## Seeking Explanations

As indicated at the start, I believe children's quest for explanations deserves and rewards special attention. Why? In part because children are so interested in explanations. And in part because explanations – both getting them and generating them – turn out to be an important mechanism for learning.

First consider children's interest in explanations. In Chouinard's analyses, young children mostly asked for factual information, but even young two-year-olds asked for explanations about 5–8 percent of the time, and by 3.5 it was a third to half of their questions. In parallel, in a diary study by Callanan and Oakes (1992), adults' provision of explanations in response to their children's questions increased with the age of the child: mothers of three-year-olds reported responding with a causal explanation 32 percent of the time to their child's questions, whereas mothers of older children reported responding with a causal explanation 50–60 percent of the time.

Chouinard's examination of the CHILDES data focused on only four children and lumped together fact-seeking and explanation-seeking questions, with fact-seeking questions clearly dominating the mix. Frazier et al. (2009, 2016) specifically addressed explanation seeking via questions and did so with sizable samples of children. The primary question we addressed, to begin with, was when children ask such questions – why, why, why? – do they really want explanations? Do their questions reveal young children to be active discoverers who really seeks answers, in this case explanations, with their questions? It is possible to be rationally skeptical about that: parents and teachers often suspect that all those whys might just be to get attention, gambits to keep the conversation going, to put off bedtime.

The approach we took to answering this question was the one outlined earlier: we focused on how satisfied children were with answers they got. Assume that even young children tend to want an explanation when they ask why-questions. If so, getting an explanation in response to their questions should be more satisfying than getting nonexplanatory responses and answers. If children get a nonexplanatory response instead of an explanation, they could reveal their relative dissatisfaction by disagreeing, re-asking the original question, or providing their own explanation instead. If children get an explanatory response, they could reveal their satisfaction by agreeing or following up with a comment or question that incorporates that answer. Indeed, in careful analyses of everyday conversations with their parents, two-, three-, and four-year-olds reacted in just these fashions (Frazier et al., 2009, study 1). They evidenced relative satisfaction with explanatory responses to their why- and how-questions and dissatisfaction if parents attempted to foist off non-explanations instead.

In these everyday conversations, however, parents' explanatory responses proved longer than their non-explanations, so maybe children just prefer extended conversation rather than explanation after all. To tackle this, we brought these processes into the lab for more experimental control.

In our experimental setup (Frazier et al., 2009, study 2), preschool children interacted with an adult around a variety of items – toys, pictures, books, videos – some of which were designed to be "odd," that is, to provoke why-questions. For example, the child would see someone turn a light switch off with her foot; the child would receive paper and crayons for drawing and on opening the crayon box find nothing but orange crayons. These items successfully elicited many why-questions (e.g., "Why are they all orange?"), and in response the adult provided carefully scripted responses, all equally long, half of them providing explanations ("It was a mistake at the crayon factory") and half non-explanations ("You are right, all of them are orange"). Again, young preschoolers were typically satisfied with explanatory responses to their questions and, in stark contrast, dissatisfied with non-explanations, often asking their questions again, frowning, and offering their own explanations instead. Kurkul and Corriveau (2017) provide complementary findings.

In short, children's reactions to the different types of information they get from adults, in response to their own requests, confirms that young children are motivated to actively seek explanations. When preschoolers ask why-questions, they're not merely trying to prolong conversation, they're trying to get to the bottom of things.

## Learning from the Explanations They Request

Our findings in Frazier et al. (2009) confirmed that young children actively seek causal information; they use specific conversational strategies to obtain it, and in this process, they prefer explanations over non-explanations. But this study and others leave many additional questions unanswered, including the important question of what, if anything, children learn from the answers they receive? At a minimum do they, and how do they, recall the answers they receive?

We addressed these questions in an additional set of studies (Frazier et al., 2016). Recall data provide an opportunity to measure whether explanatory information is better retained than nonexplanatory information and potentially which parts of extended explanations were most remembered. Further, recall of *nonexplanatory* answers presented an opportunity to see if children would construct an explanation in place of the nonexplanatory information they were given, perhaps demonstrating constructive memory processes where children's drive for explanation further shapes their memories.

We used the same type of "odd" items designed to provoke why-questions from children as in our original studies (Frazier et al., 2009). For example, children heard a story about a child who put ketchup, instead of chocolate syrup, on her ice cream. This item, and others like the picture of the ordinary man in ordinary clothes with a red clown nose and the box of crayons with nothing but orange ones, again elicited many questions from children, to which an adult sometimes gave a clear explanatory answer and other times gave a clearly nonexplanatory response. After children responded to the items and after a distraction task to ensure a suitable five- to ten-minute delay, children were reminded of their question for each item and asked to recall the answer they had received.

To illuminate children's explanatory preferences and learning further, in this study, we varied the "levels" of explanation children received. Here, we examined explanations that differed in length and amount of explanatory detail. Our aim was not to precisely define "levels of detail" but to use variation in responses to answers – all of which were explanatory – to better illuminate young children's reactions to and learning from the explanations they receive. Accordingly, we intuitively devised three arguably different levels of explanations that might straightforwardly be related to children's memory and preferences using adults' ratings to help us in this process. Level 1 explanations were meant to provide minimal information but were still explanatory. For example, given the question, "Why did she pour ketchup on her ice cream?" a Level 1 explanation was, "It was a mistake." Level 2 explanations added more information, such as, "It was a mistake because she thought it was chocolate in the bottle." Level 3 explanations were still more elaborative, such as, "It was a mistake because she thought it was chocolate in the bottle, because the ketchup bottle and the chocolate bottle look the same."

Preschool children again preferred explanatory answers over nonexplanatory ones, evidencing clear satisfaction with the former and clear dissatisfaction with the latter. In addition, children (and adults as well) preferred Level 2 explanations over Level 1 explanations and found Level 3 explanations no more satisfying than the Level 2 ones.

What about learning? Here it is important to point out that preference and learning could certainly differ: children might prefer Level 2 explanations, but best recall the shorter, less complex Level 1 ones. And the learning profile might be the same *or different* for adults (e.g., adults might remember best the longer rather than shorter explanations because they provided more complete information).

Young children and adults learned from the answers they elicited by their questions – they recalled much of the explanatory information they received. And their recall of explanations – all levels of explanations – were better than their recall of non-explanations. In fact, children had difficulty accurately recalling the non-explanations they received at all. Intriguingly, both adults and children learned best from the Level 2 explanations. They recalled them *better* than the shorter, less complex Level 1 explanations (though, Level 1 explanations were recalled much better than non-explanations). They also recalled the Level 2 information best and often failed to recall the additional information presented (beyond Level 2 information) in the longer Level 3 explanations.

Arguably, the Level 2 explanations provided the right mix of simplicity and complexity. Relatedly, recent research with adults shows that adults prefer explanations that have the "explanatory virtues" of being simple yet broad or complex – explanations that cover a range of specific instances (breadth) without getting bogged down in too many details (simplicity) (see Lomborozo, 2016, for a review). Children do too, and they not only prefer such explanations they remember them best.

## Learning by Explaining

Children learn not only from the explanations that others provide but also from the answers they themselves generate in response to others' questions. Moreover, sometimes they generate answers sparked by others' questions, but they can also generate answers sparked by dissatisfaction with the answers other people provide. A thought-provoking example of this second sort occurred in our Frazier et al. (2016) study: children who received unsatisfying non-explanations often generated explanations of their own. Kurkul and Corriveau's (2017) children also did this in their everyday conversations about 10 percent of the time. Moreover, in our experimental data, on almost half the trials when they received a *non-explanation* to their why-questions, children misremembered the non-explanation as if it was an explanation. In this, they typically came up with an explanation of their own in the face of the adult's failure to do so, and then "remembered" that as what they heard. For example, given an item where a boy puts on a hat, scarf, and gloves to go outside on a hot day, and hearing the non-explanation, "He's wearing all his winter clothes," several children recalled this response as "Cause he thought it was winter." Children seemed to expect an explanation, and so they generated one and then tended to (mis)recall that rather than the experimenter's non-explanation.

Children also generate explanations in response to others' questions, of course. Systematic research has examined the benefit to them when they do so: children's learning is consequentially affected by the answers they generate in response to others' explanatory questioning.

In a microgenetic study of social cognition, Jennifer Amsterlaw and I (Amsterlaw & Wellman, 2006) demonstrated that children's explanations facilitate an understanding of false beliefs, a milestone in children's developing theory of mind. On various pretest tasks like those in Figure 4.1(a), our predominantly three-year-old participants consistently exhibited the response typical for their age, incorrectly predicting that Ann would look for the Band-Aids where they really are. Then, over a period of weeks, children participated in one of two training regimens. In an explanation condition, children received twenty-four false-belief explanation problems, many variations on tasks of the sort depicted in Figure 4.1(b), over twelve twice-weekly sessions. In this condition, children made an initial prediction – for example, said Anne will go to the unmarked box. Then they saw their prediction was incorrect (because the children were pretested to include only those consistently incorrect on false-belief prediction tests), that is, they saw Ann went to the Band-Aid box and then were simply asked, "Why did she (or he) go there?" Notably, *no* feedback was given to children on their explanations, they were simply asked to attempt one.

Children in a comparison condition also received twenty-four problems, but these were prediction tasks alone (like Figure 4.1(a), where the question is about where will Ann look and there is no question about why). A "control" group participated only in the pre- and posttests.

At posttest, children in the explanation condition significantly outperformed the comparison and control groups on both false-belief explanation and prediction tasks. Moreover, only the explanation group succeeded on a transfer problem of a sort that had never appeared in training. In sum, the explanation group developed and learned; although the comparison group received an equivalent number of false-belief problems, they learned no more than the control group. These data from the comparison group help ensure that simply asking children questions, and their answering them, does not account for the children's improvement in these studies, because in that group children were also asked questions and answered them. They were asked prediction questions. Yet those children did not improve over a baseline control group, whereas the explanation group did.

In Rhodes and Wellman (2013), we provided still further data from a still bigger sample confirming the superiority of requesting the children to explain. In these microgenetic studies children's explanations were initially poor. In their early sessions children's explanations were often inaccurate, made up, or simply "I don't know." For example, children asked to explain why the agent in Figure 4.1(b) did what he did, could and did explain the behavior by "Ann didn't want Band-Aids after all," or "I don't know." Having to supply an explanation anyway was nonetheless helpful in inducing children to get better at the false-belief explanations and their false-belief

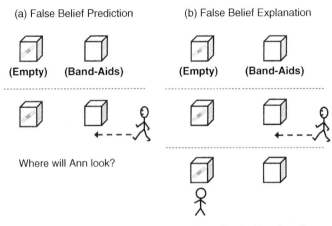

Figure 4.1 False belief tasks have children reason about an agent whose actions should be controlled by a mistaken belief. Here the child first says the Band-Aid box should have Band-Aids, but opens it to find it empty and the Band-Aids instead in the other nondescript box. Then the child is told of Ann "Who wants a Band-Aid, and has *never* seen these boxes before." In prediction tasks (a) the child is asked, "Where will Ann look?" In parallel explanation tasks (b) the child is shown that Ann goes to look in the Band-Aid box (not where the Band-Aids really are) and is asked, "Why is Ann looking there?" Correct responses to prediction tasks require the child to judge Ann will look in the Band-Aid box. Correct responses to the explanation task require the child to cite Ann's false belief or mistaken knowledge: "She thinks Band-Aids are there." "She doesn't know they're moved." "She got tricked by the picture."

predictions as well over their microgenetic sessions. Arguably, a key factor concerns the child's having to attend to mechanisms or to wrestle with explanatory reasoning, rather than accuracy per se.

In sum, (a) asking questions and receiving answers – both questions of fact and especially requests for explanations – aids children's learning; (b) asking questions and not receiving answers can sometimes do so as well; and (c) generating explanations even in the absence of feedback about their correctness also helps children learn. Furthermore, as I'll discuss in the next section, generating explanations even in the absence of feedback about their correctness allows young children to access their more advanced understandings.

## Advantaged and WEIRD or Universal?

The research I have reviewed thus far, and indeed most of the burgeoning research on children's information-seeking and explanation-seeking questions, has almost all been conducted with typically developing children, residing in WEIRD (Western, Educated, Industrialized, Rich, Developed) countries and circumstances (Henrich et al., 2010). Such children are often being raised with parents who engage them in conversation, encouraging frequent questions and frequent causal-explanatory exchanges, and helpfully providing relevant information within such parent–child interactions. This raises the question of whether children's putative questioning-asking and explanation-providing prowess is limited to those special populations and circumstances.

A good way to expand the discussion beyond "advantaged and WEIRD" children is to consider still further the special advantage that accrues in young children's reasoning and learning when children attempt their own explanations.

## Children Can Be Better at Explanations than Judgments

In our microgenetic research children's learning was better when they were required to explain than when they got extended practice at predicting. Intriguingly, in other research, children's earliest understandings can be more apparent in their explanations than their judgments.

Bartsch and Wellman (1989) provided an early example of this asymmetry in the realm of social cognition, or theory of mind. They tested preschool children on carefully comparable false-belief tasks requiring predictions versus explanations, of the sort Figure 4.1 illustrates. Young children who systematically failed false-belief predictions often provided compelling false-belief explanations. This "explanation advantage" occurred despite the fact that the probability of being correct in the prediction task was essentially 50 percent, whereas the chance of spontaneously generating a false-belief explanation (when the child could equally attempt to explain the action in terms of the external situation, the agent's desires, the agent's past overt behavior, etc.) must have been substantially less than 50 percent.

These data (see also Dunn et al., 1991) met with initial skepticism because eliciting explanations in such young children typically requires additional prompting; young children often say nothing (or "don't know") to an initial why-question and need further questions to cogently respond. Perhaps the follow-up questions overly shape children's apparently insightful responses (Perner, 1991). However, additional research shows an explanation advantage even with no additional prompting

(Robinson & Mitchell, 1995) or if researchers simply re-ask children the original question when they first say nothing or "don't know" (Bartsch et al., 2007).

Children in China provide an example of expansion to non-WEIRD samples; they come from non-Western homes and cultures. And Chinese children (summing those in mainland China with those who have immigrated to many other countries worldwide) represent about half of the children living in the world today. Moreover, Chinese children growing up in mainland China provide a strong test of the relation between explanation and prediction, because Chinese preschool children are reportedly asked many fewer explanation questions in everyday conversation than young Western children are (Miao, 1986). Nonetheless, Chinese preschoolers evidence the same advantage for explanation over prediction responses as do their Western peers (e.g., Tardif et al., 2004).

An explanation advantage is apparent not only in social-cognitive research but in the domain of naive biology as well, when preschoolers are asked to predict versus to explain illness and contamination events (Legare et al., 2009). And again, this advantage appears in Chinese children as well as Western ones (Legare et al., 2013).

Not all comparisons between predictions and explanations evidence an explanation advantage: of course, it is also possible to ask complex explanation questions where young children do poorly. One important sort of complexity probably inadvertently accounts for some findings where young children's explanations are poor in comparison to judgments (e.g., for social cognition: Wimmer & Mayringer, 1998; for illness and contamination: Au et al., 1993). Note in Figure 4.1 that the explanation questions asked children to explain the character's action. In Wimmer and Mayringer (1998), the procedure for children who first did not answer or answered inadequately was to rephrase the explanation question as, "Ann goes here, because she thinks the Band-Aids are here; why does Ann think the Band-Aids are here?" That is, the child was asked to explain the character's reasoning (her "thinking") rather than her action. Requests for metacognitive explanations of this sort (Why do you/they think that?) often lead to responses that are unclear and confused in young children. In contrast, eliciting explanations for action-events (Why did she/you do that?) proves more revealing. Metacognitive explanations are of interest and have a role to play in developing children's knowledge and reasoning (see below), but metacognitive explanations, for young children, are often unrevealing and certainly may not evidence any explanation advantage.

Finally, returning to data on children's reactions to others' explanations, Kurkul and Corriveau's (2017) research was with children in lower

SES (socioeconomic status) homes as well as those in middle-class homes. Both groups frequently asked for explanations in their everyday conversations with their caregivers, both groups reacted similarly in their responses to satisfying versus unsatisfying answers, and both groups generated and voiced their own explanations at about the same rates (10 percent of the time) when their questions received nonexplanatory responses from their caregivers. Arguably, many sorts of interactive, ask-and-respond conversational pragmatics may be widespread across the conversational lives of young children in a great many societies and circumstances (as argued by Stivers et al., 2009).

## Questions about Questions and Explanations

Like all good science, our increasing knowledge about children's quest for information via questions and explanations also provokes new questions. For example, where do the cognitive advantages of asking questions come from? Relatedly, in the explanation research, generating an explanation provides many learning advantages even in the absence of asking for and receiving explanations from others; to what extent might this apply more broadly? For example, if children make their own predictions about a phenomena, could that be as effective as asking a question? The micro-genetic research shows ways in which making predictions are not as good as being asked to produce explanations, but could making a prediction be as good as asking a question? Or more so, and in what situations? I will not list or address the many intriguing questions about questions and explanations. Instead, I will consider just one by way of example: Why might questions and explanations be so advantageous for children's comprehension and learning? That is, by what mechanisms do they operate to advance children's cognition? This is a much less researched question, but speculatively to me it seems there are several plausible mechanisms at work, all worth further research.

### Privileging the Unknown

Imagine that a child simultaneously sees two almost identical events – one (A) in accord with prior knowledge and the other (B) not – and is invited to explain whatever he or she wants. Because children like confirming established expertise, and because they have prior knowledge about it, they might well prefer to explain A. Or, because it is novel and initially unexplained, they might attempt to explain B. In fact, in just these situations preschool children consistently try to explain B, events not in accord with their prior understandings (Legare et al., 2010).

This preference, at the least, confirms again that explanations are important to children. More importantly, this preference arguably helps direct children to acquiring new information. Research with adults shows that focusing preferentially on what you don't yet know can be an effective learning mechanism (see e.g., Bjork, 2018).

## Attentional and Motivational Scaffolding

Recall that children actively ask questions and they want and seek explanations. Asking questions directs conversation and instruction to questions children are attentive to and intensely interested in, such as why things happen. Children's own motivations thus facilitate and scaffold their learning. Intrinsic motivation and rewards, rather than extrinsic ones, are known to aid learning (Lepper et al., 1973; Mueller & Dweck, 1998).

## Cognitive Scaffolding

Intuitively, it seems that causal predictions would typically be easier than causal explanations, there should be a "prediction advantage." For one thing, predictions can be achieved with simple, even nonverbal judgments, whereas explanations require more demanding verbal articulation. More substantively, explanations seem to require a deeper level of analysis too. Arguably, causal predictions can be based on detecting specific causal regularities (the relation between X and Y), and thus achieved on the basis of observing statistical regularities between specific events. In contrast, causal explanations typically require invoking more general explanatory principles (the why of an explanation). Yet, as noted above, what we often find is an "explanation advantage" instead.

Why? Consider these two scenarios. In a prediction scenario, we have a new hybrid car left overnight (in Michigan) in January. Prediction question: "What's going to happen to the car?" (Shrug.) In the parallel explanation scenario, we have the same unfortunate car and an outcome; for example, it is covered in ice. Explanation question: "Why is there ice on the car?" ("It got so cold that condensation froze on it.")

As captured here and argued by Wellman and Liu (2007), explanation can be difficult because there are multiple possibly relevant causes and frameworks to consider. But in this example explanation has a clear advantage as well: the outcome of the causal chain is specified. In this sense, explanation is a form of post-diction (as contrasted to prediction). Knowing the outcome of the relevant causal chain constrains what the reasoner need consider. Outcome information significantly reduces the problem space much as reverse engineering does. It is far easier to engineer a radically new sort of hybrid car if one has a working car to disassemble and analyze. This is why in the philosophy of science, it is an axiom that more credit accrues to theories that can make accurate predictions of as-yet-unobserved phenomena and not merely explain observed phenomena after the fact. Explanations are easier for scientific theories because there has already been a peek at the results. Explanations of the sort sought in "explanation advantage" studies with children similarly require post-diction of a known outcome.

To the extent that explanations are more constrained than predictions, leading to more accurate answers, this increased accuracy could helpfully constrain and scaffold learning. Moreover, and relatedly, children's explanations are initially more sophisticated than their predictions. That is, they are more sophisticated in being demonstrably more accurate in the explanation-advantage studies. Thus, explanations may often represent and make available children's more advanced comprehension and reasoning, thereby providing an important platform for further learning.

### Self-Explanation Effect

Instructional psychology studies with older children and adults show that, in learning from text or examples, explaining novel information to oneself facilitates learning (e.g., Chi et al., 1994). In these "self-explanation" studies, the learner's task is typically to explain the author's or the instructor's reasoning ("How do you think I knew that?"). And ask and answer their own explanatory questions about the text. Such explanation manipulations are a more effective learning strategy than merely receiving feedback (Siegler, 1995; Aleven & Koedinger, 2002), thinking out loud (Wong et al., 2002; Pine & Siegler, 2003), or reading study materials twice (Chi et al., 1994), manipulations designed to parallel any extra attention and processing required in self-explanation. Providing explanations also influences generalization and transfer. For example, school-age students who received practice on addition problems were more likely to succeed in solving transfer subtraction problems if prompted to explain the earlier addition materials (Rittle-Johnson, 2006).

In total, asking themselves for and providing explanations enhances children's learning of everyday (such as social cognition) and school-relevant (such as mathematics and science) phenomena. The youngest demonstrations (e.g., Amsterlaw & Wellman, 2006) have children explain external events and overt actions, but somewhat older children and adults benefit from attempting metacognitive explanations ("Why did I think that?") as well.

## Desirable Difficulties

In the instructional research on self-explanations and in our studies of an explanation advantage, providing an explanation is typically more difficult than simply reading or listening or observing. In our studies, at the very least explaining requires more words, more elaboration, more thought than making a simple prediction. So does asking a question as opposed to just listening or attending. As Bjork (e.g., 2018) and others have argued more difficult processing often leads to deeper processing and deeper, more elaborate processing leads to better learning and retention. An additional mechanism underlying the potency of question-asking and explanation generation in children's cognitive development therefore is that they arguably enlist the advantages of desirable difficulties.

Regardless, questions, explanations, and explanatory questions aid learning and development. Better understanding why, even if challenging, is certainly worth our attention; it's a desirable difficulty.

## Conclusions

In sum, questions and relatedly explanations characterize *and* aid childhood learning and development. They engage children and their cognitive as well as social motivations. Thus, children frequently, judiciously, and persistently engage in them. Inspired by analyses of data showing an explanation advantage in childhood reasoning, plausibly information-seeking questions more generally enlist underlying mechanisms for advancing children's quest for comprehension and learning. (1) Most basically, they elicit information from children's environments. (2) They engage children's own attentional and motivational interests. (3) They require and encourage children to focus preferentially on what they don't yet know. (4) They require deeper processing and, often, elicit some of children's best reasoning, thereby providing the cognitive advantages of desirable difficulties.

## Acknowledgments

Financial support for the research covered in this chapter has come from a MERIT award to Wellman from NICHD, from the John Templeton Foundation, and from the University of Michigan. The research was conducted in collaboration with numerous students and colleagues without whose efforts it would have been impossible to achieve. In particular (and in no particular order), Tamar Kushnir, Alison Gopnik, Candida Peterson, Brandy Frazier, Julie Song, Susan Gelman, Cristine Legare,

Kristin Lagatutta, Karen Bartsch, Jonathan Lane. I am deeply grateful to these colleagues and institutions.

## References

Aleven, V., and Koedinger, K. R. (2002). An effective metacognitive strategy: Learning by doing and explaining with a computer-based cognitive tutor. *Cognitive Science*, 26, 147–79. http://doi:10.1207/s15516709cog2602_1

Amsterlaw, J., and Wellman, H. M. (2006). Theories of mind in transition: A microgenetic study of the development of false belief understanding. *Journal of Cognition and Development*, 7, 139–72. http://doi:10.1207/s15327647jcd0702_1

Au, T. K., Sidle, A. L., and Rollins, K. B. (1993). Developing an intuitive understanding of conservation and contamination: Invisible particles as a plausible mechanism. *Developmental Psychology*, 29, 286–99. http://doi:10.1037/0012-1649.29.2.286

Bartsch, K., and Wellman, H. M. (1989). Young children's attribution of action to beliefs and desires. *Child Development*, 60, 946–64. http://doi:10.2307/1131035

Bartsch, K., Campbell, M. D., and Troseth, G. L. (2007). Why else does Jenny run? Young children's extended psychological explanations. *Journal of Cognition and Development*, 8, 33–61. http://doi:10.1080/15248370709336992

Bascandziev, I., and Harris, P. L. (2016). The beautiful and the accurate: Are children's selective trust decisions biased? *Journal of Experimental Child Psychology*, 152, 92–105. http://doi:10.1016/j.jecp.2016.06.017

Beal, C. R., and Flavell, J. H. (1982). Effect of increasing the salience of message ambiguities on kindergartners' evaluations of communicative success and message adequacy. *Developmental Psychology*, 18, 43–48. http://doi: 10.1037//0012-1649.18.1.43

Begus, K. and Southgate, V. (2012) Infant pointing serves an interrogative function. *Developmental Science*, 15, 611–17. http://doi:10.1111/j.1467-7687.2012.01160.x

Bjork, R. A. (2018). Being suspicious of the sense of ease and undeterred by the sense of difficulty: Looking back at Schmidt and Bjork (1992). *Perspectives on Psychological Science*, 13, 146–8. http://doi:10.1177/1745691617690642

Brown, R. (1973). *A first language: The early stages*. Oxford: Harvard University Press.

Callanan, M. A., and Oakes, L. M. (1992). Preschoolers' questions and parents' explanations: Causal thinking in everyday activity. *Cognitive Development*, 7, 213–33. https://doi.org/10.1016/0885-2014(92)90012-G

Chi, M. T. H., de Leeuw, N., Chiu, M., and LaVancher, L. (1994). Eliciting self-explanations improves understanding. *Cognitive Science*, 18, 439–77. http://doi:10.1207/s15516709cog1803_3

Chouinard, M. (2007). Children's questions: A mechanism for cognitive development. *Monographs of the Society for Research in Child Development*, 72, no.1, 1–129.

Dunn, J., Brown, J., Slomkowski, C., Tesla, C., and Youngblade, L. (1991). Young children's understanding of other people's feelings and beliefs:

Individual differences and their antecedents. *Child Development*, 62, 1352–66. https://doi.org/10.2307/1130811

Frazier, B. N., Gelman, S. A., and Wellman, H. M. (2009). Preschoolers' search for explanatory information within adult–child conversation. *Child Development*, 80, 1592–611. https://doi.org/10.1111/j.1467-8624.2009.013 56.x

(2016). Young children prefer and remember satisfying explanations. *Journal of Cognition and Development*, 17, 718–36. https://doi.org/10.1080/15248372.201 5.1098649

Harris, P. L. (2012). *Trusting what you're told: How children learn from others.* Cambridge, MA: Belknap Press of Harvard University Press.

Henrich, J., Heine, S.J., and Norenzayan, A. (2010) The weirdest people in the world? *Behavioral and Brain Sciences*, 33, 61–135. http://doi:10.1017/s0140525 x0999152x

Hickling, A. K., and Wellman, H. M. (2001). The emergence of children's causal explanations and theories: Evidence from everyday conversation. *Developmental Psychology*, 37, 668–83. https://doi.org/10.1037/0012-1649.37.5.668

Kemler Nelson, D. G., Egan, L. C., and Holt, M. B. (2004). When children ask, "What is it?" What do they want to know about artifacts? *Psychological Science*, 15, 384–9. http://doi:10.1111/j.0956-7976.2004.00689.x

Koenig, M. A., Clément, F., and Harris, P. L. (2004). Trust in testimony: Children's use of true and false statements. *Psychological Science*, 15, 694–8. https://doi.org/10.1111/j.0956-7976.2004.00742.x

Kurkul, K. E., and Corriveau, K. H. (2017) Question, explanation, follow-up: A mechanism for learning from others? *Child Development*, 89, 280–94. http://doi:10.1111/cdev.12726

Legare, C. H., Wellman, H. M., and Gelman, S. A. (2009). Evidence for an explanation advantage in naïve biological reasoning. *Cognitive Psychology*, 58, 177–94. https://doi.org/10.1016/j.cogpsych.2008.06.002

Legare, C. H., Gelman, S. A., and Wellman, H. M. (2010). Inconsistency with prior knowledge triggers children's causal explanatory reasoning. *Child Development*, 81, 929–44. https://doi.org/10.1111/j.1467-8624.20 10.01443.x

Legare, C. H., Zhu, L., and Wellman, H. M. (2013). Examining biological explanations in Chinese preschool children: A cross-cultural comparison. *Journal of Cognition and Culture*, 13, 67–93. https://doi.org/10.1163/156853 73-12342085

Lepper, R., Greene, D., and Nisbett, R. E. (1973) Undermining children's intrinsic interest with extrinsic reward: A test of the "overjustification" hypothesis. *Journal of Personality and Social Psychology*, 281, 129–37. http://doi:10.1037/h0035519

Lombrozo, T. (2016) Explanatory preferences shape learning and inference. *Trends in Cognitive Sciences*, 20, 748–59. http://doi:10.1016/j. tics.2016.08.001

MacWhinney, B., and Snow, C. (1990). The child language data exchange system: An update. *Journal of Child Language*, 17, 457–72. http://doi:10.101 7/s0305000900013866

Miao, X. C. (1986). Young children's understanding of interrogatives: The developmental peculiarities of answering WH questions in young children. *Psychological Science*, 5, 1–5.

Mueller, C. M., and Dweck, C. S. (1998). Praise for intelligence can undermine children's motivation and performance. *Journal of Personality and Social Psychology*, 75, 33–52. http://doi:10.1037//0022-3514.75.1.33

Perner, J. (1991). *Understanding the representational mind*. Cambridge, MA: MIT Press.

Pine, K. J., and Siegler, R. S. (2003). The role of explanatory activity in increasing the generality of thinking. Paper presented at the biennial meeting of the Society for Research in Child Development. Tampa, FL.

Revelle, G. L., Wellman, H. M., and Karabenick, J. D. (1985). Comprehension monitoring in preschool children. *Child Development*, 56, 654–63. http://doi:10.2307/1129755

Rhodes, M., and Wellman, H. (2013). Constructing a new theory from old ideas and new evidence. *Cognitive Science*, 37, 592–604. https://doi.org/10.1111/cogs.12031

Rittle-Johnson, B. (2006). Promoting transfer: The effects of direct instruction and self-explanation. *Child Development*, 77, 1–15. http://doi:10.1111/j.1467-8624.2006.00852.x

Robinson, E. J., and Mitchell, P. (1995). Making children's early understanding of representational mind: Backwards explanation versus prediction. *Child Development*, 66, 1022–39. http://doi:10.2307/1131796

Robinson, E. J., and Robinson, W. P. (1977). Development in the understanding of causes of success and failure in verbal communication. *Cognition*, 5, 363–78. https://doi.org/10.1016/0010-0277(77)90021-X

Rowland, C. F., and Pine, J. M. (2000). Subject-auxiliary inversion errors and wh-questions acquisition: What children do know? *Journal of Child Language*, 27, 157–81. http://doi:10.1017/s0305000999004055

Sabbagh, M., and Baldwin, D. A. (2001). Learning words from knowledgeable versus ignorant speakers: Links between preschoolers' theory of mind and semantic development. *Child Development*, 2, 1054–70. http://doi:10.1111/1467-8624.00334

Siegler, R. S. (1995). How does change occur: A microgenetic study of number conservation. *Cognitive Development*, 28, 225–73. http://doi:10.1006/cogp.1995.1006

Stivers, T., Enfield, N. J., Brown, P., et al. (2009) Universals and cultural variation in turn-taking conversations. *PNAS*, 106, 10587–92. http://doi:10.1073/pnas.0903616106

Tardif, T., Wellman, H. M., and Cheung, K. M. (2004). False belief understanding in Cantonese-speaking children. *Journal of Child Language*, 31, no. 4, 779–800. https://doi.org/10.1017/S0305000904006580

Wellman, H. M., and Liu, D. (2007). Causal reasoning as informed by the early development of explanations. In A. Gopnik and L. E. Schulz (eds.), *Causal learning: Psychology, philosophy, and computation* (pp. 261–79). New York: Oxford University Press. http://doi:10.1093/acprof:oso/9780195176803.003.0017

Wellman, H. M., Song, J. H., and Peskin-Shepherd, H. (2019). Children's early awareness of comprehension as evident in their spontaneous corrections of speech errors. *Child Development*, *90*, 196–209. https://doi.org/10.1111/cdev.12862

Wimmer, H., and Mayringer, H. (1998). False belief understanding in young children: Explanations do not develop before predictions. *International Journal of Behavioral Development*, *22*, 403–22. http://doi:10.1080/016502598384441

Wong, R. M. F., Lawson, M. J., and Keeves, J. (2002). The effects of self-explanation training on students' problem solving in high-school mathematics. *Learning and Instruction*, *12*, 233–62. http://doi:10.1016/s0959-4752(01)00027-5

# 5 Children's Question-Asking across Cultural Communities

*Maureen Callanan, Graciela Solis, Claudia Castañeda, Jennifer Jipson*

Young children's questions have been the focus of cognitive and language development research for many years (Piaget, 1926; Hood & Bloom, 1979; Chouinard, 2007; Frazier et al., 2009). These questions have been studied in order to better understand children's curiosity, as well as their developing language and communication skills (Hood & Bloom, 1979; Tizard & Hughes, 1984; Callanan & Oakes, 1992; Callanan & Jipson, 2001; Chouinard, 2007). Anecdotally, parents report that preschool-aged children's questions sometimes test their patience and make them wonder how best to respond. While children seem to ask questions in every community where language has been studied, it is essential to recognize that question-asking and -answering are cultural practices, and that there is likely to be cultural variation in how these practices develop (Hood et al., 1982; Vygotsky, 1987; Rogoff, 2003). It is important to consider the normative assumptions that many researchers make, and to contextualize those assumptions within the community under study.

Recognizing question-asking and -answering as cultural practices highlights both the importance of considering diverse children's experiences, but also the importance of avoiding deficit assumptions that might lead one to underestimate children's abilities or families' support for children's thinking, or to miss other curiosity-driven practices such as keen observation (Valencia & Solorzano, 1997; Rogoff, 2014; Rogoff et al., 2015). In this chapter, we first consider the challenges of avoiding deficit assumptions when investigating diversity in cognitive developmental research. We next review cross-cultural studies of children's questions, in particular, and consider the findings within the frame of avoiding deficit approaches. We then present findings from two of our studies of family conversation in different communities, focusing on children's questions.

## Avoiding Deficit Assumptions When Studying Cultural Variation

When comparing children across cultures, researchers are prone to unintentional biases that privilege their own culture. Gutiérrez and Rogoff (2003) point out that many cross-cultural researchers seem to, tacitly or explicitly, take a deficit perspective when comparing families from diverse communities to middle-class white families. Similarly, Medin et al. (2010) argue that whenever we study cultural variation we are prone to inaccurate assumptions, such as inadvertently considering our own experience as the norm, which can lead to the assumption that divergent experiences are somehow lacking.

It is also often much easier for people (including researchers) to see variability within their own cultural group and to overlook variability in other groups, a cognitive bias that can lead to deficit assumptions (Medin et al., 2010). We know that individuals within our own community have a variety of different values, preferences, and abilities, and yet it is easy for us to see other cultural groups as homogeneous along these same dimensions. Related to this point, Gutiérrez and Rogoff (2003) argue that culture should not be viewed as a "trait" or entity within all members of a given group; instead, culture is more accurately seen as a dynamic set of "repertoires of practices." It is crucial to consider children's cognitive and communicative skills, such as question-asking, within the context of the cultural practices that they engage in with their families.

Building on the arguments of Gutiérrez and Rogoff (2003) and Medin et al. (2010), Callanan and Waxman (2013) suggested that researchers should also avoid simple models where culture is considered a causal variable. We know that there are likely to be clusters of causal factors involved in anything as complex as children's cognitive development. And yet, there seems to be a strong tendency, in both research and everyday language, to use causal words such as "influence" when discussing correlational findings where associations are found between parents' behaviors and children's developmental outcomes. One example is the extensive attention given to the "30-million-word gap," based on Hart and Risley's (1995) finding that working-class parents in their sample spoke fewer words to their children than did professional parents. In recent discussions of this finding, the amount of talk used by parents is discussed as a causal factor in children's development even though the number of words parents speak can only be indirectly related to children's language skills or academic performance (see Miller & Sperry, 2012). This work has been used to justify efforts to change lower-income parents' language usage at home, while often ignoring the existing language and communication practices in the home. This is troubling, especially considering that recent data has failed to replicate the close link between income level and number of words spoken (Sperry et al., 2019). Studies of parent–child interaction must take a more nuanced perspective rather than assuming simple causal models.

Taking together these concerns about deficit assumptions, it is important for researchers to become aware of their own biases and to take a strengths-based approach when considering data that compares children from different cultural communities (Rogoff, 2003; Solis & Callanan, 2016). An important example of this approach is the work of Miller et al. (2005), who analyzed storytelling practices in two working-class communities on their own terms. Miller et al. (2005) noted some differences in the way storytelling was experienced by these children compared to what had been described in existing literature with middle-class Western children. In particular, they argued that these children experienced "positive valuing [. . .] and artful performance of personal story-telling [. . .] privileging of dramatic language and negative story content, and the *need to defend one's own point of view*" (p. 119, emphasis added). In other words, the authors concluded that children in these working-class communities were more likely to experience and observe questioning of evidence provided in storytelling contexts, such as recounting of personal events. The storyteller's perspective was not always taken at face value, and the children learned to defend their own point of view when telling a story. The authors suggest that this may contrast with expectations in middle-class homes, where children may learn to assume that they have the right to state their view without defending it. Miller et. al. (2005) also point out that "their fluent participation in personal storytelling will not necessarily be recognized for the strength that it has as they venture beyond home and community" (p. 133). In her commentary on this research, Michaels (2005) shared observations from her work on classroom science discourse, where she reported qualitative evidence that low-income children questioned evidence provided in the classroom that they could not verify. For example, Michaels and Sohmer (2000) reported that one working-class African American fourth grade girl talked about the contradiction between the earth's axis being tilted and her own embodied experience of feeling that we stand upright on the earth. Michaels and Sohmer (2000) report that they rarely saw this type of comment made by their middle-class participants, who more quickly accepted the abstract concepts without question. The authors note that the middle-class students' unquestioning style was seen as being more scientific, both by their teachers and by the researchers. And yet, in her later reanalysis, Michaels (2005) questions this earlier interpretation, noting that this sort of "struggle to square abstract scientific concepts with our bodies and our experiences represents a crucial intellectual practice" (p. 142). Michaels' insight suggests that one important question that needs to be addressed is how and when different children evaluate evidence and determine that something is worth asking a question about. Is it possible that working-class children's questions, though discounted as nonscientific, may actually show sophistication because of their attention to both the science concepts and their embodied reality?

Just as a strength-based perspective can add valuable new perspectives on children's learning, a deficit-based perspective can lead to potentially harmful misunderstandings about children's abilities. In two very different literatures, Rowley and Camacho (2015) and Stevenson and Gernsbacher (2013) point out, for example, that tests that are seen as assessing important abilities in the "normative" group can suddenly be downplayed and discounted when non-normative groups excel. In their discussion of the need for more diversity in cognitive developmental research, Rowley and Camacho (2015) argue that white students are never conceptualized as having a deficit, even though their test scores are often lower than those of Asian students. They note that "although Asian-White test score gaps are as large as White-Black or White-Latino gaps [...] they are rarely studied. When they are studied, results are often framed in terms of maladaptive cultural practices among Asian Americans rather than the academic shortcomings of White students" (pp. 683–684). In the very different literature on assessing abilities of individuals on the autism spectrum, Stevenson and Gernsbacher (2013) make a similar point. While block design tests are seen as valid measures of intellectual ability in neurotypical individuals, Stevenson and Gernsbacher argue that "Autistic individuals' strength on Block Design tests is often interpreted, not as an area of cognitive strength, but instead as an area of diagnostic weakness. For example, a popular theory proposes that ... they actually suffer from ... a reduced ability to 'see the big picture'" (p. 1).

With these issues surrounding deficit-based versus strength-based models as background, we next review research that has compared children's questions across communities, with the goal in mind of uncovering the unspoken assumptions about children's questions that may have an impact on our interpretations of the findings.

## Children's Questions in Cross-Cultural Studies

Many studies of young children's questions have focused on highly educated US or western European families, with results typically finding that children's fact-seeking and explanation-seeking questions are very frequent in the preschool years, and often lead to informative conversations with parents and others (Callanan & Oakes, 1992; Chouinard, 2007; Frazier et al., 2009). As Henrich et al. (2010) have argued, many psychological studies have been based on a very selective group of participants from Western, Educated, Industrialized, Rich, Democratic (WEIRD) societies. These so-called WEIRD samples are usually studied by researchers from similar backgrounds, making them further prone to the biases discussed by Gutiérrez and Rogoff (2003) and Medin et al. (2010). Some studies, however, have compared groups of families from diverse backgrounds, finding some variation across groups in children's questions. For example, Tizard and Hughes (1984) found differences in the types of questions asked by low-income girls compared with higher-income girls in Britain; why-questions were somewhat more frequent in middle-class homes, and yet the authors emphasize that both groups of children did ask why-questions and engage in "intellectual search." Further, both groups of children were less likely to ask why-questions at nursery school than at home. Other studies have focused on family explanatory conversations in nondominant communities. For example, Delgado-Gaitan (1994) studied Mexican immigrant families in the US and found that, though parents expressed an expectation that children should not question parents as a matter of respect, there was a sharp division between school-related topics and other topics, and Mexican immigrant parents were very open to children's questions when they saw them as part of their schooling.

In an informative recent study comparing children's questions across non-Western communities, Gauvain et al. (2013) examined extant data collected in the 1970s in four traditional non-Western communities and compared their findings to those reported by Chouinard (2007), which analyzed several US families from the CHILDES database (see also Chapter 10). Gauvain et al. (2013) found that the children in the four traditional communities differed from the CHILDES families in that they asked similar numbers of fact-seeking questions, but many fewer explanation-seeking questions. The authors argue that information-seeking questions (which include both fact- and explanation-seeking questions) may be universal but that explanation-seeking questions may be more specific to Western highly technological cultural communities. They speculate that technological societies provide children with more processes about which to ask for explanations. We question this notion, however, considering children's universal contact with natural phenomena that are causally complex and about which children and adults have wondered for centuries. Prior studies have shown that children asked many explanatory questions about the natural world and about people's behavior, and relatively fewer about technology (Callanan & Oakes, 1992).

Gauvain et al. (2013) have unquestionably provided the field a valuable dataset and an intriguing analysis. In the spirit of avoiding deficit interpretations, however, it seems crucial to take a critical approach in considering how to interpret this difference between the questions being asked by "Western" children and "traditional" children. Are the questions of the Western children necessarily more sophisticated and productive for children's learning? In Chouinard's (2007) data, and other data where Western middle-class children were found to use many explanatory questions, little insight is provided as to the contexts within which these questions were formulated and the functions they were serving. Further, it is important to keep in mind that there is no clear evidence for a direct link between incidence of why-questions in children's speech and any advantage in reasoning, learning, or understanding the world. It does make sense to predict that asking more why-questions is likely to lead to hearing more causal explanations, and that this may provide children opportunities to learn new causal links. At the same time, use of why-questions is likely a culturally learned practice (see Hood et al., 1982), and even if it fulfills an explanation-seeking function for children in so-called WEIRD communities, there may be different conversational (or even nonverbal) processes that serve similar functions in other communities.

To more deeply investigate the contribution of why-questions to children's learning, it is also important to recognize that not all why-questions may serve the same function. A distinction has been noted between single-word "why" utterances compared with much more fully formed questions that begin with the word "why" (e.g., "Why is the moon sometimes round and sometimes not?") (Callanan et al., 1995; Frazier et al., 2009). Single-word "why" questions have been observed within sequences referred to as "why-chaining," where the child follows each of the parent's answers with another "why?" In contrast, deeper why-questions contain more fully formed inquiries, and they are sometimes embedded in complex conversations that Tizard and Hughes (1984) called "passages of intellectual search," where children follow each answer with a logical and incisive follow-up question, seemingly seeking to construct a conclusive explanatory story.

Researchers have posed the question as to whether these single-word why-questions, or "simple" causal questions in Frazier et al.'s (2009) terminology, might be more focused on keeping the conversation going than on discovering a causal explanation (Callanan et al., 1995). Frazier et al. (2009) tested this question and found that children's reactions to explanations and non-explanations were equivalent whether they asked simple questions ("why?" or "how come?") or complex causal questions. In other words, even with simple questions children were more likely to agree with an explanation (11.9 percent) than with a non-explanation (4.1 percent), and more likely to re-ask the question after a non-explanation (25.6 percent) than after an explanation (9.9 percent) (Frazier et al., 2009, study 1). While we agree that this rules out the possibility that simple why-questions are never used to request explanations, and it is compelling that the data on children's reactions to explanations for simple questions mirror those for complex questions, there is still little information available for the majority of the instances where children ask causal questions. Therefore, there may still be a difference between simple versus complex causal questions – both in what they tell us about children's causal thinking, and in their potential for instigating productive conversation that can lead to learning.

When considering the importance of Gauvain et al.'s (2013) findings, one might want to ask what the data would look like if we removed children's "why-chaining" questions from the data – would the middle-income Western children still be asking more conceptual or complex why-questions? Also important to consider is whether there are alternative ways that children may engage in explanation-seeking that would not be apparent by recording their questions. For example, are there nonverbal ways of seeking explanations, possibly including quizzical expressions or keen observation that could be interpreted by adults as requests for explanations in some communities?

There are some additional questions to ask about how the methods used by Gauvain et al. (2013) differ from the methods used in the comparison studies with Western children. First, research tells us that children's questions are likely to arise more in some types of situations that in others. For example, over a number of studies in museum settings we have seen that children's causal questions were less common than we might have expected (Crowley et al., 2001; Tenenbaum & Callanan, 2008; Callanan et al., 2017). Perhaps children's questions are less likely to come up during the kinds of active exploratory behavior that are common in museum settings. This is consistent with our initial diary study, where parents' reports of the settings where children's why-questions emerge more often included reflective settings, such as riding in the car, than active play (Callanan & Oakes, 1992). Because Gauvain et al.'s (2013) data consisted largely of peer-dominated activity, perhaps these were settings where explanatory questions might be less common. Another question about different data collection strategies with the Western and non-Western samples is that Gauvain et al. (2013) report that the first verbal or nonverbal act by the child was recorded in the dataset they worked with. Does this mean that children's questions were being considered out of context? Would this data collection strategy, by definition, miss out on the ability to distinguish "why-chaining" from "passages of intellectual search"? Overall, these comparisons across studies point to the importance of including methodological diversity in our research as well as cultural diversity.

Beyond the Gauvain et al. (2013) cross-cultural comparison, other studies have considered children's questions and explanatory talk with adults in families from different economic backgrounds. In an important recent paper, Kurkul and Corriveau (2018) have studied children's questions and parents' responses in families from low-SES and mid-SES backgrounds using the Hall et al. (1984) data from the CHILDES database. Kurkul and Corriveau (2018) found that low-SES children asked fewer questions than did mid-SES children in this observational dataset, but that their ratio of explanation-seeking to fact-seeking questions was no different from that of the mid-SES children. Parents from the low-SES group were less likely, however, to give explanatory answers than were mid-SES parents. And low-SES parents were also more likely to give explanations that Kurkul and Corriveau defined as "circular." The authors argue that exposure to noncircular explanations is important for children's developing logical and scientific reasoning.

Again, with the avoidance of deficit assumptions as a goal, it seems important to critically examine the assumption that noncircular explanations are normative and that they are the main type of response to children's questions that should predict children's learning or scientific reasoning. Centuries of philosophical thinking about explanations have identified a broad range of types of explanation. Many theorists have considered Aristotle's classification of four causes to be useful; these include efficient cause (mechanistic cause or agent of change), material cause (what things are made of), final cause (also known as functional or teleological cause), and formal cause (structure or form). Clearly some of these types of causes are more valued by the dominant culture and by modern science; some are hardly considered causal at all in current thinking (Lombrozo & Vasilyeva, 2017). And yet, the preference for different types of causality has varied quite a bit across history and across cultures. Efficient cause is currently valued by modern science but the history of science reveals change over time in this preference (Kuhn, 1977; Gould, 1983). More research is needed to determine whether there are preferences for different types of causes or explanations across different cultural communities.

Further, to avoid deficit thinking, as discussed earlier, it is best to define cultural practices on their own terms, rather than in terms of what they are not. For example, Piaget (1926) characterized preschool-aged children as "pre-causal" because they did not answer questions about causality in the way that had been seen as causal in older children's and adults' reasoning. When Piaget presented a picture of a man on the ground next to a bike and asked children to complete a sentence like "the man broke his leg because . . ." he considered answers like "he ran into a tree" as causal and answers like "he broke his leg" as non-causal. In fact, the latter was considered pre-causal and used as evidence that preschoolers cannot distinguish cause from effect. Another possible interpretation of pre-schoolers' response, however, is that they are providing an interpretive cause, and saying something like "I know the man fell off his bike because he broke his leg." While certainly different from what US adults would likely say when asked for a cause, this answer still could reveal causal thinking (Donaldson, 1986; Callanan et al., 1995).

With regard to data like Kurkul and Corriveau's (2018), then, one question is whether there might be a different way to interpret the types of explanations they are observing in lower-income families. Michaels' (2005) commentary on Miller et al. (2005) provides a thought-provoking example of what this might look like. As mentioned earlier, Michaels comments that the working-class children in her studies of classroom discourse tended to use more past experience and evidential claims in their explanations than middle-class children, saying things like "It rained last night because there are puddles on the ground." Michaels (2005) speculates that these types of explanations might be used by working-class children in part because the cultural practice of explaining in their families includes justifying that you have a valid point of view (as shown by Miller et al., 2005, and discussed earlier). Also relevant is Michaels' (2005) argument mentioned earlier, that the working-class children in her studies tended to do more puzzling over how abstract notions like the tilt of the earth relate to their own personal experience (that the earth does not seem to be tilted). Michaels (2005) notes that middle-class children tend to just accept such discrepancies without puzzling as much over them. And she raises the question whether we should assume that it is necessarily better to accept what one is taught without puzzling over its inconsistencies with one's own experience.

Integrating the important research on children's questions in this section with the previous work on deficit assumptions, it becomes clear that further research is needed on how the conversational practices of asking and answering questions unfold in diverse families and communities. Taking a small step in this direction, we next consider two studies from our lab where we have looked at children's questions across communities – including a working-class community of mostly immigrant families from Mexico, a diverse middle-income community of majority European-American families, and a subgroup of Mexican-American families in the diverse community. We consider aspects of children's questions in these two datasets, considering variation across the groups with a strengths-based perspective.

### Children's Spontaneous Questions about Nature in Two Communities

One of our studies explores children's ideas about the natural world by asking parents of preschoolers to keep track of and record spontaneous conversations about nature for two weeks (Jipson & Callanan, 2014). A sub-sample from this larger study included families from a middle-income coastal community in central California with diverse demographics but a majority from European-American backgrounds, and a nearby lower-income agricultural community, with a majority of Mexican-heritage immigrant families. Families varied in levels of formal schooling from zero to nineteen years. We divided the families based on a median split, into a "higher schooling" group with at least fourteen years of schooling, and a "lower schooling" group with thirteen years of schooling or fewer.

Families either visited a lab or were visited by researchers in their home. In a videotaped session, parents read a book to their child, filled out a demographic questionnaire, and were introduced to a journal and asked to keep track of conversations about nature for two weeks. Researchers called parents to remind them to keep journal entries throughout the two weeks, and then picked up the journals at the end of the study. In the journals, parents reported the context of each conversation, how it was initiated, and as much as they could remember of the verbatim conversation. Using this dataset we analyzed parents' reports of children's questions in these diary reports to ask if there were differences between the two communities in the frequency or types of questions asked.

We identified all of the questions reportedly asked by children in the diary records and found that the two groups were similar in the number of questions asked, with an average of 6.68 questions in the more highly schooled group and 7.31 in the less highly schooled group. We then coded each of the children's questions as fact-seeking or explanation-seeking. Explanation-seeking questions were questions that usually begin with "why" or "how" and that request a causal explanation (e.g., "Why is the moon round?" "How do seeds grow?"). Fact-seeking questions were either yes/no questions, (e.g., "Can we feed the ducks?" "Are tomatoes healthy?") or questions that use words such as "what," "when," or "where" (e.g., "What's inside a leaf?" "What's a tsunami?").

To ask whether children from different family schooling backgrounds differed in the types of questions they asked, we conducted an ANCOVA on the frequency of children's questions, 2 (type of question: explanation-seeking or fact-seeking) x 2 (parents' schooling: basic schooling or higher schooling) x 2(gender), with a covariate of children's age in months. This analysis revealed two interactions after controlling for children's age. First, an interaction of question type with parents' schooling, $F (1, 30) = 21.91$, $p = 0.0001$, showed that children of parents with basic schooling asked significantly fewer fact-seeking questions ($M = 1.95$) than did children of parents with high schooling ($M = 4.03$), and children from the basic schooling group asked significantly more explanation-seeking questions ($M = 5.10$) than did children of parents with higher schooling ($M = 2.82$). The second significant interaction was between question type and children's gender, $F (1, 30) = 9.88$, $p = 0.004$; girls asked more explanation-seeking questions ($M = 4.63$) than boys ($M = 3.29$), and girls asked fewer fact-seeking questions ($M = 2.20$) than boys ($M = 3.79$). While not the focus of our study, this gender difference is also somewhat surprising given earlier studies of gender differences in conversations about STEM topics (Crowley et al., 2001; Tenenbaum & Leaper, 2003).

We had no reason to predict that children in the basic schooling group would show more frequent focus on explanation-seeking questions than those in the higher schooling group. However, it is important that they did not show less interest in explanatory questions, as might have been predicted by the research of Gauvain et al. (2013) and Kurkul and Corriveau (2018) reported earlier.

## Children's Questions in a Science Task with Parents

In another study, we considered two groups of Mexican-heritage families, differing in schooling background. In this sample there was a group of parents with "basic schooling" – meaning less than high school graduation – ranging from zero to eleven years of schooling, and a "higher schooling" group of parents who had at least twelve years of schooling, ranging from twelve to sixteen years. We considered children's questions in the context of a science activity conducted in families' homes.

The task used in this study was a "sink and float" activity where parents and children were asked to predict whether a variety of objects would sink or float, and were then given the opportunity to test their ideas. We coded a variety of aspects of parents' and children's talk and behavior in this task, but most relevant to this chapter was our measure of the types of questions that children asked. We coded two types of questions: conceptual questions (e.g., "Why didn't that one float?") and procedural questions (e.g., "Where should we put the ones that we think will sink?"). As we have reported in other papers (Solis & Callanan, 2016, unpublished data), the children from these two groups varied in the types of questions they asked during the sink and float game. Children whose parents had basic schooling were more likely to ask conceptual questions, and children whose parents had higher schooling were likely to ask more procedural questions. Again, this may seem different from what one might predict given some of the recent literature on low-income children's cognitive and language skills. However, we argue that the different questioning style of children may be related to different strategies parents took to the task. In particular, the parents with higher schooling took on a teacher-like role and focused on asking children known-answer questions and evaluating children's performance (Solis & Callanan, 2016). In contrast, the parents with basic schooling seemed to engage in the task as co-learners with their children (Solis & Callanan, 2016). Perhaps this variation in the roles where parents positioned themselves may have been related to children's relative focus on conceptual versus procedural aspects of the task.

## Conclusions

The findings presented here raise more questions about how young children develop practices of asking questions, which may help us to better understand how and what they learn from the resulting conversations. We hope to have posed some challenging questions that may help the field to move beyond deficit interpretations. For example, future research should consider carefully what counts as sophisticated reasoning, and for whom (see Medin & Bang, 2014). Importantly, the valuing of these practices is related to what gets considered a "good" question or a "bad" question in school environments, something that is admittedly quite difficult to change. Michaels (2005) pointed out that middle-class children were likely to accept abstract models without try to "square" them with their own phenomenal experience, whereas working-class children were likely to puzzle over these discrepancies. It is potentially problematic if the former is recognized as sophisticated thinking in school, while the latter may be seen as deficient just because it is different from the norm.

As the field moves forward toward better understanding of diversity in how children ask questions and learn from answers, it may be useful to keep in mind the work of Harkness and colleagues on variation in parental ethnotheories (Harkness et al., 2015). Harkness et al. (2015) define parental ethnotheories in terms of unquestioned assumptions about what children need from parents; these assumptions are argued to influence how parents create physical and social environments for their children, and caregiving behaviors. Together, these factors make up what Harkness et al. (2015) call the developmental niche in which children grow up. For example, whereas in interviews about their children, US parents tended to focus on their children's cognitive skills and how to provide stimulation to support this development, parents in Kenya were more likely to focus on children's development of responsibility, which they described as a part of social intelligence. Depending on parents' ethnotheory, children are likely to be faced with different opportunities to strengthen different skills. These findings should lead us to question normativity and complicate how we define cultural groups. Opportunities for children to ask questions, and reactions to the questions they ask, are also likely to be framed by the ethnotheories of their parents and cultural communities (Goodnow, 1990). At the same time, any cross-cultural work risks increasing the perception of homogeneity within cultures, so it is important to work to reveal the variability within cultures as well as between.

Asking questions may well be a cultural universal, and yet the findings discussed in this chapter make it clear that the types of questions that children ask, in what contexts, and with what results, vary a great deal. To understand the role of questions in children's cognitive development, much progress is needed in revealing the nature and power of this diversity.

## Acknowledgments

The research discussed in this chapter was partially supported by National Science Foundation grant DRL1217441, *My Sky Tonight*, with Astronomical Society of the Pacific as the PI organization. The work was also partially supported by the Center for Research on Education, Diversity & Excellence (CREDE), as funded by the US Department of Education. Thanks to our collaborators, to our students who assisted with data collection, coding, and analysis, and to the families who participated in these studies.

## References

Callanan, M., and Jipson, J. (2001). Explanatory conversations and young children's developing scientific literacy. In K. Crowley, C. Schunn, and

T. Okada (eds.), *Designing for science: Implications from everyday, classroom, and professional settings* (pp. 21–49). Mahwah, NJ: Erlbaum.

Callanan, M., and Oakes, L. (1992). Preschoolers' questions and parents' explanations: Causal thinking in everyday activity. *Cognitive Development, 7,* 213–33. http://doi:10.1016/0885-2014(92)90012-g

Callanan, M., and Waxman, S. (2013). Commentary on special section: Deficit or difference? Interpreting diverse developmental paths. *Developmental Psychology, 49,* 80–3. http://doi:10.1037/a0029741

Callanan, M., Shrager, J., and Moore, J. (1995). Parent-child collaborative explanations: Methods of identification and analysis. *The Journal of the Learning Sciences, 4,* 105–29. http://doi:10.1207/s15327809jls0401_3

Callanan, M., Castañeda, C., Luce, M., and Martin, J. (2017). Family science talk in museums: Predicting children's engagement from variations in talk and activity. *Child Development, 88,* 1492–1504. http://doi: 10.1111/cdev.12886

Chouinard, M. M. (2007). *Children's questions: A mechanism for cognitive development.* Monographs of the Society for Research in Child Development, *72.* Boston, MA: Blackwell.

Crowley, K., Callanan, M. A., Tenenbaum, H. R., and Allen, E. (2001). Parents explain more often to boys than to girls during shared scientific thinking. *Psychological Science, 12,* 258–61. http://doi:10.1111/1467-9280.00347

Delgado-Gaitan, C. (1994). Socializing young children in Mexican-American families: An intergenerational perspective. In P. Greenfield and R. Cocking (eds.), *Cross-cultural roots of minority child development* (pp. 55–86). Hillsdale, NJ: Erlbaum.

Donaldson, M. (1986). *Children's explanations: A psycholinguistic study.* Cambridge: Cambridge University Press.

Frazier, B. N., Gelman, S. A., and Wellman, H. M. (2009). Preschoolers' search for explanatory information within adult–child conversation. *Child Development, 80,* 1592–611. https://doi.org/10.1111/j.1467-8624.2009.01356.x

Gauvain, M., Munroe, R., and Beebe, H. (2013). Children's questions in cross-cultural perspective: A four-culture study. *Journal of Cross-Cultural Psychology, 44,* 1148–65. http://doi:10.1177/0022022113485430

Goodnow, J. J. (1990). The socialization of cognition: What's involved? In J. W. Stigler, R. A. Shweder, and G. H. Herdt (eds.), *Cultural psychology: Essays on comparative human development* (pp. 259–86). New York: Cambridge University Press. http://doi:10.1017/cbo9781139173728.008

Gould, S. J. (1983). *Hen's teeth and horse's toes.* New York: Norton.

Gutiérrez, K. D., and Rogoff, B. (2003). Cultural ways of learning: Individual traits or repertoires of practice. *Educational Researcher, 32,* 19–25. http://doi:10.3102/0013189x032005019

Hall, W. S., Nagy, W. E., and Linn, R. (1984). *Spoken words: Effects of situation and social group on oral word usage and frequency.* Hillsdale, NJ: Erlbaum.

Harkness, S., Mavridis, C. J., Liu, J. J., and Super, C. M. (2015). Parental ethnotheories and the development of family relationships in early and middle childhood. In L. A. Jensen (ed.), *Oxford library of psychology. The Oxford handbook of human development and culture: An interdisciplinary perspective*

(pp. 271–91). New York: Oxford University Press. http://doi:10.1093/oxfordh
b/9780199948550.013.17

Hart, B., and Risley, T. (1995). *Meaningful differences in the everyday experience of
young American children.* Baltimore, MD: Brookes Publishing.

Henrich, J., Heine, S., and Norenzayan, A. (2010). Beyond WEIRD: Towards a
broad-based behavioral science. *Behavioral and Brain Sciences, 33,* 111–35.
http://doi:10.1017/s0140525x0999152x

Hood, L., and Bloom, L. (1979). *What, when, and how about why:
A longitudinal study of early expressions of causality.* Monographs of the
Society for Research in Child Development, *44.* Chicago, IL: University
of Chicago Press.

Hood, L., Fiess, K., and Aron, J. (1982). Growing up explained: Vygotskians look
at the language of causality. In C. J. Brainerd and M. Pressley (eds.), *Verbal
processes in children* (pp. 265–85). New York: Springer-Verlag. http://doi:10
.1007/978-1-4613-9475-4_8

Jipson, J., and Callanan, M. (2014). *My Sky Tonight: Researching young children's
ideas about astronomy and designing informal astronomy activities for families.*
Poster presented at International Conference of the Learning Sciences.
Boulder, CO.

Kuhn, T. (1977). *The essential tension.* Chicago, IL: University of Chicago Press.

Kurkul, K. E., and Corriveau, K. H. (2018). Question, explanation, follow-up:
A mechanism for learning from others? *Child Development, 89,* 280–94. http://
doi:10.1111/cdev.12726

Lombrozo, T., and Vasilyeva, N. (2017). Causal explanation. In M. R. Waldmann
(ed.), *Oxford handbook of causal reasoning* (pp. 415–32). New York: Oxford
University Press. http://doi:10.1093/oxfordhb/9780199399550.013.22

Medin, D. L., and Bang, M. (2014). *Who's asking? Native science, western science,
and science education.* Cambridge, MA: The MIT Press.

Medin, D. L., Bennis, W., and Chandler, M. (2010). Culture and the home-field
disadvantage. *Perspectives on Psychological Science, 5,* 708–13. http://doi:10.1177
/1745691610388772

Michaels, S. (2005). Can the intellectual affordances of working-class storytelling
be leveraged in school? *Human Development, 48,* 136–45. http://doi:10.1159
/000085516

Michaels, S., and Sohmer, R. (2000). Narratives and inscriptions: Cultural tools,
power, and powerful sensemaking. In M. Kalantzis and B. Cope (eds.),
*Multiliteracies: Literacy learning and the design of social futures* (pp. 265–86).
New York: Routledge.

Miller, P. J., and Sperry, D. (2012). Déjà vu: The continuing misrecognition of
low-income children's verbal abilities. In S. Fiske and H. R. Markus (eds.),
*Facing social class: How societal rank influences interaction* (pp. 109–30).
New York: Russell Sage Foundation.

Miller, P. J., Cho, G. E., and Bracey, J. R. (2005). Working-class children's
experience through the prism of personal storytelling. *Human Development,
48,* 115–35. http://doi:10.1159/000085515

Piaget, J. (1926). *The language and thought of the child.* New York: Harcourt Brace.

Rogoff, B. (2003). *The cultural nature of human development.* New York: Oxford University Press.

Rogoff, B. (2014). Learning by observing and pitching in to family and community endeavors: An orientation. *Human Development, 57,* 69–81. http://doi:10.1159/000356757

Rogoff, B., Mejia-Arauz, R., and Correa-Chavez, M. (2015). A cultural paradigm: Learning by observing and pitching in. In M. Correa-Chávez, R. Mejía-Arauz, and B. Rogoff (eds.), *Advances in child development and behavior: Vol. 49. Children learn by observing and contributing to family and community endeavors: A cultural paradigm* (pp. 1–22). Waltham, MA: Academic Press. http://doi:10.1016/bs.acdb.2015.10.008

Rowley, S.J., and Camacho, T. C. (2015). Increasing diversity in cognitive developmental research: Issues and solutions. *Journal of Cognition and Development, 16,* 683–92. http://doi:10.1080/15248372.2014.976224

Solis, G., and Callanan, M. (2016). Evidence against deficit accounts: Conversations about science in Mexican-heritage families living in the United States. *Mind, Culture, and Activity, 23,* 212–24. http://doi:10.1080/10749039.2016.1196493

Sperry, D. E., Sperry, L. L., and Miller, P. J. (2019). Reexamining the verbal environments of children from different socioeconomic backgrounds. *Child Development* 90, 1303–1318. http://doi.org/10.1111/cdev.13072

Stevenson, J. L., and Gernsbacher, M. A. (2013). Abstract spatial reasoning as an autistic strength. *PLOS ONE, 8,* no. 3, 1–9. http://doi:10.1371/journal.pone.0059329

Tenenbaum, H. R., and Callanan, M. A. (2008). Parents' science talk to their children in Mexican descent families residing in the USA. *International Journal of Behavioral Development, 32,* 1–12. http://doi:10.1177/0165025407084046

Tenenbaum, H. R., and Leaper, C. (2003). Parent-child conversations about science: The socialization of gender inequities? *Developmental Psychology, 39,* 34–47. http://doi:10.1037/0012-1649.39.1.34

Tizard, B., and Hughes, M. (1984). *Young children learning.* Cambridge, MA: Harvard University Press.

Valencia, R. R., and Solorzano, D. G. (1997). Contemporary deficit thinking. In R. R. Valencia (ed.), *The evolution of deficit thinking: Educational thought and practice* (pp. 160–210). The Stanford Series on Education and Public Policy. London: Falmer Press.

Vygotsky, L. (1987). *Thought and Language.* Cambridge, MA: The MIT Press.

# 6    The Development of Information-Requesting Gestures in Infancy and Their Role in Shaping Learning Outcomes

*Kelsey Lucca*

One of the foundational ideas of developmental psychology, famously put forth by Piaget, is that young children are active learners (Piaget, 1954). Rather than passively absorbing information from their environment, children strategically interact with their environment in ways that maximize their potential for information gain. When children reach gaps in their knowledge, or *disequilibrium*, they seek out ways to fill those gaps – they might ask a question or explore their environment to resolve that disequilibrium and gain new knowledge. This ability to reason about what is known and unknown, and the tendency to behave in ways that maximize information gain, emerges much earlier than Piaget had originally proposed, during infancy (Begus & Southgate, 2012; Kidd et al., 2012; Harris & Lane, 2013; Xu & Kushnir, 2013; Lucca & Wilbourn, 2018; Lucca & Sommerville, 2018).

In just the first few weeks of life, infants engage with their environment in ways that directly contribute to and enhance their learning. For example, infants selectively focus their attention on informative visual and auditory stimuli in their environment, such as human faces and infant-directed speech (Cooper & Aslin, 1990; Morton & Johnson, 1991). Across the first year of life, infants' curiosity flourishes: they acquire both more advanced motor control as well as sophisticated social-cognitive capacities, which enable them to manifest their curiosity in new and different ways. While an infant's environment is full of potential sources of information, they are keenly aware that adults are particularly rich sources of information, and are highly motivated to access that information. Thus, active learning becomes even more active when young learners transition from selectively *attending* to sources of information to explicitly *requesting* information – a transition that I argue is marked by the emergence of index-finger pointing.

While the ability to request information has long been thought to be restricted to a time in development after children are able to verbally articulate questions, in this chapter I present new evidence that this ability is already present during the first two years of life, when infants begin to produce pointing gestures (Southgate et al., 2007; Lucca & Wilbourn, 2018). While most historical and mainstream theoretical accounts of early pointing maintain that infants' pointing serves either an imperative ("get me that!") or declarative ("look at that!") function, in this chapter I capitalize on recent discoveries in infant cognition to show that pointing also serves an interrogative ("what's that?") function (Begus & Southgate, 2012; Begus et al., 2014; Kovács et al., 2014; Lucca & Wilbourn, 2018). An essential component of this argument is that the early-emerging ability to request information has potent and direct implications for learning across a range of domains. In what follows, I offer ways for developmentalists to harness these findings to construct a more complete theoretical account of active learning and cognitive development more broadly.

To demonstrate how information-requesting pointing gestures help young learners actively make sense of the world around them, I first review the evidence for information-seeking during infancy, as it is manifested through attentional biases and exploratory play. I then turn to infants' burgeoning understanding of adults as reservoirs of information, and outline how infants transition from information-seeking to information-requesting through the use of pointing. Here, I propose that long before infants acquire the verbal abilities to ask questions, they are already requesting information through their pointing gestures. I then argue how interrogative pointing drives learning, specifically in the domain of language acquisition. I end by exploring how infants make the transition from information-requesting through pointing to requesting information through questions.

## How Do Infants Seek Out Information from Their Environment?

### *Infants Maximize Information Gain through Selective Attention*

In adulthood, the process of acquiring information is highly rewarding. If we don't know something, it isn't long before we Google it to find out. This process also appears to be rewarding early in life: when children don't know something, they try hard to find it out – often by asking questions (Davis, 1932). These information-seeking questions have been the subject of much research (Harris et al., 2017; Ronfard et al., 2018): What kinds of questions do children ask (Kemler Nelson et al., 2004)? When do they ask them (Chouinard, 2007)? Why do they ask them (Ruggeri & Lombrozo, 2015)? How do caregivers respond (Callanan & Oakes, 1992; Kurkul & Corriveau, 2018)? But how do infants, who are unable to verbally request information, seek out information from their environment? Relative to the research on information-seeking in older children and adults, there is a paucity of research on information-seeking during infancy. However, in recent years, with the emergence of new experimental methodologies and techniques, as well as discoveries in infants' rational and active learning, interest in this topic has surged.

One of the first ways that infants begin to actively gather information is by selectively attending to potential sources of information in their environment. Within the first month of life, newborns prefer human faces over other dynamic and salient stimuli, and infant-directed speech over adult-directed speech (Cooper & Aslin, 1990; Morton & Johnson, 1991). By seven months of age, infants preferentially allocate their attention to stimuli that are not only likely to provide information, but are also ideally suited to learn from (i.e., stimuli that are not overly predictable or overly complex; Kidd et al., 2012, 2014). Infants attend to and track the statistical regularities of information in their environment, and use these patterns to make inferences and guide future decision-making behaviors (Saffran et al., 1996; Sobel & Kirkham, 2006; Estes et al., 2013). These different forms of selective attention allow infants to maximize the amount of information they can extract from their surroundings.

*Infants Acquire Information through Exploration*

As infants develop more advanced motor control, their ability to extract information from the environment undergoes a major transition. They no longer have to rely solely on looking to get information; rather, they can actively explore their environment. Indeed, beginning very early on in development, infants are highly curious and engage in exploratory play. At the earliest stages of development, infants explore objects by putting them in their mouth. By six months of age, infants engage in a deeper level of exploration by visually inspecting objects prior to putting them in their mouth (Rochat, 1989). This multimodal exploration provides infants with important information about object properties (e.g., shape, taste, weight, texture). With more developed fine-motor control, infants start to manually explore objects more thoroughly – they bang, drop, slide, roll, and grip objects. This detailed exploration allows infants to discover the various affordances of objects (Lockman, 2000), and enhances their ability to reason about those objects (Gibson, 1988). For instance, when infants physically interact with objects, they are better able to discriminate those objects among others (Needham, 2000), and are more attentive to their intermodal properties (Eppler, 1995).

A critical question that emerges from this work is whether infants' learning is a *by-product* of their exploration, or whether their exploration is *driven* by a motivation to learn? Recent evidence provides support for the latter. When infants observe events that violate their expectations about how the physical world works, such as when an object passes through a wall (when it should have stopped upon hitting the wall) or continues to travel horizontally through space after reaching the end of a surface (when it should have dropped off), they show heightened attention towards those objects (Spelke et al., 1992; Wilcox et al., 1994). Infants' increased looking towards unexpected events suggests that they are inconsistent with their prior knowledge about the world.

As adults, we often treat events that violate our expectations as opportunities for learning, because they potentially offer new opportunities to update our knowledge states. For example, imagine going to meet a friend for coffee. You have plans to meet at 10:00, but this particular friend has a history of arriving late, so when 10:30 approaches, you don't think much about it and continue waiting. Now suppose you're going to meet a different friend who, unlike your first friend, is never late. By the time 10:30 rolls around, you've already called them several times and left messages to find out what happened. You may have only sought out information in the latter scenario because, as adults, we are strategic and selective in our investigative, information-seeking behaviors. We are keenly aware that information-seeking is only useful in contexts in which there is actually new information to be learned (i.e., when events violate our expectations). There is not much to learn from following up with the friend who is always late, but potentially much to gain by following up with the friend who is never late; they might have run into car trouble, for example, and be in need of help.

New research suggests that infants also reason in a similar way, and are aware that expectancy violations hint at the potential for novel information gain (Stahl & Feigenson, 2015). Infants are not only aware that objects/events that have violated their expectations may be ripe with new information, they also engage in selective hypothesis-testing that is specific to updating their existing representations and knowledge. For instance, when an object violates an infant's solidity expectations (i.e., it passes through a solid surface), they will bang that object on the table as if testing its solidity properties. When an object violates an infant's support expectations (i.e., it continues traveling across space without physical support), they will throw it off the table as if testing its anti-gravitational properties. Infants' sensitivity to the degree to which new information aligns or misaligns with their previous knowledge, together with their strategic exploration, has the potential to be a driver of conceptual change or theory formation. Indeed, infants are significantly more likely to learn new information about objects that have recently violated their expectations than about objects that have operated in ways consistent with their expectations/prior knowledge states (Stahl & Feigenson, 2015). In this way, infants' exploration, similar to adults', is carried out in a way that maximizes their potential for novel information gain.

Infants' active exploration not only enhances their perception of the physical world, it has also been shown to facilitate their understanding of the social world (Sommerville et al., 2005). Sommerville and colleagues (2005) gave three-month-olds experience with Velcro-covered "sticky-mittens" that allowed them to successfully and easily hold objects without needing to manually grasp and lift them. This experience facilitated infants' own ability to perform organized, goal-directed actions on objects (i.e., swipe objects while also maintaining eye contact with those objects). But perhaps more interestingly, it also facilitated their ability to form linkages between their own actions and the actions of others: infants who were given experience with sticky-mittens were significantly more likely to represent others' actions as being intentional and goal-directed in nature. Across development, infants acquire new methods of exploration, which further broadens their opportunities for learning. For instance, exploratory activity in the form of locomotion has also been linked to enhanced learning, such as improved spatial search behaviors (Bertenthal et al., 1994).

### Infants Turn to Adults for Information

While infants' exploration and direct actions on the world offer numerous opportunities for learning, it only gets them so far – the social environment also plays an essential role in constructing infants' knowledge. Even in domains where infants can learn much on their own, such as the physical features of their environment as described above, paying attention to what others are doing, or being explicitly taught, may cause infants' self-directed learning to be even more efficient and effective (Csibra & Gergely, 2009). And critically, there are entire domains of information that infants can *only* have access to by learning from others, such as culturally relevant information that is not always directly observable (e.g., societal norms and values, Legare & Nielsen, 2015; Legare & Harris, 2016). Contrary to historical accounts of early development, which viewed early learning as a passive process in which infants absorb information from their caregivers, we now know that infants are *active* learners: they view adults as rich sources of information, and are highly motivated to access that information. Research dating from the early

1980s has provided strong empirical evidence for this claim. For instance, when infants are in need of information – such as whether or not to cross a visual cliff – they routinely refer to adults to determine how to behave (social referencing; Sorce et al., 1985; Feinman et al., 1992). If an adult provides positive information, such as a joy or interest, infants will cross the visual cliff. If an adult provides negative information, such as fear or anger, infants will not cross the visual cliff. Infants are so skilled at gathering information from adults that this information need not be ostensively directed towards them: eighteen-month-olds can learn new information (e.g., words) by simply overhearing a conversation (Floor & Akhtar, 2006).

Infants not only understand that adults tend to provide information, they also have nuanced expectations about what this information should look like, who it should come from, and when it should be provided. Beginning in the first year of life, infants are sensitive to the reliability of potential informants, and expect adults to provide accurate information (Chow et al., 2008; Koenig & Woodward, 2010; Tummeltshammer et al., 2014). Moreover, infants also prioritize information that comes from reliable sources, and will selectively learn from individuals who have previously provided reliable information. Infants also use more subtle cues, such as confidence and competence, to determine credibility (Birch et al., 2010; Zmyj et al., 2010; Stenberg, 2013). This awareness directly influences learning: infants prefer to learn from individuals who provide information with high levels of certainty and competence than individuals who are less competent or confident. Similarly, infants consider age in their evaluation of who is best suited to provide information, and preferentially learn from adults over infants or young children (Zmyj et al., 2012; Kachel et al., 2018).

Infants' expectation for adults to provide information is so pervasive that it has recently been leveraged to explain a key developmental phenomenon: preference for in-group over out-group members (Begus et al., 2016). One salient marker of group membership is language. From shortly after birth, infants demonstrate a sensitivity to their native language, and by six months, infants begin to socially evaluate others based on the language they speak (Mehler et al., 1988; Kinzler et al., 2007). That is, infants prefer others who speak their native language or in their native dialect, compared to individuals who speak a foreign language or speak their native language with an accent. A recent study found that when infants encounter a native speaker they exhibit increased anticipatory theta oscillations, a signal that the brain is preparing for encoding new information, and devote more visual attention to that information when it arrives, compared to when they encounter a foreign speaker. (Klimesch, 1999; Begus et al., 2016; Marno et al., 2016). The finding that infants' in-group preference is reflected in a neural encoding of an expectation for information suggests that infants may view in-group members as potential informants, and their bias to interact with them may be driven by a desire to obtain information. Recent work has also argued that infants' bias towards interacting with prosocial, compared to antisocial, individuals may be similarly driven by a motive to affiliate with individuals who are most likely/willing to provide new information (Lucca et al., 2018b). Future work that directly and empirically tests whether infants' social decision-making is driven by a willingness and ability to learn from different types of individuals (e.g., in-group members, prosocial individuals) will be essential for substantiating these hypotheses. In doing so, findings in this vein have the potential to test whether established phenomenon surrounding infants' social preferences may be explained, at least in part, by a drive to obtain new information.

The findings reviewed above provide compelling evidence that infants are selective (as opposed to indiscriminate) in their information-seeking. Further evidence for this hypothesis comes from findings demonstrating that infants monitor their own certainty and selectively engage in increased information-seeking when new information is actually needed (Vaish et al., 2011). Infants also show heightened signs of information-seeking when they are less confident about how to solve a problem (Goupil & Kouider, 2016; Goupil et al., 2016). When infants are more confident about the solution to a problem, they will attempt to solve that problem without looking to an adult for help. To possess the kind of metacognitive awareness demonstrated by Goupil and colleagues requires infants to possess and integrate several distinct skills. First, they must assess their own knowledge and abilities, and be aware of what they can and cannot do on their own. Second, they must be able to assess the knowledge and abilities of another person to determine their role as a potential informant. Finally, in order to express their uncertainty to that person, infants must modulate their own behavior based on both their knowledge of their own skills/understanding and those of others. In this way, studying infant information-seeking has provided new information about the nature of early learning processes, and more specifically, it has challenged the long-standing notion that metacognition is restricted to older children and adults. In sum, the work reviewed above provides compelling evidence that information-seeking during infancy is finely tuned to ensure accurate and efficient transfer of information.

## Infants Construct Knowledge through Explicit Requests for Information

If infants are driven to acquire information, and understand that adults are well suited to provide them with information, then it is important to identify which behaviors, infants produce, if any, to obtain information from adults. Before producing their first words, infants produce a variety of behaviors that could serve an information-requesting function, and may appear to, but providing direct evidence of their information-requesting function is rather hard because they are not always directly observable, or can be explained by several other motives. In this section, I argue that there is a growing body of work providing direct and compelling evidence that infants' pointing gestures serve an information-requesting function.

### *An Abridged History of Infants' Pointing Gestures*

Researchers have long been interested in what infants do with their hands. In 1877, Charles Darwin made the first systematic observations of an infant's gestures. In *A Biographical Sketch of an Infant*, Darwin (1877) described how the development of infants' hands far outpaces the development of other parts of the body. Darwin argued that because infants' first "rational actions" are in the form of myriad gestures, they can serve as a window into infants' interests and thoughts. For instance, infants clap their hands to capture the attention of adults, reach their arms out to be picked up, and wave "hello" and "goodbye." In the years since Darwin's first observations, one gesture in particular has captivated developmental psychologists: pointing (Werner & Kaplan, 1963; Bruner, 1975; Murphy & Messer, 1977; Bates et al., 1979; Leung & Rheingold, 1981; Masur, 1983; Dobrich & Scarborough, 1984; Goldin-Meadow, 2007; Tomasello, 2008; Colonnesi et al., 2010).

There are several reasons why pointing has consistently captured the attention of developmental psychologists. First, infants all around the world produce index-finger pointing gestures, despite the fact that ubiquitous index-finger pointing during adulthood is not universal across cultures (Blake et al., 2003; Callaghan et al., 2011; Liszkowski et al., 2012; Salomo & Liszkowski, 2013; Cooperrider et al., 2014). Second, pointing appears to be a uniquely human behavior (Tomasello, 2006). Although nonhuman primates can be trained to produce point-like gestures in captivity (Savage-Rumbaugh, 1990; Leavens & Hopkins, 1998), there is currently no evidence that they point in the wild or in the same way that human infants do (Liszkowski et al., 2009; van der Goot et al., 2014), suggesting that the early-emerging drive to explicitly request information from others may differentiate humans from our closest primate relatives. Finally, infants' pointing gestures have strong ties to language development. They not only precede infants' first words, they also predict when those words will occur (as discussed more later in this chapter, see also Bates et al., 1979; Dobrich & Scarborough, 1984; Samuelson & Smith, 1998; Brooks & Meltzoff, 2005; Rowe et al., 2008; Colonnesi et al., 2010).

Throughout development, there is evidence that pointing gestures are intricately linked to communicative development. The earliest signs of pointing emerge between three and six months,[1] when infants first begin to extend their index finger (Trevarthen, 1977; Masataka, 1995). These early point-like gestures, or "proto-points," are more likely to occur when infants are engaged in face-to-face interactions with their care-givers (Fogel & Hannan, 1985). These proto-points are also reliably produced in combination with speech-like vocalizations (i.e., vocalizations that are syllabic with oral resonance and pitch contours; Bloom, 1988; Masataka, 1995). Importantly, this gesture–speech coupling continues throughout development. As infants gain more strength and control of their upper body at around six months, they begin to produce manual arm movements consistently alongside speech-like vocalizations (Blake et al., 1994; Franco & Butterworth, 1996; Iverson & Fagan, 2004). Between nine and twelve months, the first signs of "true" index-finger pointing begin to appear (i.e., an index finger protruded from the other fingers with the arm fully extended; Leung & Rheingold, 1981; Dobrich & Scarborough, 1984; Gredebäck & Melinder, 2010 (Carpenter et al., 1998). These fully-formed pointing gestures continue to be produced together with other communicative behaviors, such as speech-like vocalizations and gaze alternations (Bates et al., 1975; Franco & Butterworth, 1996; Esteve-Gibert & Prieto, 2014; Grünloh & Liszkowski, 2015).

*Pointing Gestures Are Intricately Linked to Language Development*

Infants' pointing gestures emerge at a critical time in their development – between nine and twelve months, as infants are entering the "social-cognitive revolution" (Tomasello, 1995). During this time, infants are rapidly acquiring a broad set of social-cognitive skills that prepare them to effectively communicate with others. For instance, infants acquire the understanding that the actions of others are intentional and goal directed (Csibra et al., 1999; Behne et al., 2005; Falck-Ytter et al., 2006) and are able to reliably follow the gaze of others in complex situations (e.g., to determine what is behind a visual barrier; Caron et al., 2002; Moll & Tomasello, 2004; Brooks & Meltzoff, 2005). At this time, infants are also

---

[1] Though there is some evidence that the first precursors of pointing may actually be present in neonates (Nagy et al., 2005).

beginning to form basic representations of the mental states of others: they know what others have and have not seen (Tomasello & Haberl, 2003). Finally, at this age, infants frequently engage in triadic interactions (i.e., interactions in which infants and adults jointly attend to an object of shared attention; Ratner & Bruner, 1978; Bakeman & Adamson, 1984; Ross & Lollis, 1987). These various social skills all contribute to infants' communicative development in that they enable infants to understand others as potential communicative partners.

That infants have the requisite skills for effective and sophisticated communication when they start pointing suggests that pointing may serve as a scaffold for language development. However, some of the strongest and clearest evidence for the link between pointing and language development comes from the fact that infants' pointing gestures are one of the strongest predictors of their early vocabulary development. The timing of infants' first pointing gestures predicts when they will comprehend and produce their first words (Harris et al., 1995; Carpenter et al., 1998). When infants first begin to point, as well as the rate at which they point at twelve months, reliably predicts how many different gestures and words these infants will comprehend at fourteen months (Fenson et al., 1994), along with their speech production rates at twenty-four months (Camaioni et al., 1991). Pointing has longer-term ramifications as well: infants' rate of pointing at fourteen months predicts their vocabulary size at forty-two months (Rowe et al., 2008). Corroborating these findings, a meta-analysis of 25 studies, including 734 infants, found a reliable and robust link between early pointing and vocabulary development (Colonnesi et al., 2010). In sum, there is overwhelming evidence that infants' early pointing gestures are intimately tied to their language development (Fenson et al., 1994; Harris et al., 1995; Carpenter et al., 1998; Iverson & Goldin-Meadow, 2005; Colonnesi et al., 2010).

The link between pointing and language development is not only correlational. New evidence suggests that it is also causal in nature. In a study conducted by LeBarton and colleagues (2015), researchers randomly assigned seventeen-month-old infants to either a "pointing intervention" condition, or a control condition. Over a six-week period, infants in both conditions were exposed to words in a storybook on a weekly basis. In the pointing intervention condition, infants were also encouraged to point while the words were introduced. After the intervention period, experimenters assessed infants' gesture use and speech production rates during parent–child interactions, as well as infants' vocabulary size as measured by a standardized vocabulary checklist. The first key finding to emerge was infants' change in gesture use: infants who were randomly assigned to the pointing intervention increased their rates of pointing, providing direct evidence that early gesture use is malleable. The second key finding to emerge was that the intervention successfully enhanced infants' vocabulary: at posttest, infants in the pointing intervention group had significantly more advanced vocabularies than infants in the control condition. These findings are important in that they demonstrate that infants' early gesture use is not fixed, and that the link between pointing and early word learning may be causal in nature, but they don't pinpoint the mechanism underlying the effect. Why might infants' increased pointing lead to subsequent gains in vocabulary development? One possibility is that infants' increase in pointing provided more opportunities for parents to comment and expand on infants' interests. Thus, infants' gestures may have influenced their vocabulary acquisition through their influence on parental speech – the more words infants hear, the more words that can potentially enter into their vocabulary. In the sections that follow, I elaborate on this possibility and expand on it by exploring how infants' own cognition may also be influenced by their gesture use.

Regardless of the precise mechanism at play, the finding that early gesture use is malleable and a direct driver of vocabulary development has a timely and critical relevance for health and educational policies. Children's early language abilities are essential for all aspects of learning and are strongly linked to positive academic, financial, and health outcomes later in life. Unfortunately, by the time children are eighteen months, there are large disparities in language abilities – children from low-income homes know significantly fewer words than infants from middle-income homes – and this gap only widens across development (Hoff, 2006). What's more, this early communication gap is first seen in early gesture use, children from low-SES homes produce fewer gestures than children from high-SES homes (Rowe & Goldin-Meadow, 2009). Thus, these findings offer one potential remedy for closing this early gap between children from diverse backgrounds.

### Why Do Infants Point?

Given that infants' pointing gestures not only *reflect* their language development, but may also *drive* it, it is imperative to understand why infants point. Unlike adults or children who can verbally articulate their goals in different settings, it is not possible to directly measure an infant's motivation for producing a given behavior. This has been a critical barrier to the study of pointing, as hypotheses about the motives of pointing must be formulated by observing naturally occurring pointing gestures, or by designing experiments that elicit pointing gestures. Since only pointing gestures, and not motivations themselves, are directly observable, these different studies have led to drastically different interpretations of pointing, which in turn, have led to much debate (see, for instance, D'Entremont & Seamans, 2007; Gómez, 2007; Southgate et al., 2007; Tomasello et al., 2007). Similar to many other areas of infant cognition, this debate centers strongly around lean versus rich interpretations of infants' motive for pointing. While some contend that infants' early pointing is driven by a motive to influence the mental states of others (rich interpretation; Tomasello et al., 2007), others maintain that infants' pointing gestures are more of a social tool, and are driven by a desire to change the behavior of others (lean interpretation; Bates et al., 1975). In what follows, I review findings in support of each of these views and marshal evidence for a new interpretation of early pointing.

Some of the first speculations on infants' motivation for pointing came from Wundt (1973) and Vygotsky (1962), who contended that infants' pointing gestures are noncommunicative, failed reaching attempts. According to their perspective, when infants point towards an object, they do so with the objective of touching, holding, or acting on that object in some way. Later, during the 1960s and 70s, a slightly more nuanced perspective emerged. Werner and Kaplan (1963) argued that infants point towards objects to hone their attention in on those objects, and individuate them amongst other objects. Bates and her colleagues (Bates et al., 1975, 1979, 1987) subsequently built on this proposal and famously dubbed infants' pointing gestures the "quintessential act of reference". According to this perspective, infants' use of their pointing gestures to refer to objects directly facilitates their ability to contemplate those objects. When an infant contemplates an object, they carefully and thoughtfully consider, think about, and reflect upon that object. Thus, there are qualitative differences in the acts of grasping, reaching, and pointing. While reaching and grasping gestures are "tied up with pragmatic things-of-action," pointing gestures are uniquely linked to a world of "contemplated objects" (Werner & Kaplan, 1963).

Collectively, these perspectives viewed infants' pointing gestures as being purely egocentric and simple manifestations of their attentional states (e.g., "I'm looking at that"; Werner & Kaplan, 1963) or imperative and reflective of their desires to obtain objects (e.g., "I want that"; Bates et al., 1975; Vygotsky, 1962). However, research conducted over the past twenty years has challenged this perspective. Currently, there is an agreement that infants point for a variety of reasons, some of which are egocentric and for the self, but others of which are deeply social in nature (Liszkowski et al., 2004). In a series of different studies using experimental techniques, researchers have provided compelling evidence that infants' points are guided by several potentially complimentary motivations to (1) share interest in some object or event (e.g., "look at that!"; Liszkowski et al., 2004), (2) help others by sharing relevant or useful information with others (e.g., "there it is!"; Liszkowski et al., 2006), or (3) request information (e.g., "what is that?"; Southgate et al., 2007). These first two motives have been studied extensively, and have a well-documented importance for early development (e.g., they support the development of uniquely human skills for cooperation and shared intentionality; Bates et al., 1975; Tomasello et al., 2007). In comparison, this third motive, information-requesting, has received far less attention.

### Infants Point to Acquire Information

The first direct evidence for an information-requesting motive of pointing came from Begus and Southgate (2012). In this study, infants were more likely to point for individuals they knew to be knowledgeable, rather than ignorant. Kovács and colleagues (2014) built on this finding by demonstrating that infants' communicative needs are filled (i.e., they produce fewer follow-up communicative behaviors) when adults respond to their pointing gestures with information, compared to when adults respond to their pointing gestures by acknowledging their interest without providing information. Although infants may produce other behaviors to request information from adults (e.g., social referencing and object-directed vocalizations may also serve this same purpose; Feinman et al., 1992; Chouinard, 2007), pointing gestures may be unique because they are such clear and salient markers of infants' interest and attention, they afford infants with a particularly effective way of signaling adults' attention and eliciting information. Indeed, caregivers spontaneously and consistently respond to their infants' pointing gestures, more so than other preverbal communicative behaviors (e.g., reaching gestures, vocalizations), with information (Kishimoto et al., 2007; Wu & Gros-Louis, 2015).

Importantly, infants do not indiscriminately point for information. Rather, infants are selective and strategic in their information-seeking, and calibrate their information requests to both the nature of the task (i.e., whether they actually need information or not) and the ability of another individual to provide that information (i.e., whether that individual is capable of providing information). A recent study conducted by Lucca and colleauges (2018b) found that when infants have evidence that their communicative partner is capable of providing information (i.e., when that individual has a demonstrated history of successfully solving the problem for which infants need help), they are significantly more likely to point than when they have evidence that their communicative partner is less likely to provide information (i.e., when they have witnessed that individual previously struggle to solve, or fail to solve, the problem for which they need help). Critically, infants only engage in this selective information-seeking when they do, in fact, need information (i.e., when the problem is not possible to solve on their own). When infants don't need information from another individual to solve a problem, they don't seek out information – regardless of how capable a communicative partner is – they instead act on the problem and solve it themselves.

## Information-Requesting Pointing Drives Learning

Although an information-requesting motive is much more selfish than more declarative (i.e., attention-sharing) motives of pointing, it may be this type of utilitarian function of pointing that makes it such a powerful, driving force for early learning and development. Pointing not only provides caregivers with a signal that their infant is seeking out information, but it is in these exact moments when infants are in an ideal position to learn – because they have an expectation information may arrive, which facilitates subsequent encoding of information. A desire to obtain information is directly related to learning because it triggers a heightened state of preparedness to receive and subsequently process information (Gruber & Otten, 2010). For example, a study conducted by Kang and colleagues (2009) found that epistemic curiosity activates the reward circuitry and memory regions in the brain. Moreover, when individuals report that they are interested in obtaining information, they respond with increased pupil dilation when that information arrives, a signal of focused attention. In addition to these physiological responses, there are also important behavioral effects: epistemic curiosity directly leads to an enhanced ability to retain new information, in both the short- and long-term (Kang et al., 2009; Gruber & Otten, 2010).

If infants point to obtain information, and information is best learned when it is explicitly sought out, then infants should learn best in the moment they point towards objects. Indeed, experimental work has documented that infants are more likely to learn new labels for objects after they've pointed towards those objects, compared to if they had expressed their interest in those objects in a way other than pointing (e.g., by reaching; Lucca & Wilbourn, 2018). Moreover, in this study infants' pointing only led to successful learning when information was provided for a pointed-to object. If the experimenter redirected the infants' attention and provided information for a not-pointed-to object, infants did not form the object–label association. These findings suggest that infants' pointing gestures do not reflect a broad, heightened state of attention for learning. Rather, the association between pointing and learning is specifically tailored to the object of interest. Importantly, this effect is seen across domains of learning: when infants point towards objects, they not only successfully learn the labels for those objects, they also demonstrate a heightened sensitivity to learn about those objects' functions (Begus et al., 2014; Lucca & Wilbourn, 2018). Understanding the contexts under which learning is optimized holds significant potential for better understanding the nature of learning, not only in infancy, but also throughout the lifespan. In sum, this work demonstrates that infants' pointing gestures lead to increased learning both externally, by increasing the amount of information they are exposed to, and internally, by signaling, or triggering, a heightened readiness to learn.

### How Does Interrogative Pointing Relate to Question-Asking?

The research reviewed above suggests that infants' pointing gestures are somewhat analogous to question-asking in older childhood. However, despite the clear parallels between pointing and question-asking, research has yet to systematically examine the two behaviors together. The one exception is a series of studies conducted by Chouinard (2007). Using a combination of data from diary studies, transcripts from the CHILDES database, and observational reports, Chouinard examined developmental differences in information-requesting behaviors in children aged one to five years. Across all ages, children's questions were primarily information-seeking in nature, as opposed to requests for attention. Children of all ages were also persistent in their pursuit of information: when they asked a question and were given an uninformative response, they persisted in their communicative requests (a signal their communicative needs were not met), more so than when they were given an informative response. In addition to these continuities in information-requesting, important developmental changes emerged as well. Specifically, children asked questions that were tailored to their developing cognitive abilities. Between one and two years of age, as children are acquiring their first words, they primarily requested labels for objects, but as children got older, between two and four years of age, their questions grew more sophisticated – they started to seek out deeper, more conceptual information about objects. By four years of age, as full-fledged theory-of-mind is emerging, children began to increase the frequency with which they asked questions about mental states. In this way, children's requests for information reflect, while also building on, their burgeoning cognitive development.

Though Chouinard (2007) provided important insights into the types of information young learners appear to be searching for when they request information, this study relied strictly on observation and parental report. That is, the researchers either observed children in a naturalistic setting or asked parents to report on their children's information-seeking behaviors. This subjectivity hinders our ability to draw definitive conclusions from this work, and know for certain whether the types of information that parents reported, or experimenters observed, were the types of information children were requesting. This is especially true for the nonverbal requests made by younger children, whose requests were not as clearly interpretable as older children's verbal requests.

To provide a more direct assessment of the types of information being requested by young children, experimental studies are necessary. The first experiment to systematically assess children's information-seeking was conducted by Kemler Nelson and colleagues (2004). In this study, experimenters elicited questions from children and manipulated the type of response given (i.e., they gave a label or function). When children, aged two to four years of age, asked generic "what's that?" questions about artifacts, they asked fewer follow-up questions after being given the object's function, compared to its label, suggesting that they are centrally concerned with understanding what novel artifacts do.

A recent study conducted by Lucca and Wilbourn (2018) extended this question into infancy to assess what kinds of information young learners request as they first begin to request information, through pointing. Following Kemler Nelson and colleagues (2004), infants were presented with novel artifacts and given the object's function (e.g., *it goes like this, arm tapping motion*), label (e.g., *it's a modi!*), or a simple acknowledgment of their interest (e.g., *wow! Look at that!*). When the experimenter responded to infants' pointing gestures with labels, infants stopped communicating – a signal that this information fulfilled their communicative request. Alternatively, when the experimenter responded to infants' pointing gestures with functions or no information about pointed-to objects, infants persisted in their communicative attempts. Infants' production of additional communicative behaviors (e.g., more pointing gestures, vocalizations) is a signal that they were *not* satisfied with receiving functions or no information (Golinkoff, 1986).

Critically, this effect was unique to pointing: if infants did not point towards an object prior to receiving information about it (e.g., if they had indicated their interest in that object by looking or reaching towards it), they produced the same number of follow-up behaviors after receiving that object's function, label, or no information. This finding demonstrates that it's not just something about receiving functions or no information that drives infants to persist in their communicative attempts. Rather, pointing gestures appear to be unique and specific requests for object labels – a finding consistent with prior work demonstrating that infants' pointing gestures, but not other expressions of interest (e.g., reaching, looking), selectively lead to enhanced learning.

Why might infants point to obtain labels for objects? This is an important question, especially since it contrasts with findings from older children, whose information requests are geared towards receiving object functions (Kelmer Nelson et al., 2004). These divergent findings point to meaningful developmental differences in the types of information infants and young children find most relevant and important. These developmental differences in information-requesting behaviors are not surprising as they directly map on to children's cognitive and linguistic development. Between six and twelve months of age, infants begin to understand that speech is a communicative tool that functions to transfer information between people (Martin et al., 2012). At eighteen months, infants enter the "vocabulary burst" and are rapidly adding new words to their lexicon (Bloom, 1973; Nelson, 1973). By this time, infants' understanding of the communicative value of words may be expanding as well. That is, infants may actively and selectively seek out labels at this age because they may be realizing that words afford them with new opportunities: the more words they have in their repertoire, the better equipped they are to effectively communicate with their care-givers – conveying more information and getting needs met more efficiently.

Infants' burgeoning understanding of the pragmatic nature of words helps reconcile the findings on information-seeking in older children. Older children have already acquired the labels for many of the objects in their environment, and may therefore be shifting towards seeking out deeper, more explanatory investigations about objects (e.g., functions). These developmental differences in preferences for labels and functions also correspond with caregivers' responses to requests for information at different points in development (Chouinard, 2007). Prior to children's second birthday, caregivers respond to information requests with labels more frequently than with functions. After children's second birthday, caregivers switch strategies, and tend to respond to information requests with functions more frequently than labels. Thus, young learners' requests for information maps onto both their emerging cognitive skills and also the types of information they are most frequently given in response to their information requests.

## Open Questions

One critical open question is how infants' pointing gestures become tools for requesting information. One possibility is that infants' pointing gestures develop out of early manual index-finger exploration. Before infants start pointing, one of their primary modes of exploration is examining objects with their index fingers (Shinn, 1900; Blake et al., 1994). Once infants are able to combine reaching with extending their index finger, they may use pointing as a means to explore objects out of reach. This type of noncommunicative pointing may help infants narrow their attention and focus on objects of interest (Werner & Kaplan, 1963; Bates et al., 1975). Alternatively, infants' pointing gestures may emerge as a non-exploratory behavior. Infants' pointing gestures may start out as imperative ("I want that!") or declarative ("Look at that!") requests. Caregivers' routine responses to these types of gestures with information may, across development, shape infants' pointing gestures into explicit requests for information. That is, infants may pick up on the pattern of pointing and receiving information in response and, through this process, acquire the understanding that their pointing gestures are an effective tool for acquiring new information.

Likely, these different mechanisms (exploratory/individualistic pointing and pointing shaped by caregiver responsiveness) work together. More research, especially with participants outside of Western Educated Industrialized Rich Democratic (WEIRD) societies, is needed to disentangle these hypotheses (Henrich et al., 2010). Although data from WEIRD populations is most represented in developmental research, these populations are not representative of all human behavior, and are by no means the norm. In fact, despite its prevalence in Western societies, the preference for pointing with an index-finger pointing is *not* universal during adulthood (Cooperrider et al., 2018).

Another important open question surrounding early information-requesting relates to the decision-making process that underlies early pointing. Requesting information is costly, especially for infants, who have limited energetic and motoric resources, which raises the question: Do infants factor the costs and benefits associated with requesting information into their decision to point in a given situation? Recent evidence suggests that, at least in some contexts, infants' behavior is modulated by the perceived costs and benefits associated with acting (Sommerville et al., 2018). Thus, it may be that similar computational processes underlie infants' decision to request information or not by pointing. Understanding how infants integrate different forms of information into their decision to request information, and how infants and adults from more representative groups use and respond to different forms of pointing (e.g., index-finger pointing, chin pointing), will elucidate which factors drive early pointing. These findings will be critical in revealing the mechanisms that underlie early information-seeking behaviors more broadly.

Once infants acquire the ability to request information through their pointing gestures, it is important to understand how they then transition into question-asking. There are obvious linguistic developments that must occur, but what other cognitive and social prerequisites are required for this transition? Moreover, what are the specific behaviors that adults are producing that scaffold and support the transition to question-asking, and what can be done to further foster this kind of curiosity-driven learning, starting in infancy and extending into early childhood? These questions are necessary for further unraveling the complexities of early information-seeking, and in doing so, providing a more complete account of how children actively make sense of the world around them.

**Conclusion**

For decades, the central focus of information-requesting has been question-asking. Here, I have argued that the seeds of information-requesting are already present during infancy, long before children can ask questions. Although both infants and older children understand that information can be transmitted socially, and are highly motivated to access this information (Gergely et al., 2007; Vaish et al., 2011; Homer & Tamis-Lemonda, 2013), investigations of social information gathering has been primarily restricted to older children (two to seven years). When older children reach a gap in their knowledge, they ask questions aimed at closing this gap (Davis, 1932; Kemler Nelson & O'Neil, 2005; Chouinard, 2007; Ruggeri & Lombrozo, 2015). This motivation to request information has long been regarded as a powerful driving force of cognitive development and the acquisition of culture, since children's questions afford them with an effective way to fill in gaps in their knowledge (Davis, 1932; Gopnik & Meltzoff, 1997).

Here, I proposed that pointing gestures in infancy are analogous to question-asking in older children because they offer an effective way for infants to signal adults' attention and elicit targeted information from them. Pointing gestures are unique in this way because they are clear and salient markers of infants' interest and attention. Indeed, caregivers respond to infants' pointing gestures, more often than other preverbal communicative behaviors, with information (Kishimoto et al., 2007;

Wu & Gros-Louis, 2015). Infants' pointing gestures do not only happen to elicit information from others. Instead, this is in an active process: infants point with the objective to obtain information from others. And, critically, infants are strategic and selective in their requests for information – infants point for specific type of information, but only when they need it, and only when there is evidence that information transfer is likely (Lucca et al., 2018a). Pointing gestures therefore allow infants to receive information at a time when they are most receptive to it – that is, when they are explicitly requesting it. Since information is best learned when it is actively sought out, infants' pointing gestures signal a critical window for early learning.

## Acknowledgments

I would like to thank the editors of this book, Lucas Butler, Kathleen Corriveau, and Samuel Ronfard, for their helpful feedback on an earlier draft of this chapter, as well as Makeba Wilbourn, Michael Tomasello, Elika Bergelson, Brian Hare, Beth Marsh, Jessica Sommerville, Selin Gülgöz, and Jin X. Goh for their thoughtful discussion on many of the ideas presented here.

## References

Bakeman, R., and Adamson, L. B. (1984). Coordinating attention to people and objects in mother-infant and peer-infant interaction. *Child Development, 55,* 1278–89. https://doi.org/10.2307/1129997

Bates, E., Camaioni, L., and Volterra, V. (1975). The acquisition of perfromatives prior to speech. *Merrill-Palmer Quarterly of Behavior and Development, 21,* 205–26.

Bates, E., Benigni, L., Bretherton, I., Camaioni, L., and Volterra, V. (1979). *The emergence of symbols: Cognition and communication in infancy.* New York: Academic Press.

Bates, E., O'Connell, B., and Shore, C. (1987). Language and communication in infancy. In J. Osofsky (ed.), *Handbook of Infant Development* (2nd ed., pp. 149–203). New York: Wiley.

Begus, K., and Southgate, V. (2012). Infant pointing serves an interrogative function. *Developmental Science, 15,* 611–17. https://doi.org/10.1111/j.1467-7687.2012.01160.x

Begus, K., Gliga, T., and Southgate, V. (2014). Infants learn what they want to learn: Responding to infant pointing leads to superior learning. *PLOS ONE, 9,* e108817. https://doi.org/10.1371/journal.pone.0108817

(2016). Infants' preferences for native speakers are associated with an expectation of information. *Proceedings of the National Academy of Sciences, 113,* 12397–402. https://doi.org/10.1073/pnas.1603261113

Behne, T., Carpenter, M., Call, J., and Tomasello, M. (2005). Unwilling versus unable: Infants' understanding of intentional action. *Developmental Psychology*, *41*, 328–37. https://doi.org/10.1037/0012–1649.41.2.328

Bertenthal, B. I., Campos, J. J., and Kermoian, R. (1994). An epigenetic perspective on the development of self-produced locomotion and its consequences. *Current Directions in Psychological Science*, *3*, 140–45. https://doi.org/10.1111/1467–8721.ep10770621

Birch, S. A. J., Akmal, N., and Frampton, K. L. (2010). Two-year-olds are vigilant of others' non-verbal cues to credibility. *Developmental Science*, *13*, 363–9. https://doi.org/10.1111/j.1467–7687.2009.00906.x

Blake, J., O'Rourke, P., and Borzellino, G. (1994). Form and function in the development of pointing and reaching gestures. *Infant Behavior and Development*, *17*, 195–203. https://doi.org/10.1016/0163–6383(94)90055–8

Blake, J., Osborne, P., Cabral, M., and Gluck, P. (2003). The development of communicative gestures in Japanese infants. *First Language*, *23*, 3–20. https://doi.org/10.1177/0142723703023001001

Bloom, K. (1988). Quality of adult vocalizations affects the quality of infant vocalizations. *Journal of Child Language*, *15*, 469–80. https://doi.org/10.1017/s0305000900012502

Bloom, L. (1973). *One word at a time: The use of single-word utterances before syntax.* The Hague, The Netherlands: Mouton.

Brooks, R., and Meltzoff, A. N. (2005). The development of gaze following and its relation to language. *Developmental Science*, *8*, 535–43. https://doi.org/10.1111/j.1467–7687.2005.00445.x

Bruner, J. S. (1975). From communication to language: A psychological perspective. *Cognition*, *3*, 255–87. https://doi.org/10.1016/0010–0277(74)90012–2

Callaghan, T., Moll, H., Rakoczy, H., et al. (2011). *Early social cognition in three cultural contexts.* Monographs of the Society for Research in Child Development, *76*. Boston, MA: Wiley-Blackwell.

Callanan, M. A., and Oakes, L. M. (1992). Preschoolers' questions and parents' explanations: Causal thinking in everyday activity. *Cognitive Development*, *7*, 213–33. https://doi.org/10.1016/0885–2014(92)90012–G

Camaioni, L., Castelli, M. C., Longobardi, E., and Volterra, V. (1991). A parent report instrument for early language assessment. *First Language*, *11*, 345–58. https://doi.org/10.1177/014272379101103303

Caron, A., Kiel, E., Dayton, M., and Butler, S. (2002). Comprehension of the referential intent of looking and pointing between 12 and 15 months. *Journal of Cognition and Development*, *3*, 445–64. https://doi.org/10.1207/S15327647JCD3,4–04

Carpenter, M., Nagell, K., Tomasello, M., Butterworth, G., and Moore, C. (1998). Social cognition, joint attention, and communicative competence from 9 to 15 months of age. *Monographs of the Society for Research in Child Development*, *63*, i–174. https://doi.org/10.2307/1166214

Chouinard, M. M. (2007). Children's questions: A mechanism for cognitive development. *Monographs of the Society for Research in Child Development*, *72*, i–129.

Chow, V., Poulin-Dubois, D., and Lewis, J. (2008). To see or not to see: Infants prefer to follow the gaze of a reliable looker. *Developmental Science, 11,* 761–70. https://doi.org/10.1111/j.1467–7687.2008.00726.x

Colonnesi, C., Stams, G. J. J. M., Koster, I., and Noom, M. J. (2010). The relation between pointing and language development: A meta-analysis. *Developmental Review, 30,* 352–66. https://doi.org/10.1016/j.dr.2010.10.001

Cooper, R. P., and Aslin, R. N. (1990). Preference for infant-directed speech in the first month after birth. *Child Development, 61,* 1584–95. https://doi.org/10.2307/1130766

Cooperrider, K., Núñez, R., and Slotta, J. (2014). The protean pointing gesture: Variation in a building block of human communication. In P. Bello, M. Guarini, M. McShane, and B. Scassellati (eds.), *Proceedings of the 36th Annual Meeting of the Cognitive Science Society* (pp. 355–60). Austin, TX: Cognitive Science Society.

Cooperrider, K., Slotta, J., and Núñez, R. (2018). The preference for pointing with the hand is not universal. *Cognitive Science, 42,* 1–16. https://doi.org/10.1111/cogs.12585

Csibra, G., and Gergely, G. (2009). Natural pedagogy. *Trends in Cognitive Sciences, 13,* 148–53. https://doi.org/10.1016/j.tics.2009.01.005

Csibra, G., Gergely, G., Bíró, S., Koós, O., and Brockbank, M. (1999). Goal attribution without agency cues: The perception of "pure reason" in infancy. *Cognition, 72,* 237–67. https://doi.org/10.1016/S0010–0277(99)00039–6

Darwin, C. (1877). A biographical sketch of an infant. *Mind, 2,* 285–94.

Davis, E. (1932). The form and function of children's questions. *Child Development, 3,* 57–74.

D'Entremont, B., and Seamans, E. (2007). Do infants need social cognition to act socially? An alternative look at infant pointing. *Child Development, 78,* 723–8. https://doi.org/10.1111/j.1467–8624.2007.01026.x

Dobrich, W., and Scarborough, H. S. (1984). Form and function in early communication: Language and pointing gestures. *Journal of Experimental Child Psychology, 38,* 475–90. https://doi.org/10.1016/0022–0965(84)90090–0

Eppler, M. A. (1995). Development of manipulative skills and the deployment of attention. *Infant Behavior and Development, 18,* 391–405. https://doi.org/10.1016/0163–6383(95)90029–2

Estes, K., Evans, J. L., Alibali, M. W., and Saffran, J. R. (2013). Can infants map meaning to newly segmented words? *Psychological Science, 18,* 254–60. https://doi.org/10.1111/j.1467–9280.2007.01885.x

Esteve-Gibert, N., and Prieto, P. (2014). Infants temporally coordinate gesture-speech combinations before they produce their first words. *Speech Communication, 57,* 301–16. https://doi.org/10.1016/j.specom.2013.06.006

Falck-Ytter, T., Gredebäck, G., and von Hofsten, C. (2006). Infants predict other people's action goals. *Nature Neuroscience, 9,* 878–9. https://doi.org/10.1038/nn1729

Feinman, S., Roberts, D., Hsieh, K. F., Sawyer, D., and Swanson, D. (1992). A critical review of social referencing in infancy. In S. Feinman (ed.), *Social referencing and the social construction of reality in infancy* (pp. 15–54). Springer.

Fenson, L., Dale, P. S., Reznick, J. S., et al. (1994). Variability in early communicative development. *Monographs of the Society for Research in Child Development, 59*, i–185.

Floor, P., and Akhtar, N. (2006). Can 18-month-old infants learn words by listening in on conversations? *Infancy, 9*, 327–39. https://doi.org/10.1207 /s15327078in0903_4

Fogel, A., and Hannan, T. E. (1985). Manual actions of nine- to fifteen-week-old human infants during face-to-face interaction with their mothers. *Child Development, 56*, 1271–9. https://doi.org/10.2307/1130242

Franco, F., and Butterworth, G. (1996). Pointing and social awareness: Declaring and requesting in the second year. *Journal of Child Language, 23*, 307–36. https://doi.org/10.1017/s0305000900008813

Gergely, G., Egyed, K., and Kiraly, I. (2007). On pedagogy. *Developmental Science, 10*, 139–46. https://doi.org/10.1111/j.1467–7687.2007.00576.x

Gibson, E. J. (1988). Exploratory behavior in the development of perceiving, acting, and the acquiring of knowledge *Annual Review of Psychology, 39*, 1–41. https://doi.org/10.1146/annurev.psych.39.1.1

Goldin-Meadow, S. (2007). Pointing sets the stage for learning language—and creating language. *Child Development, 78*, 741–5. https://doi.org/10.1111/j .1467–8624.2007.01029.x

Golinkoff, R. M. (1986). I beg your pardon? The preverbal negotiation of failed messages. *Journal of Child Language, 13*, 455–76. https://doi.org/10.1017 /s0305000900006826

Gómez, J.-C. (2007). Pointing behaviors in apes and human infants: A balanced interpretation. *Child Development, 78*, 729–34. https://doi.org/10.1111/j.1467– 8624.2007.01027.x

Gopnik, A., and Meltzoff, A. (1997). *Words, thoughts, and theories.* Cambridge, MA: MIT Press.

Goupil, L., and Kouider, S. (2016). Behavioral and neural indices of metacognitive sensitivity in preverbal infants. *Current Biology, 26*, 3038–45.

Goupil, L., Romand-Monnier, M., and Kouider, S. (2016). Infants ask for help when they know they don't know. *Proceedings of the National Academy of Sciences, 113*, 3492–6. https://doi.org/10.1073/pnas.15151 29113

Gredebäck, G., and Melinder, A. (2010). The development and neural basis of pointing comprehension. *Social Neuroscience, 5*, 441–50. https://doi.org/10 .1080/17470910903523327

Gruber, M. J., and Otten, L. J. (2010). Voluntary control over prestimulus activity related to encoding. *Journal of Neuroscience, 30*, 9793–800. https://doi .org/10.1523/jneurosci.0915–10.2010

Grünloh, T., and Liszkowski, U. (2015). Prelinguistic vocalizations distinguish pointing acts. *Journal of Child Language, 42*, 1312–36. https://doi.org/10 .1017/S0305000914000816

Harris, M., Barlow-Brown, F., and Chasin, J. (1995). The emergence of referential understanding: Pointing and the comprehension of object names. *First Language*, *15*, 19–34. https://doi.org/10.1177/014272379501500101

Harris, P. L., and Lane, J. D. (2013). Infants understand how testimony works. *Topoi*, *33*, 443–58. https://doi.org/10.1007/s11245-013–9180–0

Harris, P. L., Bartz, D. T., and Rowe, M. L. (2017). Young children communicate their ignorance and ask questions. *Proceedings of the National Academy of Sciences*, *114*, 7884–91. https://doi.org/10.1073/pnas.1620745114

Henrich, J., Heine, S. J., and Norenzayan, A. (2010). The weirdest people in the world? *Behavioral and Brain Sciences*, *33*, 61–135. https://doi.org/10.1017/S0140525X0999152X

Hoff, E. (2006). How social contexts support and shape language development. *Developmental Review*, *26*, 55–88. https://doi.org/10.1016/j.dr.2005.11.002

Homer, B. D., and Tamis-Lemonda, C. S. (2013). *The development of social cognition and communication*. Mahwah, NJ: Lawrence Erlbaum Associates.

Iverson, J. M., and Fagan, M. K. (2004). Infant vocal-motor coordination: Precursor to the gesture-speech system? *Child Development*, *75*, 1053–66. https://doi.org/10.1111/j.1467–8624.2004.00725.x

Iverson, J. M., and Goldin-Meadow, S. (2005). Gesture paves the way for language development. *Psychological Science*, *16*, 367–71. https://doi.org/10.1111/j.0956–7976.2005.01542.x

Kachel, G., Moore, R., and Tomasello, M. (2018). Two-year-olds use adults' but not peers' points. *Developmental Science*, *21* (5), e12660. https://doi.org/10.1111/desc.12660

Kang, M. J., Hsu, M., Krajbich, I. M., et al. (2009). The wick in the candle of learning. *Psychological Science*, *20*, 963–74. https://doi.org/10.1111/j.1467–9280.2009.02402.x

Kemler Nelson, D. G., and O'Neil, K. (2005). How do parents respond to children's questions about the identity of artifacts? *Developmental Science*, *8*, 519–24. https://doi.org/10.1111/j.1467–7687.2005.00443.x

Kemler Nelson, D. G., Egan, L. C., and Holt, M. (2004). When children ask *What is it?* what do they want to know about artifacts? *Psychological Science*, *15*, 384–9. https://doi.org/10.1111/j.0956–7976.2004.00689.x

Kidd, C., Piantadosi, S. T., and Aslin, R. N. (2012). The goldilocks effect: Human infants allocate attention to visual sequences that are neither too simple nor too complex. *PLOS ONE*, *7*, e36399. https://doi.org/10.1371/journal.pone.0036399

    (2014). The goldilocks effect in infant auditory attention. *Child Development*, *85*, 1795–804. https://doi.org/10.1111/cdev.12263

Kinzler, K. D., Dupoux, E., and Spelke, E. S. (2007). The native language of social cognition. *Proceedings of the National Academy of Sciences of the United States of America*, *104*, 12577–80. https://doi.org/10.1073/pnas.0705345104

Kishimoto, T., Shizawa, Y., Yasuda, J., Hinobayashi, T., and Minami, T. (2007). Do pointing gestures by infants provoke comments from adults? *Infant Behavior & Development*, *30*, 562–7. https://doi.org/10.1016/j.infbeh.2007.04.001

Klimesch, W. (1999). EEG alpha and theta oscillations reflect cognitive and memory performance: A review and analysis. *Brain Research Reviews, 29,* 169–95. https://doi.org/10.1016/S0165–0173(98)00056–3

Koenig, M. A., and Woodward, A. L. (2010). Sensitivity of 24-month-olds to the prior inaccuracy of the source: Possible mechanisms. *Developmental Psychology, 46,* 815–26. https://doi.org/10.1037/a0019664

Kovács, Á. M., Tauzin, T., Téglás, E., Gergely, G., and Csibra, G. (2014). Pointing as epistemic request: 12-month-olds point to receive new information. *Infancy, 19,* 543–57. https://doi.org/10.1111/infa.12060

Kurkul, K. E., and Corriveau, K. H. (2018). Question, explanation, follow-up: A mechanism for learning from others? *Child Development, 89,* 280–94. https://doi.org/10.1111/cdev.12726

Leavens, D. A., and Hopkins, W. D. (1998). Intentional communication by chimpanzees: A cross-sectional study of the use of referential gestures. *Developmental Psychology, 34,* 813–22. https://doi.org/10.1037//0012–1649 .34.5.813

LeBarton, E. S., Goldin-Meadow, S., and Raudenbush, S. (2015). Experimentally induced increases in early gesture lead to increases in spoken vocabulary. *Journal of Cognition and Development, 16,* 199–220. https://doi .org/10.1080/15248372.2013.858041

Legare, C. H., and Harris, P. L. (2016). The ontogeny of cultural learning. *Child Development, 87,* 633–42. https://doi.org/10.1111/cdev.12542

Legare, C. H., and Nielsen, M. (2015). Imitation and Innovation: The dual engines of cultural learning. *Trends in Cognitive Sciences, 19,* 688–99. https:// doi.org/10.1016/j.tics.2015.08.005

Leung, E. H. L., and Rheingold, H. L. (1981). Development of pointing as a social gesture. *Developmental Psychology, 17,* 215–20.

Liszkowski, U., Carpenter, M., Henning, A., Striano, T., and Tomasello, M. (2004). Twelve-month-olds point to share attention and interest. *Developmental Science, 7,* 297–307. https://doi.org/10.1111/j.1467–7687.20 04.00349.x

Liszkowski, U., Carpenter, M., and Striano, T. (2006). 12- and 18-month-olds point to provide information for others. *Journal of Cognition and Development, 2,* 173–87. https://doi.org/10.1207/s15327647jcd0702

Liszkowski, U., Schäfer, M., Carpenter, M., and Tomasello, M. (2009). Prelinguistic infants, but not chimpanzees, communicate about absent entities. *Psychological Science, 20,* 654–60. https://doi.org/10.1111/j.1467–9 280.2009.02346.x

Liszkowski, U., Brown, P., Callaghan, T., Takada, A., and de Vos, C. (2012). A prelinguistic gestural universal of human communication. *Cognitive Science, 36,* 698–713. https://doi.org/10.1111/j.1551–6709.20 11.01228.x

Lockman, J. J. (2000). A perception-action perspective on tool use development. *Child Development, 71,* 137–44.

Lucca, K., and Sommerville, J. A. (2018). The little engine that can: Infants' persistence matters. *Trends in Cognitive Sciences, 22,* 965–8. https://doi.org/10 .1016/j.tics.2018.07.012

Lucca, K., and Wilbourn, M. P. (2018). Communicating to learn: Infants' pointing gestures result in optimal learning. *Child Development*, *89*, 941–60. https://doi.org/10.1111/cdev.12707

Lucca, K., Horton, R., Xu, Y., Sedlacek, A., and Sommerville, J. A. (2018a) When to explore and when to exploit? Insights from the development of persistence during infancy. Poster presented at the Cognitive Science Society Meeting. Madison, WI.

Lucca, K., Pospisil, J., and Sommerville, J. A. (2018b). Fairness informs social decision making in infancy. *PLOS ONE*, *13*, 1–14. https://doi.org/10.1371/journal.pone.0192848

Marno, H., Guellai, B., Vidal, Y., et al. (2016). Infants' selectively pay attention to the information they receive from a native speaker of their language. *Frontiers in Psychology*, *7*, 1–11. https://doi.org/10.3389/fpsyg.2016.01150

Martin, A., Onishi, K. H., and Vouloumanos, A. (2012). Understanding the abstract role of speech in communication at 12 months. *Cognition*, *123*, 50–60. https://doi.org/10.1016/j.cognition.2011.12.003

Masataka, N. (1995). The relation between index-finger extension and the acoustic quality of cooing in three-month-old infants. *Journal of Child Language*, *22*, 247–57. https://doi.org/10.1017/s0305000900009776

Masur, E. F. (1983). Gestural development, dual-directional signaling, and the transition to words. *Journal of Psycholinguistic Research*, *12*, 93–109. https://doi.org/10.1007/BF01067406

Mehler, J., Jusczyk, P., Lambertz, G., et al. (1988). A precursor of language acquisition in young infants. *Cognition*, *29*, 143–78. https://doi.org/10.1016/0010–0277(88)90035–2

Moll, H., and Tomasello, M. (2004). 12- and 18-month-old infants follow gaze to spaces behind barriers. *Developmental Science*, *7*, 1–9. https://doi.org/10.1111/j.1467–7687.2004.00315.x

Morton, J., and Johnson, M. H. (1991). CONSPEC and CONLERN: A two-process theory of infant face recognition. *Psychological Review*, *98*, 164–81. https://doi.org/10.1037/0033-295X.98.2.164

Murphy, C., and Messer, D. (1977). Mothers, infants, and pointing: A study of a gesture. In H. R. Schaffer (ed.), *Studies in mother-infant interaction* (pp. 325–54). London: Academic Press.

Nagy, E., Compagne, H., Orvos, H., et al. (2005). Index finger movement imitation by human neonates: Motivation, learning, and left-hand preference. *Pediatric Research*, *58*, 749–53. https://doi.org/10.1203/01.PDR.0000180570.28111.D9

Needham, A. (2000). Improvements in object exploration skills may facilitate the development of object segregation in early infancy. *Journal of Cognition and Development*, *1*, 131–56. https://doi.org/10.1207/S15327647JCD010201

Nelson, K. (1973). Structure and strategy in learning to talk. *Monographs of the Society for Research in Child Development*, *38*, 1–135.

Piaget, J. (1954). *The construction of reality in the child*. New York: Routledge.

Ratner, N., and Bruner, J. (1978). Games, social exchange and the acquisition of language. *Journal of Child Language*, *5*, 391–401. https://doi.org/10.1017/S0305000900002063

Rochat, P. (1989). Object manipulation and exploration in 2-to 5-month-old infants. *Developmental Psychology*, *25*, 871–84. https://doi.org/10.1037/001 2-1649.25.6.871

Ronfard, S., Zambrana, I. M., Hermansen, T. K., and Kelemen, D. (2018). Question-asking in childhood: A review of the literature and a framework for understanding its development. *Developmental Review*, *49*, 101–20 https://doi .org/10.1016/j.dr.2018.05.002

Ross, H. S., and Lollis, S. P. (1987). Communication within infant social games. *Developmental Psychology*, *23*, 241–8. https://doi.org/10.1037/0012–1649.23 .2.241

Rowe, M. L., and Goldin-Meadow, S. (2009). Differences in early gesture explain SES disparities in child vocabulary size at school entry. *Science*, *323*, 951–3. https://doi.org/10.1126/science.1167025

Rowe, M. L., Ozçalişkan, S., and Goldin-Meadow, S. (2008). Learning words by hand: Gesture's role in predicting vocabulary development. *First Language*, *28*, 182–99. https://doi.org/10.1177/0142723707088310

Ruggeri, A., and Lombrozo, T. (2015). Children adapt their questions to achieve efficient search. *Cognition*, *143*, 203–16. https://doi.org/10.1016/j.cognition.20 15.07.004

Saffran, J. R., Aslin, R. N., and Newport, E. L. (1996). Statistical learning by 8-month-old infants. *Science*, *274*, 1926–8. https://doi.org/10.1126/science .274.5294.1926

Salomo, D., and Liszkowski, U. (2013). Sociocultural settings influence the emergence of prelinguistic deictic gestures. *Child Development*, *84*, 1296–307. https://doi.org/10.1111/cdev.12026

Samuelson, L. K., and Smith, L. B. (1998). Memory and attention make smart word learning: An alternative account of Akhtar, Carpenter, and Tomasello. *Child Development*, *69*, 94–104. https://doi.org/10.1111/j.1467–8624 .1998.tb06136.x

Savage-Rumbaugh, E. S. (1990). Language as a cause-effect communication system. *Philosophical Psychology*, *3*, 55–76. https://doi.org/10.1080/09515089 008572989

Shinn, M. W. (1900). *The biography of a baby*. Boston and New York: Houghton Mifflin.

Sobel, D. M., and Kirkham, N. Z. (2006). Blickets and babies: The development of causal reasoning in toddlers and infants. *Developmental Psychology*, *42*, 1103–15. https://doi.org/10.1037/0012–1649.42.6.1103

Sommerville, J., Woodward, A., and Needham, A. (2005). Action experience alters 3-month-old infants' perception of others' actions. *Cognition*, *72*, 181–204. https://doi.org/10.1016/j.cognition.2004.07.004

Sommerville, J., Enright, E., Horton, R., et al. (2018). Infants' prosocial behavior is governed by cost-benefit analyses. *Cognition*, *177*, 12–20. https://doi.org/10 .1016/j.cognition.2018.03.021

Sorce, J. F., Emde, R. N., Campos, J. J., and Klinnert, M. D. (1985). Maternal emotional signaling: Its effect on the visual cliff behavior of 1-year-olds. *Developmental Psychology*, *21*, 195–200. https://doi.org/10.1037/0012–1649 .21.1.195

Southgate, V., van Maanen, C., and Csibra, G. (2007). Infant pointing: Communication to cooperate or communication to learn? *Child Development*, 78, 735–40. https://doi.org/10.1111/j.1467–8624.2007.01028.x

Spelke, E. S., Breinlinger, K., Macomber, J., and Jacobson, K. (1992). Origins of knowledge. *Psychological Review*, 99 (4), 605–32. https://doi.org/10.1037/00 33-295X.99.4.605

Stahl, A. E., and Feigenson, L. (2015). Observing the unexpected enhances infants' learning and exploration. *Science*, 348, 91–4. https://doi.org/10.1126 /science.aaa3799

Stenberg, G. (2013). Do 12-month-old infants trust a competent adult? *Infancy*, 18, 873–904. https://doi.org/10.1111/infa.12011

Tomasello, M. (1995). Joint attention as social cognition. In C. Moore and P. Dunham (eds.), *Joint attention: Its origins and role in development* (pp. 103–30). Hillsdale, NJ: Erlbaum.

(2006). Why don't apes point? In N. J. Enfield and S. C. Levinson (eds.), *Roots of human sociality: Culture, cognition and interaction* (pp. 506–24). Oxford and New York: Berg.

(2008). *Origins of human communication*. Cambridge, MA: MIT Press.

Tomasello, M., and Haberl, K. (2003). Understanding attention: 12- and 18-month-olds know what is new for other persons. *Developmental Psychology*, 39, 906–12. https://doi.org/10.1037/0012–1649.39.5.906

Tomasello, M., Carpenter, M., and Liszkowski, U. (2007). A new look at infant pointing. *Child Development*, 78, 705–22. https://doi.org/10.1111/j.1467–86 24.2007.01025.x

Trevarthen, C. (1977). Descriptive analysis of infant communicative behavior. In H. R. Schaffer (ed.), *Studies in mother-infant interaction* (pp. 227–70). New York: Academic Press.

Tummeltshammer, K. S., Wu, R., Sobel, D. M., and Kirkham, N. Z. (2014). Infants track the reliability of potential informants. *Psychological Science*, 25, 1730–8. https://doi.org/10.1177/0956797614540178

Vaish, A., Demir, Ö. E., and Baldwin, D. (2011). Thirteen- and 18-month-old infants recognize when they need referential information. *Social Development*, 20, 431–49. https://doi.org/10.1111/j.1467–9507.2010.00601.x

van der Goot, M. H., Tomasello, M., and Liszkowski, U. (2014). Differences in the nonverbal requests of great apes and human infants. *Child Development*, 85, 444–55. https://doi.org/10.1111/cdev.12141

Vygotsky, L. S. (1962). *Thought and language*. Translated by E. Hanfmann and G. Vaker. Cambridge, MA: MIT Press.

Werner, H., and Kaplan, B. (1963). *Symbol formation*. New York: Wiley.

Wilcox, T., Rosser, R., and Nadel, L. (1994). Representation of object location in 6.5-month-old infants. *Cognitive Development*, 9, 193–209. https://doi.org/10 .1016/0885–2014(94)90003–5

Wu, Z., and Gros-Louis, J. (2015). Caregivers provide more labeling responses to infants' pointing than to infants' object-directed vocalizations. *Journal of Child Language*, 42, 538–61. https://doi.org/10.1017/S0305000914000221

Wundt, W. (1973). *The language of gestures*. Introduction by A. L. Blumenthal. The Hague: Mounton. (First published 1900.)

Xu, F., and Kushnir, T. (2013). Infants are rational constructivist learners. *Current Directions in Psychological Science, 22*, 28–32. https://doi.org/10.1177/0963721412469396

Zmyj, N., Buttelmann, D., Carpenter, M., and Daum, M. M. (2010). The reliability of a model influences 14-month-olds' imitation. *Journal of Experimental Child Psychology, 106*, 208–20. https://doi.org/10.1016/j.jecp.2010.03.002

Zmyj, N., Daum, M. M., Prinz, W., Nielsen, M., and Aschersleben, G. (2012). Fourteen-month-olds' imitation of differently aged models. *Infant and Child Development, 12*, 250–66. https://doi.org/10.1002/icd

# 7    Developmental Changes in Question-Asking

*Angela Jones, Nora Swaboda, Azzurra Ruggeri*

## Introduction

The French philosopher and author Voltaire once said, "Judge a man by his questions rather than by his answers." Centuries have passed since the Enlightenment, but the idea that a good question may be more valuable than a good answer applies today more than ever. The Internet has made information available at our fingertips at all times: search engines, accessed via our computers, tablets, or smart phones, allow us to look up things whenever and wherever we want – an enhanced encyclopedia of factual knowledge; forums and online communities hold vast nets of human knowledge – from the pragmatic and trivial ("How do I fix my leaking kitchen sink?") to the scholarly ("How can I create beautiful graphs using R?"). Type any question into Google and you will find an answer somewhere on the Net. This quasi-infinite space of immediately available knowledge has increased the urgency of learning how to navigate this space efficiently – it has become more and more crucial to know how to search for information, that is, to know what kind of questions to ask, how to do this effectively and reliably, how to filter and interpret the results, and how to integrate them into one's already existent body of knowledge. In this chapter, we examine children's question-asking strategies, tracing their emergence and developmental trajectory and trying to identify the factors impacting and contributing to their success.

The research we review and discuss has strong potential for informing educational practice and the development of pedagogical tools. For example, the question of how learners approach problems in which they have to figure out how different variables (e.g., water, sunlight, and fertilizer) affect an outcome measure (e.g., health of a plant; Klahr et al., 1993) by actively asking questions or intervening in a causal system has received particular attention in educational research. Over the past decades, the control of variables strategy (CVS) has emerged as a prominently advocated and researched approach and its mastery is considered a benchmark criterion within science, engineering, technology, and mathematics curricula, as part of the more general effort to equip children with the most crucial scientific thinking skills (National Research Council, 2012). The fundamental principle of CVS consists in changing one variable at a time while holding all other variables constant in order to isolate the impact of this variable on the outcome measure (Kuhn & Brannock, 1977). Although considerable effort has been invested in teaching students CVS (e.g., Kuhn & Angelev, 1976; Kuhn & Brannock, 1977; Chen & Klahr, 1999), empirical research shows that its acquisition requires extensive teaching and training (see Schwichow et al., 2016, for a review), and even if children have acquired CVS in one context, they do not readily transfer it to novel problems (e.g., Kuhn & Phelps, 1982; Klahr et al., 1993; Kuhn et al., 1995). There is some evidence that self-directed learning, wherein students explore problems on their own, as opposed to direct instruction, can result in longer-lasting acquisition and transfer of children's use of CVS to solve science-related problems (e.g., Dean & Kuhn, 2007; but see Matlen & Klahr, 2012). However, even adolescents and adults who have mastered CVS do not always rely on it (e.g., Kuhn et al., 1995). There is no doubt that CVS is an effective learning strategy. However, its superiority to alternative strategies may be limited to particular situations. Consider the following scenario: you have to figure out which of twenty switches on a poorly labeled fuse box in the basement turns on the bedroom light. According to CVS, the switches should be turned on one by one until the causally effective switch has been found. However, the optimal strategy in this particular scenario would actually be to turn on half of the switches (ten switches) to find out which subset contains the target switch (i.e., the one controlling the bedroom light), and then to repeat this process, testing half of the remaining switches until only the target switch remains. Recent evidence shows that adults readily adapt their inquiry strategy to the nature of a causal system, relying on CVS when multiple variables affect an outcome (i.e., when it is most effective) but preferring to test multiple variables at once in situations when only one or a few variables affect the outcome (e.g., as in the situation described above; Coenen et al., 2019).

This example reveals a discrepancy between advocated educational interventions, such as those promoting CVS as the hallmark of scientific reasoning, and the most recent results of research in cognitive and developmental psychology investigating how children and adults tackle reasoning problems and spontaneously engage in inquiry processes – a discrepancy that may partly explain why it is so challenging to teach children CVS. As we show in this chapter, although inquiry and question-asking skills emerge very early in childhood, their development continues throughout childhood and is closely connected to children's developing understanding and experience of the world, as well as to the development of general cognitive abilities, such as working memory, executive functions, verbal, and metacognitive skills. Combining insights on the development of children's cognitive processes that support inquiry with educational research may ultimately help in the design of stimulating learning environments and better, more effective interventions.

## Developmental Changes in Question Informativeness

It should already be clear from reading the previous chapters that asking questions is a powerful learning tool. Children ask questions about a variety of topics many times per day. Their inquiry behavior is purposeful, intended to fill a knowledge gap, to resolve some inconsistency, or to seek explanations and, more generally, to test and extend their developing understanding of the world (Piaget, 1954; Carey, 1985; Gopnik & Wellman, 1994; Chouinard, 2007; Frazier et al., 2009; Wellman, 2011; Harris, 2012).

Research to date has shown that young children ask domain-appropriate questions (Callanan & Oakes, 1992; Hickling & Wellman, 2001; Greif et al., 2006), have reasonable expectations about what responses count as answers to their questions (Frazier et al., 2009), can use the answers they receive to solve problems (Chouinard, 2007; Legare et al., 2013), and direct their questions to more reliable informants (Koenig & Harris, 2005; Birch et al., 2008; Corriveau et al., 2009; Mills et al., 2010; Mills et al., 2011). But do children ask good questions?

## A Qualitative Approach to Capture Question Informativeness

To answer this question, we first need to define what a good question is. There are many different ways to assess the quality of a question, such as its potential to stimulate a discussion or to initiate or maintain social interactions. In this chapter, we focus on questions as goal-directed behaviors intended to obtain new information. In this sense, a good question is one that is "appropriately worded to obtain the information needed to solve a problem" (Mills et al., 2011, p. 3) – that is, one that is *informative*. This definition implies that the quality of a question cannot be determined in absolute terms but depends on the kind of information that is sought, the source of this information, what the information will be used for, prior knowledge of the question asker, and the specific learning situation. For example, if one wants to find out how a new, mysterious machine works, inquiring about its color is unlikely to give useful insight into its mechanism. On the other hand, asking about the function of various buttons is more likely to be informative in this situation because it provides new information about the relevant features of the machine. However, this binary classification of questions into informative or uninformative does not offer a framework with which to assess relative degrees of informativeness – it does not specify *how much* new information a certain question provides.

A more fine-grained classification was suggested by Mosher and Hornsby (1966), who pioneered the study of children's question-asking strategies using the 20-questions game. In this game, children have to identify a target object/cause or a category of objects/causes (e.g., "What kind of objects can be found on Planet Apres?" or "Why was the man late for work today?") within a given set by asking as few yes–no questions as possible. Although the 20-questions game may appear to be very constrained and artificial at first glance, it is a classic example of sequential, binary information search, a problem that is actually a very general one encountered throughout the lifespan. Consider a Boy Scout tasked to identify the species of a wild bird with the help of a *Boy Scouts Handbook*. He may begin by looking at the bird's size (e.g., "Is it larger than a wren?"), then at the location where it was observed (e.g., "Is it high up or on the ground?"), and then at its color ("Is it brown?"). By sequentially querying different features of the bird, the Boy Scout is able to drastically reduce the number of potential alternatives at every step of the search process, converging on the target object in only a few steps. A similar process can be used for medical diagnoses: in emergency medicine, resident physicians learn to check for the presence or absence of certain physiological changes to rule out lethal conditions that can be associated with a particular complaint (e.g., Green & Mehr, 1997; Hamilton et al., 2003). Additional real-world decision-making, categorization, and causal inference tasks have been modeled with fast and frugal trees that involve sequential, binary branching (see Berretty et al., 1997; Berretty et al., 1999; Martignon et al., 2008). Thus, studying children's performance on a 20-questions game is a good compromise between experimental tractability and real-world generalizability.

Mosher and Hornsby (1966) categorized children's questions in this game as hypothesis-scanning or constraint-seeking. Hypothesis-scanning questions are tentative solutions, that is, single objects or hypotheses that are tested directly (e.g., "Is this daisy on Planet Apres?" or "Was the man late because he woke up late?"). Conversely, constraint-seeking questions aim to reduce the space of possible hypotheses by targeting categories or testing features shared by several different hypotheses (e.g., "Are flowers found on Planet Apres?" or "Was he late because of something he forgot at home?"). Constraint-seeking questions are traditionally considered more informative than hypothesis-scanning questions because they allow the question asker to rule out multiple hypotheses (objects, categories of objects, or causes) at once, thus reducing the number of questions needed to identify the solution. Following Mosher and Hornsby (1966), previous research has found that the ability to ask informative questions undergoes a large developmental change from age four to adulthood. Although preschoolers as young as four are already able to generate a majority of informative questions as opposed to redundant or uninformative questions (i.e., questions that target all or none of the hypotheses or that are completely irrelevant to the task; see Legare et al., 2013), their question generation is strongly characterized by a hypothesis-scanning approach. Indeed, preschoolers almost always ask hypothesis-scanning questions in the 20-questions game and still predominantly use this strategy until age seven (Mosher & Hornsby, 1966; Herwig, 1982; Ruggeri & Feufel, 2015; Ruggeri & Lombrozo, 2015). For example, in a traditional version of the 20-questions game, Herwig (1982) found that about 95 percent of the questions asked by pre-schoolers, 90 percent of those asked by first graders, and 83 percent of those asked by second graders were hypothesis-scanning. However, other studies found that 80 percent of the questions asked by fifth graders were constraint-seeking and that this strategy increased in prevalence until adulthood (see Ruggeri & Feufel, 2015; Ruggeri & Lombrozo, 2015).

Mosher and Hornsby (1966) replicated these findings in a less constrained version of the 20-questions game, where children aged six to eleven years were prompted to identify the cause of an event (e.g., "A man is driving down the road in his car; the car goes off the road and hits a tree.") by asking yes–no questions without being presented with a predefined set of possible hypotheses. Just like in the more constrained version of the task, younger children tended to ask mainly hypothesis-scanning questions (e.g., "Did an animal run across the road and the man tried to avoid it?"). When prompted to describe their strategies, only a few of the younger children mentioned the idea of a "general" question or of narrowing down the hypothesis space. In contrast, almost all the older children were able to articulate a more systematic strategy, with half of them mentioning the principle of asking broad questions. These results suggest that with increasing age children also develop a more explicit metacognitive understanding of the features determining a question's informativeness. We return to the role of metacognition in the development of children's question-asking strategies later in this chapter.

## Limitations of the Qualitative Approach

With their qualitative distinction between hypothesis-scanning and constraint-seeking questions, Mosher and Hornsby (1966) initiated the investigation of children's active learning through question-asking. As mentioned in the previous section, within this qualitative framework, constraint-seeking questions are more informative than hypothesis-scanning questions. However, this is not always the case. The informativeness of constraint-seeking and hypothesis-scanning questions varies depending on the characteristics of the problem under consideration, such as the number of hypotheses available and their likelihoods, as well as on the learner's prior knowledge and experiences (Todd et al., 2012; Ruggeri & Lombrozo, 2015). Imagine a scenario in which there are three equally likely candidate hypotheses. For example, you might want to find out whether mangoes, strawberries, or cherries are your best friend's favorite kind of fruit. Using a constraint-seeking approach, you could ask if her favorite fruit is red. This question would split the hypothesis space 2:1: strawberries or cherries versus mangoes. If she answers "yes," then you have eliminated mangoes and only strawberries or cherries remain. Conversely, if the answer is "no," then you have eliminated both red fruits and are left with only one possibility: mangoes must be her favorite fruit. However, in this context, a hypothesis-scanning question (e.g., "Are strawberries your favorite kind of fruit?") would also induce a 2:1 split, targeting one of three hypotheses. Therefore, in this particular situation both questions are equally informative. Moreover, if one hypothesis is much more likely to be correct than the others, then a hypothesis-scanning question that targets that single high-probability hypothesis (e.g., one that has a 70 percent probability of being correct) can be more informative than a constraint-seeking question that targets several hypotheses with a smaller summed probability (e.g., 30 percent).

Going back to our previous example, you may have seen your friend eat strawberries more often than either mangoes or cherries. From this first-hand experience, you may infer that she strongly prefers strawberries over the other two kinds of fruit. Asking directly whether strawberries are her favorite fruits with a hypothesis-scanning question is therefore likely to result in a quick win. Finally, and crucially, not all constraint-seeking questions are equally informative. Imagine that instead of three "favorite fruit" options, you have eight: red apples, cherries, strawberries, raspberries, oranges, apricots, blueberries, and melons. In this case, there are several possible constraint-seeking questions you could ask. For instance, you might again ask if her favorite fruit is red, which would target half of the available options (i.e., red apples, cherries, strawberries, and raspberries).

This question is very informative because it allows you to narrow down the hypothesis space to four options, irrespective of whether her answer is yes or no, which means you will need no more than two subsequent questions to find the answer. However, you might also ask if her favorite fruit is round. This question targets six of the eight hypotheses available (i.e., apples, cherries, oranges, apricots, blueberries, and melons). In this case, the number of subsequent questions needed to find her favorite fruit depends on whether the answer is yes or no. If she says "yes," then you are left with six options; if she replies "no," then only two options remain. Assuming that all eight fruits were initially equally likely to be her favorite, getting a "yes" answer to this question is more likely than getting a "no." In this sense, this question is not as effective as the previous one (i.e., red fruit) because it does not guarantee the fastest route to the right answer. These examples also highlight the crucial role of prior knowledge for determining the range of considered hypotheses and estimating their respective likelihoods and therefore its potential to impact question-asking efficiency.

The divergence between a constraint-seeking approach and actual question informativeness is further illustrated by two other kinds of questions that children ask: pseudo-constraint-seeking questions and confirmatory questions. Pseudo-constraint-seeking questions take the *form* of a constraint-seeking question (e.g., "Is it blue?") but target only a single object in the set (i.e., the only blue object in the set). They are as informative as the corresponding hypothesis-scanning question. Previous research with traditional 20-questions games (i.e., involving equally likely hypotheses) has found that the rate of pseudo-constraint-seeking questions increases with age (Mosher & Hornsby, 1966; Ruggeri & Lombrozo, 2015), suggesting that older children understand the form that efficient questions should take but that they sometimes fail to generate such questions in a way that actually improves informativeness. Confirmatory questions, by contrast, are redundant based on the information already gathered. Although they do not provide any new information, about 20 percent of the questions asked by four- to six-year-olds in a question-asking task were found to be confirmatory (Legare et al., 2013), and the prevalence of confirmatory questions partially explains why seven- and ten-year-olds fall short of adult levels of efficiency (Ruggeri et al., 2016).

## Quantitative Approach: Using Information Gain to Measure Question Quality

The examples above illustrate how the qualitative distinction between different question types does not necessarily map onto their actual informativeness. Given this consideration, instead of exclusively relying on the qualitative distinction between question types, previous studies have introduced a formal approach that quantifies more precisely the information gathered by children's questions (Eimas, 1970; Nelson et al., 2014; Ruggeri et al., 2016, 2017). Although several possible measures have been used to compute how informative different questions are (e.g., probability gain, impact, expected savings, path length; see Nelson, 2005), the most commonly employed is *expected stepwise information gain*. Expected stepwise information gain (EIG; see Oaksford & Chater, 1994; Steyvers et al., 2003; Nelson et al., 2010; Chin et al., 2015) measures the reduction of entropy – that is, the uncertainty as to which hypothesis is correct – upon asking a certain question (see Lindley, 1956). Within this framework, the best questions are those that maximize the reduction of entropy, allowing the learner to move from a state of uncertainty (e.g., "What kind of objects are on Planet Apres?") closer to a state of certainty (e.g., "Only birds are found on Planet Apres"). More information about the expected information gain framework, the formulas used to calculate EIG, and detailed examples can be found in Ruggeri et al. (2016, pp. 2162–3), and Ruggeri et al. (2017, pp. 3 and 12).

Generally, studies employing quantitative measures of question informativeness have confirmed earlier qualitative findings, namely, that the informativeness of children's question-asking strategies increases with age (Ruggeri & Feufel, 2015; Ruggeri & Lombrozo, 2015; Ruggeri et al., 2016). In particular, studies with preschoolers (four- to six-year-olds) have shown to what extent they have difficulties generating the most informative questions from scratch (Ruggeri et al., unpublished data).

Moreover, using a formal, quantitative approach, we can study the efficiency of children's questions in a much more fine-grained way than with a purely qualitative approach. For example, by being able to calculate the expected information gain associated with every conceivable (task-related) question, researchers can assess the quality of children's and adults' question-asking strategies in absolute terms. Indeed, within this quantitative framework, the informativeness of children's questions can be compared to an "optimal" strategy that selects the most informative question to ask at each step of the search process, or to a strategy that "randomly" selects a question among all those that could be asked. This analysis revealed that even seven-year-olds ask questions that are more informative than those generated by a computer-simulated learner that asks random questions, but that even adults tend to fall short of optimality (Ruggeri et al., 2016). Apart from the fact that even adults do not necessarily possess the cognitive resources required to perform complex computations, a likely explanation for this failure is that human decisions are influenced by considerations other than maximization of information gain. For instance, question-asking might be influenced by prior experience with the kinds of questions that are usually efficient, along with any alternative goals they might have in mind during the task (e.g., pleasing the experimenter or rapidly finishing the experiment without investing too much effort). Also, their numeracy skills, motivation, level of tiredness, and level of distraction may all impact their question-asking efficiency.

## Adaptiveness and Ecological Learning

As discussed earlier, the informativeness of question-asking strategies depends on children's prior knowledge and expectations, as well as on the task's characteristics, such as the number of hypotheses available and their likelihood. Therefore, the best question can be defined as the match between task characteristics on the one hand and the knowledge, abilities, and biases of the learner on the other (e.g., Gigerenzer et al., 1999; Ruggeri & Lombrozo, 2015). This implies that asking informative questions requires the ability to recognize, select, and generate those questions that are most informative in the particular situation. This ability to flexibly adapt active learning strategies to different situations has been referred to as *ecological learning* (Ruggeri & Lombrozo, 2015).

Ruggeri and Lombrozo (2015) investigated whether children of seven and ten years of age and adults flexibly adapt their question-asking strategies to the characteristics of a 20-questions game in which they had to find out why a man was late for work. Participants were introduced to ten candidate hypotheses, possible solutions for the game. In one condition, all hypotheses were presented as equally likely to constitute the correct solution (Uniform condition). In the other condition, a few hypotheses were presented as much more likely than the others to constitute the correct solution (Mixed condition). Confirming the results of previous studies, the authors found a steady developmental increase in children's reliance on constraint-seeking questions. However, all age groups, including seven-year-olds, asked more hypothesis-scanning questions that targeted the most likely hypothesis in the Mixed condition. These results were the first to demonstrate that children as young as seven years old are ecological learners, able to tailor the kinds of questions asked to the characteristics of the task at hand. A more recent study showed that even five-year-olds are able to dynamically reassess the informativeness of different question types depending on the situation encountered when they are allowed to select one of two preformulated questions (Ruggeri et al., 2017). In this study, Ruggeri and colleagues (2017) presented five-year-old children with a storybook describing the reasons why the monster Toma had been late for school over several days. In the Uniform condition, Toma had been late equally often for six different reasons: once he had been late because he could not find his jacket, once because he could not find his shoes, once because he could not find his books, once because his bike was broken, once because he spilled his drink, and once because he was watching television. In the Skewed condition, Toma had been late multiple times for one particular reason (i.e., on five of eight days he was late because he woke up late). On the remaining three days, he had been late because he could not find his jacket, could not find his shoes, and because his bike was broken. Children then learned that Toma was late yet again and that two of his monster friends wanted to find out why. In the Uniform condition, one monster friend asked the constraint-seeking question "Were you late because you could not find something?" (EIG: 1.0), whereas the other friend asked the hypothesis-scanning question "Were you late because your bike was broken?" (EIG: 0.66). Because in this condition all reasons were equally likely (i.e., occurred exactly once), the constraint-seeking question targeting three of the six candidate solutions (i.e., "Were you late because you could not find something?") was the most informative question. In contrast, in the Skewed condition, one friend wanted to know whether Toma had been late because he woke up late (hypothesis-scanning question, EIG: 0.94) and the other friend wanted to know whether Toma had been late because he could not find something (constraint-seeking question, EIG: 0.81). In this condition, the hypothesis-scanning question targeting the single most likely hypothesis (i.e., "Were you late because you woke up late?") was the most informative.

Children then had to indicate which of Toma's friends would find out first why Toma had been late – that is, which friend asked the more informative question. In both conditions, the majority of children selected the monster asking the question with the higher expected information gain, regardless of the question type: in the Uniform condition, 70 percent of the children selected the friend who asked the constraint-seeking question ("Were you late because you could not find something?"), whereas in the Skewed condition, 73 percent of the children selected the friend who asked the hypothesis-scanning question ("Were you late because you woke up late?"). These results, replicated across several versions of the same task, suggest that preschoolers have the computational foundations for developing successful question-asking strategies, although they do not yet rely on these when generating questions from scratch.

Further research is required to better understand why this is the case. It may be possible that, despite their early emergence, the computational and probabilistic skills underpinning efficient question-asking continue to develop and improve across childhood, thereby allowing children to ask better questions as they grow older. It may also be that these computational foundations are fully present from an early age but that children fail to integrate them with other cognitive processes, such as generating questions; possibly because of age-related limitations in cognitive processing resources. The second part of this chapter looks more closely at what is known so far about potential factors driving improvements in children's question-asking strategies, such as enhanced executive functions and cognitive processing, metacognition, and improving verbal skills.

Interestingly, despite the general developmental increase in performance observed in the 20-questions game, previous research shows that adults do not adapt their active learning strategies more promptly than children do (Ruggeri et al., 2015). On the contrary, some preliminary results seem to suggest that children can sometimes be even more sensitive to the information structure of a task than adults. For example, Ruggeri and Lombrozo (2015) presented adults and nine-year-old children with an open causal inference task, in which the goal was again to find out why a man had been late for work. However, instead of providing participants with a set of possible solutions, they told them that the solution was either *very likely* or *very unlikely*. Trying to obtain a seemingly possible quick win, children tended to start by asking a hypothesis-scanning question in the Very Likely condition, targeting hypotheses they thought had high likelihood (e.g., "Was the man late because he got stuck in a traffic jam?"), but they preferred to ask constraint-seeking questions in the Very Unlikely condition where the potential for a quick win was much lower. In contrast, adults mostly asked constraint-seeking questions in both conditions. A possible explanation for adults' overreliance on constraint-seeking questions may be that they have more frequently experienced situations where this type of question is more informative and therefore resort to constraint-seeking questions as a default strategy, knowing it would eventually, reliably lead to the solution.

## Boosting Children's Question-Asking Efficiency

Efforts to boost children's learning have resulted in the elaboration of a wide variety of pedagogical tools and educational programs, ranging from computer-assisted learning apps (e.g., Lego Education, which is designed to teach computational reasoning, or Alien Assignment, which promotes problem-solving skills and literacy; see Hirsch-Pasek et al., 2015) to teaching curricula (e.g., Young Scientist Series, Science Start,

Preschool Pathways to Science, reviewed in Klahr et al., 2011). These interventions often aim to improve skills that are fundamental to general problem-solving (e.g., reasoning about individual variables and forming testable hypotheses about their relationships). Is it possible to teach children to ask better questions?

Attempts to improve children's question-asking strategies have met with only moderate success so far (e.g., Courage, 1989; Denney, 1972; Denney et al., 1973; Denney & Turner, 1979). For instance, Courage (1989) tested four-, five-, and seven-year-old children on a 20-questions game and on a Listener game, which is very similar to the 20-questions game except the experimenter first provides a verbal clue about which object she is thinking about. Following this pretest phase, children were trained on either one or both tasks again, with the experimenter providing explicit instructions about how to ask constraint-seeking questions, which were more informative in these tasks. Only five-year-olds showed significant improvements after training (Courage, 1989). In an earlier study, Denney (1972) trained six-, eight-, and ten-year-olds by providing them with explicit examples of adult models asking either hypothesis-scanning or constraint-seeking questions while playing a short 20-questions game. Six-year-olds' rate of hypothesis-scanning versus constraint-seeking questions was unaffected at posttest, while eight-year-olds were susceptible to both training models: children who observed adults asking hypothesis-scanning questions asked fewer constraint-seeking questions at posttest (a decline of 46.8 percent) and vice versa (an increase of 18 percent). Ten-year-olds were unaffected by the hypothesis-scanning model, but those who viewed the constraint-seeking model asked more constraint-seeking questions at posttest (an increase of 26.4 percent; Denney, 1972). However, these benefits of training were short-lived and were not apparent a week after the posttest. Considering the greater success of pedagogical interventions for teaching more complex inquiry skills such as CVS (e.g., Davenport et al., 2008; Klahr et al., 2011; Matlen & Klahr, 2012; Siler et al., 2012; Chase & Klahr, 2017), it is surprising that it should be so difficult to improve children's question-asking strategies.

However, some recent interventions have proven to be partially successful. For instance, reducing demands on vocabulary and categorization in a hierarchical 20-questions game through scaffolding (i.e., telling children which object features could be used to categorize the objects at different hierarchical levels) led six-year-olds to ask more informative questions (Ruggeri et al., unpublished data). These results also provide evidence for the importance of both verbal and categorization skills in the development of children's questions and also show that a simple change to task instructions can potentially improve performance without extensive training. Likewise, in another study, prompting five- to seven-year-olds to provide explanations about evidence observed in a training phase increased the informativeness of their questions in a test phase (Ruggeri et al., 2019b).

More generally, it would be interesting to investigate how and whether attendance at preschools focusing on free or guided play (e.g., Montessori schools) or schools with an emphasis on inquiry learning (e.g., Socratic schools) has a long-lasting boosting effect on children's active learning and question-asking strategies. Training children's active inquiry skills at an early age may improve or accelerate the development of effective question-asking and information search strategies and may make learning more fun. This, in turn, may also increase curiosity and motivation as well as perseverance in the face of setbacks in the short or long term (for a review of the impact of preschool and primary school on child development, see Sylva, 1994).

## Factors Impacting Question Efficiency and Adaptiveness

As documented earlier in this chapter, a large body of work has shown that question-asking strategies undergo significant shifts around the ages of five, seven, and ten years, but it is not yet fully understood why these changes occur, why some interventions do not work, and why some are beneficial only for particular age groups. More specifically, it is not known precisely which factors drive developmental changes in question-asking, how they interact with each other, or how their relative importance changes at different developmental stages. These factors include verbal skills, categorization skills, executive functions, metacognition, probabilistic reasoning, attention, motivation, education, and socioeconomic status (SES). For instance, verbal ability has been shown to be generally associated with question informativeness in a 20-questions game played with four-, five- and six-year-olds, but this effect disappeared after controlling for age (Ruggeri et al., unpublished data). In the following sections, we focus here on some of the other contributing factors.

### Categorization Skills

Why do younger children tend to ask hypothesis-scanning questions in a 20-questions game, despite their typical inefficiency? A dominant explanation is that constraint-seeking questions require advanced categorization abilities, in particular the ability to represent, and therefore target, more abstract categories or features. Consistent with this idea, Ruggeri and Feufel (2015) found that scaffolding higher-level representations facilitated children's ability to ask constraint-seeking questions. In their study, seven- and ten-year-old children, as well as adults, were presented with twenty cards on a computer screen, each of which contained a word label (e.g., "dog" or "sheep"). Participants were randomly assigned to one of two experimental conditions based on the specificity of the label: a basic-level condition (e.g., "Dog") or a subordinate-level condition (e.g., "Dalmatian"). The authors found that participants were more likely to ask constraint-seeking questions in the former condition than in the latter, suggesting that more abstract labels facilitated a shift away from object-based reasoning when generating questions. They also found that the ability to generate more abstract features (e.g., "a dog is a mammal" or "a dog has four legs") is one factor that affects performance and that it develops within this age range (see also Herwig, 1982). It remains to be seen exactly to what extent improvements in children's categorization skills drive changes in question-asking efficiency, at which stages, and how these skills interact with verbal abilities more generally.

*Executive Functions*

Although there is no direct or definitive evidence of how executive functions drive changes in the informativeness of children's questions, recent work strongly suggests that they play a crucial role. For instance, Legare and colleagues (2013) examined how cognitive flexibility correlated with question-asking strategies in four- to six-year-olds. They presented children with a 20-questions game in which they had to find out which card of a given set turned on a magic machine, and a cognitive flexibility game in which they had to sort twelve object cards twice, once according to color and once according to their category. Higher cognitive flexibility scores were correlated with a higher proportion of constraint-seeking questions and better performance in the 20-questions game for all children, regardless of age (Legare et al., 2013). However, overall accuracy, which necessitated not only gathering information but also remembering and coordinating it in working memory, was low on this task. The authors interpreted this as evidence that young children can strategically use constraint-seeking questions to acquire relevant information before they are able to successfully coordinate and maintain that information in working memory. Along these lines, a recent study found a positive correlation between active learning performance and working memory capacity in a word-learning game (Ruggeri et al., 2019a). This points to the development of executive functions as an important factor influencing not only the formulation of effective questions but also the ability to successfully represent and use the information acquired during questioning.

Another component of executive functions that may impact question-asking ability is inhibitory control. This ability develops rapidly between the ages of four and eight (e.g., Romine & Reynolds, 2005; reviewed in Best & Miller, 2010) but continues to improve well into adolescence and adulthood, with documented refinements occurring until twenty-one years of age (Huizinga et al., 2006). The impact of inhibitory control on children's questions has not been directly investigated to date. However, since it enables goal-oriented behavior (e.g., by suppressing task-irrelevant or incorrect behaviors) and control of attention (e.g., inhibiting attention to irrelevant stimuli), it seems likely that having good inhibitory control should help children ask effective questions by keeping them focused on the task and by allowing them to inhibit less effective question-asking strategies. For instance, hypothesis-scanning questions may be a strong default strategy in early childhood, and improvements in inhibitory control may enable children who realize that this is not always the most appropriate question type to inhibit this strategy with increasing success in favor of a constraint-seeking strategy.

*Metacognition*

One reason why children's information search is generally less efficient than adults' is that they search much more exhaustively, making unnecessary queries. For example, in information board procedures, younger children (seven- to eight-year-olds) tend to search more of the available options and in a less systematic manner than older children (ten- to fourteen-year-olds; Davidson, 1991a, 1991b, 1996). This may be partly explained by children's difficulty attending to or identifying the most relevant information for a particular task (Mata et al., 2011). In addition, results of a study by Ruggeri et al. (2016) suggest that a crucial source of developmental changes in question-asking efficiency is a difference in stopping rules. In this study, children (seven- and ten-year-olds) and adults played a hierarchical version of the 20-questions game. Children asked more confirmatory questions than adults, thus continuing their search for information past the point where all the required information had been gathered, suggesting that they had more conservative stopping rules. Therefore, uncertainty monitoring may contribute to driving improvements in question-asking efficiency. Uncertainty monitoring develops during the preschool years (Lyons & Ghetti, 2011), continues to improve throughout middle childhood (Koriat & Ackermann, 2010), and predicts strategic performance (e.g., withholding a response when you are not sure about it) even in three- to five-year-olds (Lyons & Ghetti, 2013). Because having a good understanding of the state of one's own knowledge is a key requirement for knowing what information to ask about, changes in uncertainty monitoring and other components of meta-cognition may also impact question informativeness. For example, being better able to keep track of how certain they are about the correct solution in a 20-questions game may enable children to realize, consciously or not, that some questions lead to greater reductions in uncertainty than others. Therefore, one could speculate that greater reductions in uncertainty following a more informative (e.g., constraint-seeking) question may encourage children to continue asking these kinds of questions, thereby increasing their information search efficiency.

### Probabilistic Reasoning

As discussed previously, the informativeness of different questions crucially depends on the relative likelihoods of the candidate solutions. This also means that in order to ask the most informative questions, one must be able to understand and reason with frequencies and probabilities. Recent research suggests that young children, and even infants, are remarkably skilled at tracking frequencies in the environment and are capable of rudimentary probabilistic reasoning (Téglás et al., 2007; Xu & Garcia, 2008; Xu & Denison, 2009; Denison & Xu, 2010a, 2010b, 2014; Téglás et al., 2011; Denison et al., 2013). Moreover, a growing body of research suggests that infants and preschoolers use probabilistic information to form judgments, to make predictions and generalizations, and to guide information search (Kushnir & Gopnik, 2005; Gweon et al., 2010; Denison & Xu, 2014). The early emergence of this skill may explain why the ability to select the most informative questions manifests earlier than the ability to generate them from scratch (Ruggeri et al., 2017). However, although this skill emerges early in life, it requires lifelong refinement, as adolescents and even adults can struggle with certain forms of probabilistic reasoning, such as comparing fractions (e.g., Schneider & Siegler, 2010). Despite its early emergence, it is unclear how much probabilistic reasoning constrains or boosts developmental shifts in question-asking effectiveness because of this lifelong development.

### Socioeconomic Status

The propensity to ask questions in the first place should also be considered. Individual and situational variations in attention, motivation, and loquaciousness aside, social and educational factors are likely to influence how readily children ask questions and therefore how many opportunities they have to refine their strategies over time. One such factor is SES, which is a known predictor of widely used outcome measures such as IQ (Liaw & Brooks-Gunn, 1994; Smith et al., 1997; Gottfried et al., 2003). SES was found to disproportionately impact language and executive function development in preschoolers compared to other neurocognitive systems (e.g., visuomotor skills), with low-SES children performing significantly worse than mid-SES children (Noble et al., 2005). Given the influence of SES on cognition, it is also reasonable to expect that children's questions may be affected. Indeed, studies of children's interactions with parents show that children from mid-SES backgrounds ask almost double the number of questions than those from low-SES backgrounds (Kurkul & Corriveau, 2018), although the content of these questions does not differ between groups (e.g., fact-based "what-" and "where-" vs. causal "why-questions"). The responses of caregivers to causal questions also differ between socioeconomic groups, with low-SES caregivers providing lower quality answers (e.g., more circular or off-topic explanations; Kurkul & Corriveau, 2018). Because children are sensitive to the quality of responses to questions and use this as a cue to decide how many and what kind of questions to direct to an informant from a young age (Frazier et al., 2009; Harris & Corriveau, 2011), children from low-SES backgrounds might be driven to ask fewer questions in general. When they do ask questions, this comparative lack of practice may result in less efficient questions than those used by mid-SES children of the same age. To our knowledge, no study has addressed this avenue of investigation, which would provide a useful counterpoint to existing work accounting for low-SES disadvantages in school, particularly in relation to verbal skills (e.g., Walker et al., 1994; Durham et al., 2007; Rowe, 2008).

## Open Questions and Future Directions

Research on question-asking is relatively young and there are therefore many unexplored avenues of research. We believe that three questions particularly warrant further investigation. First, as highlighted in the previous section, to make further progress in understanding how and why children's question-asking strategies change, the factors driving these changes must be identified more precisely. In addition, the interactions between these factors and their relative importance at different developmental stages should also be clarified. Along the same lines, it would also be crucial to assess the cross-cultural robustness and universality of active learning strategies more generally, and of these contributing factors specifically.

Second, considering the complexity of the computations that underlie good question-asking strategies, children may evaluate the informativeness of others' questions and use this, consciously or not, as a cue to assess another person's learning ability and to identify good role models from whom to *learn how to learn*. For example, recent work with preschoolers has shown that by three years of age children infer an agent's competence from how this agent has learned (Bridgers et al., 2018) and selectively seek help from active learners. This line of inquiry would help bridge the gap between research on question efficiency and research on question-asking in its social contexts (e.g., interactions with peers, parents, and teachers).

Third, exploring novel research methods may open new perspectives on answering these questions. Complementing the earlier qualitative work with computational methods has helped researchers gain insight into the processes that underlie good question-asking strategies. However, this quantitative framework is still limited in its ecological validity: we are only able to measure question informativeness in an environment where only yes–no questions can be asked and where the hypothesis space is both constrained and predetermined. This setup is not particularly representative of naturalistic conversations, where much richer questions can be asked and where the hypotheses actually considered, as well as their likelihoods, are shaped by the question asker's prior experience and beliefs. One way to address this limitation is to elaborate a more flexible mathematical framework, as well as a behavioral paradigm in which this framework can be used. Another way would be to integrate techniques such as eye tracking, pupillometry, or electroencephalography (EEG) into the study of question-asking efficiency. This would allow researchers to investigate developmental trajectories and individual differences in more detail. For instance, increased attention to features of visual cues that aid in categorization may occur before children are able to use strategies that capitalize on categorization abilities (i.e., constraint-seeking questions). In addition, pupillometry can provide further detail by tracking changes in cognitive load associated with specific task features (Kahneman & Beatty, 1966; Wierda et al., 2012).

EEG is an even more direct measure of neural activity that would enable researchers to investigate the neural substrates of the subjective perception of question informativeness. Theta oscillations are of particular interest because they are associated with increased memory retention and anticipation of information in both adults (Guderian et al., 2009; Gruber et al., 2013) and infants (Begus et al., 2015), suggesting that prestimulus increases in theta power signal a neural state of "readiness to learn." In other words, theta power can potentially be used as a graded marker of expectation of information gain, and therefore of people's subjective assessment of question informativeness. Being able to track how this changes between individuals and across the lifespan, as well as to investigate whether this measure correlates with cognitive abilities, would greatly improve our understanding of the cognitive mechanisms underlying question-asking strategies and how they develop.

## Conclusions

In this chapter, we have reviewed much of the literature concerning how the efficiency and adaptiveness of children's questions develop. In sum, studies using both qualitative and quantitative methods have so far established three milestones in the developmental trajectory of children's question-asking strategies: at five, seven, and ten years of age. Children's question-asking abilities evolve from being able to identify good questions but not being able to spontaneously generate them at the age of five, to beginning to generate them spontaneously at age seven, and implementing efficient and adaptive question-asking strategies by the age of ten, echoing adult-level patterns of performance.

Further research is needed to gain a more complete and nuanced understanding of the processes underlying the development of question-asking. Achieving this goal will enable educators and scientists to design targeted training interventions and educational curricula to effectively support the development of these skills and provide children with a toolbox of strategies and concepts they can use to navigate the world.

## Acknowledgments

We would like to thank Björn Meder and Anita Todd for their helpful feedback and discussions.

## References

Begus, K., Southgate, V., and Gliga, T. (2015). Neural mechanisms of infant learning: Differences in frontal theta activity during object exploration modulate subsequent object recognition. *Biology Letters*, *11*, 20150041. https://doi.org/10.1098/rsbl.2015.0041

Berretty, P. M., Todd, P. M., and Blythe, P. W. (1997). Categorization by elimination: A fast and frugal approach to categorization. *Proceedings of the Nineteenth Annual Conference of the Cognitive Science Society* (pp. 43–8). Mahwah, NJ: Lawrence Erlbaum Associates.

Berretty, P. M., Todd, P. M., and Martignon, L. (1999). Categorization by elimination: Using few cues to choose. In G. Gigerenzer, P. M. Todd, and the ABC Research Group (eds.) *Evolution and cognition: Simple heuristics that make us smart* (pp. 235–54). New York: Oxford University Press.

Best, J. R., and Miller, P. H. (2010). A developmental perspective on executive function. *Child Development, 81,* 1641–60. https://doi.org/10.1111/j.1467–8 624.2010.01499.x

Birch, S. A., Vauthier, S. A., and Bloom, P. (2008). Three-and four-year-olds spontaneously use others' past performance to guide their learning. *Cognition, 107,* 1018–34. https://doi.org/10.1016/j.cognition.2007.12.008

Bridgers, S., Gweon, H., Bretzke, M., and Ruggeri, A. (2018). How you learned matters: The process by which others learn informs young children's decisions about whom to ask for help. Proceedings of the 40th Annual Meeting of the Cognitive Science Society.

Callanan, M. A., and Oakes, L. M. (1992). Preschoolers' questions and parents' explanations: Causal thinking in everyday activity. *Cognitive Development, 7,* 213–33. https://doi.org/10.1016/0885–2014(92)90012–g

Carey, S. (1985). *Conceptual change in childhood.* Cambridge, MA: MIT Press.

Chase, C. C., and Klahr, D. (2017). Invention versus direct instruction: For some content, it's a tie. *Journal of Science Education and Technology, 26,* 582–96. https://doi.org/10.1007/s10956-017–9700–6

Chen, Z., and Klahr, D. (1999). All other things being equal: Acquisition and transfer of the control of variables strategy. *Child Development, 70,* 1098–120. https://doi.org/10.1111/1467–8624.00081

Chin, J., Payne, B. R., Fu, W.-T., Morrow, D. G., and Stine-Morrow, E. A. (2015). Information foraging across the life span: Search and switch in unknown patches. *Topics in Cognitive Science, 7,* 428–50. https://doi.org/10 .1111/tops.12147

Chouinard, M. M. (2007). Children's questions: A mechanism for cognitive development. *Monographs of the Society for Research in Child Development, 72,* i–129.

Coenen, A., Ruggeri, A., Bramley, N. R., and Gureckis, T. M. (2019). Testing one or multiple: How beliefs about sparsity affect causal experimentation. *Journal of Experimental Psychology: Learning Memory and Cognition.* Advance online publication. https://dx.doi.org/10.1037/xlm0000680

Corriveau, K. H., Fusaro, M., and Harris, P. L. (2009). Going with the flow: Preschoolers prefer nondissenters as informants. *Psychological Science, 20,* 372–7. https://doi.org/10.1111/j.1467–9280.2009.02291.x

Courage, M. L. (1989). Children's inquiry strategies in referential communication and in the game of twenty questions. *Child Development, 60,* 877–86. https://doi.org/10.2307/1131029

Davenport, J. L., Yaron, D., Klahr, D., and Koedinger, K. (2008). When do diagrams enhance learning? A framework for designing relevant representations. In *Proceedings of the 8th International Conference on the Learning Sciences* (pp. 191–8). International Society of the Learning Sciences.

Davidson, D. (1991a). Children's decision-making examined with an information-board procedure. *Cognitive Development*, 6, 77–90. https://doi.org/10.1016/0885–2014(91)90007–z

(1991b). Developmental differences in children's search of predecisional information. *Journal of Experimental Child Psychology*, 52, 239–55. https://doi.org/10.1016/0022–0965(91)90061–v

(1996). The effects of decision characteristics on children's selective search of predecisional information. *Acta Psychologica*, 92, 263–81. https://doi.org/10.1016/0001–6918(95)00014–3

Dean, D., and Kuhn, D. (2007). Direct instruction vs. discovery: The long view. *Science Education*, 91, 36–74. https://doi.org/10.1002/sce.20194

Denison, S., and Xu, F. (2010a). Integrating physical constraints in statistical inference by 11-month-old infants. *Cognitive Science*, 34, 885–908. https://doi.org/10.1111/j.1551–6709.2010.01111.x

(2010b). Twelve- to 14-month-old infants can predict single-event probability with large set sizes. *Developmental Science*, 13, 798–803. https://doi.org/10.1111/j.1467–7687.2009.00943.x

(2014). The origins of probabilistic inference in human infants. *Cognition*, 130, 335–47. https://doi.org/10.1016/j.cognition.2013.12.001

Denison, S., Reed, C., and Xu, F. (2013). The emergence of probabilistic reasoning in very young infants: Evidence from 4.5- and 6-month-olds. *Developmental Psychology*, 49, 243–9. https://doi.org/10.1037/a0028278

Denney, D. (1972). Modeling and eliciting effects upon conceptual strategies. *Child Development*, 43, 810–23. https://doi.org/10.2307/1127633

Denney, D., Denney, N., and Ziobrowski, M. (1973). Alterations in the information-processing strategies of young children following observation of adult models. *Developmental Psychology*, 8, 202–8. https://doi.org/10.1037/h0034144

Denney, N., and Turner, M. (1979). Facilitating cognitive performance in children: A comparison of strategy modeling and strategy modeling with overt self-verbalization. *Journal of Experimental Child Psychology*, 28, 119–31. https://doi.org/10.1016/0022–0965(79)90106–1

Durham, R. E., Farkas, G., Scheffner Hammer, C., Tomblin, J. B., and Catts, H. W. (2007). Kindergarten oral language skill: A key variable in the intergenerational transmission of socioeconomic status. *Research in Social Stratification and Mobility*, 25, 294–305. https://doi.org/10.1016/j.rssm.2007.03.001

Eimas, P. D. (1970). Information processing in problem solving as a function of developmental level and stimulus saliency. *Developmental Psychology*, 2, 224–9. https://doi.org/10.1037/h0028746

Frazier, B. N., Gelman, S. A., and Wellman, H. M. (2009). Preschoolers' search for explanatory information within adult–child conversation. *Child Development*, 80, 1592–611. https://doi.org/10.1111/j.1467–8624.2009.01356.x

Gigerenzer, G., Todd, P. M., and the ABC Research Group (1999). *Simple heuristics that make us smart*. New York: Oxford University Press.

Gopnik, A., and Wellman, H. M. (1994). The theory theory. In L. A. Hirschfeld and S. A. Gelman (eds.), *Mapping the mind: Domain specificity in cognition and culture* (pp. 257–93). New York: Cambridge University Press.

Gottfried, A. W., Gottfried, A. E., Bathurst, K., Guerin, D. W., and Parramore, M. M. (2003). Socioeconomic status in children's development and family environment: Infancy through adolescence. In M. H. Bornstein and R. H. Bradley (eds.), *Socioeconomic status, parenting and child development* (pp. 189–207). Mahwah, NJ: Erlbaum.

Green, L., and Mehr, D. R. (1997). What alters physicians' decisions to admit to the coronary care unit? *Journal of Family Practice, 45*, 219–26.

Greif, M. L., Kemler Nelson, D. G., Keil, F. C., and Gutierrez, F. (2006). What do children want to know about animals and artifacts? Domain-specific requests for information. *Psychological Science, 17*, 455–9. https://doi.org/10.1111/j.1467–9280.2006.01727.x

Gruber, M. J., Watrous, A. J., Ekstrom, A. D., Ranganath, C., and Otten, L. J. (2013). Expected reward modulates encoding-related theta activity before an event. *Neuroimage, 64*, 68–74. https://doi.org/10.1016/j.neuroimage.2012.07.064

Guderian, S., Schott, B., Richardson-Klavehn, A., and Düzel, E. (2009). Medial temporal theta state before an event predicts episodic encoding success in humans. *Proceedings of the National Academy of Sciences of the United States of America, 106*, 5365–70. https://doi.org/10.1073/pnas.0900289106

Gweon, H., Tenenbaum, J. B., and Schulz, L. E. (2010). Infants consider both the sample and the sampling process in inductive generalization. *Proceedings of the National Academy of Sciences of the United States of America, 107*, 9066–71. https://doi.org/10.1073/pnas.1003095107

Hamilton, G. C., Sanders, A., Strange, G. S., and Trott, A. T. (2003). *Emergency medicine: An approach to clinical problem solving* (2nd ed.). Philadelphia, PA: Saunders.

Harris, P. L. (2012). *Trusting what you're told: How children learn from others.* Cambridge, MA: Harvard University Press.

Harris, P. L., and Corriveau, K. H. (2011). Young children's selective trust in informants. *Philosophical Transactions of the Royal Society B: Biological Sciences, 366*, 1179–87. https://doi.org/10.1093/acprof:osobl/9780199608966.003.0025

Herwig, J. E. (1982). Effects of age, stimuli, and category recognition factors in children's inquiry behavior. *Journal of Experimental Child Psychology, 33*, 196–206. https://doi.org/10.1016/0022–0965(82)90015–7

Hickling, A. K., and Wellman, H. M. (2001). The emergence of children's causal explanations and theories: Evidence from everyday conversation. *Developmental Psychology, 37*, 668–83. https://doi.org/10.1037//0012–1649.37.5.668

Hirsch-Pasek, K., Zosh, J. M., Michnick Golinkoff, R., et al. (2015). Putting education in "educational" apps: Lessons from the science of learning. *Psychological Science in the Public Interest, 16*, 3–34. https://doi.org/10.1177/1529100615569721

Huizinga, M., Dolan, C. V., and van der Molen, M. W. (2006). Age-related change in executive function: Developmental trends and a latent variable analysis. *Neuropsychologia, 44,* 2017–36. https://doi.org/10.1016/j .neuropsychologia.2006.01.010

Kahneman, D., and Beatty, J. (1966). Pupil diameter and load on memory. *Science, 154,* 1583–5. https://doi.org/10.1126/science.154.3756.1583

Klahr, D., Fay, A. L., and Dunbar, K. (1993). Heuristics for scientific experimentation: A developmental study. *Cognitive Psychology, 25,* 111–46. https://doi.org/10.1006/cogp.1993.1003

Klahr, D., Zimmerman, C., and Jirout, J. (2011). Educational interventions to advance children's scientific thinking. *Science, 333,* 971–75. https://doi.org/ 10.1126/science.1204528

Koenig, M. A., and Harris, P. L. (2005). Preschoolers mistrust ignorant and inaccurate speakers. *Child Development, 76,* 1261–77. https://doi.org/10 .1111/j.1467–8624.2005.00849.x

Koriat, A., and Ackerman, R. (2010). Choice latency as a cue for children's subjective confidence in the correctness of their answers. *Developmental Science, 13,* 441–53. https://doi.org/10.1111/j.1467–7687.2009.00907.x

Kuhn, D., and Angelev, J. (1976). An experimental study of the development of formal operational thought. *Child Development, 47,* 697–706. https://doi.org /10.2307/1128184

Kuhn, D., and Brannock, J. (1977). Development of the isolation of variables scheme in experimental and "natural experiment" contexts. *Developmental Psychology, 13,* 9–14. https://doi.org/10.1037//0012–1649 .13.1.9

Kuhn, D., and Phelps, E. (1982). The development of problem-solving strategies. *Advances in Child Development and Behavior, 17,* 1–44.

Kuhn, D., Garcia-Mila, M., Zohar, A., et al. (1995). Strategies of knowledge acquisition. *Monographs of the Society for Research in Child Development, 60,* i–157.

Kurkul, K. E., and Corriveau, K. H. (2018). Question, explanation, follow-up: A mechanism for learning from others? *Child Development, 89,* 208–94. https://doi.org/10.1111/cdev.12726

Kushnir, T., and Gopnik, A. (2005). Young children infer causal strength from probabilities and interventions. *Psychological Science, 16,* 678–83. https://doi .org/10.1111/j.1467–9280.2005.01595.x

Legare, C. H., Mills, C. M., Souza, A. L., Plummer, L. E., and Yasskin, R. (2013). The use of questions as problem-solving strategies during early childhood. *Journal of Experimental Child Psychology, 114,* 63–76. https://doi .org/10.1016/j.jecp.2012.07.002

Liaw, F. R., and Brooks-Gunn, J. (1994). Cumulative familial risks and low-birthweight children's cognitive and behavioral development. *Journal of Clinical Child Psychology, 23,* 360–72. https://doi.org/10.1207 /s15374424jccp2304_2

Lindley, D. V. (1956). On a measure of the information provided by an experiment. *The Annals of Mathematical Statistics, 27,* 986–1005. https://doi .org/10.1214/aoms/1177728069

Lyons, K., and Ghetti, S. (2011). The development of uncertainty monitoring in early childhood. *Child Development, 82,* 1778–87. https://doi.org/10.1111/j.1467–8624.2011.01649.x

(2013). I don't want to pick! Introspection on uncertainty supports early strategic behavior. *Child Development, 84,* 726–36. https://doi.org/10.1111/cdev.12004

Martignon, L., Katsikopoulos, K. V., and Woike, J. K. (2008). Categorization with limited resources: A family of simple heuristics. *Journal of Mathematical Psychology, 52,* 352–61. https://doi.org/10.1093/acprof:oso/9780199744282.003.0014

Mata, R., von Helversen, B., and Rieskamp, J. (2011). When easy comes hard: The development of adaptive strategy selection. *Child Development, 82,* 687–700. https://doi.org/10.1111/j.1467–8624.2010.01535.x

Matlen, B. J., and Klahr, D. (2012). Sequential effects of high and low instructional guidance on children's acquisition of experimentation skills: Is it all in the timing? *Instructional Science, 41,* 621–34. https://doi.org/10.1007/s11251-012-9248-z

Mills, C. M., Legare, C. H., Bills, M., and Mejias, C. (2010). Preschoolers use questions as a tool to acquire knowledge from different sources. *Journal of Cognition and Development, 11,* 533–60. https://doi.org/10.1080/15248372.2010.516419

Mills, C. M., Legare, C. H., Grant, M. G., and Landrum, A. R. (2011). Determining who to question, what to ask, and how much information to ask for: The development of inquiry in young children. *Journal of Experimental Child Psychology, 110,* 539–60. https://doi.org/10.1016/j.jecp.2011.06.003

Mosher, F., and Hornsby, J. (1966). On asking questions. In J. Bruner, R. Oliver, and P. Greenfield (eds.), *Studies in cognitive growth.* New York: Wiley.

National Research Council (2012). *A framework for K-12 science education: Practices, crosscutting concepts, and core ideas.* Washington, DC: The National Academies.

Nelson, J. D. (2005). Finding useful questions: On Bayesian diagnosticity, probability, impact, and information gain. *Psychological Review, 112,* 979–99. https://doi.org/10.1037/0033-295x.112.4.979

Nelson, J. D., McKenzie, C. R., Cottrell, G. W., and Sejnowski, T. J. (2010). Experience matters: Information acquisition optimizes probability gain. *Psychological Science, 21,* 960–9. https://doi.org/10.1177/0956797610372637

Nelson, J. D., Divjak, B., Gudmundsdottir, G., Martignon, L. F., and Meder, B. (2014). Children's sequential information search is sensitive to environmental probabilities. *Cognition, 130,* 74–80. https://doi.org/10.1016/j.cognition.2013.09.007

Noble, K. G., Norman, M. F., and Farah, M. J. (2005). Neurocognitive correlates of SES in kindergarten children. *Developmental Science, 8,* 78–87. https://doi.org/10.1111/j.1467-7687.2005.00394.x

Oaksford, M., and Chater, N. (1994). A rational analysis of the selection task as optimal data selection. *Psychological Review, 101,* 608–31. https://doi.org/10.1037/0033-295x.101.4.608

Piaget, J. (1954). Language and thought from a genetic perspective. *Acta Psychologica, 10,* 51–60.

Romine, C. B., and Reynolds, C. R. (2005). A model of the development of frontal lobe function: Findings from a meta-analysis. *Applied Neuropsychology, 12,* 190–201. https://doi.org/10.1207/s15324826an1204_2

Rowe, M. (2008). Child-directed speech: Relation to socioeconomic status, knowledge of child development and child vocabulary skill. *Journal of Child Language, 35,* 185–205. https://doi.org/10.1017/s0305000907008343

Ruggeri, A., and Feufel, M. (2015). How basic-level objects facilitate question-asking in a categorization task. *Frontiers in Psychology, 6,* 1–13. https://doi.org/10.3389/fpsyg.2015.00918

Ruggeri, A., and Lombrozo, T. (2015). Children adapt their questions to achieve efficient search. *Cognition, 143,* 203–16. https://doi.org/10.1016/j.cognition.2015.07.004

Ruggeri, A., Lombrozo, T., Griffiths, T. L., and Xu, F. (2016). Sources of developmental change in the efficiency of information search. *Developmental Psychology, 52,* 2159–73. https://doi.org/10.1037/dev0000240

Ruggeri, A., Sim, Z. L., and Xu, F. (2017). "Why is Toma late to school again?" Preschoolers identify the most informative questions. *Developmental Psychology, 53,* 1620–32. https://doi.org/10.1037/dev0000340

Ruggeri, A., Markant, D., Gureckis, T. D., and Xu, F. (2019a). Memory enhancements from active control of learning emerge across development. *Cognition, 186,* 82–94.

Ruggeri, A., Xu, F., and Lombrozo, T. (2019b). Effects of explanation on children's question asking. *Cognition, 191,* 103966.

Schneider, M., and Siegler, R. S. (2010) Representations of the magnitudes of fractions. *Journal of Experimental Psychology: Human Perception and Performance, 36,* 1227–38. https://doi.org/10.1037/a0018170

Schwichow, M., Croker, C., Zimmerman, C., Höffler, T., and Härtig., H. (2016). Teaching the control-of-variables strategy: A meta-analysis. *Developmental Review, 39,* 37–63. https://doi.org/10.1016/j.dr.2015.12.001

Siler, S. A., Klahr, D., and Price, N. (2012). Investigating the mechanisms of learning from a constrained preparation for future learning activity. *Instructional Science, 41,* 191–216. https://doi.org/10.1007/s11251-012-9224-7

Smith, J., Brooks-Gunn, J., and Klebanov, P. (1997). Consequences of living in poverty for young children's cognitive and verbal ability and early school achievement. In G. Duncan and J. Brooks-Gunn (eds.), *Consequences of growing up poor* (pp. 132–89). New York: Russell Sage.

Steyvers, M., Tenenbaum, J. B., Wagenmakers, E.-J., and Blum, B. (2003). Inferring causal networks from observations and interventions. *Cognitive Science, 27,* 453–89. https://doi.org/10.1207/s15516709cog2703_6

Sylva, K. (1994). School influences on children's development. *Journal of Child Psychology and Psychiatry, 35,* 135–70. https://doi.org/10.1111/j.1469–7610.1994.tb01135.x

Téglás, E., Girotto, V., Gonzalez, M., and Bonatti, L. L. (2007). Intuitions of probabilities shape expectations about the future at 12 months and beyond. *Proceedings of the National Academy of Sciences of the United States of America*, *104*, 19156–9. https://doi.org/10.1073/pnas.0700271104

Téglás, E., Vul, E., Girotto, V., et al. (2011). Pure reasoning in 12-month-old infants as probabilistic inference. *Science*, *332*, 1054–9. https://doi.org/10.1126/science.1196404

Todd, P. M., Gigerenzer, G., and the ABC Research Group (2012). *Ecological rationality: Intelligence in the world*. New York: Oxford University Press.

Walker, D., Greenwood, B., Hart, B., and Carta, J. (1994). Prediction of school outcomes based on early language production and socioeconomic factors. *Child Development*, *65*, 606–21. https://doi.org/10.2307/1131404

Wellman, H. M. (2011). Reinvigorating explanations for the study of early cognitive development. *Child Development Perspectives*, *5*, 33–8. https://doi.org/10.1111/j.1750–8606.2010.00154.x

Wierda, S. M., van Rijn, H., Taatgen, N. A., and Martens, S. (2012). Pupil dilation deconvolution reveals the dynamics of attention at high temporal resolution. *Proceedings of the National Academy of Sciences of the United States of America*, *109*, 8456–60. https://doi.org/10.1073/pnas.1201858109

Xu, F., and Denison, S. (2009). Statistical inference and sensitivity to sampling in 11-month-old infants. *Cognition*, *112*, 97–104. https://doi.org/10.1016/j.cognition.2009.04.006

Xu, F., and Garcia, V. (2008). Intuitive statistics by 8-month-old infants. *Proceedings of the National Academy of Sciences of the United States of America*, *105*, 5012–15. https://doi.org/10.1073/pnas.0704450105

# 8 Understanding Developmental and Individual Differences in the Process of Inquiry during the Preschool Years

*Candice M. Mills, Kaitlin R. Sands*

## Introduction

Children between the ages of three and five are notorious for asking questions. Anecdotally, parents express a mixture of delight, amusement, and exhaustion at the seemingly never-ending flood of questions from their preschoolers. Studies of naturalistic conversation support that at least in households of middle- to upper-socioeconomic status (SES) families, preschool-aged children ask questions at high rates. For instance, Chouinard (2007) found that preschool-aged children asked around seventy-six information-seeking questions per hour in conversations with adults, averaging out to be over one question a minute. And while some of these questions are posed simply to garner attention, in many cases, children are asking questions for the purpose of gathering information to expand their understanding of the world (e.g., Callanan & Oakes, 1992; Hickling & Wellman, 2001; Frazier et al., 2009).

The focus of this chapter is on breaking down this process of using questions to gather information from others (i.e., inquiry) into its subcomponents to better understand the circumstances under which preschool-aged children can and will ask questions to gather information from others. We see the process of inquiry involving at least four steps: determining when to engage in inquiry, deciding what to ask, selecting whom to question, and evaluating the information gathered to decide if inquiry should conclude or continue. In this chapter, we will briefly overview what we know about children's ability to succeed at each of these steps during the preschool years, followed by a discussion of possible reasons for individual differences. The chapter will conclude with open questions that we and others in the field should address in future work.

## Determining When to Engage in the Process of Inquiry

During the preschool years, we see a fascinating contradiction in children's interest in initiating the process of gathering information from others. On the one hand, preschoolers are notoriously inquisitive, asking many questions about how the world works (Chouinard, 2007). At times, they seem sensitive to what they know and do not know, being more likely to seek help for a problem that they do not know how to solve than a problem that they have seen solved before (Was & Warneken, 2017). On the other hand, preschoolers are notoriously overconfident in their knowledge and abilities. This confidence seems to lead them to feel that there is no need to ask a question because they already know something. For instance, in several studies, although preschool-aged children recognized which of a few sources was most likely to be able to provide accurate answers to some questions (e.g., where something was hidden, a challenging question requiring expertise), they would frequently attempt to guess the answer on their own instead of directing questions to the most helpful source (Robinson et al., 2011; Aguiar et al., 2012).

So what makes children feel inclined to look outside of themselves for answers to their questions? One major factor in this decision is likely to be the degree to which children feel like there is a gap in their knowledge. It can be challenging for young children to reflect on their knowledge and detect that something is missing. Indeed, children can struggle to evaluate how complete their knowledge is about a topic (Mills & Keil, 2004), particularly before the age of five or six (Taylor et al., 1994). They also sometimes conclude that if they are given possible answers to a question, they can figure out the correct answer themselves. For instance, preschool-aged children are far more likely to attempt to answer forced-choice questions and yes/no questions on their own than to answer open-ended questions about the same topics, even if there is no way they could regularly, correctly guess the right answer due to the difficulty of the questions (e.g., Waterman et al., 2001; Aguiar et al., 2012). Providing options for answering questions may give young children the sensation that they are close to the right answer, which makes it harder for them to recognize that they might not know enough to take an educated guess (for more information and other possible explanations, see Waterman et al., 2001; Aguiar et al., 2012). Thus, this research supports that young children can find it challenging to detect when their knowledge is incomplete enough that help from others would be useful.

Even if children do recognize that they have a gap in their knowledge or a question that they cannot address on their own, they have to decide whether the benefits of attempting to gather the information outweigh the costs of doing so. In some cases, a child may be driven by something called the *deprivation theory of curiosity* (or the information-gap theory of curiosity; see Jirout & Klahr, 2012; Golman & Loewenstein, 2016): the child may feel deprived by large gaps in knowledge and thus feel compelled to gather more information. In doing so, the child can reduce the feelings of deprivation, and may feel satisfaction in getting more information (or at least release from the stress of deprivation). In other cases, a child may be driven by *expected information gain*: the child may feel like there is so much to know compared to his or her initial knowledge that it seems worthwhile to engage in inquiry (e.g., Ruggeri & Lombrozo, 2015). Regardless of whether children are driven by the desire to minimize deprivation, the desire to maximize information gained, or something else, they still have to decide if that drive is high enough to override the costs involved with the various aspects of the inquiry process, like deciding whom to question or figuring out what to ask. In some cases, the process of gathering information may seem so overwhelming that children decide not to bother (see Golman & Loewenstein, 2016). In other cases, though, they initiate inquiry.

### Deciding What to Ask

Once children have decided they want to gather information from others, they need to signal to others that they need to know something and would like a response. Elsewhere in this book, research with infants and toddlers is discussed, finding that even before children are heavily verbal, they can use a gesture or a way of looking to demonstrate an interest in seeking information (see Chapters 3 and 6). During the preschool years as children become more verbal, they sometimes make a statement accompanied with a quizzical look or intonation instead of explicitly asking a question when they have something they are trying to understand (Frazier et al., 2009). These approaches are useful first steps in helping children acquire knowledge related to topics of interest. That said, in most cases, questions articulated with language allow far more precision in information gathering.

The actual ability to verbalize questions tends to develop during the second year of life, when children start to ask questions like "What's that?" By age three, children usually have integrated a number of other question words into their vocabulary, using words like "where," "when," "how," and of course "why" as a part of verbal exchanges to gather information (Tyack & Ingram, 1977; Bloom et al., 1982). Preschoolers use their questions as tools to achieve different kinds of goals, such as getting attention, continuing an interaction, or gathering specific information (Callanan & Oakes, 1992; Chouinard, 2007).

Once children are able to verbally articulate questions, they show some ability to craft different kinds of questions for different kinds of problems. For instance, in one set of studies, preschool-aged children were given opportunities to ask questions about unusual artifacts and/or unusual animals (Greif et al., 2006). Children asked different questions for artifacts (i.e., more focus on function) compared to animals (i.e., more focus on category membership and food preferences). In another set of studies, preschool-aged children were able to use questions to help them determine which of two objects was hidden inside a box (Chouinard, 2007). Thus, at least to some extent, during the preschool years, children can use questions to gather different kinds of information.

But children's ability to ask the right *kind* of questions has received far less attention. Although preschool-aged children can often articulate questions, they do not always generate effective questions: questions that are clearly on-topic and worded in a way to gather the desired information. For instance, in a set of studies conducted in our lab, we examined how preschool-aged children used questions as a tool to solve a specific problem. In most of these studies, children saw cards with images on them varying in shape and color and had to determine which card of a set of options (e.g., a blue dog, a red dog, a blue car, a red car) was hidden inside a box. Then they were given the opportunity to ask questions to one or two informants in order to solve the problem. This paradigm – similar in some ways to the classic game of "20 questions" – allowed us to measure a number of different aspects of the problem-solving process, including the characteristics of children's questions and children's overall accuracy. In general, we found stark developmental improvements in the ability to articulate effective questions between the ages of three and five (Mills et al., 2010; Mills et al., 2011). Three-year-olds knew that they needed to ask questions to figure out what was inside the box, but they frequently asked questions either irrelevant to the problem (e.g., "Is your father a firefighter?") or ineffective at narrowing down the problem space (e.g., "Is the card green?" when all four options were green). Four-year-olds tended to ask a greater proportion of effective questions than three-year-olds, and five-year-olds tended to ask more than both of the younger groups of children (Mills et al., 2010). That said, although we saw developmental improvements, children were not at ceiling in this task: for instance, four-year-olds asked roughly the same proportion of ineffective questions as effective ones.

Crucially, we have found that with enough scaffolding, preschool-aged children *can* generate questions that are primarily effective. In one study

(Mills & Landrum, 2016), children participated in several warm-up tasks before beginning a 20-questions paradigm to determine which of four cards was inside a box. The tasks were designed to help children feel comfortable asking questions (e.g., helping a shy sheep puppet ask questions to his friend) and to help children understand how pictures on cards can vary on different dimensions (i.e., both shape and color). Subsequently, the vast majority of the questions asked by four- and five-year-olds in this study were effectively worded. However, it is important to note that even if children ask effectively-worded questions, they may not ask *enough* effectively-worded questions to narrow down the problem space to one possible right answer (e.g., for a blue dog, red dog, blue car, red car, they might only ask about color and then guess from there) or to clearly understand a mechanism; this is an issue we will return to in the section of this chapter on how children determine when to conclude inquiry.

We speculate that when preschool-aged children are introduced to new kinds of problems to solve, modeling how to ask good questions for that particular kind of problem may help children feel both more comfortable asking questions and more aware of the problem space. As children get older, the amount of scaffolding needed likely depends on a number of factors, including the kind of problem and the context in which they are asking questions (e.g., with familiar caregivers at home versus with unfamiliar adults at summer camp).

The aforementioned studies in our lab focused on presenting children with constrained situations such that children felt inclined to ask questions. But another approach is to give children constrained situations *and* specific options for questions, and the children themselves have to decide which questions would be most helpful. In one such line of work (Ruggeri et al., 2017; see Chapter 7), preschool-aged children were asked to figure out why a monster named Toma was late for school. Children were presented with background data regarding why Toma was late for school in the last six to eight days to give them a sense of how likely different explanations were (e.g., being late because of something the monster could not find versus being late because of waking up late). Children then heard two monster friends each ask a question to help them determine why Toma was late (e.g., "Was Toma late because he could not find something?") and were asked to decide which friend would find out first why Toma was late that day. Five-year-olds performed at better than chance levels at selecting the most informative question based on the past explanations for why Toma was late, regardless of the characteristics of those questions (e.g., whether a question tested one specific hypothesis or strategically narrowed down the problem set to a more manageable number). Three- and four-year-olds were less successful, although *some* of these children were able to do so. We interpret this data as supporting the conclusion that preschool-aged children can sometimes articulate effective questions as well as recognize that some questions are more effective than others. Whether they will do so in a given situation, though, may depend on a number of factors, which we explore later in this chapter.

### Selecting Whom to Ask

In some cases, a question may be general enough that any adult (and perhaps any older child) could answer it accurately. In other cases, though, a child may have a specialized question regarding some kind of expertise (e.g., how to fix a broken toy) or a personal question that only a trusted confidant can answer (e.g., how to handle having made the mistake of taking a toy from the store without paying for it). Therefore, another part of the process of inquiry is to determine which source can provide accurate, trustworthy answers to one's questions.

A significant body of literature has examined young children's ability to distinguish between good and less good sources of information (also known as "selective trust"). These studies tend to provide children with one or two informants (e.g., puppets, actors on a video, confederates), give children some background about those informants, and examine whom children select as being most likely to provide a helpful response in the future (e.g., answering a question, naming an object, showing how to use a tool). In these studies, the focus is primarily on how much children understand about the characteristics needed to be a trustworthy source of information, and thus children rarely ask questions themselves. Given that the focus of this book is on questions, not selective trust, a full review of this hefty body of literature is outside of the scope of this chapter (see Mills, 2013; Sobel & Kushnir, 2013; Robinson & Einav, 2014; Harris et al., 2018). That said, we do want to highlight a few findings here.

The first is that there are developmental improvements between the ages of three and five in what children understand about the characteristics important for being a reliable source of information. Three-year-olds can sometimes recognize that someone who was accurate in the past is more likely to be a good source of information in the future, but older preschoolers are much better at this, as well as at focusing on reliability as opposed to other factors when deciding whom to trust (e.g., Mills et al., 2010). The second is that there are also developmental improvements in recognizing that different people know different things even during the preschool years, with four- and five-year-olds having a better sense of the scope of the knowledge of familiar experts, adults, and children than three-year-olds (e.g., Lutz & Keil, 2002; VanderBorght & Jaswal, 2008; Sobel & Corriveau, 2010).

Although even young preschoolers recognize that different people know different things, there is a lot that we do not know about the precision of that understanding and how it affects actual questioning behavior. The above findings regarding children's ability to distinguish between sources sometimes suggest that older preschoolers are rather sophisticated at evaluating sources of information. But it is likely that when children are in the midst of engaging in their own line of inquiry, their ability to select the best sources of information may be more variable.

One reason for this prediction is that in most of the studies examining children's ability to distinguish between sources, children are assigning experimenter-created questions to sources instead of generating questions on their own. The task of determining whether or not a source is likely to be helpful and accurate while also engaging in the task of trying to figure out how to gather information from that source may be cognitively taxing to young children. Our lab has examined this issue by conducting research in which preschool-aged children faced problem-solving tasks and had to direct questions to sources varying in characteristics in order to solve their problems. All used the 20-questions study paradigm described earlier for which children had to determine which of a set of two or four pictures was hidden inside of a box. In one study, children were introduced to two experts who could help them solve their problems: one expert who knew all about the color of the card inside the box, and one expert who knew all about the shape of the card inside the box. In order to accurately solve some of the problems, children had to direct questions to both the color expert and the shape expert to narrow down the options to one possible solution. Three-year-olds had difficulty directing questions to correct experts, seeming to think any expert could answer their questions. Four- and five-year-olds were much better at this task, although still nowhere near perfect performance (Mills et al., 2010).

In another set of studies, preschoolers were presented with two possible sources similar to a traditional selective trust paradigm. During a training phase, one informant demonstrated a history of accurately answering questions, while another informant demonstrated either inaccuracy or ignorance. During the test phase, four- and five-year-olds were given the opportunity to question whoever they wanted to solve the problems. In initial studies, five-year-olds were better than four-year-olds at directing the majority of their questions to the more accurate source, although some children – even five-year-olds – did not clearly distinguish between the sources (Mills et al., 2011). With a longer training phase for children to learn how the two informants typically answer questions, four- and five-year-olds performed much better (Mills & Landrum, 2016). These findings support that questioning appropriate sources can be challenging for young children, but experience with possible sources for a particular problem can help children more successfully direct their questions to more reliable sources.

Another reason for why children's ability to direct questions to appropriate experts may be overestimated in past research is that experiments have tended to give children two contrasting sources that they can access immediately. In real life, determining whom to question is more complicated. In some cases, real-life questioning behavior is affected by weighing the costs and benefits of gathering information. For example, a child might have a lingering question to ask a teacher, but the teacher might be busy helping another student and only another child is nearby ready to talk. In moments like these, children must consider whether it is worthwhile to ask their question to the nearby child who also appears to be confused, wait until a better source is available, or just not bother with asking the question. Research suggests that when preschoolers encounter costs, such as having to wait to gather information from others, they are often deterred by these costs and choose to settle for less accurate information (Brosseau-Liard, 2014; Rowles & Mills, 2019). More research is needed to understand the circumstances in which children will care enough about gathering information that they will find someone knowledgeable to ask, regardless of how much effort it takes.

In reflecting on the factors that influence to whom children direct their questions, it is important to be mindful that when children are asking questions of others in everyday life, they may sometimes be more motivated to build relationships with others rather than to gather accurate information (though sometimes their goal includes both activities; e.g., Jaswal & Kondrad, 2016). Recent research with preschool-aged children has demonstrated that they can be pulled in multiple directions when seeking information from others. Four- and five-year-old children were given a puzzle box to solve and two informants were available to offer help in solving the puzzle box. One informant was socially engaged but not competent at using the puzzle box while the other informant was not socially engaged but knew how to solve the puzzle. Across two studies, despite explicitly recognizing which informant had been more competent and which had been more socially engaged, preschool-aged children did not show a consistent preference seeking help from one informant over the other; if anything, on average, children leaned towards requesting information from the socially engaged source over the more competent one (Rowles & Mills, 2018). Our speculation is that children were more comfortable interacting with the socially engaged source, making them more focused on social goals (e.g., interacting with someone pleasant) rather than epistemic ones (i.e., efficiently answering the paradigm's questions). These findings support that the process of determining to whom to direct one's questions is not driven purely by a drive for obtaining the most accurate information. That said, it is important to note that it is currently an open question what children understand about the multiple purposes of question-asking (e.g., epistemic, affiliative).

### Evaluating the Information Gathered to Decide if Inquiry Should Conclude or Continue

Once children have directed questions to a source, they then have to make sense of the source's response. How do children decide when the answers to their questions are "good enough," and what they should do next? The process of learning from others is often quite iterative, but we know surprisingly little about how preschool-aged children respond to the explanations they receive. Explanations can vary on a number of dimensions, including relevance, internal coherence, circularity, accuracy, and depth (Keil, 2006; Danovitch & Mills, 2018). Indeed, naturalistic observations and parent report data demonstrate that although parents do sometimes provide explanations that are relevant, clear responses to their children's questions, their responses vary drastically in their characteristics (e.g., Callanan & Oakes, 1992; Chouinard, 2007; Frazier et al., 2009; Kurkul & Corriveau, 2017). Very little research has examined how children respond to different characteristics of explanations, particularly during the preschool years. From the evidence that does exist, though, it appears that preschool-aged children at least prefer explanations that are relevant to their questions. For instance, when preschool-aged children have questions about bizarre phenomena (e.g., someone putting ketchup on ice cream; "Why did she do that?"), they are more likely to reask their original question in response to answers that are not relevant to their questions (e.g., "That looks like vanilla ice cream") than to answers that are explanations (e.g., "She thought it was chocolate syrup"; Frazier et al., 2009). Similarly, preschoolers are more likely to ask a follow-up question when their original question about an unfamiliar artifact receives a response that refers to just a name for the artifact instead of a response that explains what the object does or how it is used (Kemler Nelson et al., 2004).

Beyond this, there is a great deal unknown about how children evaluate the quality of the explanations they encounter. For instance, although there is some evidence that preschool-aged children notice when explanations are circular (Corriveau & Kurkul, 2014), they sometimes do not, and even elementary school-aged children can struggle to detect circular explanations when they are about unfamiliar topics (Mills et al., 2017). In addition, preschool-aged children have been found to have trouble recognizing that explanations that provide mechanisms in response to questions about biological processes are better than those that do not, while six-year-olds, on average, do not (Sands & Mills, 2017). In other words, there appears to be significant development during early childhood in how children evaluate explanations.

Another issue is that even explanations that are on-topic and relevant may not sufficiently answer a question, and little is known about what makes an explanation seem "sufficient" to a child. But we suspect that in many cases, children are satisfied with on-topic responses that give them some additional information, even if those responses lack depth or complete information. For example, preschoolers sometimes stop the process of inquiry once they have received one answer even if they have not gathered sufficient information to solve the problem with certainty (Mills et al., 2011), and they sometimes appear to accept both short and detailed on-topic explanations equally, even if the more detailed explanations could be seen as more complete (Frazier et al., 2016).

At some level, this should not be surprising. Even during adulthood, people are often satisfied with a basic, big picture understanding of many different phenomena, from how a helicopter flies to how kidneys filter blood (Keil, 2006). Moreover, they often do not recognize weaknesses in their knowledge unless they are asked diagnostic questions or are faced with other situations that make them realize that even though they know *something* they do not know *enough* (Rozenblit & Keil, 2002). With young children still developing the ability to reflect on their own knowledge and thinking, it is likely that once they are given some information that is relevant to a gap in their knowledge, they often feel satisfied and confident that they know the rest. These ideas connect back to the first step of the inquiry process: deciding when to initiate inquiry. Just as children may decide not to engage in inquiry because their initial knowledge seems complete enough, children may also decide to discontinue inquiry after receiving a small amount of information if, again, they feel like their knowledge is satisfactory. Examining the circumstances for which children can detect that there is more left to know and choose to pursue that understanding is an important issue for future research.

## Understanding Individual Differences

Although children appear to improve drastically in their inquiry skills during the preschool years, it is important to be mindful that there appear to be significant individual differences as well. In fact, evidence supports that there is great variability even within the preschool years at each step of the inquiry process: how frequently children ask questions (e.g., Chouinard, 2007), what kinds of questions children ask (e.g., Mills et al., 2011), how children approach different sources of information (e.g., Jaswal et al., 2014), and how children respond to explanations varying in quality (e.g., Frazier et al., 2009). A number of different factors are likely to contribute to individual differences in inquiry.

### Social Cognition

Social cognitive skills are likely to influence success at any step that involves thinking about knowledge states in the self or in others. For instance, social cognitive skills may help a child determine whether it makes sense to seek out information from someone else or go with the child's own knowledge based on what each source is likely to know. There is some evidence to support this: in one study, three- to five-year-olds with greater theory of mind skills were more likely to seek help on a challenging line drawing interpretation problem than children with lower theory of mind skills (Coughlin et al., 2015).

Children with better social cognitive skills may also be better at recognizing who might be the best source to answer their questions. For example, false belief performance correlated with greater accuracy at identifying which of two informants was likely to give accurate information based on informant history (e.g., DiYanni et al., 2012; Lucas et al., 2013; see also Brosseau-Liard et al., 2015). Thus, preschoolers' understanding that other people have different thoughts and beliefs likely informs their ability to make inferences about another person's knowledge states and suitability to answer preschoolers' questions.

### Language

Language skills vary tremendously during the preschool years, and so it is likely that both receptive and expressive language play roles in how children approach inquiry. For instance, children with greater vocabularies and more comfort producing "how-" and "why-questions" are likely to be more effective at information gathering (Mills et al., 2015). Children with stronger receptive language skills are also likely to be better at evaluating the explanations they receive, and indeed, there is evidence to support this, at least during the elementary school years (Mills et al., 2017). We suspect that this is true during the preschool years as well, but this is an avenue for future research.

### Executive Function

Executive function skills may relate to success at several different parts of the inquiry process. When it comes to deciding what to ask, a big part of being able to articulate an effective question relates to the ability to understand what the problem actually is. If a problem is really complex, having greater executive functioning skills may contribute to success at understanding the problem and thus at coming up with appropriate questions for that particular problem. And indeed, there is some evidence to support that this is the case. In one study using a 20-questions-type format, four- through six-year-olds had to ask questions to determine which of a large array of cards was hidden in a box. Children who performed better on a cognitive flexibility task were more likely to ask more effective questions and more likely to narrow down the possibilities to the correct answer (Legare et al., 2013).

When it comes to making sense of different possible sources of information, children with greater inhibitory control skills may be better at resisting the urge to accept all sources of information as accurate and trustworthy. Indeed, 2.5–3.5-year-olds with better inhibitory control skills are better at resisting someone's misleading claims than children with lower skills (Jaswal et al., 2014). In addition, preschool-aged children with better inhibitory control skills are more willing to wait to gather information from an appropriate expert instead of accepting information from a less optimal one (Rowles & Mills, 2019).

We also suspect that executive function skills could influence both initiation and cessation of inquiry. The ability to inhibit one's belief that he or she already knows something might relate to the interest in initiating the process of gathering information from others (although this process may be complicated; see Coughlin et al., 2015). Working memory skills might make it easier to recognize that there is a contradiction in what someone is saying, which might indicate that there is something that could be clarified with a question. Additional research is needed to better understand the relationship between different components of executive function skills and different components of inquiry.

*Domain-Specific Interest and Knowledge*

Children can vary drastically in their knowledge and their interest for specific domains, and we speculate that both of these factors can influence how children approach inquiry. When it comes to making the decision to engage in inquiry, in cases when children are really interested in a topic (e.g., dinosaurs), they may be far more likely to carefully monitor what they know or do not know and pursue gaps in their knowledge so that they feel satisfied with what they know. In other words, domain-specific interest likely influences decisions about whether to engage in inquiry and how far to take it (but see Jirout & Klahr, 2012, on the idea of individual differences in domain-*general* interest in gathering information).

Domain-specific knowledge may be important in how children generate questions. Having greater amounts of background knowledge can mean that someone needs to ask fewer questions to feel satisfied with one's learning compared to someone who knows nearly nothing (e.g., Miyake & Norman, 1979). But it can also mean that when a child does have questions, the quality of the questions is likely to be more sophisticated because the child has a better sense of what to ask. For example, in one study, children with higher levels of background knowledge about ecology asked higher-level questions about ecology than children with lower levels of background knowledge (Taboada & Guthrie, 2006). In another, children asked more sophisticated questions for domains for which they were likely to have strong background knowledge than for less familiar domains (Ruggeri & Feufel, 2015).

Domain-specific knowledge also likely helps with other aspects of inquiry. For instance, having greater knowledge in a certain domain may make it easier to understand what different people are likely to know about that domain, which may be helpful for selecting the best source for a question (e.g., Lutz & Keil, 2002; Landrum & Mills, 2015). Domain-specific knowledge may also help children better understand the explanations that they receive related to that domain (Sands & Mills, 2017). Thus, we think it is important for future research examining children's question-asking skills to assess both interest and background knowledge for that particular domain, when relevant and possible.

*Caregiver Input*

Inquiry by its very nature requires gathering information from others, and there is evidence to support that there is great variation in inquiry both between and within families. For instance, mid-SES caregivers have been found to be more likely than low-SES caregivers to provide explanations and not non-explanations in response to children's questions (Kurkul & Corriveau, 2017). Caregivers also respond differently to questions depending on the setting (e.g., Jipson et al., 2018) and family stress levels (e.g., Thompson et al., 2016).

It is quite possible that children are affected by the input they receive from their caregivers such that the kinds of responses children get when they ask questions influences the way they approach asking questions in the future. There is some evidence to support this possibility: for instance, mid-SES children, who tend to receive explanations from their caregivers frequently, have been found to ask questions more frequently than low-SES children (Tizard & Hughes, 1984; Kurkul & Corriveau, 2017). Children from mid-SES families are also much more likely to provide their *own* explanations after hearing an inadequate explanation from a caregiver than children from low-SES families (Kurkul & Corriveau, 2018). But much more research is needed to better understand the relationship between caregiver input and how children approach inquiry (see Chapter 11).

*Culture*

Research examining question-asking across different cultures has found that although preschool-aged children in non-Western societies do sometimes ask information-seeking questions, very few of those questions appear to be requests for explanations (Gauvain et al., 2013; see Chapter 10). There are many possible reasons for cross-cultural differences that do not have to do with children's ability to articulate a question. For instance, researchers have speculated that children in non-Western countries do not ask as many why-questions to their parents because such questions are viewed more as a challenge to adult authority and thus are not as valued as other types of questions (Gauvain et al., 2013). So, although children across cultures are capable of asking questions from a young age, they may not be as inclined to do so.

It is also important to note that even if there are cultural and individual differences in how parents approach their children's questions, we need to be careful about concluding that one particular approach is universally better for long-term outcomes than another. Engaging in inquiry is an important way for children to gather information in some circumstances, like when learning about a new animal or witnessing an event that is hard to understand without clarification from someone else. But there are plenty of other ways for children to learn, like through direct instruction, modeling, and overhearing. The strategies that children use to learn about the world around them can and should depend on the context (see Ronfard et al., 2018). Additional research is needed to better understand both the characteristics of cultural differences in inquiry as well as the consequences of those differences (see Chapters 5 and 10).

## Conclusions

All of these steps – determining when to engage in inquiry, deciding what to ask, selecting whom to question, and evaluating the information gathered to decide if inquiry should conclude or continue – are important in inquiry. Moreover, all of the steps can be challenging on their own; together, sometimes the cognitive load may be straining and may make children feel too intimidated to move forward. And yet if a child decides to accept information from any source, to craft a vague question, to accept an unclear response, or of course to not initiate the process of inquiry to begin with, the child may not advance forward in knowledge. Understanding how to promote successful inquiry is an important issue for future research.

If encouraging inquiry during this age range is important in some circumstances, how do we do so, particularly given that young children can be so overconfident in what they know or believe? To address this question, it is worthwhile to reflect on the cost-benefit analysis that children likely undertake when determining whether or not to engage in inquiry; to increase rates of effective inquiry, the costs need to decrease and/or the benefits need to increase. Decreasing the costs might involve doing things like helping children feel more comfortable asking questions to a particular source (i.e., the person appears interested in addressing the questions, and children understand a problem space well enough to be able to recognize what they know and what they do not know). Increasing the benefits might occasionally involve extrinsic rewards; after all, some studies have found that children are more likely to assign questions to appropriate experts when the benefits of accuracy are higher (e.g., a tangible reward for accuracy, like a sticker) rather than when they are lower (e.g., no reward; Aguiar et al., 2012). But in other cases, making inquiry seem beneficial may involve making a gap in knowledge seem fascinating and utterly important to understand.

Overall, we believe that inquiry often has great value. In most cases, children cannot learn everything that they need to know about the world purely from observation, and so it is crucial for them to develop the skills needed to effectively gather information from other sources. Some of these skills will likely develop as children do, given that certain domain-general skills like intelligence, executive function skills, theory of mind, and working memory capacity develop with age and seem to relate to children's success on different parts of the inquiry process. But we should also be mindful that input from others – both in terms of how we relay the value of question-asking and how we model the process of engaging in inquiry – is likely to shape how children themselves approach inquiry.

## References

Aguiar, N. R., Stoess, C. J., and Taylor, M. (2012). The development of children's ability to fill the gaps in their knowledge by consulting experts. *Child Development, 83*, 1368–81. https://doi:10.1111/j.1467-8624 .2012.01782.

Bloom, L., Merkin, S., and Wootten, J. (1982). "Wh"-questions: Linguistic factors that contribute to the sequence of acquisition. *Child Development, 53*, 1084–92. https://doi:10.2307/1129150.

Brosseau-Liard, P. E. (2014). Selective, but only if it is free: Children trust inaccurate individuals more when alternative sources are costly. *Infant and Child Development, 23*, 194–209. https://doi:10.1002/icd.1828.

Brosseau-Liard, P., Penney, D., and Poulin-Dubois, D. (2015). Theory of mind selectively predicts preschoolers' knowledge-based selective word learning. *British Journal of Developmental Psychology, 33*, 464–75. https://doi:10.1111 /bjdp.12107.

Callanan, M. A., and Oakes, L. M. (1992). Preschoolers' questions and parents' explanations: Causal thinking in everyday activity. *Cognitive Development, 7*, 213–33. https://doi:10.1016/0885-2014(92)90012-G.

Chouinard, M. M. (2007). Children's questions: A mechanism for cognitive development: IV. Children's questions about animals. *Monographs of the Society for Research in Child Development, 72*, 58–82. https://doi:10.1111/ j.1540-5834.2007.00416.

Corriveau, K. H., and Kurkul, K. E. (2014). "Why does rain fall?": Children prefer to learn from an informant who uses noncircular explanations. *Child Development, 85*, 1827–35. https://doi:10.1111/cdev.12240.

Coughlin, C., Hembacher, E., Lyons, K. E., and Ghetti, S. (2015). Introspection on uncertainty and judicious help-seeking during the preschool years. *Developmental Science, 18*, 957–71. https://doi:10.1111/desc.12271.

Danovitch, J. H., and Mills, C. M. (2018). Understanding when and how explanation promotes exploration. In M. Saylor and P. Ganea (eds.), *Active learning from infancy to childhood: Social motivation, cognition, and linguistic mechanisms* (pp. 95–112). Cham, Switzerland: Springer International.

DiYanni, C., Nini, D., Rheel, W., and Livelli, A. (2012). "I won't trust you if I think you're trying to deceive me": Relations between selective trust, theory of mind, and imitation in early childhood. *Journal of Cognition and Development, 13*, 354–71. https://doi:10.1080/15248372.2011.590462.

Frazier, B. N., Gelman, S. A., and Wellman, H. M. (2009). Preschoolers' search for explanatory information within adult–child conversation. *Child Development, 80*, 1592–611. https://doi:10.1111/j.1467-8624.2009.01356.

Frazier, B. N., Gelman, S. A., and Wellman, H. M. (2016). Young children prefer and remember satisfying explanations. *Journal of Cognition and Development*, *17*, 718–36. https://doi:10.1080/15248372.2015.1098649.

Gauvain, M., Munroe, R. L., and Beebe, H. (2013). Children's questions in cross-cultural perspective: A four-culture study. *Journal of Cross-Cultural Psychology*, *44*, 1148–65. https://doi:10.1177/0022022113485430.

Golman, R., and Loewenstein, G. (2016). Information gaps: A theory of preferences regarding the presence and absence of information. *Decision*, *5*, 143–64. https://doi:10.1037/dec0000068.

Greif, M. L., Kemler Nelson, D. G., Keil, F. C., and Gutierrez, F. (2006). What do children want to know about animals and artifacts? Domain-specific requests for information. *Psychological Science*, *17*, 455–59. https://doi:10.1111/j.1467-9280.2006.01727.

Harris, P. L., Koenig, M. A., Corriveau, K. H., and Jaswal, V. K. (2018). Cognitive foundations of learning from testimony. *Annual Review of Psychology*, *69*, 251–73. https://doi:10.1146/annurev-psych-122216-011710.

Hickling, A. K., and Wellman, H. M. (2001). The emergence of children's causal explanations and theories: Evidence from everyday conversation. *Developmental Psychology*, *37*, 668–83. https://doi:10.1037/0012-1649.37.5.668.

Jaswal, V. K., and Kondrad, R. L. (2016). Why children are not always epistemically vigilant: Cognitive limits and social considerations. *Child Development Perspectives*, *10*, 240–44. https://doi:10.1111/cdep.12187.

Jaswal, V. K., Pérez-Edgar, K., Kondrad, R. L., et al. (2014). Can't stop believing: Inhibitory control and resistance to misleading testimony. *Developmental Science*, *17*, 965–76. https://doi:10.1111/desc.12187.

Jipson, J. L., Labotka, D., Callahan, M. A., and Gelman, S. A. (2018). How conversations with parents may help children learn to separate the sheep from the goats (and the robots). In M. M. Saylor and P. Ganea (eds.), *Active learning from infancy to childhood: Social motivation, cognition, and linguistic mechanisms* (pp. 189–212). Cham, Switzerland: Springer International.

Jirout, J., and Klahr, D. (2012). Children's scientific curiosity: In search of an operational definition of an elusive concept. *Developmental Review*, *32*, 125–60. https://doi:10.1016/j.dr.2012.04.002.

Keil, F. C. (2006). Explanation and understanding. *Annual Review of Psychology*, *57*, 227–54. https://doi:10.1146/annurev.psych.57.102904.190100.

Kemler Nelson, D. G., Egan, L. C., and Holt, M. B. (2004). When children ask, "What is it?" what do they want to know about artifacts? *Psychological Science*, *15*, 384–9. https://doi:10.1111/j.0956-7976.2004.00689.

Kurkul, K. E., and Corriveau, K. H. (2017). The uncontrollable nature of early learning experiences. *Behavioral and Brain Sciences*, *40*, e331. https://doi:10.1017/S0140525X17001017.

    (2018). Question, explanation, follow-up: A mechanism for learning from others? *Child Development*, *89*, 280–294. https://doi:10.1111/cdev.12726.

Landrum, A. R., and Mills, C. M. (2015). Developing expectations regarding the boundaries of expertise. *Cognition*, *134*, 215–31. https://doi:10.1016/j.cognition.2014.10.013.

Legare, C. H., Mills, C. M., Souza, A. L., Plummer, L. E., and Yasskin, R. (2013). The use of questions as problem-solving strategies during early childhood. *Journal of Experimental Child Psychology*, *114*, 63–76. https://do i:10.1016/j.jecp.2012.07.002.

Lucas, A., Lewis, C., Pala, F., Wong, K., and Berridge, D. (2013). Social-cognitive processes in preschoolers' selective trust: Three cultures compared. *Developmental Psychology*, *49*, 579–90. https://doi:10.1037/a0029864.

Lutz, D. J., and Keil, F. C. (2002). Early understanding of the division of cognitive labor. *Child Development*, *73*, 1073–84. https://doi:10.1111/1467-8624.00458.

Mills, C. M. (2013). Knowing when to doubt: Developing a critical stance when learning from others. *Developmental Psychology*, *49*, 404–18. https://doi:10 .1037/a0029500.

Mills, C. M., and Keil, F. C. (2004). Knowing the limits of one's understanding: The development of an awareness of an illusion of explanatory depth. *Journal of Experimental Child Psychology*, *87*, 1–32. https://doi.org/10.1016/j .jecp.2003.09.003

Mills, C. M., and Landrum, A. R. (2016). Learning who knows what: Children adjust their inquiry to gather information from others. *Frontiers in Psychology*, *7*, 1–12. https://doi:10.3389/fpsyg.2016.00951.

Mills, C. M., Legare, C. H., Bills, M., and Mejias, C. (2010). Preschoolers use questions as a tool to acquire knowledge from different sources. *Journal of Cognition and Development*, *11*, 533–60. https://doi:10.1080/15248372 .2010.516419.

Mills, C. M., Legare, C. H., Grant, M. G., and Landrum, A. R. (2011). Determining who to question, what to ask, and how much information to ask for: The development of inquiry in young children. *Journal of Experimental Child Psychology*, *110*, 539–60. https://doi:10.1016/j.jecp.2011.06.003.

Mills, C. M., Landrum, A. R., Campbell, I. L., and Rowles, S. P. (2015). Learning who knows what: Children adjust their inquiry to gather information from others. Poster presented at the 2015 meeting of the Cognitive Development Society, Columbus, Ohio.

Mills, C. M., Danovitch, J. H., Rowles, S. P., and Campbell, I. L. (2017). Children's success at detecting circular explanations and their interest in future learning. *Psychonomic Bulletin & Review*, *24*, 1465–77. https://doi:10 .3758/s13423-016-1195-2.

Miyake, N., and Norman, D. A. (1979). To ask a question, one must know enough to know what is not known. *Journal of Verbal Learning and Verbal Behavior*, *18*, 357–64. https://doi:10.1016/S0022-5371(79)90200-7.

Robinson, E. J., and Einav, S. (eds.). (2014). *Trust and skepticism: Children's selective learning from testimony*. New York: Psychology Press.

Robinson, E. J., Butterfill, S. A., and Nurmsoo, E. (2011). Gaining knowledge via other minds: Children's flexible trust in others as sources of information. *British Journal of Developmental Psychology*, *29*, 961–980. https://doi:10.1111 /j.2044-835X.2011.02036.x.

Ronfard, S., Zambrana, I. S., Hermansen, T. K., and Kelemen, D. (2018). Question-asking in childhood: A review of the literature and a framework for understanding its development. *Developmental Review, 49*, 101–20. https://doi:10.1016/j.dr.2018.05.002.

Rowles, S. P., and Mills, C. M. (2019). "Is it worth my time and effort?": How children selectively gather information from experts when faced with different kinds of costs. *Journal of Experimental Child Psychology, 179*, 308–323. doi: 10.1016/j.jecp.2018.11.016

Rowles, S. P., and Mills, C. M. (2018). Preschoolers sometimes seek help from socially engaged informants over competent ones. *Cognitive Development, 48*, 19–31. https://doi.org/10.1016/j.cogdev.2018.06.006

Rozenblit, L., and Keil, F. (2002). The misunderstood limits of folk science: an illusion of explanatory depth. *Cognitive Science, 26*, 521–62. https://doi:10.1207/s15516709cog2605_1.

Ruggeri, A., and Feufel, M. A. (2015). How basic-level objects facilitate question-asking in a categorization task. *Frontiers in Psychology, 6*. https://doi.org/10.3389/fpsyg.2015.00918

Ruggeri, A., and Lombrozo, T. (2015). Children adapt their questions to achieve efficient search. *Cognition, 143*, 203–16. https://doi:10.1016/j.cognition.2015.07.004.

Ruggeri, A., Sim, Z. L., and Xu, F. (2017). "Why is Toma late to school again?" Preschoolers identify the most informative questions. *Developmental Psychology, 53*, 1620–32. https://doi:10.1037/dev0000340.

Sands, K. R., and Mills, C. M. (2017). Accepting or discerning: Do preschoolers have preferences for certain types of explanations of biological causality? Poster presented at the meeting of Cognitive Development Society, Portland, OR.

Sobel, D. M., and Corriveau, K. H. (2010). Children monitor individuals' expertise for word learning. *Child Development, 81*, 669–79. https://doi:10.1111/j.1467-8624.2009.01422.x.

Sobel, D. M., and Kushnir, T. (2013). Knowledge matters: How children evaluate the reliability of testimony as a process of rational inference. *Psychological Review, 120*, 779–97. https://doi:10.1037/a0034191.

Taboada, A., and Guthrie, J. T. (2006). Contributions of student questioning and prior knowledge to construction of knowledge from reading information text. *Journal of Literacy Research, 38*, 1–35. https://doi:10.1207/s15548430jlr3801_1.

Taylor, M., Esbensen, B. M., and Bennett, R. T. (1994). Children's understanding of knowledge acquisition: The tendency for children to report that they have always known what they have just learned. *Child Development, 65*, 1581–604. https://doi:10.2307/1131282.

Thompson, R. B., Foster, B. J., and Kapinos, J. R. (2016). Poverty, affluence and the socratic method: Parents' questions versus statements within collaborative problem solving. *Language & Communication, 47*, 23–9. https://doi:10.1016/jlangcom.2015.11.003.

Tizard, B., and Hughes, M. (1984). *Young children learning*. London: Fontana.

Tyack, D., and Ingram, D. (1977). Children's production and comprehension of questions. *Journal of Child Language, 4*, 211–24. https://doi:10.1017/S0305000900001616.

VanderBorght, M., and Jaswal, V. K. (2008). Who knows best? Preschoolers sometimes prefer child informants over adult informants. *Infant and Child Development, 18*, 61–71. https://doi:10.1002/icd.591.

Was, A. M., and Warneken, F. (2017). Proactive help-seeking: Preschoolers know when they need help, but do not always ask for it. *Cognitive Development, 43*, 91–105. https://doi:10.1016/j.cogdev.2017.02.010.

Waterman, A. H., Blades, M., and Spencer, C. (2001). Interviewing children and adults: The effect of question format on the tendency to speculate. *Applied Cognitive Psychology, 15*, 521–31. https://doi:10.1002/acp.741.

# 9 "Why Are There Big Squares and Little Squares?"

## How Questions Reveal Children's Understanding of a Domain

*Dave Neale, Caroline Morano, Brian N. Verdine,*
*Roberta Michnick Golinkoff, Kathy Hirsh-Pasek*

MOM: (pointing to a wooden shape) "That one's a square."
ALICE: "Why are there big squares and little squares?"

Alice's mom did not answer her question, and that is hardly surprising – to an adult, the question may appear nonsensical and impossible to answer. To three-year-old Alice, however, it is clearly a question worth asking. This indicates something about her current understanding of the nature of geometric shape categories, which represent a crucial part of early learning (Resnick et al., 2016). If her question was posed in relation to many other domains of knowledge that Alice has encountered, such as animals or artifacts, her question would be perfectly logical. Consider instead the questions "Why are there big dogs and little dogs?" or "Why are there big shoes and little shoes?" Each of these questions has a logical answer grounded in a domain-specific framework that defines what constitutes possible and relevant knowledge in that domain. Alice may be making a form of category error, because the domain of geometry differs in some fundamental ways from most other domains she has encountered. This suggests that domains differ not only in the specific knowledge linked to each domain, but also in how one approaches the *act of knowledge acquisition itself* – through, for example, questioning.

One way in which children learn to divide up the world is linked to the notion of nominal and natural kinds (Keil, 1989). Traditionally, natural kinds are viewed as classes of things which would exist regardless of human intervention, for example, animals, plants, and minerals. Nominal kinds are classes of things where cultural convention has dictated the defining features and boundaries of the class, for example, artifacts (such as tables), kin relations, or occupations (such as professor). However, Keil (1989) argues that kinds should be seen as continuous rather than dichotomous and proposes a *kind continuum*. The continuum ranges from pure nominal kinds, where the entities are precisely defined and noncausal (e.g., shapes and numbers), to pure natural kinds, where there can be vagaries in definitions, and the entities exist in a complex and rich causal world (e.g., animals and plants). Keil considers shapes as a "pure nominal kind," because their definitions are highly precise and fixed, and they do not exert any causal influence or depend on any causal mechanisms. They can be a part of a causal system, but only when applied by a causal agent (e.g., an architect using numbers and shapes to design a building). This causal distinction is evident in the fact that people do not tend to talk about shapes and numbers in terms of their *effects* on the world. By contrast, adults may often talk to children about how a computer can run a program or how an animal can bite. Shapes are very different from the other domains studied so far in the question-asking literature, which focuses primarily on the other parts of Keil's continuum, i.e., natural kinds and causal relationships. Consequently, shapes represent a valuable means of illustrating our main argument in this chapter: that children's questioning in a domain reveals their thinking about knowledge acquisition, rather than simply their domain-specific knowledge.

Furthermore, studying children's questions about shapes is important because while shape knowledge is critical for a variety of professions, such as architects, engineers, and mathematicians, the benefits of shape knowledge extend into cognitive areas such as mathematics abilities and spatial thinking (Levine et al., 2012, Mix & Cheng, 2012; Verdine et al., 2014). Shape knowledge supports the development of children's "cardinal knowledge, composition, decomposition, and the number line" (Resnick et al., 2016, p. 258). Higher levels of shape knowledge have been linked to better mental manipulation skills, e.g., the ability to imagine how a 2D figure might look when rotated by mentally visualizing the movements (Cross et al., 2009). These mental manipulation skills are one component of spatial abilities, which are strongly connected to STEM fields (Wai et al., 2009; Newcombe & Frick, 2010; Uttal, et al., 2013; Verdine et al., 2014). The US government has recognized the critical nature of fostering shape knowledge, as the Common Core State Standards now require teachers to instruct children on shapes during preschool and kindergarten (National Governors Association Center for Best Practices, 2010). Under these standards, it is required for students to learn shape names, becoming familiar with shapes in a variety of orientations and presentations. Additionally, by kindergarten, the standards posit that students should be able to compare and create more complex shapes. Furthermore, geometry, like mathematics and language, represents one of the core symbolic systems of modern human societies. Symbolic systems are representational tools that are not only important on a social level, but also on an individual level as a means of representing thoughts and ideas (Vygotsky, 1962, 1978).

Despite the importance of early shape knowledge, research has shown that children struggle to develop a coherent understanding of the defining properties of shapes through elementary school (Satlow & Newcombe, 1998). The defining features are the essential components of a shape (e.g., a triangle's defining feature is that it has three sides). Shapes also have non-defining characteristics that can be altered without changing the shape category (e.g., a triangle can be big or small). Because children often have difficulty identifying the defining features of shapes, many have commented that we need to find ways to support children's early shape knowledge, and their awareness of the importance of defining features (Schwartz et al., 1979; Verdine et al., 2014; Resnick, et al., 2016).

Such an awareness constitutes part of an individual's broad conceptualization of a domain. A child who is aware that shapes have specific defining features, along with a variety of malleable non-defining features, knows something about *what constitutes relevant knowledge* in the shape domain. In contrast, a child may know that a triangle always has three sides, but be unaware that all shapes are defined by a similar set of specific rules, and so will not attempt to seek out those defining rules for other shapes. Greif and colleagues (2006) point out that Children's questions "reveal what they themselves consider important in creating a new conceptual category" (p. 458). Consequently, children's questions can be a way to assess this understanding of what constitutes relevant and important knowledge in a domain. Indeed, questions have a long history of being viewed as an epistemic tool, in that they reflect how an individual engages in and conceptualizes the acquisition of new knowledge (Berlyne & Frommer, 1966). Perhaps part of the explanation for why preschoolers struggle to learn about the defining features of shapes is that they have little conception of what constitutes relevant shape knowledge or how to go about acquiring it.

In this chapter, we outline empirical support for the idea that children's questions show us not only what a child knows in a given domain, but how that child is conceptualizing and approaching the act of knowledge acquisition itself. In this way, studying the questions children ask provides information that cannot be gleaned from studies which simply test children's domain-specific knowledge. This information is valuable for researchers and educators because a child's conceptualization of knowledge acquisition will guide the way they approach learning in a domain. The more effectively they can guide their learning, the more they can take control of it, and children learn best when they are active participants in the learning experience (Choi et al., 2018). To illustrate this point, we will present two case studies. First, we will examine existing research into children's questions about animals, to show how this idea applies in relation to an extensive body of research that includes analyses of children's questioning behavior. Second, we will detail the findings from our own study into children's questions about shapes, to see how preschoolers' approach to knowledge acquisition differs in a domain composed of pure nominal kinds rather than natural kinds. Our results suggest that, in contrast to the animal domain, three-year-olds demonstrate very little awareness of relevant information in the shape domain. We conclude by considering why this might be the case and suggesting some ways it could be rectified.

We have chosen to use animals as an example of a natural kind because the animal domain is also one area of knowledge that children encounter from an early age. Children may see some animals (e.g., dogs, squirrels, and birds) in their everyday lives and have gained information about various animals' properties through firsthand experience. Animals may similarly appear in many popular forms of media aimed at children, such as books, television shows, and electronic apps. Furthermore, the evidence base on preschoolers' animal knowledge is substantial.

## How Questions Reveal Children's Conceptualization of a Domain: The Case of Animal Knowledge

Clear support for the assertion that children's questions can reveal what they consider to be relevant information about a domain comes from studies looking at preschoolers' questions about animals. Although there has been much research into children's conceptualization of the animal domain, the majority of the paradigms used limit researchers' ability to understand what features children *prioritize* as relevant and useful in their own self-directed learning. To show how questions make a unique contribution to understanding domain-specific development, we first review non-question research into preschoolers' animal knowledge.

Fouquet and colleagues (2017) looked at children's understanding of the distinction between artifacts and animals. They found that children understood animals to have properties associated with life, such as movement and growth, but had a harder time extending these properties to plants. While children performed relatively accurately when attributing properties to animals, the paradigm used in Fouquet et al. (2017) limited children's expressions to some extent. Children had to decide which objects and animals could be the subject of specific verbs, and so were unable to indicate what verbs they would elect to use for various stimuli.

Other studies also use close-ended tasks with limited options to assess children's knowledge of specific animal properties. Gelman and Markman (1986) asked children whether or not a given property could be applied to an animal or artifact, and found that children largely relied on perceptual cues when classifying animals. Similarly, Dolgin and Behrand (1984) explored *children's answers* to adults' questions about animals and objects, asking children twenty different questions which focused on the difference between animate objects and inanimate objects. Results showed children have a well-developed understanding of the properties of familiar animals at three years old, but give no information about which of these properties children would naturally view as most relevant or essential to the domain.

In the studies described above, researchers are constraining the domain space, limiting the options to what *they believe* is important information in the animal domain. Consequently, the results give us information on what children know about animals, but they do not show us how children perceive the knowledge space of the animal domain. What do children consider the most important and relevant properties of exemplars? When presented with a novel exemplar, what do they feel they should know, and when do they consider that they know enough? This information is crucial, because what a child considers important and relevant will drive and structure their self-directed learning. Children's growing awareness of relevant knowledge will allow them to interrogate the knowledge space more effectively.

So how much awareness of relevant knowledge in the animal domain do preschoolers display through their questioning? Greif and colleagues (2006) showed three- to five-year-old children sixteen objects; eight of which were novel artifacts (e.g., a "crullet" was a meatball-maker; the assigned function was to make balls out of playdough) and eight of which were unfamiliar but real animals (e.g., tapir). Children were instructed to choose a box and experimenters revealed a photograph inside, asking children, "What do you want to know about that thing?" Children were prompted to ask as many questions as they would like until satisfied. The experimenters provided accurate answers to each question, but always responded with the object's name when asked ambiguous questions. Ambiguous questions gave no clear indication of the expected form of the response, e.g., "What is it?" is ambiguous, whereas "What is it called?" or "What is it for?" are not. Trials continued until children saw all the items. Children were more likely to ask questions about functions (e.g., "What does it do?") for artifacts than animals and were more likely to ask about category membership (i.e., "Is it a dog?") for animals than artifacts. In addition, children were more likely to ask follow-up questions about habitat for animals. Children were able to ask relevant questions for each category. When presented with animals, they asked about name, eating behaviors, reproduction, and habitat, but asked no questions about function.

This means that by three years old, children's questions indicate that they have a basic awareness of what constitutes relevant information concerning animals. They even ask about nonobvious, generalizable properties, such as habitat. However, this study only speaks to what children will ask when shown pictures of animals in a very specific and controlled experimental context.

By contrast, a study by Chouinard and colleagues (2007) looked at the questions of 112 children in the naturalistic context of a visit to a zoo. In such a freeform environment, and faced with real animals, children may ask a broad range of questions. Chouinard et al. (2007) categorized children's questions into 14 types, including label questions, various types of generalizable properties (e.g., function of parts of animals, whether a specific animal lays eggs), and theory-of-mind (ToM) questions (including references to emotions). Using the data provided by Chouinard et al. (2007), we grouped all questions concerning generalizable properties, and then looked at the change over time in the percentage of these generalizable property, name, and ToM questions from two to four years of age.

At two years of age, 45 percent of children's questions were about animal names, but 15 percent were about animal properties and 5 percent were about internal states. By age three, the percentage of name questions decreased to 30 percent, and the percentage of questions about properties rose to 20 percent, demonstrating a growing awareness that the obvious (e.g., number of legs) and nonobvious (e.g., diet) features of an animal constitute relevant information. By the age of four, there was also a rise in the number of questions concerning internal states, to 9 percent, suggesting children are beginning to attach more relevance to knowing how an animal feels or thinks.

Important and unique information can be gained from studying how preschoolers' questions change. The majority of studies into early animal knowledge show us what children know and do not know about animals. For example, even at age two, they understand animals to have properties relevant to living things, they rely on perceptual cues to classify animals, and they have little knowledge of unfamiliar animals. However, they do not show us anything about the information children prioritize as significant in the animal domain. But preschoolers' questions about animals suggest that from an early age children are aware of many relevant features, including diet, habitat, and even emotions and internal states. As far as we are aware, outsides the questions literature, no studies have investigated children's knowledge of animals' internal states, which shows how question research can reveal unexplored aspects of children's conceptualization of domain-relevant knowledge. In the next section, we review studies into children's shape knowledge in the preschool years, and then discuss how question research can similarly contribute to this research base.

## Questions and Children's Developing Conceptualization of the Shape Domain

Young children demonstrate an ability to ask relevant questions about animals and artifacts from two years of age. Research has shown that pre-schoolers consider relevant questions to concern behavior, change over time and habitat (Kemler Nelson et al., 2004; Greif et al., 2006; Chouinard et al., 2007). But what do preschoolers consider relevant questions for geometric shapes, where the within-domain entities have no salient functions, do not change over time, and interrelate through theoretical principles rather than through habitat or behavior? We know little about how preschoolers use questions to acquire early geometric knowledge. And as we have stated, it is important to understand not only children's developing knowledge in a domain, but also how they conceptualize relevant knowledge and how they approach the act of knowledge acquisition itself. Knowing this, we can support them in understanding the knowledge space of a domain and how to direct their own domain-specific learning.

One of the main developmental trends in shape knowledge is the increasing ability to recognize a variety of shapes as valid, including atypical instances of common shapes such as triangles and rectangles. Atypical versions of shapes are challenging for children, who initially have difficulty identifying which features define a shape category and which features can be altered without calling the shape by a different name. For example, when a triangle's sides are made longer or shorter, its appearance may change significantly. However, neither the lengths of the sides nor the degrees of the angles are what makes it a triangle; the important detail is the number of closed sides. Shapes can be seen as more or less "typical." Typical shapes are generally equilateral, with sides of equal length. Atypical shapes are still valid instances but have longer or shorter sides, nonstandard orientations (e.g., an upside-down equilateral triangle), and nonstandard angles, such as acute triangles (Satlow & Newcombe, 1998).

Verdine et al. (2016) assessed twenty-five- and thirty-month-old chil-dren's ability to discriminate between different shapes, including atypical instances, by showing them two different shapes on a screen and asking them to point to the named shape. While the twenty-five-month-olds performed slightly above chance for all shape types, the thirty-month-olds performed well above chance. This developmental trend in shape discrimination abilities continues through elementary school. Satlow and Newcombe (1998) found that children's judgments about typical and nonvalid shapes showed some improvement with age from preschool to fourth grade. However, children had difficulty in accepting atypical shapes as valid instances of a shape category at all ages.

The studies discussed above show us when children can discriminate between valid and nonvalid shapes. However, similar to the studies discussed earlier which tested children's specific animal knowledge, they offer little indication of what children see as relevant information, or any indication of how they would guide their own learning in the shape domain. Studying questions is important because children might ask about the defining features of a shape before they know what those defining features are. Specifically, questions can show us when and how children become *aware* that certain properties – e.g., angles, number of sides – *are relevant knowledge for shapes*, whether or not they actually know those properties for any given shape. More broadly, children's questions reveal not only what they know, but what they think about the act of knowledge acquisition itself.

The research suggests that between thirty months and three years children begin to apply shape names to less typical examples of shapes. Is this ability to recognize atypical exemplars reflected in an expanded awareness of what constitutes relevant shape knowledge? Or are children simply learning what constitutes valid and invalid shapes based on nondefining characteristics, via exposure to multiple exemplars over time? Studying three-year-olds' questions about shapes can provide some answers – if their increased shape knowledge is still grounded in simple visual recognition rather than defining principles, their questions will be very limited in nature. In contrast, if their increased shape knowledge is grounded in their developing awareness of relevant properties in the shape domain, they should ask a broader range of questions, concerning properties such as sides, similarities to other shapes, and perhaps similarities to objects in the world ("embedded shapes").

As pointed out earlier, there is no prior research looking at preschoolers' questions about shapes. Therefore, we lack an evidence base similar to that we used regarding animals. However, as an initial foray into preschoolers' shape questions, we analyzed an existing dataset from a previous study that coded for the nature of the conversations between parents and three-year-old children during play with shapes (Verdine et al., 2019). Through coding children's questions, we aimed to see how three-year-olds' awareness of relevant knowledge regarding shapes compared to that for animals.

**Standard Shape Condition**

2 identical sets of 10 standard shapes

**Alternate Shape Condition**

10 alternate shapes                    10 standard shapes

**Tablet Condition**

Main Menu          Quizzing          Flash Cards          Puzzle

Figure 9.1 Example stimuli for the three conditions in Verdine et al. (2019). Reprinted from *Early Childhood Research Quarterly*, *46*, B. N. Verdine, L. Zimmerman, L. Foster, M. A. Marzouk, R. M. Golinkoff, K. Hirsh-Pasek, & N. S. Newcombe, Effects of geometric toy design on parent–child interactions and spatial language, pp. 126–141, Copyright (2019), with permission from Elsevier.

Sixty parent–child dyads in the Verdine et al. (2019) study were assigned to one of three toy conditions: a *standard* condition, an *alternate* condition, and a *tablet* condition (Figure 9.1). In each condition, toys included ten shape categories. In the standard condition, there were two identical sets of ten canonical shape types (e.g., two equilateral triangles). In the alternate condition, children saw ten standard shapes and ten alternate versions. In the tablet condition, children and parents played an app called, "Shapes Toddler Preschool" by Toddler Teasers that randomly presented the same ten standard shape types used in the two other conditions.

Parents were asked to play with their children for ten minutes and to teach their children the names of the ten target shapes. In the standard and alternate conditions, research assistants provided parents with additional suggestions of activities that would mimic the games in the tablet condition.

All children's questions were first coded as information-seeking (questions that probe for facts or an explanation) or non-information-seeking (e.g., asking permission, seeking attention, or clarifying a previous statement). The non-information-seeking questions were not analyzed further. Because we were interested in questions as a means for a child to guide their own learning, we first coded children's questions as prompted by the parent, or as unprompted, i.e., generated by the child without any evident support (Table 9.1). Unprompted questions were considered an expression of the child's self-directed inquiry. Then, each question was coded for the topic (Table 9.2).

Our analysis of questions using this coding scheme revealed some interesting patterns. As the data did not meet the assumptions required for parametric analyses, we chose to use non-parametric tests. Children asked more information-seeking questions in the two physical toy conditions, both standard ($M = 2.80$, $SD = 3.22$) and alternate ($M = 5.20$, $SD = 5.47$), than in the tablet condition ($M = 0.85$, $SD = 1.31$). An Independent-Samples Kruskal-Wallis test revealed a significant difference between groups in the number of information-seeking questions children asked, $X^2(2) = 14.40$, $p = .001$, with a mean rank score of 39.75 for alternate, 32.27 for standard, and 19.48 for tablet. Children asked significantly more information-seeking questions in the alternate condition (*median* = 3.50) compared to the tablet condition

Table 9.1 *Coding scheme for the context of information-seeking questions*

| Code | Definition | Example |
|---|---|---|
| Prompted | Question is on a topic immediately following from parent's preceding conversational turn | P: "What do you think it is?" C: "Is it a triangle?" |
| Unprompted | Question is not on a topic immediately following parent's preceding conversational turn | P: "I wonder what we could make." C: "Is that a circle?" |

Table 9.2 *Coding scheme for the topic of information-seeking questions asked by parents and children*

| Code | Definition | Hypothetical Examples |
|------|-----------|----------------------|
| Identity | Seek to identify the label of a specific shape | "What is this one called?" "Is that a square?" |
| Comparisons to Real-World Objects | Question highlights a comparison between a specific shape and another non-shape object | "Which shape looks like a slice of pizza?" |
| Defining Spatial Properties | Questions on what defines a shape, or a specific shape's sides, corners, or angles | "Why is it a triangle?" "How many corners does a square have?" |
| Non-Defining Spatial Properties | Questions about properties such as size or color | "Is the triangle bigger than the circle?" |
| Location | Ask the location of a specific shape within the room | "Where is the square?" |
| Non-Shape Topics | Question topic does not fit into any of the above categories | "How many windows are in our house?" |

(*median* = 0.00), $p = .001$. The comparison between the standard condition (*median* = 2.00) and the tablet condition (*median* = 0.00) for children's information-seeking questions was marginally significant ($p = .054$).

As all the shapes on the app were standard shapes, we can make a direct comparison to the physical standard shape condition. Children asked significantly fewer questions about shapes of the *same format* when engaging with electronic, rather than physical modalities. Indeed, children asked so few questions in the tablet condition we were forced to exclude it from the next stage of analysis concerning the topic of children's questions. This finding has implications for our understanding of electronic apps as a learning tool. One possible interpretation of the lack of questions in the tablet condition is that as the tablet presents an interactive application, children felt little need to also interact with their parent. In other words, the cyclical action-response loop of social interaction was replaced by the action-response loop of the application. Another interpretation is that perhaps children did have questions in the tablet condition, but felt no need to vocalize them, as they could address them by interacting with the application. If, for example, they wondered which shape was a triangle, they could make a guess by selecting a shape and seeing if they were right or wrong by the response given on the screen. Therefore, it is not possible to make any conclusions about how the tablet condition

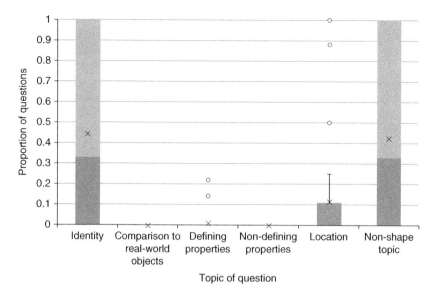

Figure 9.2 The proportion of children's questions on each topic, out of all information-seeking questions (line = median, x = mean, circles = outliers).

affected children's learning experience, but we can conclude that it did alter the social nature of the interaction. What this may mean for children's learning is a question for future research.

The next stage of analysis was to look at children's questions by topic in the standard and alternate conditions. Figure 9.2 shows the proportion of questions on each topic, represented as a box plot because the data deviated substantially from normality. There were no significant differences in the topics of children's questions between the two physical material conditions (standard and alternate), so the figure combines both conditions. Children asked almost exclusively about shape names and location of shapes in the room. Out of the 184 information-seeking questions asked by children, only 3 concerned shape properties. The latter were all about the non-defining property of size. Consequently, these results suggest that three-year-old children's awareness of relevant knowledge for shapes is primarily limited to identifying shape names.

Next, because we were using unprompted questions as an indicator of children's self-directed learning, we looked at how many unprompted questions about shapes children asked in the different conditions. We hypothesized that children would ask more unprompted questions about shapes when they were playing with unfamiliar shapes than when they were playing with familiar shapes. All questions on non-shape topics were excluded, as we were only interested in how the materials may affect children's shape learning. An Independent-Samples Mann-Whitney test revealed a marginally significant difference between conditions in the proportion of unprompted questions about shapes children asked, $U = 182.00$, $z = 1.75$, $p = .09$., with a mean rank score of 19.61 for alternate and 13.87 for standard. These results represent tentative support for the hypothesis that unfamiliar or atypical play materials are associated with a higher number of unprompted questions from children. In turn, this suggests that exposure to a varied range of exemplars may relate to children's curiosity and self-directed inquiry. Previously, researchers have successfully elicited causal questions in young children through presenting them with unusual, surprising stimuli (Frazier et al., 2009, 2016). As children appear to express interest in asking questions about unusual stimuli in these studies, unfamiliar, atypical shape exemplars may similarly elicit more unprompted questions in children. We will now consider why three-year-olds' awareness of relevant knowledge for shapes appears so different from that for animals.

### The Challenge of Shape Learning

When faced with a novel animal, why does a three-year-old know they should ask about name, diet, behavior, and habitat, but when faced with a novel shape, they only ask for its name? What makes understanding the important features of shapes so much harder than understanding the important features of animals?

Perhaps the challenge arises from the fundamental differences between shapes and animals, as discussed earlier in this chapter. Given that young children exhibit a bias towards treating all objects, even inanimate ones, as agents (Kelemen, 1999a, 1999b), and show a high level of interest in causality (Frazier et al., 2009; Corriveau & Kurkul, 2014), it could be that because shapes are non-agent, noncausal, pure nominal kinds (Keil, 1989) children struggle to accommodate them into one of their most fundamental schematics for interpreting the world.

Another important way in which shape learning differs from learning about animals is the role of number. Numbers, like shapes, are pure nominal kinds on Keil's continuum. Numbers are essentially a way of modeling the world, by allocating an abstract representation of quantity to distances, times, lengths, ages, and anything else conducive to being measured. In a sense, they are more abstract than shapes, having no physical instantiations at all and existing only as properties of sets or measurements. Unlike animals or tools, every defining feature of a shape is numerical: the number of sides, the length of sides, the degrees of the angles. Thus, an understanding of the defining features of shapes must be accompanied by a certain level of understanding regarding number and measurement. Perhaps preschool children's shape knowledge is constrained by their number and math knowledge. Some support for this hypothesis comes from research showing that early number competency predicts early shape knowledge (Hornung et al., 2014).

However, there is another potential reason for preschoolers' lack of awareness of relevant knowledge for the shape domain. The results of our study suggest that exposure to multiple, diverse shape exemplars may have triggered more unprompted questions from preschoolers about those exemplars. But how varied is the range of exemplars preschoolers will tend to encounter? Resnick et. al. (2016) examined commercially available books, shape-sorter toys, and electronic apps about shapes made for children in the US. They found that the materials widely available for children include only limited variation of the shape categories, presenting mostly standard versions of shapes. For example, while 90 percent of the apps had equilateral triangles, only 45 percent of the apps had non-canonical triangles. In addition, while 60 percent of shape-sorter toys had standard stars, no shape-sorter toys had non-canonical stars. In fact, likely only adding to the confusion, books frequently use 3D geometric figures which they label with 2D shape names. Spheres like the sun, oranges, and soccer balls are used for circles and things like the pyramids are used for triangles. Atypical and embedded shapes may promote children's question-asking and their domain-specific learning, but they do not appear to be gaining much exposure to these shape types through commercially available materials. Therefore, it could be beneficial for preschool centers to acquire more diverse shape exemplars. This relatively simple and inexpensive act could have a significant impact on children's question-asking behavior and learning in the shape domain.

Further support for children's self-directed learning about shapes could come in the form of guided play. During guided play, adults follow children's lead, providing appropriate scaffolding to help guide their learning (Weisberg et al., 2013). Research has shown that guided play produces strong benefits for children in various domains, such as language and math (Pellegrini & Galda, 1990; Campbell et al., 2001; Marcon, 2002). Guided play has also been studied in children's learning of shapes. Fisher and colleagues (2013) taught 70 four- and five-year-old children about the properties of shapes in three different pedagogical conditions: guided play, didactic instruction, and free play. In guided play, the researcher demonstrated the similarities between atypical and typical versions of a shape and then had the child explore the shapes by touching or tracing the images and constructing their own shapes with construction sticks. Children who were taught using guided play performed significantly better on a shape sorting task than children in the other two conditions. Children in the guided play condition were more likely to accept both standard and atypical versions of shapes and to reject nonvalid instances of shapes than children in the other conditions. Because guided play involves following children's lead, it gives children agency to explore what they want to know. Therefore, it is an ideal context for children to ask questions and direct their own learning. With an adult available to answer and stimulate new questions, children's questions during guided play may fall just on the sweet spot of what they are unsure of and want to know more about. As far as we are aware, no research has yet looked at children's questioning behavior during guided play. Future research should examine how children's question-asking differs in various contexts, including guided play, direct instruction, and free play.

## Conclusion

The development of shape knowledge is an area in which investigating the role of questions has major potential. Unlike paradigms which test the extent of children's domain knowledge, question research indicates children's level of awareness about the relevance of types of domain-specific knowledge, and this can drive their self-directed learning.

Our initial study into questions about shapes suggests that three-year-olds' questions about shapes are much more limited in range than their questions about animals (Greif et al., 2006; Chouinard et al., 2007). With shapes, they asked almost exclusively about names. In contrast, the evidence shows that from two years of age children demonstrate a high degree of awareness about what constitutes relevant information in the animal domain. There is reason to suspect that learning about shapes, as a pure, nominal kind and a domain grounded in quantification and measurement, is simply more challenging. However, the scarcity and limited range of shape exemplars in children's daily environments may also be contributing to their lack of shape knowledge at age three.

Our initial investigation into children's questions about shapes is limited in that it only involved three-year-olds and no other age groups. Consequently, we were unable to establish any developmental trajectory for children's question-asking about shapes. Research with older preschool children is needed to identify the point at which they begin to ask questions about defining shape features. Also, our results are based on one specific context. Chouinard et al.'s (2007) study of children's questions in the zoo revealed a larger range of questions than the more limited context used by Greif et al. (2006). Similarly, three-year-olds may ask more varied questions regarding shapes in other contexts.

It is also important to note that the learning challenge outlined in this chapter may not be limited to shapes, but could apply to other cultural symbolic systems as well. Preschool children also express confusion over the meaning of number words (Condry & Spelke, 2008) and we could find no research looking at their questioning behavior in this other symbolic domain. Children may struggle to ask relevant questions about numbers during the preschool years, and this is something future studies should investigate.

In conclusion, preschool children's question-asking behavior is an important indicator of their awareness of what constitutes relevant knowledge in a given domain. Questions also represent an important learning tool in that they help children direct their own learning. Given the importance of early shape learning, more studies should investigate preschoolers' questions regarding shapes. In geometry, there is no valid answer to the question "Why are there big squares and little squares?" but knowing this requires an awareness of the nature and limits of domain-specific knowledge. With better educational resources and adult support, we may be able to promote more relevant question-asking behavior and more effective learning, helping children develop their crucial awareness of the abstract symbolic systems on which human society and culture depend.

### Acknowledgments

This research was supported by grants to the last two authors from the National Institutes of Health Stimulus Grant 1RC1HD0634970-01, the National Science Foundation via the Spatial Intelligence and Learning Center (SBE-1041707), and the Institute of Education Sciences through Grant R305A140385.

The authors thank the following people for their work on this project: Laura Zimmermann and Natalie Brezack, for coordinating aspects of the project and data collection; Sandy Abu El Adas, Kyla Amick, Emma Blackney, Kim Cummings, Jessica Curran, Brendan Czupryna, Laura DiRusso, Emily Horwitz, Paige McHale, Shannon McLaughlin, Adam Rosen, Alexa Rubilotta, Kelly Sassa, Olivia Smith, Hannah Straub, Dunia Tonob, Natalie Wallace, Ori Zaff. We would also like to thank the Spatial Intelligence and Learning Center and their Spatial Network for their consultation at various stages of this project.

## References

Berlyne, D. E. and Frommer, D. (1966). Some determinants of the incidence and content of children's questions. *Child Development*, *37*, 177–89. https://doi.org/10.2307/1126438

Campbell, F. A., Pungello, E. P., Miller-Johnson, S., Burchinal, M., and Ramey, C. T. (2001). The development of cognitive and academic abilities: Growth curves from an early childhood educational experiment. *Developmental Psychology*, *37*, 231–42. https://doi.org/10.1037/0012–1649.37.2.231

Choi, K., Lapidow, E., Austin, J., Shafto, P., and Bonawitz, E. (2018). Preschoolers are more likely to direct questions to adults than to other children (or selves) during spontaneous conversational acts. https://doi.org/10.31219/osf.io/tj42

Chouinard, M. M., Harris, P. L., and Maratsos, M. P. (2007). Children's questions: A mechanism for cognitive development. *Monographs of the Society for Research in Child Development*, *72*, i–129.

Condry, K. F., and Spelke, E. S. (2008). The development of language and abstract concepts: The case of natural number. *Journal of Experimental Psychology: General*, *137*, 22–38. https://psycnet.apa.org/doi/10.1037/0096–3445.137.1.22

Corriveau, K. H., and Kurkul, K. E. (2014). "Why does rain fall?": Children prefer to learn form an informant who uses noncircular explanations. *Child Development*, *85*, 1827–35. https://doi.org/10.1111/cdev.12240

Cross, C. T., Woods, T. A., and Schweingruber, H. (2009). *Mathematics learning in early childhood: Paths toward excellence and equity*. Washington, DC: The National Academies Press.

Dolgin, K. G., and Behrend, D. A. (1984). Children's knowledge about animates and inanimates. *Child Development*, *55*, 1646–50. https://doi.org/10.2307/1130034

Fisher, K., Hirsh-Pasek, K., Newcombe, N., and Golinkoff, R.M. (2013) Taking shape: Supporting preschoolers' acquisition of geometric knowledge. *Child Development*, *17*, 1872–8. https://doi.org/10.1111/cdev.12091

Fouquet, N., Megalakaki, O., and Labrell, F. (2017). Children's understanding of animal, plant, and artifact properties between 3 and 6 years. *Infant and Child Development*, *26*, 1–13. https://doi.org/10.1002/icd.2032

Frazier, B. N., Gelman, S. A., and Wellman, H. M. (2009). Preschoolers' search for explanatory information within adult–child conversation. *Child Development*, *80*, 1592–611. https://doi.org/10.1111/j.1467–8624.2009.01356.x

  (2016). Young children prefer and remember satisfying explanations. *Journal of Cognition and Development*, *17*, 718–36.

Gelman, S. A., and Markman, E. M. (1986). Young children's inductions from natural kinds: The role of categories and appearances. *Child Development*, *58*, 1532–41. https://doi.org/10.2307/1130693

Greif, L. M., Kemler Nelson, D. G., Keil, F. C., and Gutierrez, F. (2006). What do children want to know about animals and artifacts? *Psychological Science*, *16*, 455–9. https://doi.org/10.1111/j.1467–9280.2006.01727.x

Hornung, C., Schiltz, C., Brunner, M., and Martin, R. (2014). Predicting first-grade mathematics achievement: The contributions of domain-general cognitive abilities, nonverbal number sense, and early number competence. *Frontiers in Psychology*, 5, 1–18. https://doi.org/10.3389/fpsyg.2014.00272

Keil, F. C. (1989). *Concepts, kinds, and conceptual development*. Cambridge, MA: MIT Press.

Kelemen, D. (1999a). The scope of teleological thinking in preschool children. *Cognition*, 70, 241–72. https://doi.org/10.1016/s0010-0277(99)00010-4

(1999b). Why are rocks pointy? Children's preference for teleological explanations of the natural world. *Developmental Psychology*, 35, 1440–52. https://doi.org/10.1037/0012–1649.35.6.1440

Kemler Nelson, D., Chan, E. L., and Holt, M. B. (2004). When children ask, "What is it?" what do they want to know about artifacts? *Psychological Science*, 15, 384–9. https://doi.org/10.1111/j.0956–7976.2004.00689.x

Levine, S. C., Ratliff, K. R., Huttenlocher, J., and Cannon, J. (2012). Early puzzle play: A predictor of preschoolers' spatial transformation skill. *Developmental Psychology*, 48, 530–42. https://doi.org/10.1037/a0025913

Marcon, R. (2002). Moving up the grades: Relationships between preschool model and later school success. *Early Childhood Research and Practice*, 4, 517–30.

Mix, K. S., and Cheng, Y. L. (2012). The relation between space and math: developmental and educational implications. *Advances in Child Development and Behavior*, 42, 197–243. https://doi.org/10.1016/B978-0–12-394388-0.00006-X

National Governors Association Center for Best Practices (2010). *Common Core State Standards for mathematics*. Washington, DC: National Governors Association Center for Best Practices, Council of Chief State School Officers.

Newcombe, N. S., and Frick, A. (2010). Early education for spatial intelligence: Why, what, and how. *Mind, Brain, and Education*, 4, 102–11, https://doi.org/10.1111/j.1751-228X.2010.01089.x.

Pellegrini, A. D., and Galda, L. (1990). Children's play, language, and early literacy. *Topics in Language Disorders*, 10, 76–88. https://doi.org/10.1097/00011363–199006000–00008

Resnick, I., Verdine, B. N., Golinkoff, R., and Hirsh-Pasek, K. (2016). Geometric toys in the attic? A corpus analysis of early exposure to geometric shapes. *Early Childhood Research Quarterly*, 36, 358–65. https://doi.org/10.1016/j.ecresq.2016.01.007

Satlow E., and Newcombe N. S. (1998). When is a triangle not a triangle? Young children's developing concepts of geometric shape. *Cognitive Development*, 13, 547–59. https://doi.org/10.1016/s0885-2014(98)90006-5

Schwartz, M., Day, R. H., and Cohen, L. B. (1979). Visual shape perception in early infancy. *Monographs of the Society for Research in Child Development*, 4, 1–63.

Uttal, D. H., Meadow, N. G., Tipton, E., et al. (2013). The malleability of spatial skills: A meta-analysis of training studies. *Psychological Bulletin*, 193, 352–402. https://doi.org/10.1037/a0028446

Verdine, B. N., Irwin, C. M., Golinkoff, R. M., and Hirsh-Pasek, K. (2014). Contributions of executive function and spatial skills to preschool mathematics achievement. *Journal of Experimental Child Psychology, 126,* 37–51. https://doi.org/10.1016/j.jecp.2014.02.012

Verdine, B. N., Lucca, K. R., Golinkoff, R. M., Hirsh-Pasek, K., and Newcombe, N. S. (2016). The shape of things: The origin of young children's knowledge of names and properties of geometric forms. *Journal of Cognitive Development, 17,* 142–61. https://doi.org/10.1080/15248372.2015.1016610

Verdine, B. N., Zimmermann, L., Foster, L., et al. (2019). Effects of geometric toy design on parent-child interactions and spatial language. *Early Childhood Research Quarterly, 46,* 126–41. https://doi.org/10.1016/j.ecresq.2018.03.015

Vygotsky, L. (1962). *Thought and language.* Cambridge, MA: MIT Press. (1978). *Mind in society: The development of higher psychological processes.* Cambridge, MA: Harvard University Press.

Wai, J., Lubinski, D., and Benbow, C. P. (2009). Spatial ability for STEM domains: Aligning over 50 years of cumulative psychological knowledge solidifies its importance. *Journal of Educational Psychology, 101,* 817–35. https://doi.org/10.1037/a0016127

Weisberg, D. S., Hirsh-Pasek, K., and Golinkoff, R. M. (2013). Guided play: Where curricular goals meet a playful pedagogy. *Mind, Brain, and Education, 7,* 104–12. https://doi.org/10.1111/mbe.12015

# 10 Children's Questions in Social and Cultural Perspective

*Mary Gauvain, Robert L. Munroe*

Young children are curious about the world and they use a variety of behaviors to explore and learn about it (Engel, 2015). This process is founded in adaptation and reflects children's need to understand and connect with their social and physical environment. Children's exploratory behaviors are evident at birth and change with age as their skills develop. Whereas very young infants rely largely on observation, using vision and other senses (e.g., smell, touch) to identify and learn about objects and people, older infants can move around on their own to explore the many sights, sounds, and events around them. From the outset, these explorations are greatly aided by other people, especially caregivers, who guide children's selection and interpretation of information and provide safety and security when children experience uncertainty or fear (Bowlby, 1969).

Beyond infancy, children often use language to learn about the world. They show great interest in the names of people and objects along with the categories they belong to, which provides insight into the nature of these entities and helps organize children's expanding knowledge base (Nelson, 2007). The rapid increase in vocabulary between two and three years of age is an outgrowth of this process (Nelson, 1973). During this same age period, children increasingly initiate conversations with more experienced partners and they start to use another linguistic method to explore the world – they ask questions (Smith, 1933; Tyack & Ingram, 1976; Hood et al., 1979; Harris, 2012). Children's spontaneous or self-initiated questions are conducive to learning because they signal a child's interest to other people, who can then help the child learn more about it (Bruner, 1975, 1981). For instance, by asking questions children can get assistance as they develop concepts in various domains (e.g., biology, social rules; Carey, 1985). Because these exchanges can contribute to intellectual growth, children's questions, especially those that seek explanation or "why-questions," are posited as a mechanism for cognitive development (Chouinard, 2007).

The general claim that children's question-asking behavior benefits learning is undeniable. If a child, or anyone for that matter, generates a question of interest to them, and it is answered in an informative and sincere way and the questioner attends to the reply, the individual's knowledge will increase (Grice, 1989). However, the deeper claim that children's questions are a mechanism for cognitive development requires more scrutiny. Not only is it necessary to specify what is meant by mechanism, it is important to clarify exactly what role children's questions play in cognitive development. The content and occurrence of children's questions, especially across social and cultural contexts, also need to be examined. This last issue is particularly important because of an implicit assumption of universality in much of the research on children's question-asking behavior. However, supporting evidence is limited because this research has been mainly carried out in social and cultural settings where questions from young children are encouraged and supported. These settings also tend to have a tradition of formal schooling, which is related to how parents and children talk to one another outside of school (Rogoff, 2003; Greenfield, 2009). Some evidence, described later, suggests that there may be substantial differences across developmental contexts in children's question-asking behavior, especially in questions that seek explanation.

Here we discuss children's questions as a form of social and cultural behavior. Our approach is based on the sociocultural perspective, especially the idea that cultural practices and tools, including language, mediate individual functioning and help shape cognitive development (Vygotsky, 1987; Cole, 1996). We also draw on theories of language socialization that emphasize how, over development, children learn to use language in ways that are appropriate in the social and cultural setting in which they live (Ochs & Schieffelin, 1984). To be clear, we do not take issue with the idea that children have great curiosity about the world, a characteristic that leads them to seek out opportunities for learning. Rather, we are concerned with the form this curiosity takes and its relation to the social and cultural context of development.

In the next section, we review research on children's use of question-asking behavior, including explanatory questions. We then turn our discussion to sociolinguistic views of the development of children's communicative competence. To illustrate our position, we describe our research comparing children's information-seeking questions in Western and non-Western settings. Findings suggest that the pattern of caregiver–child interaction described in Western, middle-class families around these questions may not be applicable to all societies or to all social groups within a society. In particular, this research challenges the assumption of universality of children's explanation-seeking questions and, in so doing, opens discussion about the role of these questions in cognitive development.

## Children's Efforts to Learn by Asking Questions

Research on the cognitive function of children's questions has concentrated on two types of knowledge- or information-seeking questions: those that request factual information (e.g., "Where are you going?" "What's in your hand?") and those that ask for explanation (e.g., "Why are you doing that?" "How does that work?"). Explanation-seeking questions, in particular, have garnered substantial attention from researchers because of their potential in helping children learn about causal relations in the physical and social world. Indeed, almost a century ago, Piaget (1923) saw children's questions as efforts to understand causality and resolve problems of incommensurate understanding, or disequilbrium, between what the child knows and how the world or objects in the world appear to operate. More recently, Dunn (1988) proposed that children's explanation-seeking questions are largely about social causation, especially the motives or intentions behind human behavior. Subsequent research has shown that both types of concerns motivate children's explanatory questions, but by and large, questions about persons (activities and states) are more common than questions about objects or physical phenomena (Hickling & Wellman, 2001).

But do children's explanatory questions actually stimulate conversations that might lead to advances in causal understanding? The evidence is equivocal. Research using naturalistic observations and parental reports has found that when parents respond to children's explanatory questions with explanations, children raise more questions, which suggests that these types of responses from parents stimulate more interest in children (Callanan & Oakes, 1992). However, it may be that children ask further questions because of the content of the parents' explanations. Callanan and Jipson (2001) found that parents' responses to children's explanatory questions were often incomplete and, in some cases, incorrect. Children's follow-up questions may simply be greater effort to get at the explanation they seek.

Other research that used the CHILDES child language database (MacWhinney & Snow, 1985, 1990) has probed this issue by using transcripts of six preschool-age children (Frazier et al., 2009). The researchers investigated how children reacted to adult responses to children's explanatory questions. Children asked more follow-up questions when adults provided explanatory versus nonexplanatory information, which suggests that the children were seeking this type of information and not just trying to initiate or sustain a conversation. This result was replicated in a subsequent experimental study in which preschoolers interacted with an experimenter in a situation that provoked questions from the children. The children's questions were followed with various scripted responses from the experimenter, both explanatory and nonexplanatory. Again, children reacted differently to explanatory and nonexplanatory information. They were more responsive in a substantive way to the former and when explanatory information was not provided, children continued to request it. Also, children remembered informative explanations but not uninformative ones (Frazier et al., 2016). This research suggests that through their questions, children seek information relevant to learning and that they evaluate responses in this light.

Chouinard (2007) also used the CHILDES database to study the transcripts of four children beginning when they were two years of age. Data were recorded in the children's home and most of their questions were addressed to parents (usually mother). From the longitudinal dataset, which covered the time from when the children were two up to five years of age, there were approximately 100,000 child utterances and 17 percent (17,000) of them were information-seeking questions. Beginning around age three, almost one-quarter (23–26 percent) of these questions sought explanation rather than isolated factual information. In follow-up research, Chouinard carried out experimental work with US children to investigate children's learning following their explanatory questions and found evidence that learning was taking place. Four-year-olds who asked explanatory questions were able to get information that changed their current knowledge state, which, in turn, helped them solve a problem.

Taken together, these studies indicate that young children ask information-seeking questions with great frequency and they often seek causal explanations in their questions. Moreover, when children receive explanations they seem to be more satisfied with the response than when they do not receive explanations, which suggests they can distinguish causal information from other types of responses. Finally, when children obtain explanations, they are able to carry out cognitive tasks more effectively, indicating they have learned from the response. This pattern has been borne out using various methods including naturalistic observations, diary studies, analysis of extant data sets of child language, and laboratory observations of children's questions and their related behaviors. The variety of methods is impressive and attests to the difficulty in studying children's spontaneous questions. However, a major shortcoming in this research is lack of attention to the social and cultural settings in which children produce information-seeking questions.

## The Social and Cultural Context of Children's Question-Asking Behavior

Through the process of socialization children become members of their cultural group. Cognitive development is affected by socialization because the social and cultural context provides the core experiences, interactions, and tools through which children learn and develop knowledge and skills (Cole, 1996; Gauvain & Perez, 2015a). Language is integral to this process (Vygotsky, 1987) and it plays a dual role. Not only does much of socialization occur through language, children are socialized to use language (Ochs, 1986). Learning about and through language largely occurs in everyday interactions between young and more experienced community members.

All languages have rules that govern their structure and use. These rules include pragmatics, the communicative function and use of language, which defines the preferred and expected manner of communication in social situations (Hymes, 1974). During socialization, children learn to use language, including asking questions, in ways that are context sensitive and socially acceptable in their community (Slobin et al., 1996; Ochs & Schieffelin, 2011). In doing so, children show agency in language socialization and display their membership in the community (Heath, 1983; Sterponi, 2010).

It is especially important that children learn to use language in ways that respect the social roles and status of community members – a practice that will help prepare children for their future roles and relationships in the community (Ochs, 1986). This understanding is marked linguistically in many ways, including syntax (e.g., appropriate use of formal and informal verbs) and various pragmatic forms (e.g., politeness, honorific and respectful language, different speech volume or registers across settings such as home and church). As young as three years of age, children use context-sensitive language. For instance, they speak in a different register depending upon the person to whom they are talking (Andersen, 1990). They also use language in ways that acknowledge culturally appropriate social positions, for example, they are aware of who can or should be spoken to, allowed and prohibited topics, how to address and listen to others, and the types of responses that are expected (Sterponi, 2010).

Young children also know how to make requests that evoke the action of another person. Preschool-age children make requests with varying degrees of directness ranging from direct commands or imperatives (e.g., "Give me the (toy) car") to less direct need statements or questions (e.g., "I need the car" "Would you give me the car?") to indirect directives or hints (e.g., "I like the blue car the most"; Ervin-Tripp, 1982). Between ages three and four, children's requests reflect social factors such as the status of the listener or interpersonal goals, for instance, they use less direct requests with higher status persons or when they are trying to be polite or especially nice (e.g., when they want to get a treat from another person; Bates, 1976). As Kyratzis and Cook-Gumperz (2015) explain, "pragmatic choices, in something as apparently simple as request forms, reveal the real complexities of the discourse knowledge necessary for children to become competent communicators in everyday settings" (p. 684).

Information-seeking questions (e.g., "Where is the car?") differ from requests in that they ask for knowledge instead of overt action. Despite this difference, research on children's requests may be instructive regarding children's information-seeking questions. This research demonstrates that young children know that inquiries are social instruments, that is, they can be used to help children get something they want from another person. The research also indicates that young children know about and can use inquiries that vary in directness and, additionally, they adjust the directness of the inquiry to the social situation.

Observations of children's spontaneous explanatory questions during free play and other activities suggest that these questions emerge gradually over the preschool years and reflect the development of pragmatic skills (James & Seebach, 1982). Whereas the explanatory questions of three- and four-year-old children in this study were mostly information-seeking (e.g., "Why are we doing this?"), five-year-olds also asked such questions for conversational and directive purposes (e.g., when passing a book to the teacher a child asked, "Why don't we read this one?").

Thus, even before children begin formal schooling, they have learned socially appropriate ways of interacting with and learning from other people in their community. Research on the development of requests provides insight into what young children may understand about information-seeking questions, including their awareness of socially appropriate forms of questioning. Next, findings from research on children's questions in different social and ethnic communities in Western, industrialized societies and small-scale traditional societies are described. This research underscores the significance of the social and cultural context to the production of children's questions, particularly questions that seek explanation or causal information.

### Children's Questions across Social Contexts in Western and Industrialized Societies

Research conducted in Western industrialized societies shows that children's question-asking behavior varies according to the social surrounds.

It also demonstrates that the production of explanatory questions varies by social context (Tizard & Hughes, 1984; Hart & Risley, 1992).

A study conducted in the United Kingdom examined the rate and types of young children's explanatory questions at home and in nursery school in relation to family social class and parental responses to the questions (Tizard et al., 1983). Results indicate that children asked more explanatory questions at home, averaging 26 questions an hour (range 8–145); at school the rate was much lower, averaging 1 question an hour (range 0–46). Social class was a contributing factor in that girls (only girls were in the study) from middle-class families had a proportionally higher rate of questions in their talk both at home and at school than did girls from working-class families. Although there were very few explanatory questions in either social class group, children from middle-class families posed more of these questions than children from working-class families. The rate of explanatory questions was not related to child IQ, but it was related to quality of maternal response to these questions. Middle-class mothers provided more responses described as extensive than working-class mothers.

In further analysis of the language environment and communicative exchanges of the mothers and children, Tizard and Hughes (1984) found that children from working-class families were as competent as children from middle-class families in conceptual and logical thinking. Rather, what differed was the frequency of certain types of questions in the two groups, what the researchers described as a difference in language style. A feature of this style is that mothers who asked more questions of their children, had children who asked more questions of their mothers, and middle-class dyads displayed this pattern more than dyads in working-class families.

In a study using the CHILDES database, Kurkul and Corriveau (2018) corroborated these findings. These researchers examined caregivers' responses to four- to five-year-old children's explanation-seeking questions in relation to family socioeconomic status (SES). Although the proportion of explanatory questions asked by children in middle-SES and low-SES families was similar at about 25 percent of their information-seeking questions overall, children in middle-SES families asked almost twice the number of such questions than children in low-SES families. Additionally, whereas middle-SES caregivers often offered explanations in response to children's explanatory questions, low-SES caregivers rarely did. Also, the quality of the responses from caregivers differed. Middle-SES caregivers provided more causal information and low-SES caregivers used more circular responses (e.g., "It's that way because it is"). The researchers suggest that children in middle-SES families generate more questions than children in low-SES families because they receive more satisfying responses from their caregivers. For Corriveau and colleagues, this pattern could have implications when children enter school in that children from low-SES families will have had less exposure to the types of explanations and explanation-seeking questions that are favored in the classroom.

Heath (1983) came to a similar conclusion in research investigating the early communicative experiences, including types of questions, of children from two ethnic groups, African American and European American, both of whom lived in working-class communities in the southeastern United States. There was a difference in the types of questions the children in these two groups asked. The African American children tended to ask one-off questions about events, objects, and people in the immediate setting, especially when they were new or the children were unsure of them. In contrast, the European American children tended to ask questions during conversations with their parents that involved mutual questions and answers. These observations suggest that the manner and social situations of children's questions differs across ethnic communities even among families in the same social class. For Heath, these differences have significance beyond the home context in that the conversations of the European American parents and children resemble, and possibly function as training for, the types of exchanges children will experience later in school. In this way, caregiver–child interactions around children's questions may have consequences beyond the immediate situation if they help prepare children for experiences in other societal institutions (Schieffelin & Ochs, 1984).

Looking at an industrialized community in a different cultural setting, Nakamura (1996) found that Japanese children's use of polite language when making requests varies by social context. Japan has an elaborate system of polite language and demeanor that even young children are expected to learn. In this study, three-, four-, and five-year-old middle-class children living in Tokyo were observed over a period of a year in different home contexts, such as during role play, object play, and when interacting with different partners, including parents, peers, and familiar and unfamiliar adults. These young children used a variety of polite expressions and their use varied by social context. During requests, children used polite forms in appropriate social contexts, such as when they addressed unfamiliar adults and during role play when they pretended to be a person of high status (e.g., a doctor). They used direct informal request forms with their mothers. This pattern is similar to that reported for middle-class children in the United States; however, consistent with Japanese cultural values, there is greater emphasis on polite forms in that setting.

Other research has demonstrated that children's explanatory questions in the same household are interpreted differently by parents depending on the content of the question. In observations of the conversations of Mexican American parents and their young school-age children, Delgado-Gaitan (1994) found the parents welcomed and supported children's questions when they pertained to school matters. However, when the children asked questions on other topics, such as family routines, parents found these questions to be defiant and challenging to parental authority and they were discouraged.

Across these studies, we see that social and cultural conventions of language use regulate the manner and frequency with which children request help and information from others. There are individual differences in how parents within a society encourage and respond to children's questions as well as differences across cultural contexts regarding speech forms that are acceptable and those that are not. Although reasons for these variations have not received much study, research on child socialization points to several potential contributing factors such as parent occupational and educational backgrounds, including future aspirations for their children (Tudge, 2008), and regular patterns of parent–child discourse, such as parents' responsiveness when conversing with their children about various topics (Fivush & Nelson, 2006; Laible & Song, 2006; Bornstein et al., 2007). Child characteristics, such as language and self-regulatory skills as well as children's interest in and motivation to have conversations about various topics, may also play a role (Foster, 1986; Laible et al., 2015).

Evidence of variation in children's production of a specific type of question – those that seek explanation – is especially interesting in this regard. Differences in the manner and rate of explanatory questions are found when comparing children across social class, ethnic groups in the same social class, and different cultural communities. These patterns, along with evidence of variation within the same family context depending on the content of children's questions (Delgado-Gaitan, 1994), suggest that the high levels of children's explanatory questions reported in some research may represent certain family contexts and perhaps certain topics of discussion in families, even for children living in middle-class homes in Western industrialized societies (e.g., see Harris, 2007; Maratsos, 2007). These findings call for more study of children's question-asking behavior across diverse social and cultural contexts (Bornstein, 2002).

Finally, it may be that the reasons for variation in children's question-asking behavior, especially explanatory questions, within a society differ from the reasons behind cultural variation in this behavior. Whereas the former may be explained best by family socialization factors, such as those just mentioned, variation across cultures may be more reflective of community-level values and practices. In our view, seeking a single explanation for children's question-asking behavior is, at present, ill-advised given the lack of research on social and cultural factors that underlie this behavior. We return to this issue later, but first we describe our research on cultural variation in children's questions.

## Children's Questions in Small-Scale Traditional Societies

In our research we have studied children's information-seeking questions in small-scale traditional societies (Gauvain et al., 2013). The data were collected by R. H. and R. L. Munroe in 1978–9 in four communities, the Garifuna (Belize), Logoli (Kenya), Newars (Nepal), and Samoans (American Samoa) (Munroe et al., 1984; Gowdy et al., 1989). The sample included 192 children, with 48 children (12 each at three, five, seven, and nine years of age, evenly divided by gender) in each community. The communities differ geographically and historically and, at the time of data collection, had no contact with each other.

### The Four Communities

The purpose of the original research was to study the development of gendered behaviors and understanding (Munroe et al., 1984). Information about children's questions is available in the naturalistic observations collected by the researchers at the time. Sociodemographic background information was also collected on sample children and their families and these data were used to examine whether socioeconomic status related to the frequency of children's question-asking behavior. The descriptions below pertain to the communities at the time the data were collected. Estimates of time use, represented as proportions of daylight activities dedicated to subsistence work, were derived from systematic naturalistic observations of the adults in the four communities (Munroe & Munroe, 1990a, 1990b, 1991; Munroe et al., 1997).

*Garifuna*    The Garifuna, an Arawak-speaking group, live in southern Belize. Community members, also referred to as the Black Carib, are descendants of African slaves who settled in Central America in the 1800s following a period in the islands of the Caribbean. By 1978–9, they had mostly relinquished subsistence farming and fishing, food was purchased locally, half of the men (50 percent) worked in wage labor employment in the town, and only 6 percent of the adults' daily activities was devoted to subsistence work. In 1979 the per capita income of Belize was $1,001 per year. Both primary and secondary schools were available. Children were expected to attend secondary school and many parents had done so. The main school was run by the Roman Catholic Church (there was also a small American-run Protestant school), with an American clerical hierarchy and some American teachers.

*Logoli*   The Logoli are members of an equatorial, Bantu-speaking group living near Lake Victoria in Kenya, East Africa. In the late 1970s they lived on dispersed patrilocal, patrilineal homesteads, farmed subsistence products such as maize and beans, and kept cattle. When the data were collected, few Logoli men (3 percent) were employed in wage labor in the village, and 19 percent of the adults' daily activities was devoted to subsistence work. The per capita income of Kenya at the time was $380 per year. Only primary school was available and it was run by Kenyan administrators and taught by Kenyans, though the school still reflected its curricular origins in British colonial education. An examination at the end of primary school was structured so that only a small minority of children was allowed to pursue secondary education.

*Newars*   The Newars are Tibeto-Burman speaking members of a farming caste in the Kathmandu Valley of Nepal. In the late 1970s, they lived in a compact village surrounded by terraced rice fields. All the households possessed and cultivated patrimonial land. At the time of data collection, few Newar men (15 percent) participated in wage labor in the village and 26 percent of the adults' daily activities was devoted to subsistence work. The per capita income in Nepal in the late 1970s was $130 per year. Only a government-supported primary school was present in the village. The educational system was indigenous and a local villager was the instructor in the school that two-thirds of older sample children attended.

*American Samoa*   The sample of American Samoans consisted of village-dwelling members of a Polynesian island culture. In 1978–9, some families continued traditional growing of taro and raising of domesticated pigs. Most men (87 percent) worked in wage labor, often in US development programs, and only 13 percent of the adults' daily activities was devoted to subsistence work. The per capita income in American

Samoa at the time was $5,210 per year. Primary and secondary school were available, with children expected to finish secondary school as had most parents. The school system was supported by US funding and included the presence of some American teachers.

When the data were collected, a degree of monetization had occurred in all four communities. This process was facilitated by the presence of local wage earners, commuters, and remittees who were partially dependent on community members temporarily working in urban areas or even foreign countries. Children participated to some extent in the money economy in all four communities, but it was most extensive among the Garifuna and Samoans where children frequently shopped. In 1978–9, the Samoans and Garifuna were also experiencing other societal-level changes. Both villages had airfields with regularly scheduled flights, medical facilities with a resident physician, large religious structures, multiple shops, and commercial accommodations for visitors. None of these amenities was available among the Logoli or the Newars. Thus, despite an ongoing decline in subsistence activities in the samples, all four communities retained enough of their aboriginal customs that they could be validly labeled as representing "small-scale traditional" societies (Gauvain & Munroe, 2009).

*Naturalistic Observations*    Observations were carried out by trained observers in each site. An event-sampling technique was used to gather information on young children's talk during social interaction (Munroe & Romney, 2006). The sample included twenty-four children ($N = 96$) from each of the four cultures, with half of the children three years of age and half five years of age. For six weeks, children were observed in their natural settings one to several times a day. A total of thirty to thirty-five observations per child was collected on a schedule so that all children were observed at a similar time of day. For each observation, the observer sought out the scheduled child, recorded background information including the setting and personnel present, and then recorded the first (and only the first) verbal or nonverbal (physical aggression or touching) social act performed by the child. We examined the *verbal* social acts, or utterances, only, which comprised 89 percent of the observed behaviors. The observers, who were fluent in English and the local language, translated the utterances into English.

There were 2,705 utterances in total, averaging 28 per child. The utterances were coded for the type and content of the questions and the social setting; reliabilities were very good to excellent. There were 269 (10 percent) of the total utterances identified as questions that

Table 10.1 *Content codes for information-seeking questions with definitions from Chouinard (2007) and examples from the four-culture data*

| Code | Definition | Example |
|------|-----------|---------|
| Label | Name of object, or to what a name applies | "Matuala, what are we eating?" (Samoa, 3-year-old) |
| Appearance | Visible property of an object | No instances |
| Property | Permanent property of an object | "Where is the edge of it?" Samoa, 5-year-old |
| Function | Function of an object | "Can I eat the fruit that dropped from the tree?" (Logoli, 5-year-old) |
| Part | Part of an object | No instances |
| Activity | Activity of an object, person, or animal | "Are you finished combing my hair?" (Garifuna, 3-year-old) |
| State | Temporary state of something | "Is it too hot?" (Newar, 5-year-old) |
| Count | Number of, existence of something | "How many seeds should I put in every hole?" (Logoli, 5-year-old) |
| Possession | Who something belongs to, or if someone has possession of something | "Is this mine?" (Garifuna, 5-year-old) |
| Location | Where something is or belongs | "Where is my brother?" (Newar, 3-year-old) |
| Hierarchy | How different category labels relate to one another | No instances |
| Generalization | A category as a whole | No instances |
| Theory of Mind | Beliefs, desires, mental states, or personality of a person | "Do you want to play with me?" (Samoa, 3-year-old) |
| Identity | What makes something what it is | "Who give you that piece of yam you are eating?" (Garifuna, 3-year-old) |
| General Information | News about someone or someplace | "Did you win your match?" (Logoli, 3-year-old) |

sought information. Each information-seeking question was coded as either explanatory or fact-seeking, following the method of Chouinard (2007). Questions that included any of the terms "why," "how," or "what about" were coded as explanatory, and all others were coded as fact-seeking. Examples of explanatory questions are "Why are you laughing, Talonga?" (three-year-old Samoan female, Samoa) and "Why did you keep the tail on this kite?" (five-year-old male, Newar). Examples of fact-seeking questions are "What is her name again?" (three-year-old female, Belize) and "Are you going to take your meal?" (five-year-old male, Nepal). Question content was coded using Chouinard's fourteen-item coding scheme (see Table 10.1). We added one code that pertained to General Information, defined as a request for news from elsewhere (e.g., "What news do you have?" three-year-old female, Logoli). These codes are mutually exclusive. We also coded whether any questions, regardless of type or content, concerned a future-oriented behavior (e.g., "Ma, which dress will I put on after I bathe?" three-year-old female, Garifuna) or a past event or memory (e.g., "Tafeo, did you see the cat?" five-year-old female, Samoa). For social setting, we coded the personnel present when children asked the question as well as the person to whom the child directed the question. The following categories of persons were identified: mother, father, other adult, older child or adolescent (9–16 years), younger child (3–8 years), infant (0–2 years).

*Children's Questions*    When we compared the number of children's information-seeking questions across the four cultures, we found no differences, so we collapsed the data and compared it with extant data from Western samples (Chouinard, 2007). This comparison yielded no difference in the number of fact-seeking questions. However, the proportion of explanation-seeking questions in our four-culture sample was much lower, making up fewer than 5 percent of the children's questions compared with around 25 percent in the Western sample.

Twelve of the ninety-six children in the four-culture sample asked no questions, and of the remaining eighty-four children, seventy-four asked fact-seeking questions but did not ask any explanatory questions. The three- and five-year-old children did not differ in the total number of questions or number of fact-seeking questions they asked. Also, socio-economic status was unrelated to the number of questions children asked, both within and across the culture groups. The same was true of child gender except in one instance: whereas Garifuna male children asked the majority of questions (67 percent), Logoli boys asked fewer questions (40 percent) than did girls.

Of the ten children who asked an explanatory question, half were three years of age and half were five years of age. Nine of these children asked only one such question and one child, a Newar three-year-old boy, asked three. This particular child is worth remarking upon for several reasons. The overall percentage of his information-seeking questions (fact-seeking and explanatory questions combined) was the sixth highest of all children among the ninety-six in the full sample. This child was the only one in the entire sample who was the offspring of a storekeeper in the village. This boy's mother was absent from the village and his father owned a small shop. This child was in the shop all the time and his questions were not directed toward his father but to others in the vicinity. We suspect that the child's unique experience in the shop, a setting in which questions are often asked as customers seek out goods to buy, influenced the boy's pattern of social interaction.

Taken together, these results indicate that children living in small-scale traditional communities and children living in Western industrialized settings ask questions at similar rates. Children are curious and they use questions to learn about the world. However, relative to children in Western societies, children in small-scale traditional societies ask very few explanatory questions. Possible explanations for this difference are discussed later. First, we describe the content and social contexts of children's question-asking behavior in the four-culture and Western samples.

### What Did the Children Ask About and to Whom?

There were similarities and differences across the Western and four-culture samples in the content of children's questions. For both groups, most questions were about activity and location. In the four-culture sample, the number of questions about location and activities did not differ by child age.

Western children often asked about state, label, and identity, which was also evident in our four-culture sample. Similar to the Western data, the younger (three-year-old) children in our sample asked more questions about label than the older (five-year-old) children. This result led Chouinard (2007) to conclude that, compared with older preschoolers, younger children are more focused on learning basic facts about the world and they use questions to do so, a point with which our data concur. In our sample, five-year-old children asked more questions about state than younger children did, which was also consistent with the Western data.

Theory of Mind (ToM) questions, which ask about what someone wants, is thinking, or believes, also occurred at similar rates in the Western and non-Western samples. Unlike the Western data, the rate of these questions in our sample did not increase with child age, but these questions did make up a substantial portion (17.5 percent) of the children's questions overall. In the Western sample, ToM questions were asked mostly of adults (usually parents, who were often the only other interlocutors available), whereas in the four-culture sample these questions were asked largely of other children, even though parents were often available. This result is consistent with research conducted in other small-scale traditional communities in Western Samoa (Ochs, 1988), Inuit in Canada (Crago, 1992), and Kaluli in Papau New Guinea (Schieffelin, 1990) where it is inappropriate to inquire explicitly about what someone else is thinking. Over the preschool years children begin to appreciate different points of view and they have interest in what others think (Doherty, 2009). Our data suggest that children pursue this interest while at the same time they abide by the pragmatics or social constraints of language use in their culture. In some social settings, such as the four communities we studied, ToM questions may be seen as intrusive, perhaps even confrontational, and therefore disruptive of established respect and authority relations between adults and children. However, as our data show, young children still asked ToM questions and they mainly did so of other young children, often infants. For instance, a three-year-old Samoan boy asked a male infant "Do you want to play with me?" and a five-year-old Newar boy asked an infant girl "Do you feel it?" As to the other content areas, questions about possession (4 percent) and identity (5 percent) were infrequent and at similar rates for three- and five-year-olds. There were very few or no questions in the other content areas (range 0–3).

There was no difference across the four culture groups in information-seeking questions that concerned future behaviors (Logoli = 6; Garifuna = 16; Newar = 14; Samoa = 14). Three-year-old children asked 18 of these questions while five-year-old children asked 32 of them. Of the 5 memory questions asked, 4 were posed by five-year-old children; and as to culture group, Samoan children asked 4 and 1 was asked by a Garifuna child. Thus, in terms of cognition more generally, children in the four cultures asked questions that took the point of view of others and displayed concern with future activities and memory for events. The age-related patterns observed are consistent with extant research on the development of future-oriented thinking and memory in early childhood (Gauvain & Perez, 2015a). In other words, the children's questions give evidence of complex thought and, therefore, there is no reason to assume a gulf in cognitive activity between them and children living in Western industrialized societies based on their question-asking behaviors. In other words, we need to look elsewhere to explain the different patterns of explanatory questions in the Western and non-Western comparative samples.

As to the social setting of children's questions, the US children in the comparison sample were observed only at home and, unsurprisingly, the great majority of their questions were addressed to parents (usually mother). Children in the non-Western samples were mainly observed outdoors near their homes, which allowed us to investigate children's questioning when the social surrounds include individuals besides the parents. Across the four communities, the mean number of participants per setting (besides the observed child) was slightly over four persons. The usual social scene was peer-group dominated and only 27 percent of the questions were directed to a parent (the mother, occasionally the father). Although about three-fourths of the children's questions were peer directed, for three content categories – state, ToM, and identity – the rate was even higher with 17 of 18 (94 percent) questions about state, 39 of 44 (89 percent) questions about ToM, and 11 of 13 (85 percent) questions about identity aimed at peers or younger children. There were no content categories for which parents were asked an unusually high percentage of questions. When addressing parents, our sample children mostly asked about activities ("Are we going by school today?") and location, although these questions occurred in large numbers to nonparents also. Finally, we found no differences in the rate of children's fact-seeking questions that were asked of parents or nonparents. However, children did appear to ask parents fewer explanatory questions than they asked of others. Of the twelve explanatory questions, only two were directed toward parents. And, as previously stated, several were directed at shoppers in a parent's store. This rate is low compared with the Western data, where children were mainly in the company of parents. Nevertheless, the small, albeit relative, rate of explanatory questions to parents in the non-Western samples is significant and needs to be accounted for.

To summarize, the content of children's questions is largely consistent across the non-Western and Western samples. However, the social situation in which children are learning to use language differs dramatically across these two types of cultural settings, a factor we contend contributes in important ways to children's question-asking behaviors.

### *What Do These Results Tell Us?*

These data show that children living in Western, industrialized societies and in small-scale traditional communities ask information-seeking questions at similar rates. However, relative to children living in Western settings, children living in small-scale traditional societies ask very few explanatory questions. The rarity of explanatory questions in our four-culture sample is provocative and, initially, we found this pattern puzzling. But further consideration of the findings from a sociocultural perspective led to some possible interpretations.

We believe the low rate of explanatory questions among children living in these four small-scale traditional communities relative to Western middle-class children may reflect two factors. First, in small-scale traditional societies, there is often unspoken acceptance of greater authority of adults vis-à-vis children; for a child to ask "why" would challenge that authority (LeVine, 1970). Second, in these societies, there may not be a great need for children to ask adults explanatory questions. Children can see their meaningful part in a relatively stable socioeconomic fabric and may seldom need to ask for explanations. In contrast, in industrial societies, question-asking (at least in the middle class; Tizard & Hughes, 1984) is seen as a "teachable moment." Also, less opportunity to observe adults in their occupational settings (i.e., "authentic activities"; Rogoff, 2003) and demands of life (e.g., new objects and devices) may make asking explanatory-type questions adaptive for children. (In fact, the use of certain technology for many different types of activities may exacerbate these patterns by making the activities of adults even more mysterious to children. The same instrument – a smartphone, tablet or computer – may be used to socialize with friends and family, read the news, be entertained, keep lists, shop, bank, work, and so forth. But to a young child, these behaviors would look the same, although at times the child may detect differences in the parent's urgency or affect.)

There was evidence in our sample consistent with the interpretation that authority relations in a society may play an important role in children's question-asking behavior. Recall that the lowest percentage of questions, overall, was among the Logoli children of Kenya. LeVine (1973) has argued that a primary socio-behavioral pattern in sub-Saharan Africa involves social distance between persons differing in age and sex. This includes an emphasis on the authority of elders and the compliance, obedience, and responsibility of those who are younger (Doob, 1965). Asking of questions by children would implicitly violate these norms of conformity. Indeed, asking for explanations – which the Logoli children did not do at all – would do so even more. Similar hierarchical patterns of caregiver–child interaction have been reported in Western Samoa, which is also a highly stratified society (Ochs, 1982). Young children in this community are expected to understand and abide by social expectations regarding interpersonal respect in the manner in which they talk to others, especially elders.

Yet, in regards to explanatory questions, it is difficult to understand a phenomenon's near absence. In looking for a clue, it is worth considering what occurs in situations like those reported for US children. It is almost startling to read in the CHILDES transcripts the never-let-up why-type questions asked by the children. For instance, in one case the child was looking at pictures in a book alongside his mother, and the following exchange occurred (MacWhinney & Snow, 1985):

MOTHER (MO): "he's a little boy who's painting."
CHILD (CH): "why he painting?"
MO: "because he likes to paint."
CH: "why he like to paint?"

MO: "because it's fun."
CH: "why it's fun?"
MO: "because it's something he like[s] to do."
CH: "why he like to do it?"

In contrast, in our four cultures, the children mostly asked spontaneous, one-off questions designed to get immediate, relevant information. Continuously asking "why," as the child does in the above example,
would more than likely be regarded as insolent. This interpretation was
borne out in interviews with the mothers in these four societies in which
a large majority stated that children should be obedient, responsible, and
respectful, as well as engaged in household chores and subsistence work.
These responses are consistent with Serpell's (2017) sociocultural
description of intelligence that includes social responsibility as an important dimension.

It is important to stress that the three- and five-year-old children in
these four non-Western cultures were not silent. Even though these
children were not asking many explanatory questions, they were participating in and learning about the world around them. Children were
observed working in various capacities on their own and alongside other
children and adults (Gauvain & Munroe, 2009). The work often involved
practices and tools typical of the setting, including those related to clean-
ing up, preparing food, caring for younger children, and generally helping
out around the house (e.g., gardening, tending to animals, running
errands). They were observed in various forms of play including formal
rule-based games, role playing, and play with toys and other objects. They
were also observed handling conventional learning materials, such as
books and writing supplies.

By and large, the children's days were full of activities that made sense in
the communities in which they lived, but which differ sharply from the
experiences of many children living in Western, industrialized settings.
Children in these four cultures were exposed to and involved in the activities
of adults in the community on an ongoing and regular basis, which provided
them with substantial opportunity to observe mature behaviors practiced in
their communities and even begin to learn some of them under the tutelage
or watchful eyes of more experienced community members. The children in
our sample, both three- and five-year-olds, were observed talking with others
and asking questions about things that interested them. These experiences
provided children with culturally organized and supported opportunities for
cognitive development (Nerlove & Snipper, 1981). The sole difference in
children's question-asking behavior in these four cultures and the Western
comparison data was in the use of explanatory questions. These findings

suggest that children's use of explanation-seeking questions varies across social and cultural settings and that social factors within cultural settings regulate their frequency and, perhaps, contribution to cognitive development.

There are, of course, limitations in the comparisons on which this conclusion is based. Perhaps most importantly, the social partners of the children in the Western sample were generally the parents whereas in the non-Western samples the social scene usually involved several nonparental adults and other children. This difference, however, yielded some insights about the presence of parents with respect to children's question-asking. In addition, the fact that the Western sample included a small set of observed children ($N = 4$) was offset to some extent by the size of the database (17,000 information-seeking questions). Our relatively small number of total utterances (fewer than 300 information-seeking questions) was balanced, in a sense, by a total sample approaching 100 children. Also, the number of culture groups is very small and needs to be expanded as research continues on this topic. It is also important to remember that the culture groups we studied were representative of only certain traditional ways of life, mainly agriculturally based subsistence societies, and do not tell us about question-asking in, say, hunter-gatherer societies or even in the larger cities of the nations in which the sample children were living. Finally, the data were collected several decades ago and patterns may have changed in these four cultures. Given that data from the Western comparison sample were collected around the same time, this concern can be raised of them as well.

## Conclusions

We began by describing children's great curiosity and eagerness to learn about the world. Children's ability, beginning around age three, to ask questions about what interests them is certainly an important part of this endeavor. However, separating children's questions from their social and cultural context of expression undermines the larger goal of describing how children learn about the world, of which question-asking behavior is one part.

In order to learn socially, children need to acquire and use language in ways that are appropriate in their community (Ochs & Schieffelin, 1984). Children's questions, like other aspects of language use, are subject to social and cultural rules and expectations, including what information can or should be exchanged and with whom. To study the connection between social and cultural context and children's question-asking behavior, we reviewed research conducted in socially diverse settings in

Western, industrialized societies and small-scale traditional societies. This inquiry revealed substantial variation in children's question-asking behavior, especially questions that seek explanation. These contrasting results make assumptions about the universality of children's explanation-seeking questions troubling. That is, if explanation-seeking questions are an important mechanism for cognitive development, where does this conclusion leave children who live in social and cultural settings where language socialization does not emphasize or encourage such forms of speech? In probing this issue, we did not consider that children in some cultures are less curious about the world or less capable of asking questions. Indeed, our data suggest the exact opposite. Children in the small-scale traditional communities we studied were active participants in daily life and in the conversations that surrounded them. When they wanted to know something, they asked questions of others. We contend that children around the world are equally able in this regard and we know of no evidence, including ours, that refutes this claim.

Instead, in our research, we found a discrepancy between the rate of children's explanatory questions and extant data from Western samples, a difference that was not expected when we launched the investigation. This led us to consider social and cultural conditions that may affect the frequency of children's explanatory questions. We did not take a close look at what learning ensued from these questions because we agree that when children ask explanation-seeking questions that are responded to in a helpful manner, the exchange will benefit children's learning. Rather, our concern is that a behavior that is common in a particular social circumstance – middle-class, Western, industrialized communities – is viewed as a mechanism for cognitive development without deeper consideration of the form and function of this behavior in the social and cultural context of child development.

We suggest that a number of social and cultural factors may work against young children asking adults, including parents, for explanations, at least at the high rates seen in Western, middle-class families. One factor is simply that in some societies, such as those that are relatively stable socioeconomically, there may be a lower level of need or "demand" for these questions. Children can fit into and contribute meaningfully to family stability and well-being without constant explanation-seeking. Another factor is the personnel present. When young children spend much of their time with one other person, especially one who is much more knowledgeable than the child and, in the case of caregiver, emotionally involved, certain question-asking behaviors may be much more likely than when children are in larger social groups much of the day. There are also likely associations between societal values and other social practices and children's explanatory questioning. Two possibilities are described here, authoritarian child rearing and an emphasis on politeness and respect for authority figures – which often co-occur. The low level of explanatory questioning by children in social situations in which these values are in force suggests that pressures exerted during socialization, such as high expectations of obedience and formality when children interact with adults, regulate the presence and frequency of children's explanatory questions.

## Implications

As research on children's question-asking behavior goes forward, it is worth remembering that participants in research reported in high-impact developmental journals in 2015 represented less than 8 percent of the world's children and over 95 percent of papers were authored by scientists working in Western settings (Nielsen et al., 2017). In considering findings from diverse social and cultural contexts, the research with children living in Western, middle-class settings – who ask explanation-seeking questions at a high and regular rate – suggests to us that it may be in the industrial/post-industrial world that "the range of variation" falls outside statistically observable cross-cultural norms (Whiting, 1954). In other words, the high rates of explanation-seeking questions by middle-class children in industrial and post-industrial societies may be the outlier – the pattern that requires explication. As we noted earlier and have argued elsewhere (Gauvain & Munroe, 2012), there may be adaptational prerequisites in these societies that would tilt children toward asking explanatory questions.

In some respects, examining the contribution of children's questions to learning and cognitive development is a limited undertaking. To us, it is more useful to consider children's questions as one of a constellation of behaviors they have at their disposal to help them learn from others (Gauvain & Nicolaides, 2015). There are many spontaneous, child-generated ways that children learn socially, including the allocation of attention (Adamson & Bakeman, 1991; Chavajay & Rogoff, 1999), tendencies to imitate (or not) the behaviors of others (Lyons et al., 2007), observation (Lancy, 1996; Gaskins & Paradise, 2010), conversations and sharing of information (Haden et al., 2001; Gauvain & Perez, 2015b), listening in on the conversations of others (Rogoff, 2003), openness to instruction and guided participation (Rogoff, 1990; Gauvain, 2001), various forms of cultural learning (Tomasello et al., 1993), and participation, both direct and peripherally, in household and community activities (Lave & Wenger, 1991; Rogoff et al., 2003). Children engage in all these ways of learning, albeit with different rates and forms across social and cultural settings. And all of them demonstrate the active role of children in shaping their own development (Kessen, 1979).

The issues for us, then, are how do children go about selecting among these various modes of learning in specific circumstances and how do these modes fit together in the culture? During socialization, children learn *how to learn* from other people in their community and they use information in specific situations, including input from others, to guide them as to what to do. Some of this learning may be overt; and some may be embedded in other practices, such as language socialization as we discuss here. As this long list of ways of learning suggests, the ability for children to learn from other people is over-determined, and it needs to be – it is essential to children's survival. Yet in order to learn successfully from other community members, children need to adhere to the values and practices of the community. Even in cultures where children's explanatory questioning is encouraged and frequent, sociocultural values and practices impose limits on these questions. For instance, in middle-class Western households certain questions, which Harris (2012) labels as taboo, are likely to be met with disapproval and discouraged (e.g., "Why is Grandpa fat?" "Mommy, why doesn't Daddy love you anymore?").

Children's questions, and the interactions they promote, serve immediate functions along with broader social and cultural goals. These goals include preparing children to adapt to other societal institutions and expectations (Ochs & Schieffelin, 1984). Improved understanding of children's explanatory questions across diverse social and cultural contexts is important for clarifying the role these questions play in cognitive development. There is also a need for research that probes the role of children's questioning in other areas of psychological growth, including social and emotional realms (Pretacznik-Gierowska & Ligeza, 1990; Laible et al., 2015). It will also be important to discover if children's questioning changes as cultures change. As mentioned previously, one of the important features of industrial and technological societies is an ever-expanding availability of new material forms or tools to support human activity. These features, which are closely tied to the widespread process of globalization, may alter how children interact with others. Research on the increased availability of formal schooling in a community has shown that parent–child interaction changes by incorporating ways that help prepare children for the demands of school, such as new forms of questions by parents toward children (e.g., questions with known answers). Along similar lines, we expect that in a changing society in which more resources and tools are available to support everyday life, children's experiences will change considerably, including the ways in which children talk with others and the type and amount of information they feel compelled to seek out through questions.

## Acknowledgments

The fieldwork described in this chapter was supported by a grant from the National Science Foundation awarded to Robert L. and Ruth H. Munroe. We thank the villagers, participants, and local experimenters for their cooperation, Sarah Ingalls and Jason Rivera for assistance in coding, and Ronald Macaulay, Susan Seymour, and Claudia Strauss for comments on the research. Robert L. Munroe passed away on May 14, 2018, and this chapter is dedicated to his memory.

## References

Adamson, L. B., and Bakeman, R. (1991). The development of shared attention during infancy. In R. Vasta (ed.), *Annals of child development* (vol. 8, pp. 1–41). London: Kingsley.

Andersen, E. S. (1990). *Speaking with style: The socio-linguistic skill of children.* London: Routledge.

Bates, E. (1976). *Language and context: The acquisition of pragmatics.* New York: Academic Press.

Bornstein, M. H. (2002). Toward a multiculture, multiage, multimethod science. *Human Development, 45,* 257–63. https://doi.org/10.1159/000064986

Bornstein, M. H., Hendricks, C., Haynes, O. M., and Painter, K. M. (2007). Maternal sensitivity and child responsiveness: Associations with social context, maternal characteristics, and child characteristics in a multivariate analysis. *Infancy, 12,* 189–223. https://doi.org/10.1111/j.1532–7078 .2007.tb00240.x

Bowlby, J. (1969). *Attachment and loss; Vol. 1: Attachment.* London: Hogarth Press.

Bruner, J. S. (1975). The ontogenesis of speech acts. *Journal of Child Language, 2,* 1–20. https://doi.org/10.1017/s0305000900000866

  (1981). The pragmatics of acquisition. In W. Deutsch (ed.), *The child's construction of language* (pp. 39–56). London: Academic Press.

Callanan, M. A., and Jipson, J. L. (2001). Explanatory conversations and young children's developing scientific literacy. In K. Crowley, C. D. Schunn, and T. Okada (eds.), *Designing for science: Implications from everyday, classroom, and professional settings* (pp. 21–49). Mahwah, NJ: Erlbaum.

Callanan, M. A., and Oakes, L. M. (1992). Preschoolers' questions and parents' explanations: Causal thinking in everyday activity. *Cognitive Development, 7,* 213–33. https://doi.org/10.1016/0885–2014(92)90012–g

Carey, S. (1985). *Conceptual change in childhood.* Cambridge, MA: MIT Press.

Chavajay, P., and Rogoff, B. (1999). Cultural variation in the management of attention by children and their caregivers. *Developmental Psychology, 35,* 1079–90. https://doi.org/10.1037/0012–1649.35.4.1079

Chouinard, M. M. (2007). Children's questions: A mechanism for cognitive development. *Monographs of the Society for Research in Child Development, 72,* i–112.

Cole, M. (1996). *Cultural psychology: A once and future discipline.* Cambridge, MA: Harvard University Press.

Crago, M. (1992). Communicative interaction and second language acquisition: An Inuit example. *TESOL Quarterly, 26,* 487–505. https://doi.org/10.2307 /3587175

Delgado-Gaitan, C. (1994). Socializing young children in Mexican-American families: An intergenerational perspective. In P. M. Greenfield and R. R. Cocking (eds.), *Cross-cultural roots of minority child development* (pp. 55–86). Hillsdale, NJ: Erlbaum.

Doherty, M. J. (2009). *Theory of mind: How children understand others' thoughts and feelings.* New York: Psychology Press.

Doob, L. W. (1965). Psychology. In R. A. Lystad (ed.), *The African world* (pp. 373–415). London: Pall Mall Press.

Dunn, J. (1988). *The beginnings of social understanding.* Cambridge, MA: Harvard University Press.

Engel, S. (2015). *The hungry mind: The origins of curiosity in children.* Cambridge, MA: Harvard University Press.

Ervin-Tripp, S. M. (1982). Ask and it shall be given you: Children's requests. In H. Byrnes (ed.), *Contemporary perceptions of language: Interdisciplinary dimensions* (pp. 232–45). Washington, DC: Georgetown University Press.

Fivush, R., and Nelson, K. (2006). Parent-child reminiscing locates the self in the past. *British Journal of Developmental Psychology, 24,* 235–51. https://doi.org /10.1348/026151005x57747

Foster, S. H. (1986). Learning discourse topic management in the preschool years. *Journal of Child Language, 13,* 231–50. https://doi.org/10.1017 /s0305000900008035

Frazier, B. N., Gelman, S. A., and Wellman, H. M. (2009). Preschoolers' search for explanatory information within adult-child conversation. *Child Development, 80,* 1592–611. https://doi.org/10.1111/j.1467–8624 .2009.01356.x

Frazier, B. N., Gelman, S. A., and Wellman, H. M. (2016). Young children prefer and remember satisfying explanations. *Journal of Cognition and Development, 17,* 718–36. https://doi.org/10.1080/15248372.2015.1098649

Gaskins, S., and Paradise, R. (2010). Learning through daily life. In D. Lancy, J. Bock, and S. Gaskins (eds.), *The anthropology of learning in childhood* (pp. 85–117). Lanham, MA: AltaMira Press.

Gauvain, M. (2001). *The social context of cognitive development.* New York: Guilford.

Gauvain, M., and Munroe, R. L. (2009). Contributions of societal modernity to cognitive development: A comparison of four cultures. *Child Development, 80,* 1628–42. https://doi.org/10.1111/j.1467–8624.2009.01358.x

   (2012). Cultural change, human activity, and cognitive development. *Human Development, 55,* 205–28. https://doi.org/10.1159/000339451

Gauvain, M., and Nicolaides, C. (2015). Cognition in childhood across cultures. In L. A. Jensen (ed.), *The Oxford handbook of human development and culture: An interdisciplinary perspective* (pp. 198–213). New York: Oxford University Press.

Gauvain, M., and Perez, S. M. (2015a). Cognitive development and culture. In R. M. Lerner (series ed.), and L. Liben and U. Müller (vol. eds.), *Handbook of child psychology and developmental science: Cognitive processes* (7th ed., vol. 2) (pp. 854–96). New York: Wiley.

  (2015b). The socialization of cognition. In J. Grusec and P. Hastings (eds.), *Handbook of socialization: Theory and research* (2nd ed., pp. 566–89). New York: Guilford.

Gauvain, M., Munroe, R. L., and Beebe, H. (2013). Children's questions in cross-cultural perspective: A four-culture study. *Journal of Cross-Cultural Psychology*, *44*, 1148–65. https://doi.org/10.1177/0022022113485430

Gowdy, P. D., Munroe, R. H., and Munroe, R. L. (1989). Independence of action and measured cognitive performance among children from four cultures. In D. M. Keats, D. Munro, and L. Mann (eds.), *Heterogeneity in cross-cultural psychology* (pp. 382–91). Amsterdam: Swets & Zeitlinger.

Greenfield, P. M. (2009). Linking social change and developmental change: Shifting pathways of human development. *Developmental Psychology*, *45*, 401–18. https://doi.org/10.1037/a0014726

Grice, H. P. (1989). *Studies in the way of words*. Cambridge, MA: Harvard University Press.

Haden, C. A., Ornstein, P. A., Eckerman, C. O., and Didow, S. M. (2001). Mother–child conversational interactions as events unfold: Linkages to subsequent remembering. *Child Development*, *72*, 1016–31. https://doi.org/10.1111/1467–8624.00332

Harris, P. L. (2007). Commentary: Time for questions. *Monographs of the Society for Research in Child Development*, *72*, 113–20. https://doi.org/10.1111/j.1540–5834.2007.00421.x

  (2012). *Trusting what you're told: How children learn from others*. Cambridge, MA: Harvard University Press.

Hart, B., and Risley, T. (1992). American parenting of language-learning children: Persisting differences in family-child interactions observed in natural home environments. *Developmental Psychology*, *28*, 1096–105. https://doi.org/10.1037//0012–1649.28.6.1096

Heath, S. B. (1983). *Ways with words: Language, life and work in communities and classrooms*. Cambridge: Cambridge University Press.

Hickling, A. K., and Wellman, H. M. (2001). The emergence of children's causal explanations and theories: Evidence from everyday conversation. *Developmental Psychology*, *37*, 668–83. https://doi.org/10.1037//0012–1649.37.5.668

Hood L., Bloom, L., and Brainerd, C. J. (1979). What, when, and how about why: A longitudinal study of early expressions of causality. *Monographs of the Society for Research in Child Development*, *44*, 1–47.

Hymes, D. (1974). *Foundations in sociolinguistics: An ethnographic approach*. Philadelphia: University of Pennsylvania Press.

James, S. L., and Seebach, M. A. (1982). The pragmatic function of children's questions. *Journal of Speech and Hearing Research*, *25*, 2–11. https://doi.org/10.1044/jshr.2501.02

Kessen, W. (1979). The American child and other cultural inventions. *American Psychologist*, *34*, 815–20. https://doi.org/10.1037//0003-066x.34.10.815

Kurkul, K. E., and Corriveau, K. H. (2018). Question, explanation, follow-up: A mechanism for learning from others? *Child Development*, *89*, 280–94. https://doi.org/10.1111/cdev.12726

Kyratzis, A., and Cook-Gumperz, J. (2015), Child discourse. In D. Tannen, H. E. Hamilton, and D. Schriffin (eds.), *The handbook of discourse analysis* (2nd ed., vol. 1) (pp. 681–704). Malden, MA: Wiley Blackwell.

Laible, D., and Song, J. (2006). Constructing emotional and relational understanding: The role of affect and mother-child discourse. *Merrill-Palmer Quarterly*, *52*, 44–69. https://doi.org/10.1353/mpq.2006.0006

Laible, D., Thompson, R. A., and Froimson, J. (2015). Early socialization: The influence of close relationships. In J. Grusec and P. Hastings (eds.), *Handbook of socialization: Theory and research* (2nd ed., pp. 35–59). New York: Guilford.

Lancy, D. F. (1996). *Playing on the mother ground: Cultural routines for children's development*. New York: Guilford.

Lave, J., and Wenger, E. (1991). *Situated learning: Legitimate peripheral participation*. New York: Cambridge University Press.

LeVine, R. A. (1970). Cross-cultural study in child psychology. In P. H. Mussen (ed.), *Carmichael's manual of child psychology* (3rd ed., vol. 2) (pp. 559–612). New York: Wiley.

  (1973). Patterns of personality in Africa. *Ethos*, *1*, 123–52. https://doi.org/10.1525/eth.1973.1.2.02a00010

Lyons, D. E., Young, A. G., and Keil, F. C. (2007). The hidden structure of overimitation. *Proceedings of the National Academy of Sciences*, *104*, 19751–6. https://doi.org/10.1073/pnas.0704452104

MacWhinney, B., and Snow, C. E. (1985). The Child Language Data Exchange System (CHILDES). *Journal of Child Language*, *12*, 271–94. https://doi.org/10.1017/s0305000900006449

  (1990). The child language data exchange system: An update. *Journal of Child Language*, *17*, 457–72. https://doi.org/10.1017/s0305000900013866

Maratsos, M. P. (2007). Commentary. *Monographs of the Society for Research in Child Development*, *72*, 121–6. https://doi.org/10.1111/j.1540–5834.2007.00425.x

Munroe, R. L., and Munroe, R. H. (1990a). *Black Carib time allocation*. New Haven, CT: HRAF Press.

  (1990b). *Samoan time allocation*. New Haven, CT: HRAF Press.

  (1991). *Logoli time allocation*. New Haven, CT: HRAF Press.

Munroe, R. L., and Romney, A. K. (2006). Gender and age differences in same-sex aggregation and social behavior. *Journal of Cross-Cultural Psychology*, *37*, 3–19. https://doi.org/10.1177/0022022105282292

Munroe, R. H., Munroe, R. L., Shwayder, J. A., and Arias, G. (1997). *Newar time allocation*. New Haven, CT: HRAF Press.

Munroe, R. H., Shimmin, H. S., and Munroe, R. L. (1984). Gender understanding and sex role preference in four cultures. *Developmental Psychology*, *20*, 673–82. https://doi.org/10.1037/0012–1649.20.4.673

Nakamura, K. (1996). The use of polite language by Japanese preschool children. In D. I. Slobin, J. Gerhardt, A. Kyratzis, and J. Guo (eds.), *Social interaction, social context, and language: Essays in honor of Susan Ervin-Tripp* (pp. 235–50). Mahwah, NJ: Erlbaum.

Nelson, K. (1973). Structure and strategy in learning to talk. *Monographs of the Society for Research in Child Development*, *38*, 1–135. https://doi.org/10.2307 /1165788

(2007). *Young minds in social worlds: Experience, meaning, and memory.* Cambridge, MA: Harvard University Press.

Nerlove, S. G., and Snipper, A. S. (1981). Cognitive consequences of cultural opportunity. In R. H. Munroe, R. L. Munroe, and B. B. Whiting (eds.), *Handbook of cross-cultural psychology* (pp. 423–74). New York: Garland STPM Press.

Nielsen, M., Haun, D., Kärtner, J., and Legare, C. H. (2017). The persistent sampling bias in developmental psychology: A call to action. *Journal of Experimental Child Psychology*, *162*, 31–38. https://doi.org/10.1016/j .jecp.2017.04.017

Ochs, E. (1982). Talking to children in Western Samoa. *Language in Society*, *11*, 77–104. https://doi.org/10.1017/s0047404500009040

(1986). From feelings to grammar: A Samoan case study. In B. B. Schieffelin and E. Ochs (eds.), *Language socialization across cultures* (pp. 251–72). Cambridge: Cambridge University Press.

(1988). *Culture and language development.* Cambridge: Cambridge University Press.

Ochs, E., and Schieffelin, B. B. (1984). Language acquisition and socialization: Three developmental stories and their implications. In R. A. Shweder and R. A. LeVine (eds.), *Culture theory: Essays on mind, self, and emotion* (pp. 276–320). New York: Cambridge University Press.

(2011). The theory of language socialization. In E. Duranti, E. Ochs, and B. Schieffelin (eds.), *The handbook of language socialization* (pp. 1–19). Oxford: Wiley-Blackwell.

Piaget, J. (1923). *Le langage et la pensée chex l'enfant.* Neuchâtel & Paris: Delachaux & Niestlé. (1926). *The language and thought of the child.* London: Kegan Paul.

Pretacznik-Gierowska, M., and Ligeza, M. (1990). Cognitive and interpersonal functions of children's questions. In G. Conti-Ramsden and C. E. Snow (eds.), *Children's language* (vol. 7, pp. 69–101). Hillsdale, NJ: Erlbaum.

Rogoff, B. (1990). *Apprenticeship in thinking: Cognitive development in social context.* Oxford: Oxford University Press.

(2003). *The cultural nature of human development.* New York: Oxford University Press.

Rogoff, B., Paradise, R., Arauz, R. M., Correa-Chávez, M., and Angelillo, C. (2003). Firsthand learning through intent participation. *Annual Review of Psychology*, *54*, 175–203. https://doi.org/10.1146/annurev .psych.54.101601.145118

Schieffelin, B. B. (1990). *The give and take of everyday life.* New York: Cambridge University Press.

Schieffelin, B. B., and Ochs, E. (1984). *Language socialization across cultures.* New York: Cambridge University Press.

Serpell, R. (2017). How the study of cognitive growth can benefit from a cultural lens. *Perspectives on Psychological Science, 12,* 889–99. https://doi.org/10.1177/1745691617704419

Slobin, D. I., Gerhardt, J., Kyratzis, A., and Guo, J. (1996). *Social interaction, social context, and language: Essays in honor of Susan Ervin-Tripp.* Mahwah, NJ: Erlbaum.

Smith, M. E. (1933). The influence of age, sex, and situations on the frequency, form, and function of questions asked by preschool children. *Child Development, 4,* 201–13. https://doi.org/10.2307/1125682

Sterponi, L. (2010). Learning communicative competence. In D. F. Lancy, J. Bock, and S. Gaskins (eds.), *The anthropology of learning in childhood* (pp. 235–59). Lanham, MD: Alta Mira Press.

Tizard, B., and Hughes, M. (1984). *Young children learning.* London: Fontana.

Tizard, B., Hughes, M., Carmichael, H., and Pinkerton, G. (1983). Children's questions and adults' answers. *Journal of Child Psychology and Psychiatry, 24,* 269–81. https://doi.org/10.1111/j.1469–7610.1983.tb00575.x

Tomasello, M., Kruger, A. C., and Ratner, H. H. (1993). Cultural learning. *Behavioral and Brain Sciences, 16,* 495–722. https://doi.org/10.1017/s0140525x0003123x

Tudge, J. R. H. (2008). *The everyday lives of young children: Culture, class, and child rearing in diverse societies.* New York: Cambridge University Press.

Tyack, D., and Ingram, D. (1976). Children's production and comprehension of questions. *Journal of Child Language, 15,* 211–24. https://doi.org/10.1017/s0305000900001616

Vygotsky, L. S. (1987). *The collected works of L. S. Vygotsky. Vol. 1: Problems of general psychology.* Edited by R. W. Rieber and A. S. Carton. New York: Plenum Press.

Whiting, J. W. M. (1954). The cross-cultural method. In G. Lindzey (ed.), *Handbook of social psychology* (vol. 2, pp. 523–31). Cambridge, MA: Addison-Wesley.

# 11 Mothers' Use of Questions and Children's Learning and Language Development

*Imac Maria Zambrana, Tone Kristine Hermansen, Meredith L. Rowe*

## Introduction

Interacting with young children around challenging tasks provides a particularly fruitful opportunity to examine the role of parental question use in children's learning and development. Yet, few studies have examined changes over time in parents' use of different types of questions in specific learning situations. In this chapter, we present results from a longitudinal investigation of the form and function of mothers' questions to their children at ages one, two and three years in a challenging task context across a diverse sample of families in Norway. We examine the implications of these features of mothers' questions for children's concurrent task performance and later language development, and discuss our findings in relation to our understanding of the multiple purposes of mothers' questions for child development.

### The Use of Questions in Child-Directed Speech

Through the immediate and recurring everyday communicative interactions with their infants, parents are their young children's earliest guides for the acquisition of their culture's language and knowledge (Bruner, 1983; Nelson, 2017). Previous research has provided strong support for the relationship between the quantity of parental language input and children's learning and language development (e.g., Huttenlocher et al., 1991; Hart & Risley, 1995; Weisleder & Fernald, 2013). Recently, there has been an increasing recognition that specific qualities of parental input, over and above the quantity, contribute to child language development (e.g., Cartmill et al., 2013; Hirsh-Pasek et al., 2015; Rowe, 2012; Rowe et al., 2016; Snow, 1977). One such qualitative feature that parents use frequently in interactions with their young children is questions (e.g., Pan et al., 1996). Parental questions are proposed to be an important facilitator of both children's language development and learning more broadly (Fletcher et al., 2008; Blewitt et al., 2009; Kurchirko et al., 2015; Haden et al., 2016; Yu et al., 2017), with the form and function of parental questions potentially contributing to children's learning in different ways. For example, using certain *forms* of questions, such as posing wh-questions (see below) to toddlers, places linguistic demands on children to respond verbally to the query, and is found to be more predictive of children's learning than other forms of questions, such as yes/no questions, which do not require an elaborated verbal response (e.g., Rowe et al., 2016). Similarly, questions that serve certain *functions* (see below), such as pedagogical questions or questions that serve a teaching purpose (e.g., the parent knows the answer), have been proposed to play a fruitful role in children's general learning by opening up "the space of hypotheses" for exploration rather than constraining it as is the case with strictly statement-based instructions (Yu et al., 2018, p. 5), or parental questions that are truly information-seeking (e.g., the parents does not know the answer) or rhetorical (e.g., the parent does not expect an answer) (Yu et al., 2017).

*The Form of Questions*

Many studies have looked into changes and variations of specific parental question *forms* across child development and the implications of parental question forms for learning. In particular, wh-questions (e.g., what, who, where, when, why or how) are considered particularly stimulating for children's language development, as these questions ask children to elaborate beyond a yes/no answer (Cristofaro & Tamis-LeMonda, 2012; Rowe et al., 2016). A longitudinal examination of the degree to which parents ask such questions in conversations with their children found an increase in wh-questions over the first three years of the children's lives (e.g., Pan et al., 1996). Despite the fact that parents use more wh-questions as children get older, parents vary in their use of wh-questions in interactions with their children. On average, parents with a higher socioeconomic-status (SES) produce more wh-questions than parents with a low-SES background (Snow et al., 1976; Hart & Risley, 1995), and fathers are found to produce more wh-questions compared to mothers (Gleason & Greif, 1983; Tomasello et al., 1990; Leaper et al., 1998; Rowe et al., 2004; Leech et al., 2013). This variability in exposure to wh-questions is furthermore associated with children's concurrent vocabulary, their own production of such questions and their later verbal reasoning skills (Ninio, 1980; Valian & Casey, 2003; Cristofaro & Tamis-LeMonda, 2012; Rowe et al., 2016). In fact, Rowe et al. (2016) found that it was parental wh-questions and not their production of other types of questions that related to children's language development and verbal reasoning skills, supporting the unique role of this particular type of question in parents' child-directed input. They argued that the relation may be due to the turn-taking and conversational eliciting quality of wh-questions compared to other (i.e., yes/no) questions. As children become more capable of understanding and exploiting the conversational and cognitive characteristics of parental wh-questions, experience with these questions may help promote their language skills. Indeed, the study by Rowe and colleagues (2016) found that children were more likely to respond to wh-questions than other types of questions.

Although many studies have examined parental use of different question forms with their children, the majority of this work examines parental questions during free play situations with children involving book-reading and toy play. More knowledge about parental use of different questioning forms in explicit learning situations might provide further insights into its potential stimulating role for learning outcomes. One goal of this chapter is to examine whether the *form* of mothers' questions in a challenging task with their children changes over time and relates to the children's ability to complete challenging tasks as well as their later language development.

## *The Function of Questions*

Questions are not only categorized by the way they are posed linguistically, but also by their functions (e.g., the ways in which parents use questions to achieve different instructional and pedagogical information goals). That is, although all questions can broadly serve an interrogative function in communication, they can be further categorized by the diverse intents underlying the question. For example, parents can ask questions to seek new information, to encourage turn-taking in conversation, to make a point or to teach their children something (i.e., for pedagogical purposes) (see Yu et al., 2017; Ronfard et al., 2018). Questions with certain functions might be more frequently expressed in a particular form, indicating an overlay between the form and function of a question (e.g., Shatz, 1979). However, as emphasized by others (Yu et al., 2017), the form of a question does not genuinely capture the function, which might be important to understand in practical teaching and learning situations. Thus, we can learn more about the learning implications of questions by examining both their form and function simultaneously.

Both earlier and more recent work has examined the changes and implications of the *functions* of parental questions across child ages in parent–child conversations (Holzman, 1972; Shatz, 1979; Pan et al., 1996; Kuchirko et al., 2015; Yu et al., 2017). Overall, these studies suggest that the functions of parental questions change with increasing child age. In a cross-sectional study of eighteen- to thirty-four-month-olds, Shatz (1979) found that although the variety in maternal question functions produced in free play situations was similar across child age (e.g., the use of questions for the purpose of testing, floor offering, calling attention to something, giving encouragement, requesting information), mothers of older children requested more verbal replies and information, while mothers of younger children requested more actions and phrased the different functions of their questions in more recognizable forms (e.g., more routinized paradigmatic frames). Pan et al. (1996) also found an increase in how parents, for example, used wh- and yes/no questions for a wider variety of communicative intents when playing with their children at ages fourteen, twenty and thirty-two months. In another longitudinal study of preschool children (three to five years of age) and their mothers engaging in book-reading, mothers' use of referential and open-ended questions decreased with child age, while use of story-specific questions increased (Kuchirko et al., 2015). Except for the longitudinal study by Pan et al. (1996) examining changes in parents' communicative intents in play inter-actions with their young children, little such longitudinal analyses of younger children and their parents in challenging task contexts over time exist.

In particular, some of parents' questions are pedagogical in function and these may be particularly helpful for learning. Yu et al. (2017) coded parental pedagogical questions specifically directed at testing children's knowledge, using cross-sectional transcripts of everyday interactions between parents and their two- to six-year-old children from twenty-seven studies. Effectively, all parents asked a large proportion (24 percent) of questions with a pedagogical intent in everyday situations. Yet, com-pared to parents of preschoolers, parents of toddlers were more likely to follow up a pedagogical question than other questions with additional relevant statements, suggesting that they were more likely to facilitate an answer from the younger children. There were also individual differences in parental use of pedagogical questions: parents from middle-class families asked more than twice as many pedagogical questions as parents from working-class families. However, the implications of such differ-ences for child outcomes remain to be examined.

Although these findings suggest some developmental changes in the functions of parental questions in a conversational context, knowledge is lacking about whether similar changes would be apparent in more specific learning contexts. Moreover, it is not possible to determine whether the production of pedagogical questions benefits children's learning develop-ment based on these studies, as the focus was on examining the trends in the functions of the parental questions without linking it to child outcomes. In the current chapter we examine developmental trends in the functions of parental questions when engaging with their children in a challenging task where parents' interaction agendas may be particularly pedagogically tuned and ask whether the function of parental questions (i.e., the task-specific instructional and pedagogical goals) is related to children's task performance and later language skills.

### *Questioning as a Scaffolding Practice in Early Parent–Child Interactions*

Problem-solving contexts encompass a situation where parents are both stimulating their children's language development with questions, at the same time as they convey different instructional or pedagogical intents through their questions. Indeed, while the scaffolding literature has not examined how parents use questions in particular to achieve these different aims, this literature has shown that parents adjust how much information they provide based on their child's performance – increasing support when the child struggles and decreasing support as the child's performance improves (e.g., Wood et al., 1976; Wood et al., 1978; Wood et al., 1995).

One recent experimental word-learning study demonstrated how a scaffolding-like strategy, in which adults first started out with asking low-demand questions and then followed up with high-demand questions, facilitated three-year-old children's word understanding (Blewitt et al., 2009). In line with these results, and as recently stated by Yu et al. (2017), it might be particularly important to look at the role of question functions that capture the teaching intent of the parents in order to understand how questioning might facilitate a broader range of learning performances at different child ages.

### Current Study

To sum up, parents use questions as a conversational strategy, but also for pedagogical purposes (i.e., to provide and query information) in daily conversations with their children. Parents change in their question forms and functions as children get older. The current study builds on prior investigations by addressing three remaining limitations in the literature. First of all, few studies have looked at parental questions using longitudinal analyses, which makes it difficult to determine whether parents truly make developmental adjustments (Shatz, 1979; Pan et al., 1996). Moreover, few studies have looked at parents' questions in problem-solving tasks and few studies have used coding schemes that capture the variety of pedagogical questions. Finally, few studies have looked at the impact that both the form and function of parental questions have on child learning and language development. This study addresses these limitations by investigating developmental changes in mothers' use of different question types in problem-solving tasks at child ages one, two and three years, and the implications of these longitudinal questioning patterns for the children's concurrent learning and imminent language development.

We have two specific aims. Our first aim is to examine the questions mothers ask during problem-solving tasks with their children at different ages. To address this aim, we look at early patterns in the form and function of maternal questioning behavior during problem-solving task interactions with their children at one, two and three years of age. We also examine whether maternal educational level is related to the questions they ask their children in the problem-solving situation across time. Our second aim is to explore the relation between maternal questioning behaviors and their children's developmental outcomes. To address this aim, we examine the degree to which the quality of maternal questioning (i.e., the questions' form and function) is related to children's task performance and language development when accounting for maternal educational level, and the overall amount of talk that the mothers and the children produce in the problem-solving contexts.

## Methodological Approach

### Sample, Procedure and Measures

Our study took advantage of already-existing observational video recordings of structured interaction tasks of child–caregiver interactions at one, two and three years from the longitudinal Behavior Outlook Norwegian Developmental Study (BONDS). The BONDS participants, 1,157 children and their caregivers, were recruited through a routine five-month visit to child health clinics in five Norwegian municipalities in 2006–8 (Nærde et al., 2014). The observations completed around the children's first, second and third birthdays were done in a lab set up in their local municipality. A subsample was selected for the purpose of the current study, which is part of a subproject on the developmental patterns in information-seeking and provision in early childhood. From the 165 dyads for which we had available observational data of mother–child interactions at one, two and three years (many of the caregivers were fathers), we selected $N = 64$ dyads for further transcription and coding in a stratified random manner, so that the sample for the current study would represent a diverse sociodemographic range (mothers' education $M = 13.6$ years, $SD = 2.3$; mothers' age $M = 31.2$ years, $SD = 6.0$) and child gender (50 percent boys).

## The Structured Tasks

The observations at each age consisted of several tasks in addition to the problem-solving tasks included here (see Nordahl, 2014, for assessment protocol). The problem-solving puzzle tasks were chosen to be slightly too difficult for the children to solve alone in order to prompt parental engagement and support. Before starting these particular tasks, the mothers were informed about what the task was about and that they could help the child as much as they found necessary. The dyads were given a shape-sorting task (i.e., box and figures), a traditional puzzle piece task (i.e., animal and farm themed), and a complex shape-sorting task (i.e., matching three-dimensional muffin parts with similar shapes and placing them in correct spots on a baking tray) at one, two and three years, respectively. All three task situations lasted three minutes, which was enough time for most dyads to have almost completed or completed the task.

## Transcription

The video recordings of the interactions were transcribed by reliable transcribers using the CHAT conventions of the Child Language Data Exchange System (CHILDES) (MacWhinney, 2000). All of the maternal utterances in the transcripts were coded further by three trained research assistants blind to the research hypotheses to glean measures of the linguistic form and function of mothers' questions during the structured task.

## Informational Function of Mothers' Questions

All of the mothers' utterances were coded as to whether or not they were questions. We then reliably coded the informational function of the mothers' questions into three overall categories:

(1) *Direct questions* referred to all the explicit questions asked by the mother in response to the child's task performance or focus and were further coded as: *denial or skepticism* about child task behavior (e.g., "Are you sure that is right?), *alternative suggestions* for the child to try another object, location or strategy ("Want to try there instead?") and *unprompted suggestions* for the child to try a new object and sometimes a location or strategy for the new object when the child is either off-task or is attempting something else (e.g., "Should we try this one now?").

(2) *Indirect questions referred to* all indirect questions asked by the mother in response to the child's task performance or focus that were further coded as: *hints* or reminds about characteristics of the objects or task during task performances or generic information about the task

purpose and component characteristics (e.g., "Is that squared?") and *negative information* in which the mother tells the child "how not to" complete the task, often accompanied by demonstration (e.g., trying to put a piece into an incorrect spot and saying "does this fit here?").

(3) *Other function questions* captured other undefined intent questions about the task or task object (e.g., "Is that called a tractor?").

Thus, both the direct and indirect questions are considered task-specific pedagogical function questions, with the scaffolding-based distinction that direct questions are considered plain and specific in their pedagogical function, while indirect questions are considered more oblique or generic.

### Linguistic Form of Mothers' Questions

Mother's questions were categorized based on form into three groups. *Wh-questions* included all questions where the mothers used the words "what," "who," "which," "why," "when," "where" and "how." *Auxiliary questions* included all questions where the mothers used the words "could," "would," "perhaps," "think," "here," "there," "this," "that" and "hm." The mothers often formed their auxiliary questions as simple yes/no queries or by using more tentative words (e.g., "do you *think* . . .?") or words suggesting specific actions or answers (e.g., "there?" "hm, do you . . .?"). Finally, *Other form questions* captured other undefined questions that were not captured by the wh- or auxiliary questions variables.

### Child Task Performance

Every child attempt to solve the task was identified and coded as failed or successful. *Failed attempts* included task attempts that ended unsuccessfully (e.g., the child ceased the attempt or initiated a different or new attempt). *Successful attempts* included any task attempt that ended in task success. We created one variable for each age, indicating the percentage of successful attempts out of total attempts (proportions (%) of child task success at 1 year: $M = 28.22$; 2 years: $M = 37.87$; 3 years: $M = 53.14$).

### Child Language Measures and Outcome

For the purpose of statistical control, we extracted from the transcripts the total utterances about the task produced by the children during the one-year, two-years and three-years observations. Further, the children's *vocabulary comprehension* was measured at four years by the Norwegian version of the British Picture Vocabulary Scale II (BPVS-II; Dunn & Dunn, 1997). This Norwegian version consists of twelve of the fourteen original sets (Lyster et al., 2010). We used the BPVS-II raw sum scores in our analyses ($M = 41.31$, $SD = 10.22$).

## Results

First, we describe the developmental changes in the mothers' question-asking across the three ages, distinguishing between questions' informational function and linguistic form. Next, we discuss whether the mothers' educational level was associated with maternal questioning behaviors at the three time-points. Finally, we determine the degree to which the quality of mothers' question-asking in the structured task situations predicted children's concurrent task success and language outcomes at four years, when accounting for maternal education, as well as total amount of maternal and child talk during the observations.

### Do the Form and Function of Maternal Questions Change with Child Age?

As shown in Table 11.1, we found that, on average, across all ages close to 25 percent of mothers' utterances about the task are questions. Further, there was quite a bit of variability in the quantity of mothers' question-

Table 11.1  *Questions  asked  by  mothers – informational function  (N = 64)*

|  | 1 year | | 2 years | | 3 years | | T-tests of Proportions[b] |
|---|---|---|---|---|---|---|---|
|  | M (SD) | % | M (SD) | % | M (SD) | % |  |
| Total Utterances about Task | 52.13 (16.32) | 100 | 74.39 (17.82) | 100 | 59.70 (14.15) | 100 | $1 < 2 > 3^{***}$ |
| Total Questions[a] | 11.91 (6.45) | 23 | 19.52 (6.86) | 27 | 15.64 (6.38) | 26 | $1 < 2 \& 3^{\dagger}$ |
| Direct Questions | 3.95 (3.31) | 35 | 3.75 (2.94) | 21 | 1.32 (1.72) | 8 | $1 > 2 > 3^{***}$ |
| Indirect Questions | 1.34 (1.85) | 11 | 6.84 (5.37) | 33 | 7.88 (4.71) | 49 | $1 < 2 < 3^{***}$ |
| Other Questions | 6.61 (4.68) | 54 | 8.92 (4.69) | 47 | 6.44 (4.15) | 43 |  |

a Percentages are based on the total of questions about task/objects. which sums to 100%.
b Difference tests mainly comparing proportions at T1 (1), T2 (2) and T3 (3), but
  frequencies of total utterances.
*** $p < 0.001$ ** $p < 0.01$, † $p < 0.10$

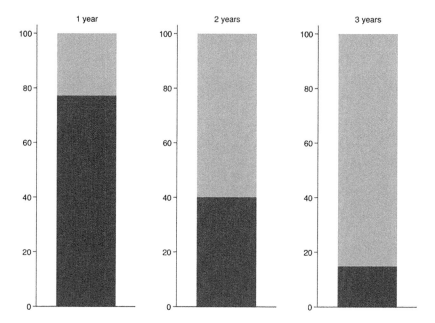

Figure 11.1 Changes in proportions of maternal direct and indirect questions (dark gray area = direct questions, light gray area = indirect questions).

asking. For example, the proportion of mothers' talk that was questions ranged from 11 to 33% at 1 years, from 18 to 45% at 2 years and from 16 to 42% at 3 years.

### Informational Function of Mothers' Questions

Table 11.1 show the developmental trends in the overall informational *function* of maternal questions. When only looking at changes in proportions of maternal direct and indirect questions, as displayed in Figure 11.1, we see a significant decrease in the amount of direct questions, and a related increase in the amount of indirect questions across time. The majority of direct questions at 1 year was unprompted suggestions, and alternative suggestions at 2 and 3 years, while the majority of indirect questions was hints at all ages.

### Linguistic Form of Mothers' Questions

When examining changes in the linguistic *form* of mothers' questions (see Table 11.2), we see that both the overall frequency and the proportion of

Table 11.2 *Questions asked by mothers – linguistic form (N = 64)*

| | 1 year | | 2 years | | 3 years | | |
|---|---|---|---|---|---|---|---|
| | **M (SD)** | **%**[a] | **M (SD)** | **%**[a] | **M (SD)** | **%**[a] | **T-tests of Proportions**[b] |
| Total Questions | 14.00 | 100 | 20.89 | 100 | 16.20 | 100 | |
| | (7.16) | | (6.57) | | (6.30) | | |
| WH-Questions | 0.84 | 6 | 7.98 | 36 | 5.50 | 33 | 1 < 2 & 3*** |
| | (1.44) | | (5.40) | | (3.85) | | |
| AUX-Questions | 9.70 | 70 | 8.47 | 41 | 6.69 | 43 | 1 > 2 & 3*** |
| | (5.50) | | (4.11) | | (3.94) | | |
| Other Questions | 3.45 | 24 | 4.44 | 22 | 4.02 | 25 | |
| | (2.62) | | (3.14) | | (3.18) | | |

*a* Percentages are based on the total of different linguistic forms questions.
*b* Difference tests comparing T1 (1), T2 (2) and T3 (3)
*** $p < .001$

mothers' WH-questions increase significantly over time, while the overall frequency and the proportion of mothers' auxiliary questions significantly decrease across time. The majority of the WH-questions were WHERE questions at 1 year, WHAT and WHERE questions at 2 years, and WHAT, WHERE and WHO questions at 3 years, while the majority of AUX-questions were SHOULD and THIS/THAT questions at 1 year, and then becoming more varied with age.

## Mothers' Question-Asking and Maternal Education

With the aim of understanding the variability in the mothers' question-asking, we examined whether the mothers' use of questions correlated with mothers' years of education. Overall, maternal education was most closely associated with total proportion of maternal utterances that were questions at 1 year ($r(62) = 0.277, p = 0.026$) and 2 years ($r(62) = 0.266, p = 0.034$), and modestly associated with mothers' indirect questions at 2 years ($r(62) = 0.243, p = 0.055$). No associations were evident between maternal education and the different question categories at child age 3 years.

## Do Maternal Questions Relate to Children's Development?

Finally, we examined the degree to which mothers' use of questions was related to children's concurrent task performance and later language development. The central question is whether mother's use of specific questioning functions or forms plays a role in children's concurrent task success and their later language comprehension at age 4.

To inform our analyses, we first examined associations between mothers' question categories at the different ages and the two child outcome measures. These analyses revealed that it was only maternal questioning at child age 2 years that related to concurrent task success and child language at 4 years. Direct questions and AUX-questions at 2 years were both negatively related to child task success at 2 years ($r = -0.303$, $p <0.05$ and ($r = -0.382$, $p <0.01$, respectively) and child language at 4 years ($r = -0.296$, $p <0.05$ and $r = -0.286$, $p <0.05$, respectively), while WH-questions at 2 years were positively related to child language at 4 years ($r = 0.317$, $p <0.05$). We therefore only focused on predicting child task success and later language abilities from the mothers' questioning strategies during the 2-year interaction.

### Child Concurrent Task Success

As shown in Table 11.3 (first column) we tested the role of AUX-questions at 2 years upon child concurrent task success and found that the proportion of mothers' AUX-questions at 2 years was a negative predictor of child task success, even when controlling for maternal education, as well as maternal and child utterances about task.

When testing the role of direct questions at 2 years (see Table 11.3, second column), we found that the proportion of mothers' direct questions at 2

Table 11.3 *The impact of mothers' question-asking at 2 years on child task success at 2 years (N = 64)*

| Outcome | | Child task success at 2 years | | | |
|---|---|---|---|---|---|
| Models | | AUX-Questions | | Direct Questions | |
| Steps | Predictor | B (SE) | R2 | B (SE) | R2 |
| 1 | Education | 0.117 (0.90) | 0.002 | 0.023 (0.93) | 0.002 |
| 2 | Mother Total Utterances | 0.000 (0.12) | 0.002 | −0.071 (0.13) | 0.002 |
| 3 | Child Total Utterances | 0.095 (0.16) | 0.018 | 0.050 (0.17) | 0.018 |
| 4 | Mother Question Category[a] | −0.399 (0.11)** | 0.113* | −0.309 (0.15)* | 0.100 |

a Mother question category is either AUX-Questions or Direct Questions
** $p < 0.01$, * $p < 0.05$

years negatively predicted task success, when accounting for the same control variables.

In a final model (not shown) we included the control variables and both mothers' AUX-questions and direct questions simultaneously and found that the five predictors explained approximately 18 percent of the variance in task performance. In this model the proportion of mothers' AUX-questions remained a significant negative predictor of task performance, but the proportion of direct questions did not.

### *Child Language Comprehension at Four Years*

Table 11.4 presents the analysis predicting child language comprehension at age 4 years. In the first model we tested the role of WH-questions at 2 years, and found that mothers WH-questions at 2 years positively predicted child language at 4 years, while controlling for maternal education, as well as maternal and child total utterances about task at 2 years.

When testing the role of auxiliary questions at 2 years (see Table 11.4, second column), we found this to be a significant negative predictor of child language at 4 years.

Finally, when testing the role of direct questions at 2 years (see Table 11.4, third column), the analyses revealed that the proportion of mothers' direct questions at 2 years was a significant negative predictor of child language at 4 years.

Table 11.4 *The impact of mothers' question-asking at 2 years on child language comprehension at 4 years (N = 64)*

| Outcome | | Child Language at 4 Years | | | | | |
|---|---|---|---|---|---|---|---|
| Models | | WH-Questions | | AUX-Questions | | Direct Questions | |
| Steps | Predictors | $B$ (SE) | $R^2$ | $B$ (SE) | $R^2$ | $B$ (SE) | $R^2$ |
| 1 | Education | 0.156 (0.56) | 0.021 | 0.190 (0.57) | 0.021 | 0.114 (0.57) | 0.021 |
| 2 | Mother Total Utterances | −0.153 (0.08) | 0.025 | −0.086 (0.07) | 0.025 | −0.159 (0.08) | 0.025 |
| 3 | Child Total Utterances | 0.084 (0.11) | 0.062 | 0.168 (0.10) | 0.062 | 0.117 (0.11) | 0.062 |
| 4 | Mother Question Category[a] | 0.342 (0.07)* | 0.159[†] | −0.317 (0.07)* | 0.158[†] | −0.305 (0.09)* | 0.141[†] |

*a* Mother question category is either WH-Questions, AUX-Questions or Direct Questions
* $p < .05$, † $p < .10$

To sum up the results, the mothers show a clear decrease in their use of both questions that are direct in their informational intent and or simpler (auxiliary) in their form over time. Moreover, using more direct and simple questions at two years is negatively related to both concurrent child task success at two years, as well as children's language comprehension at four years. Contrary, the use of questions that are indirect in intent or consist of the wh-form increases between the child ages of one and three years, and especially the use of wh-questions at two years is positively related to children's language comprehension at four years. In the following we discuss some potential explanations and implications of these diverse patterns.

## Conclusion

The results of the current study are consistent with and build upon prior work on the developmental changes in and implications of mothers' question-asking for children's language development. First and foremost, the patterns of change in mothers' use of questions with different functions in the current interactions with their children around challenging tasks concur with existing theoretical and empirical research on scaffolding (Wood et al., 1976, 1978, 1995). In line with the scaffolding literature the current investigation shows that maternal questions in particular are used to manage the amount of direct assistance given during task interactions (Wood et al., 1976). By becoming more indirect and less direct in the functions of their questions as the children get older, mothers are essentially leaving their questions more open-ended and subsequently letting the child take more of the responsibility for the task. As suggested by the findings of Yu et al. (2018) the use of pedagogical questions involving hints and prompts rather than direct instructions in the form of statements may encourage children to explore on their own and in this way increase their potential for task success and learning. The direct questions (e.g., instructions formulated as queries or suggestions) might then constitute a middle ground between the indirect pedagogical questions and direct statement-based instructions. By providing an explicit point of egress for the child at the same time as being presented as a suggestion only, direct questions might indeed give "some of the control back to the child" and in this way promote child exploration (Yu et al., 2018, p. 7), as well as child generic inferences about ways to solve the task.

This change in the functions of maternal questions as the children get older is also accompanied by an equivalent change in the question forms that mothers use when they query their children during the puzzle task performances. The maternal question forms are becoming increasingly linguistically demanding and complex (e.g., increasing use of wh-questions). These findings complement studies with cross-sectional designs or with a focus on conversational or play contexts (e.g., Pan et al., 1996; Kuchirko et al., 2015), by showing that when interacting with their children around challenging tasks, mothers adjust the questions they formulate *and* the pedagogical intent they seek to accomplish with these questions as their children get older. The current study, therefore, informs our understanding of how maternal questions are used for pedagogical purposes and as a means of scaffolding the children's task performances. This sheds light on the naturally occurring learning processes happening in mother–child interactions over time and effectively shows that many children will have an extensive understanding of how questions are used as pedagogical tools even before entering more formal educational settings.

However, the results suggest that some children experience a reduced exposure to questions in this particular context. Importantly, the education effect was primarily for the proportion of task related utterances that were questions, which suggests a difference in scaffolding strategies (questioning vs. non-questioning) by educational level. This, together with the trend for mothers with lower education levels to ask relatively fewer indirect questions at two years, is aligned with the findings by Yu et al. (2017), in which working-class parents asked less pedagogical questions to their children than middle-class parents across contexts. The current study builds on this work by showing how socioeconomic background might impact how parents adjust their input to their children's developmental level in challenging task settings. Specifically, across educational background the mothers show similar changes in how they use questions to scaffold their children's performances across child age (the kinds or the intents of questions asked), while the frequency in which they do these adjustments differ. Future research could identify other factors that contribute more to the variability in the relative use of the different question forms and functions.

Underscoring the importance of knowledge about what factors contribute to maternal questions, several maternal question categories were related to the children's developmental outcomes. Although previous work has found that parental wh-questions predict children's language and learning during book-reading and toy play activities, the current study shows that mothers' questioning strategies in explicit and challenging task situations at two years had differential impacts on children's concurrent task success. Specifically, it is the mothers who *are not* inclined to ask direct and simpler auxiliary questions at two years who have children who are most successful at the task at this same age. These mothers and the mothers who ask *more* wh-questions at two years also have children with better language comprehension skills at four years.

This is not the first study that shows a positive relationship between parental wh-questions and children's language development (e.g., Cristofaro & Tamis-LeMonda, 2012; Rowe et al., 2016). However, this study shows that mothers' wh-questions did not play a role in children's task success. It is also the first study showing that less demanding maternal questions, such as the auxiliary questions, are associated with lower levels of child task performance, indicating that oversimplification of maternal questions may not be of help but rather a disservice with two-year-olds. This is expected from a scaffolding perspective (Wood et al., 1976; Wood et al., 1995), as the results suggest that parents who do not show the expected change in scaffolding behavior across time (e.g., becoming increasingly indirect and demanding in their teaching intent) also have children who do less well on the task. These findings support the argument that it is not just asking questions that matters, but rather the ways in which these questions are asked and with which intent that is essential.

There might be several alternative explanations for the predictive associations found. One apparent candidate is that children who are more proficient at the task in the first place, and/or who are more advanced talkers, may also elicit more questions and more diverse questions from their mothers. There is indeed a negative relationship between mothers' use of less demanding query strategies and children's concurrent task success, as well as positive relationship between mothers' more demanding query strategies and children's language development. However, because the results stand even after accounting for the total amount of task-related talk of both the children and their mothers at two years, this cannot be the entire story. Why the association between mothers querying practices and children's learning and language outcomes is most prominent at age two years could be related to the fact that children's language is particularly blooming at this age (Brown, 1973). Increased language proficiency may make it easier for children to grasp the scaffolding nature of maternal questions, as well as to respond adequately. It might also be an age where the children are in need of more pedagogical support in such tasks. One study examining mother's object demonstrations in interactions with their infants found that the degree of demonstration by the mothers increased when the infants did not reproduce the task (e.g., they needed the demonstration), and decreased when they did reproduce the task (e.g., they did not need the demonstration), but only at an age when the infants were physically capable of performing the task (Fukuyama et al., 2015). Future research is, however, needed to understand more about the children's own contributions to the input they receive at different ages in different contexts.

All in all, the current study suggest that mothers' questions have several concurrent functions for children's cognitive and linguistic development. On the one hand, when mothers in challenging task contexts ask questions with a more demanding form, e.g., wh-questions, at an age when children start to grasp and respond to such questions, this might stimulate children's subsequent language development in much the same way as in other conversational contexts at this age. On the other hand, when mothers are adjusting to their children's developmental level by increasing the complexity of their question functions (e.g., becoming less direct and subsequently increasingly more indirect in their queries), and by decreasing the use of simpler question forms, this might stimulate children's concurrent task performance as well as their language development. Although future experimental and intervention designs are needed to disentangle the mechanisms and to determine the directions of the associations, these findings suggest that parental questions to children have important developmental implications, and that examining the function and forms of those questions is useful. Together with the existing literature, this study suggests that questions are not just a mechanism for cognitive development because they allow children to obtain the information they need, but also that parental questions scaffold children's language and possibly cognitive development more general by guiding their exploration. The longitudinal analyses further support that this is done with a truly hands-on adjustment to children's developmental level. However, it is an interdependent dance: as Roger Brown points out (1977, p. 20), caregivers' input seems to "arise ... from the nature of human children and the world they live in." Typically, parent–child interactions in the home become routinized, and one might expect parents over time to acquire a sensible understanding of the thresholds for their own teaching, as well as their children's learning potential, and that their children in return will form certain expectations about the parents' pedagogical agendas in challenging task situations.

### Acknowledgments

This research was supported by Young Research Talents grant from the Research Council of Norway, FINNUT program (project no 254974) to Dr. Zambrana.

# References

Blewitt, P., Rump, K. M., Shealy, S. E., and Cook, S. A. (2009). Shared book reading: When and how questions affect young children's word learning. *Journal of Educational Psychology*, *101*, 294–304. https://doi:10.1037/a0013844

Brown, R. (1973). *A first language: The early stages*. Cambridge, MA: Harvard University Press.

Brown, R. (1977). Introduction. In C. E. Snow, and C. Ferguson (eds.), Talking to children: Language input and acquisition Cambridge (pp. 1–27). UK: Cambridge University Press.

Bruner, J. S. (1983). *Child's talk: Learning to use language*. New York: W. W. Norton. https://doi:10.1177/026565908500100113

Cartmill, E. A., Armstrong, B. F., Gleitman, L. R., Goldin-Meadow, S., Medina, T. N., and Trueswell, J. C. (2013). Quality of early parent input predicts child vocabulary three years later. *Proceedings of the National Academy of Sciences*, *110*, 11278–83. https://doi:10.1073/pnas.1309518110

Cristofaro, T. N., and Tamis-LeMonda, C. S. (2012). Mother-child conversations at 36 months and at pre-kindergarten: Relations to children's school readiness. *Journal of Early Childhood Literacy*, *12*, 68–97. https://doi:10.1177/1468798411416879

Dunn, L. M., and Dunn, L. M. (1997). *Peabody picture vocabulary test–III*. Circle Pines, MN: American Guidance Service.

Fletcher, K. L., Cross, J. R., Tanney, A. L., Schneider, M., and Finch, W. H. (2008). Predicting language development in children at risk: The effects of quality and frequency of caregiver reading. *Early Education and Development*, *19*, 89–111. https://doi:10.1080/10409280701839106

Fukuyama, H., Qin, S., Kanakogi, Y., et al. (2015). Infant's action skill dynamically modulates parental action demonstration in the dyadic interaction. *Developmental Science*, *18*, 1006–13. https://doi:10.1111/desc.12270

Gleason, J. B., and Greif, E. (1983). Men's speech to young children. In B. Thorne, C. Kramarae, and N. Henley (eds.), *Language, gender and society* (pp. 140–51). Rowley, MA: Newbury House.

Haden, C. A., Cohen, T., Uttal, D., and Marcus, M. (2016). Building learning: Narrating and transferring experiences in a children's museum. In D. M. Sobel and J. J. Jipson (eds.), *Cognitive development in museum settings: Relating research and practice* (pp. 84–103). New York: Routledge. https://doi:978–1848724891

Hart, B., and Risley, T. R. (1995). *Meaningful differences in the everyday experience of young American children*. Baltimore, MD: Brookes Publishing. https://doi:10.1007/s00431-005-0010-2

Hirsh-Pasek, K., Adamson, L. B., Bakeman, R., et al. (2015). The contributions of early communication quality to low-income children's language success. *Psychological Science*, *26*, 1–13. https://doi:10.1177/0956797615581493

Holzman, M. (1972). The use of interrogative forms in the verbal interaction of three mothers (or other adults) and their children. *Journal of Psycholinguistic Research*, *1*, 311–36. https://doi:10.1007/BF01067786

Huttenlocher, J., Haight, W., Bryk, A., Seltzer, M., and Lyons, T. (1991). Early vocabulary growth: Relation to language input and gender. *Developmental Psychology*, 27, 236–48. https://doi:10.1037/0012-1649.27.2.236

Kuchirko, Y., Tamis-LeMonda, C. S., Luo, R., and Liang, E. (2015). "What happened next?": Developmental changes in mothers' questions to children. *Journal of Early Childhood Literacy*, 16, 498–521. https://doi:10.1177/1468798415598822

Leaper, C., Anderson, K. J., and Sanders, P. (1998). Moderators of gender effects on parents' talk to their children: A meta-analysis. *Developmental Psychology*, 34, 3–27. https://doi:10.1037/0012-1649.34.1.3

Leech, K. A., Salo, V. C., Rowe M. L., and Cabrera, N. J. (2013). Father input and child vocabulary development: The importance of wh-questions and clarification requests. *Semin Speech Lang*, 34, 249–59. https://doi:10.1055/s-0033-1353445

Lyster, S. -A. H., Horn, E., and Rygvold, A.-L. (2010). Ordforråd og ordforrådsutvikling hos norske barn og unge: resultater fra en utprøving av British Picture Vocabulary Scale II [Vocabulary and vocabulary development in Norwegian children and youth: results from the testing of BPVS-II]. *Spesialpedagogikk*, 9, 35–43.

MacWhinney, B. (2000). The CHILDES project: Tools for analyzing talk (3rd ed.). Mahwah, NJ: Erlbaum.

Nelson, K. (2017). The cultural basis of language and thought in development. In N. Budwig, E. Turiel, and P. D. Zelazo (eds.), *New perspectives on human development* (pp. 402–24). New York: Cambridge University Press.

Ninio, A. (1980). Picture-book reading in mother-infant dyads belonging to two subgroups in Israel. *Child Development*, 2, 587–90. https://doi:10.2307/1129299

Nordahl, K. B. (2014). Early father-child interaction in a father-friendly context: Gender differences, child outcomes, and predictive factors related to fathers' parenting behaviors with one-year-olds. PhD thesis. University of Bergen, Norway: Faculty of Psychology.

Nærde, A., Janson, H., and Ogden, T. (2014). *BONDS (The Behavior Outlook Norwegian Developmental Study): A prospective longitudinal study of early development of social competence and behavior problems*. Oslo, Norway: The Norwegian Center for Child Behavioral Development.

Pan, B. A., Imbens-Bailey, A., Winner, K., amd Snow, C. E. (1996). Communicative intents expressed by parents in interaction with young children. *Merrill-Palmer Quarterly*, 42, 248–67. https://doi:23087879

Ronfard, S., Zambrana, I. M., Hermansen T. K., and Kelemen, D. (2018). Question-asking in childhood: A review of the literature and a framework for understanding its development. *Developmental Review*. Advance online publication. https://doi:10.1016/j.dr.2018.05.002

Rowe, M. L. (2012). A longitudinal investigation of the role of quantity and quality of child-directed speech in vocabulary development. *Child Development*, 83, 1762–74. https://doi:10.1111/j.1467-8624.2012.01805.x

Rowe, M. L., Coker, D., and Pan, B. A. (2004). A comparison of fathers' and mothers' talk to toddlers in low-income families. *Social Development*, *13*, 278–91.

Rowe, M. L., Leech, K. A., and Cabrera, N. (2016). Going beyond input quantity: Wh-questions matter for toddlers' language and cognitive development. *Cognitive Science*, *41*, 162–79. https://doi:10.1111/j.1467-950 7.2004.000267.x

Shatz, M. (1979). How to do things by asking: Form-function pairings in mothers' questions and their relation to children's responses. *Child Development*, *50*, 1093–1099. https://doi:10.2307/1129336

Snow, C. E. (1977). Mothers' speech research: From input to interaction. In C. E. Snow and C. A. Ferguson (eds.), *Talking to children: Language input and acquisition* (pp. 31–49). Cambridge: Cambridge University Press.

Snow, C. E., Arlman-Rupp, A., Hassing, Y., et al. (1976). Mothers' speech in three social classes. *Journal of Psycholinguistic Research*, *5*, 1–20.

Tomasello, M., Conti-Ramsden, G., and Ewert, B. (1990). Young children's conversations with their mothers and fathers: Differences in breakdown and repair. *Journal of Child Language*, *17*, 115–30. https://doi:10.1017 /S0305000900013131

Valian, V., and Casey, L. (2003). Young children's acquisition of wh-questions: The role of structured input. *Journal of Child Language*, *30*, 117–44. https:// doi:10.1017/S0305000902005457

Weisleder, A., and Fernald, A. (2013) Talking to children matters: Early language experience strengthens processing and builds vocabulary. *Psychological Science*, *24*, 2143–52. https://doi:10.1177/0956797613488145

Wood, D., Bruner, J. S., and Ross, G. (1976). The role of tutoring in problem solving. *Journal of Child Psychology and Psychiatry*, *17*, 89–100. https://doi:10 .1111/j.1469-7610.1976.tb00381.x

Wood, D., Wood, H., and Middleton, D. (1978). An experimental evaluation of four face-to-face teaching strategies. *International Journal of Behavioural Development*, *1*, 131–47. https://doi:10.1177/016502547800100203

Wood, D., Wood, H., Ainsworth, S., and O'Malley, C. (1995). On becoming a tutor: Toward an ontogenetic model. *Cognition and Instruction*, *13*, 565–81. https://doi:10.1207/s1532690xci1304_7

Yu, Y., Bonawitz, E., and Shafto, P. (2017). Pedagogical questions in parent–child conversations. *Child Development*. Advance online publication. https:// doi:10.1111/cdev.12850

Yu, Y., Landrum, A. R., Bonawitz, E., and Shafto, P. (2018). Questioning supports effective transmission of knowledge and increased exploratory learning in pre-kindergarten children. *Developmental Science*, e12696. https:// doi:10.1111/desc.12696

# 12    Teaching and Learning by Questioning

*Deanna Kuhn, Anahid S. Modrek, William A. Sandoval*

Young children are known to be questioners. Their questions may at times seem endless, even random. Very often, however, young children's questions are profound and challenging to answer. Despite the wide range of forms it takes, young children's questioning is now recognized as a key tool they use to construct understanding and so deserves thoughtful attention, as the contributions to this volume attest.

Much less vivid is an image of older children and adolescents as avid questioners. A few gifted youth become passionate in exploring their interests, but more often teens are seen as more concerned with "fitting in" with their chosen identity group (Steinberg & Monahan, 2007), and less concerned with exploring why things are the way they are or how they could be different.

A simple explanation for this change from first to second decade of life is lacking. One potential culprit is traditional schooling, which emphasizes following directions and conformity over questioning (Dewey, 1997; Schank, 2011; Collins, 2017). Another proposal is that of a more intrinsic characteristic of cognitive flexibility, abundant in early life and gradually diminishing with age (Gopnik et al., 2017). We shall have more to say about each of these possibilities.

Our major message in this chapter will be that question-asking remains fully as important a mechanism of learning and teaching in later childhood and adolescence as it is in early childhood. Its relevance does not diminish. Given their importance, we also want to identify the kinds of questions adolescents ask, and how to encourage them to ask the most cognitively productive questions. Several different lines of research we describe are united in their concern with how we can design older children's and teens' learning environments in ways that capitalize on self-initiated, largely self-directed question-asking and answer-seeking (Dean & Kuhn, 2007). We will describe a number of studies we have done with various colleagues indicating that such contexts yield superior outcomes in the case of several different kinds of learning and across different student populations. Finally, we turn to research involving within-population individual variation in cognitive characteristics of students, as well as characteristics of their teachers, which are associated with variation in learning outcomes.

## Is Self-Guided Learning Necessary or Even Advisable?

Before turning to research evidence, it is well to begin by questioning basic premises. We educate young people because we believe it will serve them in their becoming thoughtful, effective adults able to contribute to the society they are part of. But there is much evidence now to suggest that even fairly well-educated adults are not necessarily strong reasoners or decision-makers (Baron, 1994; Stanovich, 1999). Perhaps, then, might teachers be better advised to focus their efforts on teaching students right answers rather than encouraging their questions? The answer must be no. We really have no choice but to aid students in becoming self-directed learners. Educators today cannot predict the specific kinds of knowledge and skills young people will need during their adult lives. The best we can do is equip them with the skills that will enable them to seek out and acquire the knowledge they find they need, if they are to be the self-starters and quick learners that employers are now of one voice in saying they want to hire (Friedman, 2014; Trilling & Fadel, 2009).

The traditional instructor lecturing as students faithfully write down what he has to say has now been replaced to a great extent by learning environments that may look radically different (Moskowitz & Lavinia, 2012). Individualization and automation are the twin virtues that modern educational technology promises. But in this new era, where is the sense of agency and the self-management that students need to develop and employers seek? Educators too seldom develop spaces that promote agency – an essential condition for self-directed exploration and learning. There do exist excellent examples of software that afford students the sense of directing their own learning. Much educational software, however, is designed to identify and remedy the gaps that an expert detects in a student's knowledge, with only a passive role accorded the student.

Young adolescents are cognitively and developmentally more able than younger children to take on a high level of independence and personal control (Pintrich & Schunk, 2002). More often than not, however, sufficient opportunities to develop and exercise their autonomy within the classroom is lacking (Feldlaufer et al., 1988). When students are offered fewer choices and fewer opportunities to assume personal responsibility, they may develop self-defeating motivational beliefs (Eccles et al., 1993).

The good news is that the skills involved in self-directed learning can be developed with consistent practice in a supportive environment where they are encouraged and valued. To initiate the process, students first need a problem – something that gives their activity a purpose. It is important, however, to be clear about what defines problem-based learning. A sequence of studies one of us has conducted with colleagues on problem-based learning (PBL) shows it to produce superior learning of new concepts (but not retention of facts), relative to direct teaching of the concepts by an instructor, in both young adolescent and adult samples (Capon & Kuhn, 2004; Pease & Kuhn, 2011; Wirkala & Kuhn, 2011). In these studies, we posed the further question, however, of whether the benefit of PBL was attributable to the encounter with a meaningful problem or the opportunity to collaborate with peers in exploring it. Among both adult and teen samples, the answer was clear. The new concepts were mastered to an equal extent whether students addressed the problem individually or in small groups (Pease & Kuhn, 2011; Wirkala & Kuhn, 2011). Working on a meaningful problem – having an opportunity to pose and answer meaningful questions – appears to be what affords PBL its primary power.

This is not to say that peer interaction never confers a benefit. In argumentation, we shall see, its role is central. In the case of PBL, however, it appears to be the problem encounter itself that is most important. Identifying whether and when collaboration provides an enhanced benefit requires close scrutiny. Collaborative learning is sometimes advocated uncritically, as the tool that will achieve any and all learning goals. It is worthwhile to analyze closely the many variants of collaborative learning settings in relation to varying kinds of learning goals, in order to identify the benefits collaboration can provide (Kuhn, 2015).

In the next two sections, we examine question-based learning and teaching processes as they occur within two broad categories that researchers have addressed largely separately, first inquiry – the seeking and meaning-making component – and then argument – the making and defending of resulting claims (Kuhn, 2005). In a final section we consider individual and subgroup variation in processes of both learning and teaching and their outcomes.

## Inquiry

Inquiry learning is a type of learning centered around self-directed exploration, investigation, and inference, where what is to be learned is not known in advance (Lehrer & Schauble, 2015). Inquiry learning skills have been studied by both science educators and cognitive developmental psychologists, with little intersection of their research efforts until recently (Sandoval, 2005). In the case of developmental psychologists, this research for many years was focused on older children's and adolescents' mastery of control of variables as an investigatory strategy (Inhelder & Piaget, 1958; Zimmerman, 2007). Since then it has become more widely recognized that there is much more to scientific thinking than conducting a controlled experiment demonstrating the effect of an antecedent variable on an outcome. In addition to mastering a broad set of conceptual and investigatory skills (Kuhn, 2011, 2016; Lehrer & Schauble, 2015), students must come to understand the epistemological foundations of science, recognizing scientific claims not simply as accumulated facts or freely chosen opinions but rather as judgments requiring evaluation in a framework of alternatives and evidence (Sandoval, 2005; Moshman, 2014; Sandoval et al., 2014; Greene et al., 2016).

In the real world, outcomes are most often the consequence not of a single cause but of multiple factors acting in concert, a fact that practicing scientists routinely take into account in their investigations. Criteria for inferring causes change during the first decades of life in ways that may appear paradoxical. Children (and sometimes even adults) are quite willing to interpret factors as causal simply because they co-occur with an outcome (Sloman, 2005). They later adopt more rigorous criteria and begin to distinguish causality from covariation and eventually may become able to eliminate potential causes via controlled comparison. Surprisingly, however, young teens (and often even adults) who show no difficulty with controlled comparison are likely to attribute an outcome to a single factor, even when they have themselves just demonstrated that other factors present also affect the outcome (Kuhn, 2012; Kuhn et al., 2015). Moreover, the single factor to which they attribute causal power shifts across instances examined, whether or not prior beliefs influence these attributions. In everyday reasoning unconstrained by consideration of specific evidence, a single favored cause is likely to suffice to explain a phenomenon. Overeating, for example, is regarded as sufficient in accounting for obesity.

Developmental studies suggest a preference for single-cause explanations is identifiable by age six (Walker et al., 2017a) and further increases thereafter. Gopnik et al. (2017) studied causal inference patterns from age four through adulthood, reporting that 90 percent of four-year-olds implicate an object merely present as causal in making a machine light. By age twelve to fourteen and into adulthood this percentage dropped to below 40 percent, even when participants had witnessed cases in which two objects had been required jointly to produce the effect (and to less than 10 percent when they had not witnessed such cases). The remaining majority named only a single causal factor. Gopnik et al. interpret this age difference as reflective of greater cognitive flexibility early in life. Yet Gopnik et al.'s data may reflect simply a weak co-occurrence criterion for causal inference early in life that with age becomes more rigorous and discriminating, mutually reinforcing the single-factor preference in attributing causality. We cannot conclude with any certainty that the second decade of life leaves children with diminished cognitive flexibility. Indeed, the line of research addressing single-cause explanation that we turn to now suggests that this preference can be overcome with engagement and practice in multivariable causal reasoning.

Single-factor causal reasoning is rarely adequate. If we want to support young people's becoming productive inquirers, in addition to a multivariable model of causality we need to promote their reasoning rigorously about evidence. Kuhn and Modrek (2018) reported weaknesses in this regard among a majority of community adults approached in an urban train station waiting room. They were asked to respond to items like this one:

Some health officials have found cancer rates higher in cities than in outer areas. Dr. J. Rawls claimed tanning salons are to blame. Circle ONE piece of evidence that would be best to use if you wanted to argue he was wrong.
A. Air pollution is a more likely cause of cancer in the city.
B. Many people who don't go to tanning salons also get cancer.
C. Many people outside the city also go to tanning salons and don't get cancer.

About half of community adults favor option A on such items, a quarter B, and a quarter C. Option A makes a second causal claim, failing to address the initial claim and as a result not serving to address the stated objective of showing this claim to be wrong. Option B cites evidence with respect to an alternative sufficient cause, i.e., the outcome may appear in the absence of the alleged cause due to another cause sufficient to produce it. It thus does not counter the claim that the initial factor is a cause. Option C, in contrast, does directly counter the claim that the initial factor is a cause, since it cites evidence that this factor failed to produce the outcome.

The multivariable conceptual framework that is needed for rich inquiry and the evidence evaluation skills associated with it are thus missing in many adults, and we don't yet know how their varying developmental and educational histories contribute to these performance differences at the adult level. The good news is that development is achievable in a context of sustained engagement and exercise. Kuhn et al. (2015) engaged young adolescents over a period of time in inquiry activities involving causal investigation and inference with respect to phenomena that can be accounted for adequately only in multivariable terms. A similar study by Jewett and Kuhn (2016) added a peer observer to the pairs of young adolescents who engaged in a goal-based, self-directed investigation of an authentic (but simplified) database regarding factors associated with teen delinquency across different states. Pairs were able with practice to make progress in drawing valid conclusions regarding contributory and noncontributory factors. Peers who merely observed did not learn as well, a finding also reported by Muldner et al. (2014), as well as in early studies by Ross and Killey (1977) and by Kuhn and Ho (1980) involving only single-factor causality. In the Kuhn and Ho and Jewett and Kuhn studies, questioning was prominent. Young investigators were regularly asked questions such as "What are you going to find out by trying that?" "What do you predict?" and "What do you think about how it's come out?" An objective, of course, was that such questioning would eventually become internally rather than externally generated.

It is notable that the only condition difference in the Jewett and Kuhn and Kuhn and Ho studies is that students in one condition selected the observations they wished to examine; in the other, students were able to observe identical data but had not selected them. We will refer to this difference as a difference with respect to autonomy or agency, as these are constructs we return to. We had no independent measures on the basis of which to claim that the selection group was more engaged (Chi, 2009), although they often appeared so. What we can say is that their selection of the information they were to observe enabled them to make better use of it. Finally, these studies suggest the problem-based context to be critical in supporting students' inquiry. There needs to be something to find out. Too often, young science students see their classroom science activities simply as helping to produce displays of what is already known and maybe interesting to look at. Instead, students need an incentive to ask questions to find out what there is to know. They also must learn to further question their own and others' answers, a foundation for critical discourse (Kuhn & Modrek, 2018).

With such practice students also acquire a set of intellectual values – values that deem activities of this sort to be worthwhile in general and personally useful. As a consequence of these values, such students believe that question-asking yields useful outcomes and they thus have the right and are right to question. Moreover, they believe that problems can be analyzed, that solutions can come from such analysis, and that they are capable of conducting it (Resnick & Nelson-LeGall, 1997).

Supporting inquiry practices in the classroom does not come easily for teachers. Teachers may hesitate to use inquiry in their classrooms due to confusion about the meaning of inquiry, the belief that inquiry instruction only works well with high-ability students, or a view of inquiry as difficult to manage (Windschitl, 2003). Teachers may assume that students already possess the cognitive skills that enable them to engage in inquiry learning activities in a way that is productive (Putnam & Borko, 2000). Educators must work to overcome these false assumptions if students are to develop skills in learning how to learn. Misconceptions, as cognitive and developmental psychologists now well know, are hard to overcome, and this difficulty applies to teachers as well as students.

Educational traditions change slowly, and teachers need continued support and guided practice if they are to change their customary classroom practices (Sandoval et al., 2016, 2017, 2018). Critical to such change is change in values. Teachers must themselves believe in the skills and practices they are seeking to develop in their students. The results we described in this section with respect to causal reasoning in an adult population suggest that some number of teachers may need to further develop their skills in reasoning and inference, as well as inquiry practices, along with the values to support them. Our major claim in this section has been the importance of students developing a sense of agency and of value in conducting their own inquiry and their learning more broadly. To achieve these goals, they need teachers who will believe in, model, and support such endeavors.

## Argument

We turn now to argument, the phase in which the inferences arising from inquiry activity are entered into a more public arena, either in an interactive context or in the context of a written argument that becomes an artifact available for inspection by others. In either case, the context is one in which claims are expected to be justified by appeal to evidence. Most often, of course, inquiry and argument are not independent (despite the research tradition of studying them separately). Nor do they occur in a strict sequence, but rather in alternating phases or cycles shaped by task demands and goals. Inquiry, however, can lead one to question a claim being made, and thus be seen as a driving factor to engaging in discourse about a claim.

Like inquiry, argument rests on a foundation of epistemological understanding (Ryu & Sandoval, 2012; Sandoval, 2015). In its absence, one fails to see the purpose of argument and hence to value the effort it entails. If knowledge consists of claims not open to question – either indisputable facts that can simply be looked up or opinions to be accepted without scrutiny as personal possessions of their holder (the stances reflected in less mature epistemological positions) – there is little purpose to argument. We can thus regard recognition of the relevance of evidence to argument as a core achievement.

Inquiry and argument share a common set of skills in the coordination of claims and evidence. Early origins of skill in coordinating claim and evidence have recently become a focus of attention among researchers of early cognitive development, who propose that both prior beliefs and new evidence influence claims to varying degrees, with explanatory activity capable of limiting as well as benefitting learning (Legare & Lombrozo, 2014; Johnston et al., 2017; Walker et al., 2017b). Walker et al. (2017b) cite sacrifice of detail, overgeneralization, and consequent reduced accuracy as potential negative effects of children engaging in explanation of their claims. Kuhn and Katz (2009) emphasized the enhanced commitment to a prior belief that explaining may risk. Walker et al.'s work addressed preschoolers' very simple, affectively neutral beliefs (e.g., which size or color of blocks make a machine go), whereas Kuhn and Katz investigated the more complex beliefs of older children, with the possibility hence more likely that being asked to elaborate these beliefs in explanations would lead them to become invested in being right about them (and hence less receptive to new evidence).

In curriculum we have developed to support development of argument skills (Kuhn et al., 2016a, 2016b; Hemberger et al., 2017; Kuhn, 2018), we have further connected inquiry and argument by encouraging young adolescents to generate their own questions, the answers to which they think might help them as they engage in electronic dialogs with peers on social and socio-scientific issues. We assist them in securing answers, sometimes first helping them to better formulate their questions into ones that allow factual answers; we also model the process, enriching their knowledge base regarding the topic with short passages of several lines presented in question-and-answer format. The rationale is to first create a need for the information they acquire. Rather than provide answers to questions students don't have, we have them first formulate the questions. In this way, we allow students to first see how such information could be useful, and then we assist them in securing it. The point is for students not just to acquire information but to see its value and therefore be disposed to apply it.

A study by Iordanou et al. (2019) shows further that in the case of topics where students have minimal prior knowledge (e.g., "Should the US Social Security system be continued or should people save on their own for their old age?"), making available a more extended collection of information in Q&A format is effective in simultaneously supporting knowledge acquisition and argumentive skill development. The Iordanou et al. study also put to an empirical test the claim that the Q&A format is more effective, in a design that allowed one group throughout their several weeks of work on the topic to choose the questions from an available set that they would gain answers to. This group was compared to a group who differed only in that they were given a text at the outset that remained available and consisted of the identical Q&A information, but compiled into a traditional text format. In their final essays on the topic, the Q&A group made greater reference to and use of this information as evidence for their claims than did the text group.

In tracing young adolescents' progress across a school year in both the dialogic and individual writing contexts, we find that in both contexts they face two challenges in coordinating claims and evidence. Although most students fairly readily master the linking of supporting evidence to a claim they make, other forms of claim–evidence coordination are more difficult. One is to use evidence seeking to weaken an opposing claim, rather than employ evidence only as support for their own claim. The second and more difficult challenge is to attempt to address evidence that appears supportive of the opposing position, rather than succumb to the temptation to simply ignore it. In these and other respects, we find that progress in the dialogic context precedes progress in individual essays, but the same sequence of steps appears in the two cases (Kuhn & Crowell, 2011; Kuhn & Moore, 2015; Paus et al., 2015; Kuhn et al., 2016a, 2016b).

Particularly notable is the greater use of prior personal knowledge in the dialogic context, we think due to the fact that the dialogic context is more authentic. In addition to its developmental roots in everyday conversation, it provides both an audience and a purpose to the activity. In the notoriously difficult context of individual essay writing, in contrast, novice writers stare alone at the empty page, laboring with uncertain purpose to fill it with what they imagine is expected of them.

How, then, can we best support the development of students' argumentation skills? Because of the advantages it affords, we have employed dialogic engagement as a path to developing the skills in individual written argument that are crucial to later academic success (Kuhn et al., 2016a, 2016b). Our program emphasizes peer-to-peer engagement, rather than relying on the teacher as a conduit in whole-class discussion, and on purposeful debate that addresses topics of relevance first to students' decision-making regarding their personal futures and then regarding the futures of their community, nation, and world (Kuhn, 2018). Through sustained peer engagement, students develop the norms of discourse that reinforce accountability to one another (Kuhn & Zillmer, 2015). We have found that an effective addition to practice with peers is engaging in argumentive dialogs with an older, more capable person, whose contributions to the dialog reflect more sophisticated argument forms (Papathomas & Kuhn, 2017). Also key is the question-asking component of the activity: "What questions would you like answers to that might help you in your debate on this topic?" is a prompt introduced regularly at the beginning, until students take full charge of their questioning – a point at which the border between inquiry and argument fades.

## Developing Teachers' Skills

How can teachers best support the development of the cognitive skills of argument and inquiry, as these become increasingly critical in the second decade of life? And how can we teach teachers how to do so? With respect to both inquiry and argument, we have already pointed to dimensions of educational settings that we see as critical. Activities must be experienced as purposeful and goal-directed, with actors playing a major role in setting individual goals and directing their own activity and experiencing a sense of agency in so doing, and in seeing their skills develop with engagement and practice. In a word, they need intellectual autonomy.

Is there evidence that learners who experience these learning conditions fare better than those who do not or who experience them to a lesser extent? Studies of individual and group differences among both learners and teachers have the potential to yield such evidence. We have studied individual differences in inquiry learning in low-, middle-, and high-SES middle-school students, asking what self-regulatory skills are needed to facilitate effective learning, distinguished from academic achievement, in classrooms. Self-regulation is a broad construct, usefully divided into subtypes, notably behavioral and cognitive. Behavioral regulation entails on- vs. off-task behaviors. Although cognitive regulation and behavior regulation were related, it was cognitive, not behavioral, regulation that predicted students' performance on multiple self-directed learning tasks across these different socioeconomic groups (Modrek & Kuhn, 2017; Modrek et al., 2018).

These patterns, however, did not fully extend to the high-SES, high-achieving, economically affluent sample (Modrek & Kuhn, 2017). Although these affluent students were for the most part high academic achievers and had higher scores on behavior regulation (as assessed by an observational classroom measure), they did not perform as well as the middle-class sample on the cognitive regulation test. They also performed less well than the middle-class sample on the self-directed learning task. Moreover, for this group higher behavior regulation was associated with lower cognitive regulation. Again, however, cognitive regulation, but not behavior regulation, predicted learning effectiveness. Why then did their cognitive regulation waver in both the test and learning contexts? The answer may lie in their having formed other values regarding what leads to success. Posttest questionnaires revealed these students' beliefs that it is more important to memorize what the teacher is saying than to understand the lesson and "... learning and memorizing are the same thing" (Modrek & Kuhn, 2017). Despite high academic performance, intellectual agency and autonomy thus appear to have been compromised among these students.

What, then, can teachers do, and what types of learning environments should they create, to support the development of autonomous, inquisitive learners? Recent preliminary findings come from a teacher professional development project (Sandoval et al., 2018) that aims to help teachers shift their practice toward the kinds of learning that relies on students' joint construction of knowledge and of the practices that create such knowledge. The project seeks to help teachers (a) open up their instructional activities to give students more agency and responsibility to negotiate and enact practices of experimentation, modeling, data analysis, and, argument, and (b) learn productive talk moves to help manage students' question-asking and discourse that are the product of these activities. This focus emerged from analysis of the difficulties teachers had in the first year of PD to legitimately open space for students to exercise epistemic agency (Sandoval et al., 2016, 2017). Participants were seventh to twelfth grade students and teachers from a large school district in the Western US, serving a largely Latino population, about one-third English-language learners and over two-thirds qualifying for free or reduced-prince lunch.

One of our questions was what levels of agency teachers believe students should have in their own learning, using an adaptation of a scale by Eccles and colleagues (1991). For example, two of its questions were, "Do your students have a say about how investigations are run during science class?" and, "Do you think students should have a say in this?" Students were asked similar questions. At the beginning of the intervention, students tended to report receiving less autonomy than their teachers reported giving them, while middle-school students generally reported wanting more autonomy than their teachers wished to give them. Approximately two years into the intervention, teachers' desire to give autonomy increased. Middle-school students showed susceptibility to this change and in fact showed narrower differences in their reports of autonomy of their teachers.

To examine classroom processes, we analyzed videos of 250 classroom lessons, using a low-inference discourse observation protocol (LIDO; Michaels & O'Connor, 2015) that counts categories of teacher and student talk moves expected to be consequential for productive discussion (see Table 12.1). Three codes for teacher talk address dialogic scaffolds (T1–T3) and correspond to codes for student dialogue (S1–S3). Three other teacher codes (T4–T6) characterize teachers' questions. One code for student talk (S4) concerns whether students ask questions, and two (S5, S6) how students respond to questions.

We recognize there are too many potential additional differences across individuals and across groups to allow us to infer causal relations with any certainty. Still, preliminary correlational results are suggestive. Teachers who engage in more dialogic scaffolds (T1–T3) have students who actively respond to another student's question (S1), add to or reference another student's claim (S2), or provide evidence to support their reasoning (S3). Most notable, by the end of the second year of professional development, when teachers actively attempted to get students to continue speaking (T3), students more often provided evidence to support their own claims (S3) and directly responded to other students' claims and questions (S2).

Table 12.1 *LIDO codes for teacher and student contributions to whole-class discussions*

| Code | Description | Code | Description |
|---|---|---|---|
| | **Dialogic Scaffolds** | | **Student Dialogue** |
| T1 | Get student(s) to respond to another student's turn | S1 | Addresses another student |
| T2 | Ask student to explain, clarify, or provide explanation | S2 | Refers to another student's contribution |
| T3 | Attempts to get student to continue speaking | S3 | Provides evidence or reasoning to support claim |
| | **Teacher Questions** | | **Student Responses** |
| T4 | Poses truly open, contestable question | S4 | Student asks teacher question about lesson content |
| T5 | Poses semi-open question, with a circumscribed answer set | S5 | Other elaborated turn, longer than a simple clause |
| T6 | Poses a closed, uncontestable question, or a test question | S6 | Turn is a simple clause or less |

During a randomly selected lesson on temperature that we observed, the teacher employs questions as a way to get students not only to reason more effectively, but eventually to also ask questions of their peers:

### Code Speaker Dialogue

[T6] TEACHER: Where do you want to stay when it's really hot?

[S6] STUDENT 8: The lowest level.

[T2] TEACHER: How come? Because you realize when you walk up the stairs to the second floor, what's happening?

[S6] STUDENT 8: It's hotter.

[S6] STUDENT 12: You get tired.

[T5] TEACHER: So what does that tell you? Ready? So what can you infer, that hot air –

[S6] STUDENT 8: Hot air goes up.

[T6] TEACHER: Rises, right?

[S6] STUDENT 8: Yeah. It rises.

[T6] TEACHER: Ariana, you said that the molecules of the hot water will – what's the I word you used?

[S6] STUDENT 12: Inflate.

[T1] TEACHER: Inflate. Any questions about what she said?

Notice as the discussion proceeds, how the teacher continues to use questions to encourage student discussion, in addition to promoting thinking about multiple causes. Rather than providing praise or confirmation, she responds with questions as a means of encouraging students to question their own answers.

[T2] TEACHER: So who is ready to share out your answer to the first question?

[T2] TEACHER: ... So the first question. Who can tell me what might be some of the possible causes for the different rates of diffusion? Why is the food coloring traveling a lot faster in the hot water? Who can tell me the first. Go ahead, Alice.

[S3] STUDENT 13: You're making it so hot it's expanding.

[T6] TEACHER: So expanding in liquid?

[S6] STUDENT 13: Yes.

[T2] TEACHER: Expanding means the molecules are going to do this. Ok. Alice, can you choose one person please to give me another possible cause?

[T2] TEACHER: Allen go back. Give me a possible cause. I need you to participate in this. You're thinking about this. Hurry. What would be a possible cause of why it went through a lot faster in the hot water versus the cold water?

[S3] STUDENT 14: Because hot makes everything like liquidy.

[S6] STUDENT 15: Liquidy.

[T2] TEACHER: Ok. Can I hear Hank?

[S3] STUDENT 16: In the cold water the food coloring kind of like froze a little. Then in the hot water –

[T2] TEACHER: Ok. Hank, your reason?

[S3] STUDENT 16: The food coloring?

[T2] TEACHER: Same question, possible cause.

[S3] STUDENT 16: The food coloring expanded faster in the hot water because heat makes liquids and food coloring has liquid. So it –

[T2] TEACHER: Evaporate? Did I hear that? No? What did you say?

[S6] STUDENT 17: I heard it.

[S6] STUDENT 16: Heat makes liquid and liquids keeps heating the liquid and expands.

[T2] TEACHER: Expands so same word that she used. Ok. Elijah, can I hear your explanation please? What is your possible cause for the differing rates of diffusion?

[S6] STUDENT 18: It melted faster in the hot.

[T2] TEACHER: Ok. So instead of the word melted you might use the word diffuse but you didn't tell me why. I'll come back. Alice?

[S3] STUDENT 13: The diffusion was at a very small rate in the cold because it would have _____ temperature.

[T4] TEACHER: Ok. So what's happening in the microscopic molecular level?

[S6] STUDENT 13: It stopped.

[T5] TEACHER: It stopped. Ok. That's a new way of thinking. It stopped. Maybe you can write that. Add that.

[S6] STUDENT 18: It froze.

[T2] TEACHER: Elijah? It stopped, it froze. Write that. Any other possible ways that –

[S6] STUDENT 19: It freezes, miss. It froze.

[T2] TEACHER: Any other possible ways?

[S3] STUDENT 19: When it's colder and it's hotter different atoms.

[T4] TEACHER: Did you guys hear him? So Elijah said maybe the atoms are different. Good. Moving on. Ready Adam? Last question, I want to hear this. Ok. So do you think that same pattern where it's always going to be like that diffusing a lot faster in the hot and the cold would be the same for all liquid substances? Yes or no and why? I want him to answer first. Let's say compare water to another liquid substance what do you think? Do you think that same temperature pattern would be the same like true for all? What do you think, Adam?

[S6] STUDENT 20: Yes.

[T3] TEACHER: Ok. How come? Justify.

[S3] STUDENT 20: The molecules. The temperature makes the molecules either move a lot faster or slow down.

Of particular interest in this discussion is the teacher's consistency in asking students to explore alternative causes. With minimal input, she gives students opportunities to construct their own knowledge. While this is only one transcript from a growing video corpus, it is suggestive of what effective teacher talk can do. Effective teaching, we suggest, is less about the quantity or even quality of information a teacher provides and more about a teacher's well-posed, well-timed, and thought-provoking questions. Teachers may struggle to cede control to their students, but their learning to do so appears worth the effort.

## Conclusions

A teacher's instructional style shapes the context, the world, a student learns in and interacts with. Recent studies of children in the first decade of life have suggested a trade-off between instruction and exploration, with autonomy supporting young children's exploration. In the presence of a teacher, learners expect information to be provided to them (Shafto & Goodman, 2008; Shafto et al., 2012). As teachers provided more input, young children were observed to constrain their exploration (Gweon & Schulz, 2008; Gweon et al., 2014). Interactive, inquisitive, and discourse-focused teaching, in contrast, encourages exploration and inquiry (Reiser et al., 2001; Sandoval et al., 2002; Sandoval & Reiser, 2004).

During the second decade of life, which we have focused on in this chapter, the stakes may become even higher. In the second decade, some degree of autonomy may be a condition for teens to buy into intellectual pursuits, beyond the minimum required of them. This sense of autonomy and agency is also what they will be most likely to need in the workplace, as we noted earlier. Trade-offs between explicit direct instruction and autonomy are to some extent likely to be ones of trade-off between short-term and long-term goals. We must have both in mind. Ideally, learners will come to command a great quantity and variety of knowledge while at the same time remaining in charge of doing so.

For their part, the teachers, parents, and other adults in adolescents' lives must not merely allow but also help to create the time and space for teens to engage deeply in the intellectual skills of inquiry and argument that have been the topic of this chapter. Intellectual skills and values develop slowly, with sustained practice, and the conducive time and space must be maintained if these skills and values are to prosper. As we also have stressed, teachers must learn to cede control to an extent that allows students as much autonomy as possible in choosing questions that they find authentic and worthy of pursuit. Teachers also must learn to cede control in letting students engage and address one another directly, allowing them to develop the norms of discourse that reinforce accountability to one another. In sum, arranging an environment rich in purposeful questions to ask, along with opportunity to collaborate in addressing them, will go a long way in developing the senses of autonomy and agency that have been a theme here and that will serve young people well in the decades beyond their school years.

## Acknowledgments

Some of the work described here was supported by the National Science Foundation (NSF); DRL award #1503511.

## References

Baron, J. (1994). *Thinking and deciding* (2nd ed.). Cambridge: Cambridge University Press.

Capon, N., and Kuhn, D. (2004). What's so good about problem-based learning? *Cognition and Instruction*, *22*, 61–79. https://doi:10.1207/s1532690Xci2201_3

Chi, M. (2009). Active–constructive–interactive: A conceptual framework for differentiating learning activities. *Topics in Cognitive Science*, *1*, 73–105. https://doi:10.1111/j.1756-8765.2008.01005.x

Collins, A. (2017). *What's worth teaching? Rethinking curriculum in the age of technology*. New York: Teachers College Press.

Dean Jr, D., and Kuhn, D. (2007). Direct instruction vs. discovery: The long view. *Science Education*, *91*, 384–97. https://doi:10.1002/sce.20194

Dewey, J. (1997). *Experience and education*. Free Press. Reprint edition. Originally published in 1938.

Eccles, J. S., Buchanan, C. M., Flanagan, C. et al. (1991). Control versus autonomy during early adolescence. *Journal of Social Issues*, *47*, 53–68. https://doi:10.1111/j.1540-4560.1991.tb01834.x

Eccles, J. S., Midgley, C., Wigfield, A. et al. (1993). Development during adolescence: The impact of stage-environment fit on young adolescents' experiences in schools and in families. *American Psychologist*, *48*(2), 90–101. https://doi:10.1037/0003-066X.48.2.90

Feldlaufer, H., Midgley, C., and Eccles, J. S. (1988). Student, teacher, and observer perceptions of the classroom environment before and after the transition to junior high school. *The Journal of Early Adolescence*, *8*, 133–56. https://doi:10.1177/0272431688082003

Friedman, T. (2014, February 22). How to get a job at Google. [Reporting on an interview with Laszlo Bock, vice president of people operations at Google Inc.] *The New York Times*.

Gopnik, A., O'Grady, S., Lucas, C. et al. (2017). Changes in cognitive flexibility and hypothesis search across human life history from childhood to adolescence to adulthood. *Proceedings of the National Academy of Sciences*, *114*, 7892–99. https://doi:10.1073/pnas.1700811114

Greene, J., Sandoval, W., and Braten, I. (eds.) (2016). *Handbook of epistemic cognition*. New York: Routledge.

Gweon, H., and Schulz, L. (2008). Stretching to learn: Ambiguous evidence and variability in preschoolers' exploratory play. In *Proceedings of the 30th annual meeting of the Cognitive Science Society* (pp. 570–4).

Gweon, H., Pelton, H., Konopka, J. A., and Schulz, L. E. (2014). Sins of omission: Children selectively explore when teachers are under-informative. *Cognition*, *132*, 335–41. https://doi:10.1016/j.cognition.2014.04.013

Hemberger, L., Kuhn, D., Matos, F., and Shi, Y. (2017). A dialogic path to evidence-based argumentive writing. *Journal of the Learning Sciences, 26,* 575–607. https://doi:10.1080/10508406.2017.1336714

Inhelder, B., and Piaget, J. (1958). *The growth of logical thinking from childhood to adolescence.* New York: Basic Books. https://doi:10.1037/10034-000

Iordanou, K., Kuhn, D., Matos, F., Shi, Y., and Hemberger, L. (2019). Learning by arguing. *Learning and Instruction, 63.* https://doi.org/10.1016/j.learninstruc.2019.05.004

Jewett, E., and Kuhn, D. (2016). Social science as a tool in developing scientific thinking skills in underserved, low-achieving urban students. *Journal of Experimental Child Psychology, 143,* 154–61. https://doi:10.1016/j.jecp.2015.10.019

Johnston, A. M., Johnson, S. G., Koven, M. L., and Keil, F. C. (2017). Little Bayesians or little Einsteins? Probability and explanatory virtue in children's inferences. *Developmental Science, 20,* e12483. https://doi:10.1111/desc.12483

Kuhn, D. (2005). *Education for thinking.* Cambridge, MA: Harvard University Press.

(2011). What is scientific thinking and how does it develop? In U. Goswami (ed.), *Handbook of childhood cognitive development* (pp. 497–523, 2nd ed.). Oxford: Blackwell.

(2012). The development of causal reasoning. *WIREs Cognitive Science.* https://doi:10.1002/wcs.1160

(2015). Thinking together and alone. *Educational Researcher, 44,* 46–53. https://doi:10.3102/0013189X15569530

(2016). What do young science students need to know about variables? *Science Education, 100,* 392–403. https://doi:10.1002/sce.21207

(2018). *Building our best future: Thinking critically about ourselves and our world.* New York: Wessex Learning. https://doi:10.1080/00098655.2018.1480742

Kuhn, D., and Crowell, A. (2011). Dialogic argumentation as a vehicle for developing young adolescents' thinking. *Psychological Science, 22,* 545–52. https://doi:10.1177/0956797611402512

Kuhn, D., and Ho, V. (1980). Self-directed activity and cognitive development. *Journal of Applied Developmental Psychology, 1,* 119–33. https://doi:10.1016/0193-3973(80)90003-9

Kuhn, D., and Katz, J. (2009). Are self-explanations always beneficial? *Journal of Experimental Child Psychology, 103,* 386–94. https://doi:10.1016/j.jecp.2009.03.003

Kuhn, D., and Modrek, A. (2018). Do reasoning limitations undermine discourse? *Thinking and Reasoning, 24,* 97–116. https://doi:10.1080/13546783.2017.1388846

Kuhn, D., and Moore, W. (2015). Argumentation as core curriculum. *Learning: Research and Practice, 1,* 66–78. https://doi:10.1080/23735082.2015.994254

Kuhn, D., and Zillmer, N. (2015). Developing norms of discourse. In L. Resnick, C. Asterhan, and S. Clarke (eds.), *Socializing intelligence through academic talk and dialogue* (pp. 77–86). Washington, DC: American Educational Research Association. https://doi:10.3102/978-0-935302-43-1_6

Kuhn, D., Ramsey, S., and Arvidsson, T. S. (2015). Developing multivariable thinkers. *Cognitive Development, 35,* 92–110. https://doi:10.1016/j.cogdev.2014.11.003

Kuhn, D., Hemberger, L., and Khait, V. (2016a). *Argue with me: Argument as a path to developing students' thinking and writing* (2nd ed.) New York: Routledge. https://doi:10.4324/9781315692722

(2016b). Tracing the development of argumentive writing in a discourse-rich context. *Written Communication, 33,* 92–121. https://doi:10.1177/0741088315617157

Legare, C., and Lombrozo, T. (2014). Selective effects of explanation on learning during early childhood. *Journal of Experimental Child Psychology, 126,* 198–212. https://doi:10.1016/j.jecp.2014.03.001

Lehrer, R., and Schauble, L. (2015). The development of scientific thinking. In L. Liben and U. Mueller (vol. eds.) and R. Lerner (series ed.), *Handbook of child psychology and developmental science* (pp. 1–44), vol. 2: Cognitive process (7th ed.). Hoboken, NJ: Wiley. https://doi:10.1002/9781118963418.childpsy216

Michaels, S., and O'Connor, C. (2015). Conceptualizing talk moves as tools: Professional development approaches for academically productive discussion. In L. Resnick, C. Asterhan, and S. Clarke (eds.), *Socializing intelligence through academic talk and dialogue* (pp. 347–62). Washington, DC: American Educational Research Association. https://doi:10.3102/978-0-935302-43-1_27

Modrek, A., and Kuhn, D. (2017). A cognitive cost of the need to achieve? *Cognitive Development, 44,* 12–20. https://doi:10.1016/j.cogdev.2017.08.003

Modrek, A. S., Kuhn, D., Conway, A., and Arvidsson, T. S. (2018). Cognitive regulation, not behavior regulation, predicts learning. *Learning and Instruction.* https://doi:10.1016/j.learninstruc.2017.12.001

Moshman, D. (2014). *Epistemic cognition and development: The psychology of justification and truth.* Psychology Press.

Moskowitz, E., and Lavinia, A. (2012). *Mission possible: How the secrets of the Success Academies can work in any school.* John Wiley & Sons.

Muldner, K., Lam, R., and Chi, M. (2014). Comparing learning from observing and from human tutoring. *Journal of Educational Psychology, 106,* 69–85. https://doi:10.1037/a0034448

Papathomas, L., and Kuhn, D. (2017). Learning to argue via apprenticeship. *Journal of Experimental Child Psychology, 159,* 129–39. https://doi:10.1016/j.jecp.2017.01.013

Paus, E., Macagno, F., and Kuhn, D. (2015). Developing argumentation strategies in electronic dialogs: Is modeling effective? *Discourse Processes, 53,* 280–97. https://doi:10.1080/0163853X.2015.1040323

Pease, M., and Kuhn, D. (2011). Experimental analysis of the effective components of problem-based learning. *Science Education, 95,* 57–86. https://doi:10.1002/sce.20412

Pintrich, P. R., and Schunk, D. H. (2002). *Motivation in education.* Upper Saddle River, NJ: Merrill.

Putnam, R. T., and Borko, H. (2000). What do new views of knowledge and thinking have to say about research on teacher learning? *Educational Researcher*, 29, 4–15. https://doi:10.3102/0013189X029001004

Reiser, B. J., Tabak, I., Sandoval, W. A., et al. (2001). BGuILE: Strategic and conceptual scaffolds for scientific inquiry in biology classrooms. In S. M. Carver and D. Klahr (eds.), *Cognition and instruction: Twenty-five years of progress* (pp. 263–305). New York: Psychology Press.

Resnick, L. B., and Nelson-Le Gall, S. (1997). Socializing intelligence. In L. Smith, J. Dockrell, and P. Tomlinson (eds.), *Piaget, Vygotsky and beyond: Central issues in developmental psychology and education* (pp. 145–58). London: Routledge.

Ross, H. S., and Killey, J. C. (1977). The effect of questioning on retention. *Child Development*, 48, 312–14. https://doi:10.2307/1128919

Ryu, S., and Sandoval, W. (2012). Improvements to elementary children's epistemic understanding from sustained argumentation. *Science Education*, 96, 488–526. https://doi:10.1002/sce.21006

Sandoval, W. A. (2005). Understanding students' practical epistemologies and their influence on learning through inquiry. *Science Education*, 89, 634–56. https://doi:10.1002/sce.20065

(2015). Science education's need for a theory of epistemological development. *Science Education*, 98, 383–87. https://doi:10.1002/sce.21107

Sandoval, W. A., and Reiser, B. J. (2004). Explanation-driven inquiry: Integrating conceptual and epistemic scaffolds for scientific inquiry. *Science Education*, 88, 345–72. https://doi:10.1002/sce.10130

Sandoval, W. A., Deneroff, V., and Franke, M. L. (2002). Teaching, as learning, as inquiry: Moving beyond activity in the analysis of teaching practice. Paper presented at the Annual Meeting of the Educational Research Association. New Orleans, LA.

Sandoval, W. A., Sodian, B., Koerber, S., and Wong, J. (2014). Developing children's early competencies to engage with science. *Educational Psychologist*, 49, 139–52. https://doi:10.1080/00461520.2014.917589

Sandoval, W. A., Kawasaki, J., Cournoyer, N., and Rodriguez, L. (2016). Secondary teachers' emergent understanding of teaching science practices. In C. K. Looi, J. L. Polman, U. Cress, and P. Reimann (eds.), *Proceedings of the transforming learning, empowering learners: The international conference of the learning sciences (ICLS) 2016* (Vol. 2, pp. 737–74). Singapore: ISLS.

Sandoval, W. A., Cournoyer, N., Eggleston, N., Modrek, A., and Kawasaki, J. (2017). Secondary teachers' struggles to create coherent NGSS instruction. Paper presented at the NARST Annual Meeting. San Antonio, TX.

Sandoval, W. A., Kwako, A., Modrek, A. S., and Kawasaki, J. (2018) Patterns of classroom talk through participation in discourse-focused teacher professional development. In *Proceedings of the 13th International Conference of the Learning Sciences: Volume 2* (pp. 760–7). International Society of the Learning Sciences.

Schank, R. (2011). *How cognitive science can save our schools*. New York: Teachers College Press.

Shafto, P., and Goodman, N. D. (2008). Teaching games: Statistical sampling assumptions for pedagogical situations. In *Proceedings of the Thirtieth Annual Conference of the Cognitive Science Society* (pp. 1632–7).

Shafto, P., Goodman, N. D., and Frank, M. C. (2012). Learning from others: The consequences of psychological reasoning for human learning. *Perspectives on Psychological Science, 7*(4), 341–51. https://doi:10.1177/1745691612448481

Sloman, S. (2005). *Causal models: How people think about the world and its alternatives.* New York: Oxford University Press. https://doi:10.1093/acprof:oso/9780195183115.001.0001

Stanovich, K. (1999). *Who is rational? Studies of individual differences in reasoning.* Mahwah, NJ: Erlbaum. https://doi:10.4324/9781410603432

Steinberg, L., and Monahan, K. C. (2007). Age differences in resistance to peer influence. *Developmental psychology, 43*(6), 1531–43. https://doi.org/10.1037/0012-1649.43.6.1531

Trilling B, and Fadel, C. (2009). *Twentieth century skills: learning for life in our times.* San Francisco, CA: John Wiley & Sons.

Walker, C. M., Bonawitz, E., and Lombrozo, T. (2017a). Effects of explaining on children's preference for simpler hypotheses. *Psychonomic Bulletin & Review, 24*, 1538–47. https://doi:10.3758/s13423-016-1144-0

Walker, C. M., Lombrozo, T., Williams, J. J., Rafferty, A. N., and Gopnik, A. (2017b). Explaining constrains causal learning in childhood. *Child Development, 88*, 229–46. https://doi:10.1111/cdev.12590

Windschitl, M. (2003). Inquiry projects in science teacher education: What can investigative experiences reveal about teacher thinking and eventual classroom practice? *Science Education, 87*(1), 112–43. https://doi:10.1002/sce.10044

Wirkala, C., and Kuhn, D. (2011). Problem-based learning in K-12 education: Is it effective and how does it achieve its effects? *American Educational Research Journal, 48*, 1157–86. https://doi:10.3102/0002831211419491

Zimmerman, C. (2007). The development of scientific thinking skills in elementary and middle school. *Developmental Review, 27*, 172–223. https://doi:10.1016/j.dr.2006.12.001

# 13 Asking "Why?" and "What If?"

## The Influence of Questions on Children's Inferences

*Caren M. Walker, Angela Nyhout*

### Introduction

In learning about the world, we often form inferences on the basis of sparse data. Despite this challenge, children are prolific learners. Very young children form, test, and rationally revise hypotheses in building informal theories in a variety of domains (Carey, 1985; Keil, 1992; Wellman & Gelman, 1992; Gopnik & Meltzoff, 1997). Preschoolers use data from interventions to infer causal structure (Schulz et al., 2007) and use patterns of dependence to learn about causes in various domains, even when the evidence they observe conflicts with their prior knowledge (Gopnik et al., 2001; Schulz & Gopnik, 2004). Toddlers interpret patterns of data to infer unobserved causes (Kushnir et al., 2003) and even abstract relations (Walker & Gopnik, 2014, 2017). In this chapter, we describe a growing body of research that demonstrates the efficacy of specific questions in supporting children's ability to access these intuitive reasoning skills and apply them to tasks involving sophisticated causal and scientific thinking.

In particular, we will consider three candidate questions that are likely to promote learning and inference in explicit causal reasoning tasks: explanation ("why?" questions), multiple explanation ("why else?" questions), and counterfactuals ("what if?" questions). We describe the distinct mechanisms by which each of these questions likely results in unique types of inferences, and review existing empirical support from both children and adults providing evidence for their effectiveness. We argue that the particular question posed carries selective effects on a learner's inferences, depending upon the evidence available, the state of their prior knowledge, and the relation of that prior knowledge to the true state of the world.

In exploring the role of specific questions for causal learning in early childhood, we begin with a brief review of the well-established research on the efficacy of prompts for explanation, focusing on the developmental literature. We then offer a novel proposal, drawing on the adult research, that engaging children in the evaluation of alternative outcomes via prompting for multiple explanations or consideration of counterfactuals may provide a different avenue for fostering distinct sets of causal reasoning skills. Finally, we turn to a discussion of the relation between the content and process of children's reasoning in response to these questions, and end with some suggestions for future research.

## Explanation: Asking "Why?"

### *Why Are Prompts to Explain Effective?*

Explanation questions – questions of the form "why did $X$ happen?" – have been extensively studied in the developmental literature to date. The benefits of self-explanation have been observed in a broad range of learners, from preschoolers to adults, and across a variety of knowledge domains and educational contexts, including both formal and informal learning environments (e.g., Chi et al., 1989; Chi et al., 1994; Crowley & Siegler, 1999; Siegler, 2002; Legare & Lombrozo, 2014; Walker et al., 2014). Here we will focus on developmental findings that have examined the effects of generating explanations on early learning in young children.

First, some accounts suggest that "why?" questions engage domain general processes that are not necessarily unique to explanation. For example, the act of generating an explanation has been proposed to increase attention and task engagement (Siegler, 2002). Others have suggested that cognitive benefits result from the fact that explaining is a goal-directed (Nelson, 1973) or constructive process, in which the learner is asked to go beyond the information that is explicitly provided (Chi, 2009). Explanations have also been suggested to help learners to identify gaps or inconsistencies in their existing knowledge (Chi, 2000). On each of these views, non-explanation tasks that serve to engage the same mechanisms should similarly enhance learning.

More recent accounts have instead emphasized the unique and selective effects of explanation, which carry advantages over those conferred by other learning strategies. In particular, the act of explaining appears to recruit attention to specific types of hypotheses that capture the characteristics of *good* explanations – those that are broad (Lombrozo, 2012; Williams & Lombrozo, 2010, 2013; Walker et al., 2016b), generalizable (Legare, 2012; Walker et al., 2014; Walker & Lombrozo, 2017), and simple (Walker et al., 2017). According to this view, explanation serves to constrain learning and inference, leading the learner to privilege certain hypotheses, even at the expense of others.

In line with this proposal, children who are asked to explain during learning are more likely to privilege a hypothesis that accounts for the greatest proportion of the data observed. For example, Walker and colleagues (2016b) showed five-year-old children patterns of evidence (blocks activating a novel toy) that were compatible with two candidate causal hypotheses, and varied the level of consistency of each hypothesis with their prior beliefs. In a first study, children observed the causal efficacy of blocks varying along two dimensions that were matched in terms of prior knowledge: one dimension (e.g., the top color) covaried perfectly with the machine's activation, while the second dimension (e.g., the front color) co-occurred with the effect 75 percent of the time. When children's prior beliefs about the efficacy of each hypothesis were matched, those who explained were more likely than children in a control group to favor the hypothesis with perfect covariation.

Next, children were presented with evidence that was equally consistent with the two candidate hypotheses – block color and block size – which both perfectly covaried with the effect. However, pilot data had indicated that children favored block size as the more likely causal mechanism. In this case, when the two hypotheses were matched in terms of the number of observations, children who explained favored the hypothesis that was most compatible with their prior belief (size) more often than controls. In a final study, prior belief (size), which accounted for 75 percent of the data, was pit against current observations (color), which accounted for 100 percent of the data. In this case, explainers were more likely than controls to favor the 75 percent size hypothesis, consistent with their prior beliefs, even though this hypothesis accounted for fewer observations in the current context. Thus, children who explained tended to privilege the hypothesis with the broadest *scope*: the hypothesis that was consistent with both their prior beliefs *and* the current data. Similar results have also been found with adults (e.g., Williams & Lombrozo, 2010, 2013; Williams et al., 2013).

Relatedly, Walker and colleagues (2014) found that explaining led children to form generalizations on the basis of inductively rich properties of objects (i.e., those properties that are likely to be informative for future cases). Specifically, preschoolers who explained were more likely to override salient perceptual information to make inferences about objects' hidden properties on the basis of common causal affordances. Using a well-established causal learning paradigm, preschoolers observed a series of objects that either activated or failed to activate a toy. Children were then shown a target block that activated the toy, a perceptually matched block that did not, and a causally matched block that activated the toy, but was perceptually dissimilar to the target block. Children were asked to either explain *why* or report *whether* each block made the toy activate. The experimenter then revealed that the target block contained a hidden internal part, and asked the child to select which of the other two blocks – the perceptual match or causal match – shared the same internal part. Children who had *explained* the outcome were significantly more likely to select the causally matched block – generalizing according to the blocks' shared causal status – than children who were asked to *report* on the outcome. In a second study, children who explained were also more likely to extend a category label on the basis of the objects' shared causal status. When told that the target block was a "blicket," and asked which other block was also a blicket, explainers were more likely to select the causal match over the perceptual match than children in the control condition. A final study revealed that these effects likely resulted from children's increased attention to a cluster of correlated, inductively rich properties (causality, category labels, and internal parts), which selectively impaired their memory for an uncorrelated, but highly salient perceptual feature (i.e., stickers placed on each object).

This tendency for explainers to privilege information about causal mechanisms at the expense of noncausal, perceptually salient properties has been reported in other contexts as well (Legare & Lombrozo, 2014). For example, Legare and Lombrozo (2014) familiarized preschool-aged children with a novel toy composed of interlocking gears and cranks of varying sizes and colors, which was designed to cause a fan to turn. Children were asked to explain how the toy worked, or to engage in a control activity (observing or describing). One of the gears was then surreptitiously removed. Children who had generated explanations were more likely to select a functionally correct replacement gear that was perceptually dissimilar from the original when compared with controls. They were also more likely to successfully construct a novel (functional) gear arrangement on their own. On the other hand, the non-explainers were better able to recall salient noncausal information (i.e., the color of the missing gear). Interestingly, these results were observed regardless of the specific prompts provided; those in the control condition who *spontaneously* explained showed similar effects.

In addition to selectively boosting attention to hypotheses that are broad and generalizable, explanation has also been shown to increase children's tendency to favor *simplicity* (i.e., privileging a single, unifying cause over multiple causes). Walker and colleagues (2017) presented four-, five-, and six-year-olds with a garden consisting of four quadrants of plants, two "healthy" and two "unhealthy," and directed them to consider the two plots of "unhealthy" plants. The evidence was consistent with a single common cause (both were planted in the same type of soil) or two independent causes (one plot had a broken sprinkler, the other lacked sunlight). Children were prompted to explain *why* or report *whether* the plants were sick in each quadrant. After being presented with a novel garden at test, children were asked to predict which plants were unhealthy. Five-year-olds who had explained favored the simpler, common cause at a higher rate than those who had reported, indicating that explanation heightens children's sensitivity to simplicity as a basis for favoring one hypothesis over another. Interestingly, however, this condition difference did not extend to four- or six-year-olds: four-year-olds showed no preference for the simpler hypothesis in either condition, and six-year-olds preferred the simpler hypothesis in both conditions. The authors proposed that a combination of factors may account for these developmental differences. For example, they note that the youngest children in their sample may have lacked the requisite domain knowledge to engage with the task (i.e., variables related to plant growth), leading to a null result. They also suggest several possible explanations for the consistent simplicity preference found in six-year-olds. One possibility is that older children spontaneously recruit simplicity as a basis for evaluating hypotheses. Another is that they are more likely to spontaneously explain (even without a prompt to do so), which would lead them to privilege simpler hypotheses across conditions. A third possibility is that the simpler hypothesis (i.e., soil color) may have been less salient than the complex hypothesis (i.e., sunlight and water), in light of children's prior knowledge. If so, the more salient complex hypothesis might have competed against the simpler hypothesis for *both* five- and six-year-olds; however, while five-year-olds required the help of an explanation prompt to overcome it in favor of the simpler alternative, six-year-olds did not.

Taken together, each of the cases presented above could also be interpreted as evidence that explanation leads learners to favor more *abstract* hypotheses in the service of generalization. Indeed, several previous accounts of the effects of explanation suggest a direct or indirect relation to abstraction (e.g., Lombrozo & Carey, 2006). For example, given that the instance being explained is related to a more general framework (Lombrozo, 2006, 2012; Wellman & Liu, 2007; Williams & Lombrozo, 2010, 2013), explanation may draw the learner's attention towards more abstract features (Walker & Lombrozo, 2017). Several recent studies directly assessing this interpretation have provided some support for this claim (e.g., Walker et al., 2016a; Walker & Lombrozo, 2017). First, Walker and colleagues (2016a) found that generating explanations in a causal learning paradigm facilitated three- and four-year-olds in learning and applying abstract relational rules (i.e., "same" and "different"). Later, Walker and Lombrozo (2017) reported that prompting five- and six-year-olds to explain during a storybook reading bolstered their ability to identify and extend abstract moral themes from fictional stories – a notoriously challenging task for young children (e.g., Narvaez et al., 1999). In this study, an experimenter read storybooks designed to convey a particular moral theme (e.g., tolerance), periodically interrupting the story to ask children to either *explain* why an event occurred or *report* whether an event had occurred. Even though the explanation prompts did not specifically direct children's attention to the moral theme, those who were prompted to explain were more likely to recognize and generalize the theme across a range of dependent measures. In contrast, children who were asked to report were more likely to respond on the basis of surface features and similarities in stories, in line with previous research.

## *Summary and Limitations of Explanation*

Together, the studies reviewed above demonstrate the *selective* effects of explanation, though as noted above, these effects are not universally beneficial. First, when children are prompted to explain how a novel toy works, they are more likely to learn and generalize on the basis of inductively rich (e.g., causal, categorical, internal, mechanistic) properties, at the expense of learning and remembering perceptual information. Second, when presented with competing hypotheses, children who explain tend to favor simpler over complex hypotheses, as well as those with greater scope (often drawing on prior knowledge). In some cases, this tendency may come at the expense of identifying the correct hypotheses when it conflicts with prior beliefs, accounts for fewer observations, or posits multiple independent causes.

Research with adults has similarly demonstrated that prompts to explain can lead learners to *over*generalize at times, by identifying broad patterns and ignoring exceptions or counterexamples that may be present in the data (Williams et al., 2013). Explanation has also been shown to lead adults to privilege conceptual learning at the expense of procedural learning (Berthold et al., 2011), and to lead school-aged children to focus on information about causal mechanisms, overlooking potentially relevant covariation patterns (Kuhn & Katz, 2009). We can conclude, therefore, that while explanation affords clear benefits when the primary learning goal includes attention to abstract features and the formation of broad generalizations, it is unlikely to confer these same benefits in other learning contexts. As we will argue in the following sections, some of these undesirable effects might be mitigated by relying on different types of questions, including requests for *multiple* explanations, or prompts to consider counterfactual alternatives.

## Multiple Explanation: Asking "Why Else?"

Patterns of data often afford more than one plausible explanation. Although prompting children (and adults) to explain the evidence they observe typically leads them to privilege broad generalizations (Walker et al., 2016b, 2017), it is often the case that more than one hypothesis fits this description, or that a narrower hypothesis may better account for the data. After generating an initial explanation, searching for additional explanations may therefore help the learner to better localize the best fit hypothesis. Consistent with this idea, experiments in which *multiple* requests for an explanation are provided have resulted in debiased learning and reasoning in adults.

### Why Are Multiple Prompts to Explain Effective?

In line with Kahneman and Tversky's (1982) simulation heuristic, researchers have proposed that consideration of multiple alternatives leads individuals to adopt a "mental simulation mindset" (Fischoff, 1982; Galinsky & Moskowitz, 2000; Hirt & Markman, 1995; Galinsky & Moskowitz, 2000; Hirt et al., 2004). This proposal was based on the observation that adults who generate a *single* explanation, especially when explaining social phenomena, show a number of biases in subsequent prediction and interpretation of related evidence (e.g., Ross et al., 1977; Anderson et al., 1980). According to Koehler (1991), these individuals tend to adopt a conditional reference frame under which a focal hypothesis is assumed to be true, and this frame is then used as a lens through which the learner interprets relevant evidence. Considering counter-explanations or multiple explanations was therefore proposed to "break this inertia," causing the learner to shift away from this single, focal hypothesis to consider a range of possibilities (Hirt & Markman, 1995). Empirical evidence in support of this view has demonstrated that adults who are asked to produce *multiple* explanations show a corresponding attenuation in various types of biased reasoning, including biases in prediction (Hirt & Markman, 1995; Hirt et al., 2004) and hindsight bias (Sanna et al., 2002; Sanna & Schwarz, 2003).

Attempts to localize the mechanism underlying these effects led Hirt and Markman (1995) to develop two distinct proposals, which are both (appropriately) outlined in the same paper. First, they considered the possibility that generating multiple explanations facilitates easier access to arguments in support of the *specific* explanations they have generated, by way of the availability heuristic. Further, by entertaining more than one explanation, individuals may also express increased uncertainty about the likelihood of each of these specific alternatives, leading to decreased bias in a focal hypothesis. Next, they proposed an alternate process: that multiple explanations may invoke a domain-*general* "mindset" in which the contents and focus of each explanation need not be task-specific. In support of this second proposal, they found that individuals who explained a specific outcome (e.g., a win by the Red Sox) showed an explanation bias – increased confidence in the explained outcome – relative to individuals who also explained alternate outcomes (e.g., a win by the Blue Jays) (Lord et al., 1984; Hirt & Markman, 1995). On the other hand, individuals who generated multiple explanations showed debiased reasoning, even when the explanations were about unrelated events (e.g., winner of the best sitcom) (Hirt et al., 2004), indicating a *general* openness to alternatives. However, the longevity of this effect remains unknown.

In addition to debiasing adults' predictions, multiple explanations have also been credited with attenuating the effects of the hindsight bias (Koriat et al., 1980; Fischhoff, 1982), in which individuals consistently overestimate their ability to have predicted events that have already occurred (Fischhoff, 1975). For example, adult reasoners often view the outcome of an election as inevitable and predictable, even when all indications prior to election night suggest that it would be a tight race. In a series of studies, Sanna and colleagues asked participants to explain alternate outcomes to a war, a college football game, or an election (Sanna et al., 2002; Sanna & Schwarz, 2003). They found that those individuals who generated *two* alternatives were less likely to show hindsight bias across the board.

As in the research on the effects of requests for a single explanation, requests for multiple explanations may also include certain drawbacks. In particular, when adults are asked to generate *too many* explanations in a given task, their reasoning is no less biased than baseline (Sanna et al., 2002; Hirt et al., 2004). When generating explanations, individuals tend to evaluate their plausibility – not only in terms of their content – but also in terms of the *ease* with which they bring examples to mind (i.e., accessibility experiences; Schwarz, 1998; Schwarz & Vaughn, 2002). Therefore, if generating alternatives is perceived as difficult, as is typically the case when individuals are asked to generate several explanations, they may end up concluding that the initial explanation or hypothesis was the correct one after all. Similarly, when individuals are asked to generate an *implausible* explanation (e.g., a win by a poorly performing team), their judgments also tend to revert back to the original, focal hypothesis (Hirt & Markman, 1995).

## When Might Multiple Explanations Support Learning and Inference in Childhood?

To our knowledge, previous research has not directly examined the use of multiple explanation prompts to debias reasoning in children. However, the ability to generate multiple explanations is likely supported by the same suite of cognitive abilities that underlies the representation of multiple possibilities (Horobin & Acredolo, 1989; Hirt et al., 2004). Although some have suggested that acknowledging the presence of more than one possibility poses a significant challenge for young children (e.g., Horobin & Acredolo, 1989; Beck et al., 2006), others have forwarded the opposite claim, demonstrating that they may engage with alternate possibilities more readily than older children and adults (German & Defeyter, 2000; Lucas et al., 2014).

Like adults, children appear to express a number of biases in prediction, explanation, and hypothesis-testing. For example, children begin to express the fundamental attribution error as early as six years of age, tending to prefer trait explanations over situational explanations for an individual's behavior (Seiver et al., 2013). Children also express a bias towards teleological explanations when reasoning both about artifacts and natural kinds (Kelemen, 1999), as well as essentialist explanations when reasoning about biological and psychological events (Taylor, 1996; Gelman, 2003; Taylor, Rhodes, & Gelman, 2009). We are therefore currently exploring whether asking children to generate multiple explanations for an observed phenomenon could help increase their consideration of alternate possibilities and decrease fixation on an initial explanation (e.g., that someone is exhibiting a behavior because of their membership in a particular group), which can have pernicious social consequences (e.g., Rhodes et al., 2018).

Relatedly, fixating on an initial hypothesis has also been shown to lead to biases in children's evidence-seeking and hypothesis-testing. Several studies indicate that when children have a strong belief in a hypothesis (Penner & Klahr, 1996) or are motivated to produce a specific outcome (Zimmerman & Glaser, 2001), they tend to engage in biased hypothesis-testing, seeking to confirm, rather than disconfirm their initial hypothesis (Kuhn & Phelps, 1982). If their commitment to a particular hypothesis leads them to engage in hypothesis-confirmation, then asking children to generate alternate explanations could reduce this tendency (Galinsky & Moskowitz, 2000). There is at least one piece of suggestive evidence indicating that hypothesis-testing may be facilitated by exposure to *contrastive beliefs* in childhood as well. Across three experiments, Cook and Schulz (2009) found that children were better able to conduct a controlled test of a hypothesis after they heard contrasting hypotheses about which variables affect how far a ball travels on a ramp (e.g., "Bob thinks the height of the ramp matters, and Emily thinks the type of ball matters") than children in a control condition. Although children were not prompted to generate multiple explanations, a similar mechanism may underlie both instances, since those who encountered contrastive beliefs had the opportunity to consider alternatives. In fact, according to Mercier and Sperber (2011), engaging in argumentation through dialogue or group reasoning leads to more objective inferences via exposure to multiple explanations. This type of reasoning has also been proposed to foster awareness of epistemology of science – that scientific claims are subject to scrutiny, requiring evaluation within a framework of alternatives (Moshman, 2015; Greene et al., 2016; Kuhn et al., 2017). Although these explanations are typically provided by others in a social context, Mercier and Sperber note that individual learners may be able simulate these benefits by "distance[ing] themselves from their own opinion, to consider alternatives and thereby become more objective" (2011, p. 72). Future research should therefore investigate the process by which self- versus other-generated beliefs and explanations might influence children's hypothesis-testing.

### *Summary and Limitations of Multiple Explanations*

Research with adults has found that prompting individuals to generate multiple explanations attenuates bias on various reasoning tasks, as long as individuals are not asked to generate too many alternatives (Hirt & Markman, 1995; Sanna et al., 2002; Sanna & Schwarz, 2003; Hirt et al., 2004). Here, we have outlined several proposals regarding how these findings may extend to children. First, multiple explanations could be particularly supportive in cases where children are biased towards certain types of highly salient explanations (e.g., essentialist explanations; Gelman, 2003) by prompting them to consider alternatives. Second, these prompts could serve to debias hypothesis-testing following the generation of an initial hypothesis (Kuhn & Phelps, 1982). Asking children for more than one explanation may also be preferable to requests for single explanations in at least two contexts: (1) when the initial search is biased, due to a strongly held prior theory or interest in a particular outcome, and (2) when the true hypothesis does not conform to the explanatory virtues of simplicity, breadth, etc.

At present, the proposals we have outlined about the specific impact of multiple explanations on learning and inference in childhood remain largely speculative. Empirical work is underway to investigate whether prompts to generate multiple explanations support children's hypothesis-testing in the context of both controlled laboratory settings and ecologically valid classroom settings. That said, there is an important methodological issue that future studies exploring the role of multiple explanations on children's inferences will have to carefully address. In particular, previous research by Gonzalez and colleagues (2012) indicates that the use of repeated questions in a developmental paradigm introduces a set of pedagogical inferences. In this study, preschoolers who were asked a neutral question ("Is that your final guess?") after making a selection were more likely to switch their answer when the adult speaker was perceived as knowledgeable than when she was perceived as ignorant. Children might similarly interpret an experimenter's request for a second explanation as a pedagogical cue that their first response was incorrect. Although these effects may be mitigated, this caveat is not trivial. If future research finds that multiple explanations indeed bolster children's learning, it will be critical to discern whether this advantage is conferred by the process of engaging with alternatives or due to this pedagogical inference.

Finally, in the next section, we consider the influence of counterfactual ("what if?") questions on children's learning and inference. We propose that the process underlying the generation of multiple explanations and counterfactuals are likely quite similar: both involve considering alternatives to a focal hypothesis, explanation, or event. However, there are also important potential differences between the two. Whereas multiple explanations involve accounting for evidence or generating predictions in more than one way, counterfactuals involve *changing* a particular causal variable and reasoning about the outcomes of that change. Thus, while both question-types may guide the learner to consider alternatives, counterfactuals are predicted to have the additional benefit of supporting causal inference and scientific reasoning by mentally manipulating events in a manner that is analogous to hypothesis-testing. Additionally, because counterfactuals explicitly require the individual to consider a premise that contrasts with actual events, they may lead the learner to elevate possible hypotheses that are initially lower-probability, or even counterintuitive.

## Counterfactuals: Asking "What If?"

Both children and adults spend a large amount of time entertaining thoughts about what did not or will not happen. This type of thought – termed *counterfactual thinking* – has been suggested to support a range of judgments and decisions (Byrne, 2016). Counterfactuals help us to understand the causes of past events, including both small scale (e.g., Spellman & Mandel, 1999) and historically significant events (Tetlock & Belkin, 1996), to plan for the future (Epstude & Roese, 2008; Markman et al., 2008), and to ascribe moral judgments (e.g., Branscombe et al., 1996). Commonly framed as conditional *if-then* statements, counterfactuals allow individuals to make a range of causal inferences from "If there was no icy patch, then I would not have fallen" to "If there was no ice age, then there would be no Yosemite Valley."

In the following section, we suggest that entertaining counterfactual questions may help even the youngest learners to not only consider alternative hypotheses, but to identify lower-probability hypotheses that they may not have otherwise considered. Scientific progress, in particular, often relies upon radically rethinking current dogmas and challenging intuitions. Many scientific discoveries, including the discovery of germs, the realization that the Earth is round, and the theory of evolution by natural selection, resulted from positing counterintuitive hypotheses. We therefore consider how engaging in counterfactual thinking might similarly guide and support children's causal learning in the context of scientific reasoning.

However, before turning to the existing findings supporting this proposal, we should first establish a working definition of counterfactual reasoning in this context, given the lively debate surrounding the presence of these abilities in young children (e.g., Weisberg & Gopnik, 2013; Beck, 2016). For example, several previous empirical and theoretical accounts of the development of counterfactual reasoning have focused exclusively on past counterfactuals (e.g., Beck et al., 2006; Rafetseder & Perner, 2014), suggesting that this ability may not reach maturity until well into middle childhood (Beck & Riggs, 2014), or even adolescence (Rafetseder et al., 2013). Recent research opposing these views has demonstrated that, given a sufficiently clear and simple task, children will readily engage in counterfactual reasoning as early as the preschool years (Buchsbaum et al., 2012; Gopnik & Walker, 2013; Nyhout & Ganea, 2019; Walker et al., unpublished data), even according to the strictest definition (e.g., Perner & Rafetseder, 2011). For our present purposes, we will leave this debate aside to take a much broader view of counterfactual reasoning, which includes hypothetical questions about the past, present, and future, as well as conditionals.

## Why Are Counterfactual Questions Effective?

In line with the research on the effectiveness of multiple explanation, research on counterfactual questions was initially separated into two broad camps: (1) those that suggest that counterfactual questions lead the learner to consider the *specific* alternative hypotheses that are generated (e.g., Harris et al., 1996; Roese & Olson, 1997; Tetlock & Lebow, 2001; Byrne, 2005), and (2) those that suggest they prime the learner to consider alternatives more broadly (Galinsky & Moskowitz, 2000). However, an additional third camp (3) proposes that engagement with counterfactuals may have a more directed effect on *causal reasoning*, allowing the learner to conduct imagined interventions on a causal system (Woodward, 2007; Buchsbaum et al., 2012; Gopnik & Walker, 2013; Walker & Gopnik, 2013a, 2013b). We review evidence for each of these accounts below.

In line with the first camp – that simulating counterfactuals facilitates *specific* causal inferences – research with adults has demonstrated that considering a counterfactual scenario makes the parallel causal inference more accessible (Roese & Olson, 1997; Tetlock & Lebow, 2001; for a review, see Byrne, 2005). For example, in one study, adults witnessed a simple causal event (e.g., a ball hitting a lever and a light switching on) and were then asked *causal* ("Did the ball hitting the lever make the light come on?") and *counterfactual* questions ("If the ball had not hit the lever, would the light have come on?") (Roese & Olson, 1997). Participants who were first asked the counterfactual question verified the causal question more quickly than those who were asked the causal question first. However, being asked the causal question first did not similarly facilitate reasoning about the counterfactual. These results suggest that counterfactual questions may support specific causal inferences. Proponents of this proposal (e.g., Byrne, 2002) argue that individuals generally only consider a single possibility when representing a causal relation (e.g., the ball hitting the lever and the light switching on), but consider two possibilities when representing a counterfactual (e.g., the ball hitting the lever, and the ball not hitting the lever).

In the second camp, researchers have proposed that, like multiple explanations, counterfactual questions invoke a "mindset" that is broadly open to alternatives, leading to generally debiased reasoning. In support of this claim, Galinsky and Moskowitz (2000) presented adult participants with a vignette about a narrow miss that has been demonstrated to induce consideration of counterfactual alternatives. After reading this vignette (or a control vignette), participants were provided with an unrelated task in which they were tasked with determining whether an individual was an introvert or an extrovert. They were told that a number of personality tests had indicated that the individual was likely an extrovert, and asked to select from a list of questions to assess whether this was correct. Those participants who had read the vignette designed to induce counterfactual thinking were significantly more likely to select items that were hypothesis *disconfirming* (e.g., "What factors make it hard for you to open up to people?") than those who read a control vignette. Participants in the control condition were more likely to show a typical confirmation-biased pattern, selecting more items to confirm the focal hypothesis (e.g., "What do you like about parties?"). The authors concluded that the counterfactual prime invoked a general *mental simulation mindset*, leading adults to entertain the alternative hypothesis (i.e., that the individual was an introvert), which prompted them to seek the critical evidence needed to disambiguate between these possibilities. These priming effects suggest that engagement with counterfactuals need not be tied to the specific alternatives considered. Instead, consideration of *any* alternatives can be used to invoke this mindset (Galinsky & Moskowitz, 2000). This may be a particularly important feature to consider when applying these principles to influence reasoning in young children, who often struggle to produce accurate (or even relevant) verbal responses to questions that are posed.

Finally, the third camp has emphasized the nature of the relationship between causal and counterfactual reasoning: counterfactual dependence is the defining feature of causal knowledge (i.e., the statement *X causes Y* implies the counterfactual that *a change to X would lead to a change to Y*) (e.g., Pearl, 2000; Woodward, 2003; Gopnik & Schulz, 2007; Schulz et al., 2007). Counterfactuals therefore act as input to causal judgments (e.g., Mackie, 1974; Lewis, 1986). When thinking counterfactually, the learner changes the value of the variable of interest and considers its downstream effects on other variables within the causal system – a process that is structurally identical to what we do in science. In this way, counterfactuals have been interpreted to serve as a form of thought experimentation or *imagined intervention* on the causal world (Sloman 2005; Gopnik 2009; Gopnik & Walker, 2013; Walker & Gopnik, 2013a, 2013b; Walker et al., in preparation).

### When Might Counterfactuals Support Learning and Inference in Childhood?

Given these diverse mechanisms, counterfactual questions likely support a range of early learning and reasoning tasks. In fact, past research has suggested that introducing counterfactual prompts in the form of pretend or fantastical scenarios facilitates early success in deductive reasoning, an otherwise challenging task for children (e.g., "Let's pretend that fish live in trees. Tot is a fish. Does Tot live in a tree?") (e.g., Dias & Harris, 1988, 1990; see Harris, 2000, for a review). Other prior work has suggested that encouraging children to think counterfactually leads them to engage in more sophisticated forms of causal inference (e.g., McCormack et al., 2013). For example, when adult learners observe that cause $A$ is associated with an outcome, and then observe that the combination of $A$ and $B$ is associated with the same outcome, they commonly block the inference that $B$ is causal (Dickinson, 2001; De Houwer et al., 2005). It has been argued that the reasoning process underlying this inference involves counterfactuals of the form "if B were causal, there would have been a stronger outcome" (Mitchell et al., 2005). Between the ages of five and seven years, children increasingly make these adult-like inferences (McCormack et al., 2009; Simms et al., 2012), and there is some evidence that these abilities appear even earlier (Schulz & Gopnik, 2004; Sobel et al., 2004).

To explore whether counterfactual questions might facilitate the early appearance of these inferences, McCormack and colleagues (2013) introduced five- to seven-year-old children to a toy robot that lit up and produced sound when given certain causal foods. Two causal foods given in combination had an additive effect – the light and sound produced were more intense. Children were assigned to either a *counterfactual* or *factual* condition and were asked corresponding questions after observing foods given to the robot. For example, those in the counterfactual condition were asked to imagine what would have happened if a non-causal food were causal, whereas those in the factual condition were asked to report what had happened. At test, five-year-olds who answered counterfactual questions showed significantly higher levels of blocking than those who received factual questions, boosting their performance to a level similar to that of older children. The authors concluded that engaging children in counterfactual thinking selectively increased the likelihood that they would reason correctly about causal cues. A subsequent control study demonstrated that these effects were not due to increased engagement in the task.

In the following section, we expand upon these previous findings to describe a novel proposal (in collaboration with Dr. Patricia Ganea), regarding the role of counterfactuals in scaffolding the development of scientific reasoning skills. Decades of research have indicated that children struggle with many of the most critical elements of formal scientific inquiry (see Zimmerman, 2007, for a review), often manipulating multiple variables at a time (Chen & Klahr, 1999), prioritizing producing an effect over genuine discovery (Kuhn & Phelps, 1982), and engaging in biased interpretation of evidence (Amsel & Brock, 1996; Penner & Klahr, 1996). The majority of developmental research has focused on children's ability to conduct a controlled test of a hypothesis – an ability termed the control of variables strategy (CVS) (Klahr, 2000; Zimmerman, 2000; Kuhn, 2002). Rather than engaging in correct CVS, which involves isolating a single variable and holding all others constant, elementary-aged children often manipulate multiple variables at a time, creating a confounded test of a hypothesis (Schauble, 1996; Chen & Klahr, 1999; Klahr & Nigam, 2004; Zimmerman, 2007).

We propose that since counterfactual reasoning and CVS both require isolating a single variable and reasoning about (or measuring) downstream effects, counterfactual prompts may scaffold children's early ability to conduct a controlled experiment by considering the outcomes produced by each variable under investigation. Despite theoretical accounts connecting counterfactual and scientific reasoning in children (Gopnik & Walker, 2013; Walker & Gopnik, 2013a, 2013b; Rafetseder & Perner, 2014; Wenzelhuemer, 2009), it is only very recently that researchers have begun to investigate this link empirically. In one study that is currently underway (Nyhout et al., 2019), we find initial support for the claim that counterfactual questions support children's developing ability to conduct a controlled test of a hypothesis. After observing an adult actor correctly isolate a variable in an experimental context (i.e., examining factors related to motion on an incline), children given prompts to consider *counterfactual alternatives* are better able to subsequently conduct their own controlled experiment than controls, even when provided with a different set of variables to assess. These preliminary results are the first to suggest that counterfactual questions may directly support the control of variables strategy. In this case, counterfactual questions were task-specific: children were directed to consider alternatives about features of causal systems (e.g., ramp height) they were asked to assess. Future studies will consider whether this intervention will also lead children to generalize the control of variables strategy to a novel experimental context.

In addition to prompting reflection about the potential outcomes of specific interventions, counterfactual questions may also enable the consideration of multiple, alternative hypotheses in order to select the one that is most consistent with the observed data. This may be particularly useful in cases where an individual holds a prior theory that is incompatible with the evidence. Although individuals frequently encounter data that contrast with their existing theories (Chinn & Brewer, 1998; Zimmerman, 2007), these anomalies may not be integrated into a learner's existing theory due to their failure to notice, correctly interpret, generalize, or remember this evidence (Chinn & Brewer, 1998). To give anomalous data due consideration, a learner should reason counterfactually: "*If my prior hypothesis were true, the observed evidence would not have occurred.*" However, previous research indicates that children typically do not engage in this thought process spontaneously upon encountering anomalous data (Chinn & Brewer, 1998; Chinn & Malhotra, 2002). Counterfactual questions may therefore make patterns of causal contingency more explicit for these young learners.

To explore this, Engle and Walker (2018) asked whether leading children to harness their intuitive causal reasoning skills by way of counterfactuals may scaffold their ability to notice anomalies, using a task similar to the one described above in subsection Why Are Prompts to Explain Effective? (Walker et al., 2016b, experiment 1). To review, Walker et al. (2016b) found that when two candidate causes were matched in terms of their prior probability, children who explained preferred the hypothesis in which no anomalies were observed (the cause that accounted for 100 percent of the data). Engle and Walker modified this paradigm to replace "why?" questions with "what if?" questions, and added an additional generalization phase in which children were asked to make predictions about a novel set of blocks. Results indicate that children who were asked a counterfactual question (e.g. "What if my block had been yellow? Would my toy have lit up, or not?") were significantly more likely to privilege and extend the 100 percent cause than children who were asked to report what had actually happened (e.g., "What happened when I put this red one on top? Did my toy light up, or not?"). The authors conclude that counterfactual questions likely serve to draw attention to the presence of anomalous data. In this case, the *effects* of explanation and counterfactual prompts are similar, although the underlying mechanisms are likely to be different. Ongoing work aims to pull apart the effects of the two prompts by introducing prior knowledge. Walker et al. (2014, experiment 3) found that when the 75 percent candidate cause was more consistent with prior knowledge (i.e., block size), children who *explained* preferred that hypothesis, ignoring the presence of anomalous data. In contrast, preliminary data suggests that counterfactual questions support the recognition of anomalies, even in cases in which the learner holds an incompatible belief.

### Summary and Limitations of Counterfactual Questions

An emerging body of research demonstrates that counterfactual questions likely serve as useful pedagogical tools during childhood, supporting performance on a range of skills relevant to scientific reasoning, including causal inference, hypothesis testing, and anomaly detection. Because this work is still in its early stages, we cannot yet pinpoint the precise mechanism(s) by which counterfactual questions confer their benefits in each of these cases. As with repeated requests for explanation (see Summary and Limitations of Multiple Explanations), additional research should consider pedagogical effects of counterfactual questions, which may lead children to make assumptions about the accuracy of their knowledge. Future work should also investigate the robustness of these findings across contexts. Although the phrasing of both explanation and multiple explanation prompts are generally quite constrained (e.g., "Why did that happen?"), this is not the case with counterfactuals. In the initial developmental studies reviewed above, most counterfactual questions have focused on close departures from reality (e.g., asking the child to imagine that a block was a different color), directing attention to the causal variable. It remains an open question whether counterfactuals that do *not* point the learner towards the relevant simulation would similarly support learning. As noted previously, asking children to consider radical departures from the real world has been shown to engage logical reasoning (e.g., Dias & Harris, 1988, 1990; Harris, 2000). However, it is currently unknown whether asking children to consider distant counterfactuals would support or disrupt causal learning (e.g., Hirt & Markman, 1995; Galinsky & Moskowitz, 2000).

## Conclusions and Future Directions

In this chapter, we have reviewed theories and findings on the role of three types of questions in supporting children's learning. These questions produce both overlapping and distinct effects on children's inferences. Explanation questions – questions of the form, "Why did $X$ happen?" – lead children to privilege abstract hypotheses that are broad, simple, and generalizable. However, in some contexts, a prompt to explain may lead the learner astray, causing them to discount evidence that is incompatible with their prior theories or to overlook more complex or narrow (e.g., perceptually based) hypotheses. When asked to generate *multiple* explanations (i.e., "Why else?"), however, individuals show an attenuation in biased reasoning on the basis of prior beliefs. Multiple explanations may therefore help children to consider alternatives and seek hypothesis-disconfirming evidence. Finally, counterfactual questions – those of the form "What if $X$ had happened?" – which guide individuals to perform mental simulations and interventions on causal models, may similarly scaffold their ability to consider and test alternatives (particularly those with lower prior probability) to an initial hypothesis. Together, these questions may serve to guide even the youngest learners to arrive at a conclusion that best fits the available evidence. Future work will also investigate how these different types of questions may complement one another to support learning and inference.

### Does the Answer Matter?

Additional research is needed to better understand the relationships between the question posed, the answer produced, and the pattern of inferences that are supported. However, several of the findings described above provide initial evidence that the benefits of question-asking may be *separable* from the particular answer that is generated. For example, children who are prompted to explain tend to provide more mature patterns of inferences than controls, even when they fail to provide the correct explanation (e.g., Walker, et al., 2014). That is, the act of generating an explanation (i.e., the *process* of explaining) appears to impact reasoning independently of the content of the explanation they happen to produce (i.e., the *product* of explaining) (Wilkenfeld & Lombrozo, 2015). A number of proposals are available to explain these effects. For example, generating a poor or incomplete explanation may help the learner to identify gaps in their current knowledge or theory (e.g., Chi et al., 1994), triggering exploration (e.g., Legare, 2012). It is also possible that the act of explaining serves to constrain the hypotheses that are generated in the first place, restricting the learner to consider only those that support broad generalization (Walker et al., 2014; Walker et al., 2017; Walker & Lombrozo, 2017).

Similar findings also appear in the adult research examining multiple explanations and counterfactuals. In some cases, these questions are proposed to support learning and inference by invoking a mindset that is open to alternative possibilities, even those unrelated to the specific alternative that was initially considered (Kahneman & Tversky, 1982; Hirt & Markman, 1995; Galinsky & Moskowitz, 2000; Hirt et al., 2004). In other words, the cognitive effects of responding to a question are likely not entirely reducible to the benefits of identifying and producing the correct answer.

### More Questions about Questions ... and Future Directions

There are, of course, a variety of open questions left to be examined. Although the majority of findings reviewed above report effects of experimenter-presented prompts, self-directed questions are expected to produce parallel effects. Again, the *process* of generating a response has been proposed to be far more important that the particular context in which it appears (Legare & Lombrozo, 2014). This is good news, since there is significant value in identifying simple prompts to engage cognitive processes supporting learning and transfer that can easily be integrated in a variety of educational settings, including learning environments in which no instructor is present. That said, as noted above (Summary and Limitations of Multiple Explanations and Summary and Limitations of Counterfactual Questions), there are likely important interactions between these findings and the presence (or absence) of pedagogical cues. In fact, a growing literature has begun to examine potential differences between pedagogical and non-pedagogical questions on reasoning (Gonzalez et al., 2012; Yu et al., 2017). Although this topic is beyond the scope of the current chapter, these interactions represent an important avenue for future research.

In future work, it will also be important to further explore the scope of these effects across a variety of learning contexts, including naturalistic settings (e.g., parent–child conversations, classrooms, museums), and across knowledge domains (e.g., informal and formal biological, physical, and psychological learning and inference). To this end, we are currently working with museum partners to build a hands-on exhibit for an observational study looking at the role of counterfactual questions in children's hypothesis-testing. We will be looking at the role of these prompts in various delivery formats, including questions that are spontaneously generated by parents and children, questions that are prompted through strategically placed signage, and pedagogical questions posed directly by museum staff.

Finally, open questions remain regarding the extent to which children *spontaneously* generate explanations and consider alternatives. This is an area of significant individual differences, and likely changes over the course the development (Walker et al., 2017). Children who frequently engage in self-explanation or who spontaneously entertain alternative possibilities may be more successful learners to begin with. The extent to which these individual differences are influenced by the sociocultural context, as well as other cognitive abilities, including verbal skills, flexible thinking, and uncertainty monitoring, will be an important focus for future work.

In sum, we have reviewed both theoretical and empirical evidence exploring the role of three types of questions in supporting distinct kinds of learning in childhood. We have argued that each of these questions is likely supported by a unique set of underlying mechanisms, and that each produces selective effects on children's causal and scientific reasoning. In all cases, however, asking questions can encourage even the youngest learners to go beyond their immediate observations to arrive at novel inferences.

## Acknowledgments

Many of the ideas that appear in this chapter were inspired through conversation and collaboration with the following individuals: Jae Engle, Patricia Ganea, Disha Goel, Alison Gopnik, Alana Iannuzziello, Tania Lombrozo, and Valentina Mancuso. Thanks also to members of the Early Learning & Cognition Lab at UCSD for their critical feedback and efforts towards data collection.

## References

Amsel, E., and Brock, S. (1996). The development of evidence evaluation skills. *Cognitive Development*, *11*, 523–50. https://doi:10.1016/S0885-2014(96)90 016-7

Anderson, C. A., Lepper, M. R., and Ross, L. (1980). Perseverance of social theories: The role of explanation in the persistence of discredited information. *Journal of Personality and Social Psychology*, *39*, 1037–49. https://doi:10.1037/h0077720

Beck, S. R. (2016). Why what is counterfactual really matters: A response to Weisberg and Gopnik. *Cognitive Science*, *40*, 253–6. https://doi:10.1111/cogs .12235

Beck, S. R., and Riggs, K. J. (2014). Developing thoughts about what might have been. *Child Development Perspectives*, *8*, 175–9. https://doi:10.1111/cdep.12082

Beck, S. R., Robinson, E. J., Carroll, D. J., and Apperly, I. A. (2006). Children's thinking about counterfactuals and future hypotheticals as possibilities. *Child Development*, *77*(2), 413–26. https://doi:10.1111/j.1467-8624.2006.00879.x

Berthold, K., Röder, H., Knörzer, D., Kessler, W., and Renkl, A. (2011). The double-edged effects of explanation prompts. *Computers in Human Behavior*, *27*, 69–75. https://doi:10.1016/j.chb.2010.05.025

Branscombe, N. R., Owen, S., Garstka, T. A., and Coleman, J. (1996). Rape and accident counterfactuals: Who might have done otherwise and would it have changed the outcome? *Journal of Applied Social Psychology*, *26*, 1042–67. https://doi:10.1111/j1559-1816.1996.tb01124.x

Buchsbaum, D., Bridgers, S., Weisberg, D. S., and Gopnik, A. (2012). The power of possibility: Causal learning, counterfactual reasoning, and pretend play. *Philosophical Transactions of the Royal Society B: Biological Sciences*, *367*, 2202–12. https://doi:10.1098/rstb.2012.0122

Byrne, R. M. (2002). Mental models and counterfactual thoughts about what might have been. *Trends in Cognitive Sciences*, *6*, 426–31. https://doi:10.1016 /S1364-6613(02)01974-5

  (2005). *The rational imagination: How people create alternatives to reality.* Cambridge, MA: MIT Press.

  (2016). Counterfactual thought. *Annual Review of Psychology*, *67*, 135–57. https://doi:10.1146/annurev-psych-122414-033249

Carey, S. (1985). *Conceptual change in childhood.* Cambridge, MA: MIT Press/ Bradford Books.

8

Chen, Z., and Klahr, D. (1999). All other things being equal: Acquisition and transfer of the control of variables strategy. *Child development, 70,* 1098–120. https://doi:10.1111/1467-8624.00081

Chi, M. T. (2000). Self-explaining expository texts: The dual processes of generating inferences and repairing mental models. In R. Glaser (ed.), *Advances in instructional psychology* (pp. 161–238). Hillsdale, NJ: Lawrence Erlbaum Associates, Inc.

(2009). Active-constructive-interactive: A conceptual framework for differentiating Learning activities. *Topics in Cognitive Science, 1,* 73–105. https://doi:10.1111/j.1756-8765.2008.01005.x

Chi, M. T., Bassok, M., Lewis, M. W., Reimann, P., and Glaser, R. (1989). Self-explanations: How students study and use examples in learning to solve problems. *Cognitive Science, 13,*145–82. https://doi:10.1207/s15516709cog1302_1

Chi, M. T., De Leeuw, N., Chiu, M. H., and LaVancher, C. (1994). Eliciting self-explanations improves understanding. *Cognitive Science, 18,* 439–77. https://doi:10.1207/s15516709cog1803_3

Chinn, C. A., and Brewer, W. F. (1998). An empirical test of a taxonomy of responses to anomalous data in science. *Journal of Research in Science Teaching, 35,* 623–54. 3.0.CO;2-O",1,0,0>https://doi:10.1002/(SICI)1098-2736(199808)35:6<623::aid-tea3>3.0.CO;2-O

Chinn, C. A., and Malhotra, B. A. (2002). Children's responses to anomalous scientific data: How is conceptual change impeded? *Journal of Educational Psychology, 94,* 327–43. https://doi:10.1037//0022-0663.94.2.327

Cook, C., and Schulz, L. (2009). "Bob thinks this but Emily thinks that": Contrastive beliefs in kindergartners' scientific reasoning. *31st Annual Proceedings of the Cognitive Science Society Conference.* Amsterdam, Netherlands.

Crowley, K., and Siegler, R. S. (1999). Explanation and generalization in young children's strategy learning. *Child Development, 70,* 304–16. https://doi:10.1111/1467-8624.00023

De Houwer, J., Vandorpe, S., and Beckers, T. (2005). Evidence for the role of higher order reasoning processes in cue competition and other learning phenomena. *Learning & Behavior, 33,* 239–49. https://doi:10.3758/BF03196066

Dias, M. G., and Harris, P. L. (1988). The effect of make-believe play on deductive reasoning. *British Journal of Developmental Psychology, 6,* 207–21. https://doi:10.1111/j.2044-835X.1988.tb01095.x

Dias, M. G., and Harris, P. L. (1990). The influence of the imagination on reasoning by young children. *British Journal of Developmental Psychology, 8,* 305–18. https://doi:10.1111/j.2044-835X.1990.tb00847.x

Dickinson, A. (2001). The 28th Bartlett Memorial Lecture: Causal learning. An associative analysis. *Quarterly Journal of Experimental Psychology, 54B,* 3–25. https://doi:10.1080/713932741

Engle, J., and Walker, C. M. (2018). Considering alternatives facilitates anomaly detection in preschoolers. In N. Miyake, D. Peebles, and R. P. Cooper (eds.), *Proceedings of the 40th Annual Conference of the Cognitive Science Society.* Madison, WI: Cognitive Science Society.

Epstude, K., and Roese, N. J. (2008). The functional theory of counterfactual thinking. *Personality and Social Psychology Review, 12*, 168–92. https://doi:10.1177/1088868308316091

Fischhoff, B. (1975). Hindsight is not equal to foresight: The effect of outcome knowledge on judgment under uncertainty. *Journal of Experimental Psychology: Human Perception and Performance, 1*, 288–99. https://doi:10.1037/0096-1523.1.3.288

(1982). Debiasing. In D. Kahneman, P. Slovic, and A. Tversky (eds.), *Judgment under uncertainty: Heuristics and biases* (pp. 422–44). Cambridge: Cambridge University Press.

Galinsky, A. D., and Moskowitz, G. B. (2000). Counterfactuals as behavioral primes: Priming the simulation heuristic and consideration of alternatives. *Journal of Experimental Social Psychology, 36*, 384–409. https://doi:10.1006/jesp.1999.1409

Gelman, S. A. (2003). *The essential child: Origins of essentialism in everyday thought.* Oxford Series in Cognitive Dev. https://doi:10.1093/acprof:oso/9780195154061.001.0001

German, T. P., and Defeyter, M. A. (2000). Immunity to functional fixedness in young children. *Psychonomic Bulletin & Review, 7*, 707–12. https://doi:10.3758/BF03213010

Gonzalez, A., Shafto, P., Bonawitz, E. B., and Gopnik, A. (2012). Is that your final answer? The effects of neutral queries on children's choices. In *Proceedings of the Annual Meeting of the Cognitive Science Society* (vol. 34, no. 34).

Gopnik, A. (2009). *The philosophical baby: What children's minds tell us about truth, love, and the meaning of life.* New York: Farrar, Straus, & Giroux. https://doi:10.1080/13698036.2010.488018

Gopnik, A., and Meltzoff, A. N. (1997). *Words, thoughts, and theories.* Cambridge, MA: MIT Press.

Gopnik, A., and Schulz, L. (eds.) (2007). *Causal learning: Psychology, philosophy, and computation.* Oxford: Oxford University Press. https://doi:10.1093/acprof:oso/9780195176803.001.0001

Gopnik, A., and Walker, C. M. (2013). Considering counterfactuals: The relationship between causal learning and pretend play. *American Journal of Play, 6*, 15–28.

Gopnik, A., Sobel, D. M., Schulz, L. E., and Glymour, C. (2001). Causal learning mechanisms in very young children: Two-, three-, and four-year-olds infer causal relations from patterns of variation and covariation. *Developmental Psychology, 37*, 620–9. https://doi:10.1037/0012-1649.37.5.620

Greene, J., Sandoval,W., and Braten, I. (eds.) (2016). *Handbook of epistemic cognition.* New York: Routledge. https://doi:10.4324/9781315795225

Harris, P. L. (2000). *The work of the imagination.* Blackwell Publishing. https://doi:10.1093/mind/111.442.414

Harris, P. L., German, T., and Mills, C. (1996). Children's use of counterfactual thinking in causal reasoning. *Cognition, 61*, 233–59. https://doi:10.1016/S0010-0277(96)00715-9

Hirt, E. R., and Markman, K. D. (1995). Multiple explanation: A consider-an-alternative strategy for debiasing judgments. *Journal of Personality and Social Psychology*, *69*, 1069–86. https://doi:10.1037/0022-3514.69.6.1069

Hirt, E. R., Kardes, F. R., and Markman, K. D. (2004). Activating a mental simulation mind-set through generation of alternatives: Implications for debiasing in related and unrelated domains. *Journal of Experimental Social Psychology*, *40*, 374–83. https://doi:10.1016/j.jesp.2003.07.009

Horobin, K., and Acredolo, C. (1989). The impact of probability judgments on reasoning about multiple possibilities. *Child Development*, 183–200. https://doi:10.2307/1131084

Kahneman, D., and Tversky, A. (1982). The simulation heuristic. In D. Kahneman, P. Slovic, and A. Tversky (eds.), *Judgement under uncertainty: Heuristics and biases* (pp. 201–8). Cambridge: Cambridge University Press. https://doi:10.1017/CBO9780511809477.015

Keil, F. C. (1992). *Concepts, kinds, and cognitive development*. Cambridge, MA: MIT Press.

Kelemen, D. (1999). Function, goals and intention: Children's teleological reasoning about objects. *Trends in Cognitive Sciences*, *3*, 461–8. https://doi:10.1016/S1364-6613(99)01402-3

Klahr, D. (2000). *Exploring science*. Cambridge, MA: MIT Press.

Klahr, D., and Nigam, M. (2004). The equivalence of learning paths in early science instruction effects of direct instruction and discovery learning. *Psychological Science*, *15*, 661–7. https://doi:10.1111/j.0956-7976.2004.00737.x

Koehler, D. J. (1991). Explanation, imagination, and confidence in judgment. *Psychological Bulletin*, *110*, 499–519. https://doi:10.1037/0033-2909.110.3.499

Koriat, A., Lichtenstein, S., and Fischhoff, B. (1980). Reasons for confidence. *Journal of Experimental Psychology: Human Learning and Memory*, *6*, 107–18. https://doi:10.1037/0278-7393.6.2.107

Kuhn, D. (2002). What is scientific thinking and how does it develop? In U. Goswami (ed.), *Blackwell handbook of childhood cognitive development* (pp. 371–93). Oxford: Blackwell Publishing.

Kuhn, D., and Katz, J. (2009). Are self-explanations always beneficial? *Journal of Experimental Child Psychology*, *103*, 386–94. https://doi:10.1016/j.jecp.2009.03.003

Kuhn, D., and Phelps, E. (1982). The development of problem-solving strategies. *Advances in Child Development and Behavior*, *17*, 1–44. https://doi:10.1016/S0065-2407(08)60356-0

Kuhn, D., Arvidsson, T. S., Lesperance, R., and Corprew, R. (2017). Can engaging in science practices promote deep understanding of them? *Science Education*, *101*, 232–50. https://doi:10.1002/sce.21263

Kushnir, T., Gopnik, A., Schulz, L., and Danks, D. (2003). Inferring hidden causes. In *Proceedings of the Annual Meeting of the Cognitive Science Society* (vol. 25, no. 25).

Legare, C. H. (2012). Exploring explanation: Explaining inconsistent evidence informs exploratory, hypothesis-testing behavior in young children. *Child Development*, *83*, 173–85. https://doi:10.1111/j.1467-8624.2011.01691.x

Legare, C. H., and Lombrozo, T. (2014). Selective effects of explanation on learning during early childhood. *Journal of Experimental Child Psychology*, *126*, 198–212. https://doi:10.1016/j.jecp.2014.03.001

Lewis, D. (1986). *Counterfactuals*. Cambridge, MA: Harvard University Press.

Lombrozo, T. (2006). The structure and function of explanations. *Trends in Cognitive Sciences*, *10*, 464–70. https://doi:10.1016/j.tics.2006.08.004

    (2012). Explanation and abductive inference. In K. J. Holyoak and R. G. Morrison (eds.), *Oxford handbook of thinking and reasoning* (pp. 260–76). https://doi:10.1093/oxfordhb/9780199734689.013.0014

Lombrozo, T., and Carey, S. (2006). Functional explanation and the function of explanation. *Cognition*, *99*, 167–204. https://doi:10.1016/j.cognition.2004.12.009

Lord, C. G., Lepper, M. R., and Preston, E. (1984). Considering the opposite: A corrective strategy for social judgment. *Journal of Personality and Social Psychology*, *47*, 1231–43. https://doi:10.1037/0022-3514.47.6.1231

Lucas, C. G., Bridgers, S., Griffiths, T. L., and Gopnik, A. (2014). When children are better (or at least more open-minded) learners than adults: Developmental differences in learning the forms of causal relationships. *Cognition*, *131*, 284–99. https://doi:10.1016/j.cognition.2013.12.010

Mackie, J. L. (1974). Truth, probability, and paradox: A reply to James E. Tomberlin's review. *Philosophy and Phenomenological Research*, *34*, 593–4. https://doi:10.2307/2106821

Markman, K. D., McMullen, M. N., and Elizaga, R. A. (2008). Counterfactual thinking, persistence, and performance: A test of the reflection and evaluation model. *Journal of Experimental Social Psychology*, *44*, 421–8. https://doi:10.1016/j.jesp.2007.01.001

McCormack, T., Butterfill, S., Hoerl, C., and Burns, P. (2009). Cue competition effects and young children's causal and counterfactual inferences. *Developmental Psychology*, *45*, 1563–75. https://doi:10.1037/a0017408

McCormack, T., Simms, V., McGourty, J., and Beckers, T. (2013). Encouraging children to think counterfactually enhances blocking in a causal learning task. *Quarterly Journal of Experimental Psychology*, *66*, 1910–26. https://doi:10.1080/17470218.2013.767847

Mercier, H., and Sperber, D. (2011). Why do humans reason? Arguments for an argumentative theory. *Behavioral & Brain Sciences*, *34*, 57–74.

Mitchell, C. J., Lovibond, P. F., and Condoleon, M. (2005). Evidence for deductive reasoning in blocking of causal judgments. *Learning and Motivation*, *36*, 77–87. https://doi:10.1016/j.lmot.2004.09.001

Moshman, D. (2015). *Epistemic cognition and development: The psychology of justification and truth*. New York: Psychology Press. https://doi:10.1080/02698595.2015.1195150

Narvaez, D., Gleason, T., Mitchell, C., and Bentley, J. (1999). Moral theme comprehension in children. *Journal of Educational Psychology*, *91*, 477–87. https://doi:10.1037/0022-0663.91.3.477

Nelson, K. (1973). Structure and strategy in learning to talk. *Monographs of the Society for Research in Child Development*, 38. https://doi:10.2307/1165788

Nyhout, A., and Ganea, P. A. (2019). Mature counterfactual reasoning in 4- and 5-year-olds. *Cognition*, *183*, 57–66.

Nyhout, A., Iannuzziello, A., Walker, C.M., & Ganea, P. (2019). Thinking counterfactually supports children's ability to conduct a controlled test of a hypothesis. In A. Goel, C. Seifert, & C. Freska (Eds.), *Proceedings of the 41st Annual Meeting of the Cognitive Science Society*. Montreal, CA: Cognitive Science Society.

Pearl, J. (2000). Causal inference without counterfactuals: Comment. *Journal of the American Statistical Association*, *95*(450), 428–31. https://doi:10.2307 /2669380

Penner, D. E., and Klahr, D. (1996). The interaction of domain-specific knowledge and domain-general discovery strategies: A study with sinking objects. *Child Development*, *67*, 2709–27. https://doi:10.2307/1131748

Perner, J., and Rafetseder, E. (2011). Counterfactual and other forms of conditional reasoning: Children lost in the nearest possible world. In C. Hoerl, T. McCormack, and S. Beck (eds.), *Understanding counterfactuals/ understanding causation* (pp. 90–109). New York: Oxford University Press. https://doi:10.1093/acprof:oso/9780199590698.003.0005

Rafetseder, E., and Perner, J. (2014). Counterfactual reasoning: Sharpening conceptual distinctions in developmental studies. *Child Development Perspectives*, *8*, 54–8. https://doi:10.1111/cdep.12061

Rafetseder, E., Schwitalla, M., and Perner, J. (2013). Counterfactual reasoning: From childhood to adulthood. *Journal of Experimental Child Psychology*, *114*, 389–404. https://doi:10.1016/j.jecp.2012.10.010

Rhodes, M., Leslie, S. J., Saunders, K., Dunham, Y., and Cimpian, A. (2018). How does social essentialism affect the development of inter-group relations? *Developmental Science*, *21*. https://doi:10.1111/desc.12509

Roese, N. J., and Olson, J. M. (1997). Counterfactual thinking: The intersection of affect and function. *Advances in Experimental Social Psychology*, *29*, 1–59. https://doi:10.1016/S0065-2601(08)60015-5

Ross, L. D., Lepper, M. R., Strack, F., and Steinmetz, J. (1977). Social explanation and social expectation: Effects of real and hypothetical explanations on subjective likelihood. *Journal of Personality and Social Psychology*, *35*, 817–29. https://doi:10.1037/0022-3514.35.11.817

Sanna, L. J., and Schwarz, N. (2003). Debiasing the hindsight bias: The role of accessibility Experiences and (mis)attributions. *Journal of Experimental Social Psychology*, *39*, 287–95. https://doi:10.1016/S0022-1031(02)00528-0

Sanna, L. J., Schwarz, N., and Stocker, S. L. (2002). When debiasing backfires: Accessible content and accessibility experiences in debiasing hindsight. *Journal of Experimental Psychology: Learning, Memory, and Cognition*, *28*, 497–502. https://doi:10.1037/0278-7393.28.3.497

Schauble, L. (1996). The development of scientific reasoning in knowledge-rich contexts. *Developmental Psychology*, *32*, 102–19.

Schulz, L. E., and Gopnik, A. (2004). Causal learning across domains. *Developmental Psychology*, *40*, 162–76. https://doi:10.1037/0012-1649 .40.2.162

Schulz, L. E., Gopnik, A., and Glymour, C. (2007). Preschool children learn about causal structure from conditional interventions. *Developmental Science, 10*, 322–32. https://doi:10.1111/j.1467-7687.2007.00587.x

Schwarz, N. (1998). Accessible content and accessibility experiences: The interplay of declarative and experiential information in judgment. *Personality and Social Psychology Review, 2*, 87–99. https://doi:10.1207/s15327957pspr0202_2

Schwarz, N., and Vaughn, L. A. (2002). The availability heuristic revisited: Ease of recall and content of recall as distinct sources of information. In T. Gilovich, D. Griffin, and D. Kahneman (eds.), *Current perspectives on judgment under uncertainty* (2nd ed). Cambridge: Cambridge University Press. https://doi:10.1017/CBO9780511808098.007

Seiver, E., Gopnik, A., and Goodman, N. D. (2013). Did she jump because she was the big sister or because the trampoline was safe? Causal inference and the development of social attribution. *Child Development, 84*, 443–54. https://doi:10.1111/j.1467-8624.2012.01865.x

Siegler, R. S. (2002). Microgenetic studies of self-explanation. In N. Granott and J. Parziale (eds.), *Microdevelopment: Transition processes in development and learning* (pp. 31–58). https://doi:10.1017/CBO9780511489709.002

Simms, V., McCormack, T., and Beckers, T. (2012). Additivity pretraining and cue competition effects: Developmental evidence for a reasoning-based account of causal learning. *Journal of Experimental Psychology: Animal Behavior Processes, 38*, 180–90. https://doi:10.1037/a0027202

Sloman, S. (2005). *Causal models: How people think about the world and its alternatives.* Oxford: Oxford University Press. https://doi:10.1093/acprof:oso/9780195183115.001.0001

Sobel, D. M., Tenenbaum, J. B., and Gopnik, A. (2004). Children's causal inferences from indirect evidence: Backwards blocking and Bayesian reasoning in preschoolers. *Cognitive Science, 28*, 303–33. https://doi:10.1207/s15516709cog2803_1

Spellman, B. A., and Mandel, D. R. (1999). When possibility informs reality: Counterfactual thinking as a cue to causality. *Current Directions in Psychological Science, 8*, 120–3. https://doi:10.1111/1467-8721.00028

Taylor, M. G. (1996). The development of children's beliefs about social and biological aspects of gender differences. *Child Development, 67*, 1555–71. https://doi:10.2307/1131718

Taylor, M. G., Rhodes, M., and Gelman, S. A. (2009). Boys will be boys; cows will be cows: Children's essentialist reasoning about gender categories and animal species. *Child development, 80*(2), 461–81. https://doi:10.1111/j.1467-8624.2009.01272.x

Tetlock, P., and Belkin, A. (1996). *Counterfactual thought experiments in world politics.* Princeton, NJ: Princeton University Press.

Tetlock, P. E., and Lebow, R. N. (2001). Poking counterfactual holes in covering laws: Cognitive styles and historical reasoning. *American Political Science Review, 95*, 829–43. https://doi:10.1017/S0003055400400043

Walker, C. M., and Gopnik, A. (2013a). Causality and imagination. In M. Taylor (ed.), *Oxford handbook of the development of the imagination* (pp. 342–58). https://doi:10.1093/oxfordhb/9780195395761.013.0022

Walker, C. M., and Gopnik, A. (2013b). Pretense and possibility: A theoretical proposal about the effects of pretend play on development: Comment on Lillard, Lerner, Hopkins, Dore, Smith, & Palmquist (2013). *Psychological Bulletin, 139*, 40–4. https://doi:10.1037/a0030151

Walker, C. M., and Gopnik, A. (2014). Toddlers infer higher-order relational principles in causal learning. *Psychological Science, 25*, 161–9. https://doi:10.1177/0956797613502983

Walker, C. M., and Gopnik, A. (2017). Discriminating relational and perceptual judgments: Evidence from human toddlers. *Cognition, 166*, 23–37. https://doi:10.1016/j.cognition.2017.05.013

Walker, C. M., and Lombrozo, T. (2017). Explaining the moral story. Invited paper for Special issue: Moral learning in *Cognition, 167*, 266–81.

Walker, C. M., Lombrozo, T., Legare, C., and Gopnik, A. (2014). Explanation prompts children to privilege inductively rich properties. *Cognition, 133*, 343–57. https://doi:10.1016/j.cognition.2014.07.008

Walker, C. M., Bridgers, S., and Gopnik, A. (2016a). The early emergence and puzzling decline of relational reasoning: Effects of knowledge and search on inferring abstract concepts. *Cognition, 156*, 30–40. https://doi:10.1016/j.cognition.2016.07.008

Walker, C. M., Buchsbaum, D., Banerjee, E., & Gopnik, A. (in prep). Imagining interventions: Complex causal reasoning in pretend play.

Walker, C. M., Lombrozo, T., Williams, J. J., Rafferty, A. N., and Gopnik, A. (2016b). Explaining constrains causal learning in childhood. *Child Development, 88*, 229–46. https://doi:10.1111/cdev.12590

Walker, C. M., Bonawitz, E., and Lombrozo, T. (2017). Effects of explaining on children's preference for simpler hypotheses. Invited paper for *Special issue: The process of explanation* in *Psychonomic Bulletin & Review*. https://doi:10.3758/s13423-016-1144-0

Weisberg, D. S., and Gopnik, A. (2013). Pretense, counterfactuals, and Bayesian causal models: Why what is not real really matters. *Cognitive Science, 37*, 1368–81. https://doi:10.1111/cogs.12069

Wellman, H. M., and Gelman, S. A. (1992). Cognitive development: Foundational theories of core domains. *Annual review of psychology, 43*, 337–75. https://doi:10.1146/annurev.ps.43.020192.002005

Wellman, H. M., and Liu, D. (2007). Causal reasoning as informed by the early development of explanations. In A. Gopnik and L. Schulz (eds.), *Causal learning: Psychology, philosophy, and computation*. https://doi:10.1093/acprof:oso/9780195176803.003.0017

Wenzlhuemer, R. (2009). Counterfactual thinking as a scientific method. *Historical Social Research/Historische Sozialforschung, 34*, 27–54. https://doi:10.11588/heidok.00019676

Wilkenfeld, D. A., and Lombrozo, T. (2015). Inference to the best explanation (IBE) versus explaining for the best inference (EBI). *Science & Education, 24*, 1059–77. https://doi:10.1007/s11191-015-9784-4

Williams, J. J., and Lombrozo, T. (2010). The role of explanation in discovery and generalization: Evidence from category learning. *Cognitive Science, 34,* 776–806. https://doi:10.1111/j.1551-6709.2010.01113.x

Williams, J. J., and Lombrozo, T. (2013). Explanation and prior knowledge interact to guide learning. *Cognitive Psychology, 66,* 55–84. https://doi:10.1016/j.cogpsych.2012.09.002

Williams, J. J., Lombrozo, T., and Rehder, B. (2013). The hazards of explanation: Overgeneralization in the face of exceptions. *Journal of Experimental Psychology: General, 142,* 1006–14. https://doi:10.1037/a0030996

Woodward, J. (2003). *Making things happen: A theory of causal explanation.* Oxford: Oxford University Press.

(2007). Interventionist theories of causation in psychological perspective. In A. Gopnik and L. Schulz (eds.), *Causal learning: Psychology, philosophy, and computation* (pp. 19–36). https://doi:10.1093/acprof:oso/9780195176803.003.0002

Yu, Y., Bonawitz, E., and Shafto, P. (2017). Pedagogical questions in parent–child conversations. *Child Development* (online first). https://doi:10.1111/cdev.12850

Zimmerman, C. (2000). The development of scientific reasoning skills. *Developmental Review, 20,* 99–149.

(2007). The development of scientific thinking skills in elementary and middle school. *Developmental Review, 27,* 172–223. https://doi:10.1016/j.dr.2006.12.001

Zimmerman, C., and Glaser, R. (2001). Testing positive versus negative claims: A preliminary investigation of the role of cover story on the assessment of experimental design skills. *CSE Technical Report.* https://doi:10.1037/a0017162

# 14 What Makes a Good Question? Towards an Epistemic Classification

*Jonathan Osborne, Emily Reigh*

## Introduction

Questioning is one of the most important epistemic cognitive acts. The answer to the question "how do you know?" or "why do you believe that?" lies at the basis of all arguments. The answer to the causal question of "why does that happen?" is the foundation of the critical disposition that is so commonly cited as one of the aspirations of science education (Millar & Osborne, 1998; National Research Council, 2012). As Cuccio-Schirripa and Steiner (2000) have stated, "Questioning is one of the processing skills which is structurally embedded in the thinking operations of critical thinking, creative thinking, and problem solving" (p. 210). In short, asking questions are one of the primary tools that students can use to facilitate and scaffold the construction of knowledge. Thus, questions serve an epistemic function by helping students to construct a knowledge and understanding of the entities, categories, and concepts that are commonly used in the world, their interrelationships, and the warrants and justification for their existence. In this chapter, we examine how questions have been classified to argue that none of these schemas focus on their primary function – the construction of knowledge. We then explore their function within the context of science to develop a schema which we argue is of greater utility.

Despite the value of asking questions in constructing knowledge, students rarely ask questions in classroom (Dillon, 2004). In contrast, teachers *do* ask many questions. However, their function is primarily pedagogic rather than epistemic, and they are often used as a rhetorical act to establish common knowledge (Edwards & Mercer, 1987; Wells, 2007). When asked by teachers, their uncharacteristic function is revealed by the fact that it *is the person who knows* who asks the question (Edwards & Mercer, 1987; Lemke, 1990; Cazden, 2001). To be used epistemically, questions must be asked either by the person who does not know or used rhetorically as an artifact to engage and challenge the student by stimulating their curiosity about the explanation that is to follow. For instance, "What is the largest mammal on the planet?" or "How do we know that matter is made of atoms?"

As Dillon (2004) summarizes, "classroom discourse normatively proceeds in a way that rules out student questions, while other powerful conditions and facts of life give students good reasons not to ask" (p. 7). Indeed, Dillon and his coworkers went to 27 social studies classrooms in 6 schools to determine the frequency of student questions. Choosing social studies specifically, as it more readily affords opportunities for open-ended discussion, they found only 11 student questions in 27 randomly selected 10-minute segments of classroom talk. In contrast, questions constituted 60 percent of teacher talk. In summary, teachers asked over 80 questions per hour compared to the 2 per hour asked by students. Such findings have been confirmed by a number of other classroom studies, which have found that students ask from 1.3 to 4.0 questions per lesson (Fenclova, 1978; Good et al., 1987). Furthermore, these findings stand in stark contrast to the finding of Chouinard (2007) that young children aged 2 to 5 typically ask 70–80 questions per hour in their home environment. Tizard et al. (1983), likewise, found that girls with a mean age of 4 asked anywhere between 8 and 108 questions per hour in working class homes and 18–145 in middle-class homes. However, at school the rate dropped to 0–20 for working-class girls and 0–46 for middle-class girls. The issue raised by these findings is why are there so few student questions in the classroom if it is clearly such an important epistemic act – the basis for the construction of knowledge and the interrogation of flawed ideas – especially when young children ask so many questions outside the classroom?

One reason for the absence of student questions in the classroom is that the teacher maintains tight control over discourse. One of the most pervasive classroom interaction patterns is triadic discourse in which the teacher poses a question, a student gives an answer, and the teacher evaluates the student's response (Lemke, 1990; Cazden, 2001). By controlling the organization of the interaction with students, the teacher also controls the theme of the discourse; the teacher sets the topic and controls both the way the topic unfolds and the pace of its development. Moreover, the teacher uses other tactics to control discourse, such as marking the importance or asserting the irrelevance of particular student contributions, in order to push the lesson along a predetermined path (Lemke, 1990). Given the teacher's domination of both the organization and theme of classroom conversation, student questions break the interactional rules that the teacher tries to impose on the classroom and are thus generally avoided.

Not only do teachers organize discourse to discourage student questions, but they also afford students few opportunities to elaborate answers to the questions they pose. Systematic research conducted by Rowe (1974) has shown that teachers rarely wait more than 3 seconds for a response to the questions they ask. Indeed, the average "wait time" found by Rowe was 0.9 seconds. Surprisingly, the study showed that when 97 of the teachers in the research were trained to extend the time they waited to more than 3 seconds, the student responses increased from an average of 8 to 27 words; the mean number of unsolicited responses per lesson went up from 5 to 17; the failure to respond diminished from 7 occasions to 1 per lesson; the quality of students reasoning improved; and the range and type of student contributions quadrupled. In addition, there was a notable effect on teachers. They became more flexible in the types of questions they posed, asking fewer but better questions – better in the sense that they sought less to test pupils' knowledge but more to develop and probe their understanding. Thus, rather than asking a definitional question such as "What is the symbol for potassium?" they asked more leading or probing questions such as "Can anybody explain what the difference is between mass and weight?" The change in students' responses also led teachers to report higher expectations for lower achieving students. In many senses, given the clear empirical evidence for the value of wait time found in the research of Budd and others (e.g. Tobin, 1987), pausing for an answer is the educational equivalent of washing hands in a hospital – the single action which has the maximal role in diminishing the spread of disease (Gawande, 2007). All physicians know this to be so, even though they consistently fail to sustain this practice. In education, we are less sure that all teachers know about the research on wait time. Hence, if more teachers were aware of its potential, they might also wait longer for an appropriate response and significantly improve the classroom environment and learning outcomes.

## Existing Frameworks to Classify Questions

Given the high frequency of teacher questions, then, it is important that they ask good questions – good in the sense that they are both cognitively demanding *and* encourage students to do the epistemic work of constructing knowledge. The question we ask, then, is what schema for classifying questions would enable us to distinguish the wheat from the chaff when it comes to classroom questions. For we can only teach pre- and in-service teachers how to ask better questions if we can readily recognize and classify their attributes. However, entities only exist once they are defined either in terms of their observable features or theoretical characteristics. This is the point made forcefully by Bowker and Star (1999), who showed how the introduction of the Nursing Intervention Classification system as a way of formalizing the professional knowledge of nurses contributed to the increased professionalization of nursing.

In their analysis, these authors identified three essential elements that explain how the introduction of a successful, practicable classification of the knowledge required for professional practice is a key aspect of any profession. First, a good classification system enables comparability of practice by building a common understanding of the practice itself and facilitating discourse and communication. Second, it makes the practice visible, transforming the tacit into something that is recognized and shared by the profession. In essence, it helps to identify what the skilled practitioner knows. Finally, it enables control to ensure that the practice is enacted in ways that are professionally recognized to be effective, ensuring stability over time. Without such a classification system, there is no agreed body of knowledge about the practice, how it is defined, and how it is enacted. In short, if teachers' questions cannot be conceptualized and their quality evaluated using a communal, shared language, there is no common understanding of how they differ and what might make one better than another given the context of its use.

So, what schemas exist for categorizing questions to which we might turn which meet these requirements? Since different kinds of questions make different cognitive demands, questions can be classified according to the level of thought required in formulating an answer. Bloom's taxonomy (Bloom, 1956), for example, includes a hierarchy of levels that range from knowledge through comprehension, application, analysis, synthesis, and evaluation. Although this taxonomy was originally devised for formulating questions by the teacher as part of planning the objectives for teaching or assessment, it can also be applied to teacher and student questions in the context of classroom conversations. The taxonomy has since been revised (Anderson et al., 2001) to accommodate a more highly differentiated range of cognitive processes that are subsumed under the six major categories, namely; remember, understand, apply, analyze, evaluate, and create.

The most well-known application of this schema is the simple binary division between "shallow" questions, which only use the bottom level of Bloom's taxonomy (commonly called "closed" questions), and more demanding questions that could be classified at levels two to six of the schema (commonly called "open" questions). In their research on tutoring, Graesser and Person (1994) found that only 8 percent of student questions were of the open type. "Open" questions are simply questions that have a plurality of answers. "Closed" questions, in contrast, have a singular answer. The archetypal version of a closed question is one demanding recall e.g., "What is the chemical symbol for calcium?" And because recall questions are the least cognitively demanding, such questions are commonly regarded as having limited value. However, it is possible to ask a closed question that is also cognitively demanding. For instance, the question "What is the difference between photosynthesis and respiration?" is both cognitively demanding, in that it requires the cognitive acts of comparing and contrasting, and yet is closed in that there is only one answer which defines each construct – showing that respiration is essentially the combustion of sugar and that photosynthesis is, as it name implies, the synthesis of sugars. If the attribute of a better question is that it makes higher order cognitive demands, as the authors contend, then the framework of "open" and "closed" questions is insufficient for demarcating the good question from the poor question. In essence, the scheme fails the comparability test as it neither acknowledges that all closed questions are not of equal worth nor considers the purpose or the context of the question.

Another schema for categorizing teacher questions, applied to questions found in textbooks, was developed by Pizzini and Shepardson (1991), who suggested that questions could be one of three types – input, processing, output. Input questions were seen as the least cognitively demanding since they only require students to recall information or derive it from sense data. Processing-level questions demand more in that they ask students to draw relationships among data, while output questions, the most cognitively demanding type, require students to go beyond the data in new ways to hypothesize, speculate, generalize, create, and evaluate. However, a problem with this scheme is that the labels "input," "processing," and "output" do not sufficiently describe the cognitive levels that they represent. Moreover, these labels fail to indicate the cognitive processes associated with the questions, which makes the value of such a schema questionable as they do not communicate well the difference between the types of questions and their cognitive demand or epistemic intent.

A different way of classifying questions was proposed by de Jesus and colleagues (2003), who attempted to develop a bipolar division instead of the more common unipolar constructs to categorize student questions. These authors argue that classifying questions using a unipolar construct (such as openness) is implicitly, if not explicitly, value laden in that asking open questions is always deemed better than asking closed questions. Furthermore, they argue that a unipolar classification of questions does not allow for notions of context, situation, task, preference, intention, strategy, or goal which, taken together, could account for the fact that a recall question requiring confirmation might be appropriate for a given context. Instead, if questions were to be classified using a bipolar con-struct, each pole would have "adaptive value so that the quality of the questions asked would depend on the nature of the situation, the lear-ner's preferred style of working, and the requirements of the task in hand" (p. 1028).

Based on this conceptualization, the above authors placed questions on a continuum ranging from "confirmation" questions at one end to "trans-formation" questions at the other end, rather than on levels of a hierarchy. Confirmation questions clarify information and detail, differentiate between fact and speculation, tackle issues of specificity, and ask for exemplification and/or definition. Transformation questions, on the other hand, involve some restructuring or reorganization of the students' understanding. They tend to be hypothetic-deductive, seek extensions in knowledge, explore argumentative steps, identify omissions, examine structures in thinking, and challenge accepted reasoning. The authors emphasize that both kinds of questions are necessary and that they complement one another – the type of question that is appropriate to ask depends on the nature of the situation and the requirements of the task at hand. However, while having value in recognizing that evaluating the appropriateness of a question depends on the context of its use, such a schema does not provide sufficient guidance as to how the context makes a question transformative or how it makes it confirmatory. Moreover, these authors argue that both types of questions can be impor-tant but provide little guidance that would help an independent observer to make a judgment of their value. Essentially, the scheme still fails to provide a language to describe the epistemic function of the question and how the question might aid in the construction of knowledge. While it does bring into being two important notions of "transformative" and "confirmatory," it does little to go beyond that.

Yet another perspective to classifying students' questions was offered by Watts and colleagues (1997), who described three categories of students' questions that illuminated distinct periods in the process of conceptual change in science: "consolidation questions" where students attempt to confirm explanations and consolidate understanding of new ideas, "exploration questions" where students seek to expand their knowledge and try out the constructs, and "elaboration questions" through which students attempt to examine claims and counterclaims, reconcile different understandings, resolve conflicts, test circumstances in which they might apply, and examine ideas and their consequences. This taxonomy classifies questions according to the stages through which a student's understanding progresses. Although it reflects a developmental progression in students' scientific thinking, we would argue that it has still failed to relate the nature of the question to its function in science and learning science. As we discuss beneath, science is an attempt to answer three core questions. Any attempt to classify questions that lacks a framework embedded in the types of questions that science asks makes it difficult to evaluate the significance of any question for learning science.

So, what do all of these varied attempts at classification point to? Clearly that context matters. If the underlying premise of either a teacher or student question is a request for information, then a well-framed, closed question is appropriate. If I do not know what the French verb "avoir" means and then ask for its meaning with examples of its use, this is a perfectly valid, and more importantly, appropriate question. In contrast, if I am trying to build a conceptual understanding of the concepts of heat and temperature, then an appropriate question to be asked is "What is the difference between heat and temperature?" Such a contrast forces the identification of the attributes, the ways in which they are both distinct and similar. The function of questions in classrooms then is to assist in the *epistemic work* of building knowledge. That knowledge may vary from simple definitions, to explication of an idea, to warrants for belief but, in all cases, the information helps to enlarge our knowledge and understanding of the world and context that surrounds us.

As Chouinard (2007) has shown, it is not for nothing that the young child asks so many questions. Her detailed study of a set of longitudinal data of the CHILDES database (MacWhinney & Snow, 1985) reports transcribed audiotapes of verbatim conversations between 4 target children, age 2–5 and their parents. These conversations were recorded at regular intervals over several years of the child's development and represent an exact record of every question asked by the child during the recording sessions, along with the exact responses they received. Applying a set of codes, she provides detailed analyses of the frequency and types of questions these children asked. The total data set comprised 24,741 questions gathered over 229.5 hours of conversation. Children averaged 107 questions per hour while engaged in conversation with adults. Moreover, 71 percent of the children's questions were information-seeking and 15 percent were explanation-seeking, showing that the overwhelming majority had the epistemic function of seeking knowledge about the world.

Thus, if the function of a question is fundamentally epistemic – to contribute to building knowledge in the learner – it would make logical sense to classify any question in terms of its key purpose – its function within the discipline. The sciences seek to answer three overarching questions (Osborne, 2011; National Research Council, 2012). These are:

- what exists – an ontological question
- why does it happen – a causal question
- how do we know – what might be termed a fundamental or basic epistemic question

At one level, there are simple ontic questions about observable entities – for instance, different types of birds, mammals, insects, types of clouds, plants or rock types. Answering such questions requires knowledge of the criteria that distinguishes one entity from another. Merely knowing the name of an entity is of little conceptual value. As Feynman so elegantly points out, he learnt this at an early age when his father revealingly told him that a bird has a different name in every language and that, even though he might know the name in every language, he really knew very little (Feynman, 1999). Only by closely observing the bird, its features and its behavior, would he really begin to know what the name meant. Establishing the criteria that define an entity or a concept is therefore highly dependent on the question of "How do A and B differ?" or "How are A and B similar?" Any question that requires comparison and contrast is therefore a key ontic question. What this means is that within this category of ontic questions, some questions are better than others.

The next category of questions is those that serve the production of causal explanations. These are questions of the form "what causes A?" For instance, what causes a rainbow? Why do some things float and others sink? What causes thunder and lightning? Why is the sky blue? Such questions force an elaborated response and the construction of a causal mechanism. For instance, Olbers famously asked the question in 1823 "Why is the sky dark at night" theorizing that, if the universe was infinite, there should be a star at every point in the night sky which would make the sky light. Since it was dark, the universe could not be infinite. This example also illuminates another function of good causal questions – that they are creative or imaginative and require the invention of new entities – in Olber's case a finite universe.[1] Thus, causal questions are fundamental to doing the epistemic work of explaining the material world (and also the social world).

Finally, there are basic or fundamental epistemic questions. Such questions ask for justification asking how we know in a wide range of cases across different domains, for instance, that it will rain tomorrow, that climate change is happening, or that the universe started with a big bang. A key goal of the sciences is to enable students to give explanations, such as how we know that the Earth is not flat, that a plant gets most of its "food" from synthesizing

---

[1] It should be noted that Olber's argument was flawed because he did not know about the existence of another ontic entity, namely, the fact that light in an expanding universe is shifted towards the red end of the spectrum. In short, visible light becomes invisible light.

Table 14.1 *Categories of scientific questions with related question stems*

| Category | Question Stems |
| --- | --- |
| Ontic Questions | What is …? |
| | What do X need to …? |
| | What did you notice about …? |
| | What is the purpose of …? |
| | What is the nature of …? |
| | What is another example of …? |
| | What is the difference between … and …? |
| | How is … similar to …? |
| | What does … mean? |
| Causal Questions | Why did X happen? |
| | What makes X happen? |
| | How does …… affect ………? |
| | Explain why …? |
| | What would happen if … were …? |
| | How does … work? |
| Epistemic Questions | How do you know …? |
| | What is the evidence for …? |
| | Which is the best argument for …? |
| | Why is … important? |
| | How would you justify the claim that …? |
| | What is a counterargument to …? |

carbon dioxide, or how we know that diseases are spread by tiny living microorganisms that we cannot see. Justifications for these beliefs are rooted in the empirical evidence that supports their causal explanations, which in themselves are the product of the human imagination. Asking, and answering these questions, is essential if the learner is to understand the nature of the sciences and how they justify what we ask students to believe.

Thus, our argument is essentially that there are only three categories of questions and that these questions do the work of constructing knowledge – ontic questions, causal questions, and epistemic questions. However, it follows that no epistemic work will be done if such questions are not asked by either teachers or students, and if teachers are not cognizant of the function of a question. A good question then is one that is fit for its purpose. Making that judgment, however, will only be possible if the person asking a question has a clear understanding of what the function of such questions are and the stems that might initiate such questions. Table 14.1 beneath illustrates typical question stems and the categories that they support.

Table 14.2 *Categories of scientific questions with examples*

| Category | Examples |
| --- | --- |
| Ontic Questions | What did you notice about the gravel? |
| | Where did the water go from the shirt? |
| | What happened when the chemicals were mixed? |
| | What are the problems with overfishing? |
| Causal Questions | How does a switch in a circuit work? |
| | Why was there warm, fresh water in the ocean? |
| | What if I were to keep this plant in the closet? What would happen to the plant? |
| | Can anyone explain why the cup with the lid weighs a different amount from the cup without the lid? |
| Epistemic Questions | Which is the best snack, mini bagel or an energy bar? |
| | What made you test/choose "x" to see if it was iron or steel? What surprised you? |
| | How much salt can be dissolved and how will you know? |

Table 14.2 shows a dataset of questions classified using the above schema. These questions were generated by teachers who were video recorded for the PRACTISE project, a collaboration between our group and the Lawrence Hall of Science that provided professional development to prepare elementary teachers' use of argumentation to support student learning in science. The particular focus was on instructional strategies to support whole-class discourse. As part of the data collection process, we collected the focal questions that teachers used to initiate the discussion.

Out of a total of 106 questions collected from this study, the overwhelming majority (72 percent) were ontic questions, 19 percent were causal, and 7 percent were epistemic questions.

The prevalence of ontic questions is in some sense explicable. School science, particularly at the elementary level, introduces students to the ontic zoo that we as a culture use to describe the material world. The study of the material world requires the delineation of entities and concepts. Words act as labels for the ontic zoo that science brings into being, helping to demarcate one species from another, denote a specific process, or define a concept. Without the use of words to demarcate and categorize, science would be impossible, as words enable a shared meaning which facilitates communication (Montgomery, 1996). While words serve as a referent to a concept for an experienced scientist, for the learner of science the meaning of all new language has to be interpreted and constructed anew using figurative and metaphoric language (Sutton, 1996). Finally, much of the language of science draws on unfamiliar academic vocabulary (Fillmore & Snow, 2002) – the form of language that is used to attain "conciseness, achieved by avoiding redundancy; using a high density of information-bearing words, ensuring precision of expression; and relying on grammatical processes to compress complex ideas into few words" (Snow, 2010). Thus as Ogborn et al. (1996, p. 47) have pointed out:

Eating becomes digestion; falling becomes the effect of gravity; our stable home, the Earth, becomes a rocky ball hurtling through space; what parents pass to their children becomes DNA; feeling unwell becomes an affair of microbes; plugging in the electric kettle becomes a current flowing under a potential difference; and so on. It is not enough to say that these transformations just involve knowing a bit more, they change the inhabitants of the world.

The construction of such ontic entities that are the foundation of the scientific worldview clearly is no mean task. Hence, questions that elicit the use of such terminology in an appropriate manner clearly have a role to play in school science. However, there are two concerns with the absence of causal and epistemic questions in this dataset, which are possibly representative of the typical questions posed by teachers across elementary science settings.

First, there is the issue that the ultimate goal of science is the construction of explanatory models (Schauble, 1996; Thagard, 2008). Such models provide causal explanations for why there is a rainbow, why the sky is blue, and what causes disease. The ontic zoo we invent is a necessary requirement, essentially a precursor to the production of such causal explanations. For instance, Darwin's development of his theory of evolution – the core explanatory mechanism of much of contemporary biology – was dependent on careful and painstaking observations of the different species of finches on the Galápagos Islands. These observations led him to ask the causal question of how such variation could exist within species in close proximity to one another. The overemphasis on the definitional aspect of science – essentially a style of reasoning that requires categorization and classification (Crombie, 1994) – means that students will be presented an impoverished view of science. Impoverished, that is, as students will not be exposed to what Harré (1984) has called the crowning glory of science – the explanatory theories that not only help us understand the material world but have also been applied to immeasurably improve the human condition, freeing it from the ravages of disease, hunger, and physical labor and providing us with tools and artifacts for communication and entertainment. For, as Harré states, "in them [theories] our understanding of the world is expressed" (p. 168).

Humans seek causal explanations for the world that surrounds them and a failure to provide such explanatory tools would in part explain the negative attitudes engendered by school science education in many students (Osborne et al., 2003).

The second concern is the paucity of epistemic questions. In one very true sense, the worldview that students are being asked to accept can very much be seen as a set of "crazy" ideas, in the sense that these ideas challenge commonsense conceptions. Science, for instance, asks students to believe that day and night are caused not by a moving Sun – something which daily observation would suggest – but by a spinning Earth; or that our species has not existed forever but evolved from other species over millions of years; or that infections are caused by tiny living microorganisms present throughout the air; or that the continents were once one. The list is too long to provide here. If this is so, then students have a legitimate right to know. For as Norris (1997, p. 252) argues:

> To ask of other human beings that they accept and memorize what the science teacher says, without any concern for the meaning and justification of what is said, is to treat those human beings with disrespect and is to show insufficient care for their welfare. It treats them with a disrespect, because students exist on a moral par with their teachers, and therefore have a right to expect from their teachers reasons for what their teachers wish them to believe. It shows insufficient care for the welfare of students, because possessing beliefs that one is unable to justify is poor currency when one needs beliefs that can reliably guide action.

However, the critical disposition which is seen as the hallmark of the scientist can only be fostered if students are encouraged to ask questions about how we know. As Rogers (1948) long ago argued, "we should not assume that mere contact with science, which is so critical, will make the students think critically" (p. 7). Rather, students will only develop this disposition if epistemic questions are a feature of the classroom discourse. The contention of this chapter is that the presence or absence of such questions cannot be seen until we have a schema that identifies the types of questions teachers ask. Only then can we identify the poverty or richness of the epistemic discourse in a given classroom.

## Implications for the Classroom

The argument we have advanced here has sought to show that questions have an epistemic function that can be foregrounded through a classification scheme. Asking teachers to use such a scheme to classify their own questions as a training exercise would help them to realize the predominant nature of their own questions. However, as valuable as such insights might be, human beings do not readily and easily change well-established practices (Claxton, 1988). Change poses a threat to the need to feel confident, competent, in control, and comfortable. Rather we would contend that a concerted effort is needed to persuade science teachers that students need to be given more opportunities to ask questions that do the epistemic work we have described above. Simply put, good thinkers are good questioners but the ability to ask a good question needs to be explicitly taught.

Three promising programs can be found in the work of Alison King, Tony Ryan, and Sarah Michaels and Cathy O'Connor. King (1990) conducted an extensive program of work with college undergraduates that taught them how to use a set of generic question stems to engage in a reciprocal peer-questioning procedure. This procedure trained students to ask questions that, from the perspective of our framework, represented explanatory (or causal) and epistemic questions. As a result of this questioning, students gave more detailed explanations and demonstrated higher achievement than students using a discussion approach or those using an unscaffolded questioning approach. Such guided reciprocal peer-questioning works, King argued, by promoting peer interaction and improving the quality of questioning, which in turn shapes peer responses.

In a further study, King (1992) trained students to use her generic question stems as a means of summarizing what they had learnt in lectures. Another group was trained in self-questioning and a third control group simply reviewed their lecture notes. While students trained in summarizing remembered more of the lecture in an immediate posttest, self-questioners performed better than the summarizers a week later and significantly better than the note-taking group a week later. King's work suggests that asking students to engage in the use of causal and epistemic questions not surprisingly fosters the epistemic work that supports the effective construction of knowledge. Unfortunately, if students are left to ask questions on their own, they tend to ask what we would describe as factual, ontic questions rather than asking causal and epistemic questions that require more cognitive effort (King, 1990). Using generic question stems to teach students how to ask better questions is therefore a key pedagogic practice. Importantly, what King's work also shows is that the ability to ask questions is malleable – if students are explicitly taught how to answer questions, they get better.

Modeling such questions is therefore important. One such approach is the very pragmatic approach taken by Ryan (1990). Drawing heavily on the work of Dalton (1985), who developed a set of approaches to stimulating creative thinking, Ryan has developed a set of generic questions and prompts for students to engage in epistemic, causal, and creative thinking. Using the visual metaphor of a "key" question, he shows how to ask

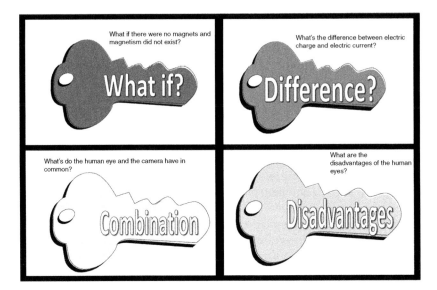

Figure 14.1  Illustration of Dalton's (1985) "key question" framework.

questions that engage students in thoughtful reflection and require them to do meaningful epistemic work (see Figure 14.1).

Difference questions are powerful in that they force comparison and contrast, therefore fostering a deeper understanding of categories of concepts – essentially a more cognitively demanding ontic question. Illustrative examples include "what's the difference between ...":

- velocity and speed?
- power and energy?
- mass and weight?
- insects and spiders?
- photosynthesis and respiration?
- hydrogen and helium?

Likewise, "what if ..." can be used to explore causal and epistemic thinking with questions such as, what if:

- water boiled at 70 Celsius?
- humans were twice as tall as they are now?
- there were no insects?
- we were all to become vegetarian?

When such question stems are presented in such a clear and visually recognizable manner, they emphasize the importance of asking questions and model for students the essence of a question that requires thought and reflection. Asking good questions is a cognitive performance that is acquired, like any proficient performance, through persistent practice (Ericsson et al., 1993). Like all competencies, it needs to be both modeled and taught explicitly. Not surprisingly, in the absence of a cognitive framework for what makes a good question, teachers will struggle to foreground its importance to students.

The third example is to be found in the work of Resnick, Michaels, and O'Connor (Michaels et al., 2008; Resnick et al., 2010). Their primary goal is to examine how classroom discourse can be made cognitively and epistemically productive. Their essential argument is that deliberative discourse needs to be taught. Discourse moves that support such an approach are seen as supporting talk that is accountable to the community that engages in such discourse, accountable to standards of good reasoning, and accountable to the construction to knowledge. Students who learn in classrooms guided by such standards will become socialized into communities of practice in which respectful and grounded discussion can be undertaken. They outline a set of normative goals for discussion to help students engage in deliberative discourse, shown on the left of Table 14.3, which are supported by a set of nine teacher talk moves, shown on the right of Table 14.3. All of the teacher talk moves are questions with the exception of wait time.

Table 14.3 *Teacher goals and talk moves*

| Discourse Goal | Supporting Teacher Talk Move |
|---|---|
| 1. To help individual students share, expand, and clarify their own thoughts | • Using wait time |
| | • Say more, e.g., can you say more about that?/ What do you mean by that?/Can you give an example? |
| | • So are you saying . . .? |
| 2. To help students listen carefully to one another | • Who can rephrase or repeat . . . What was said by . . .? |
| 3. To help students deepen their reasoning | • Why do you think that? |
| | • What is your evidence? |
| | • How do you know? |
| | • Does it always work that way? |
| | • What about the idea that . . . [counterexample]? |
| 4. To help students engage with other's reasoning | • Do you agree/disagree with X? (And why?) |
| | • Who can add onto the idea that X is putting forward? |
| | • Who can explain what X means when she says . . .? |
| | • Why do you think X said that? |

The generic nature of these stems makes them difficult to classify using our schema, but they clearly support epistemic or causal reasoning forcing the students to do epistemic work of constructing knowledge collaboratively.

How might these be used to support student questioning? First, it is important for teachers to model the kinds of questions that encourage the type of thought that should be a feature of any learning environment. If teachers rarely ask causal or epistemic questions of their students, students will not be provided with any conception of what makes a more cognitively demanding question. In short, how can they enact what they do not see? Using Ryan's simple approach, for instance of reversing the process of questioning by stating "If 'X' is the answer, what are three questions that might have been asked" shows one way of training students to ask questions themselves. Going beyond this, teachers could provide students King's or Ryan's question stems and ask them to generate a selection of questions themselves which they might ask to test if their fellow students had understood the topic.

Ultimately, the issue here is that both teachers and student need support to ask better questions. Teachers need a structured and explicit way of relinquishing the control of questioning which does not leave them feeling that they have no control of the discourse. Students need to see better questions modeled by their teachers, learn how to ask them, and be supported with opportunities to ask questions and improve their facility with questions that stimulate higher order reasoning. Only then, will the classroom begin to develop a community that asks questions of one another and replicate the nature of a scientific community where questions are asked, evidence requested, and arguments had about the competing merits of different conceptions.

There now exists a body of work undertaken over the past thirty years which points, albeit in different ways, to the importance of promoting better questions in the classroom. Yet, research suggests that these practices are rarely enacted in the classroom (Newton et al., 1999; Chin & Osborne, 2008; Chin & Osborne, 2010). How then to begin to base common pedagogic practice on this research remains the challenge for this and future generations. Our view is that a first step is defining what constitutes a valuable and valued question. Only when we are clear about what we want, can we point to the kind of questions that should be part of the common repertoire of teaching science. We see the arguments made in this chapter as a contribution to that goal.

## Summary

Question generation is one of the cognitive processes that supports reasoning and knowledge acquisition (Graesser et al., 1996; Kintsch, 1998) as questions can guide the activation, construction, and integration of relevant concepts. Indeed, some theories of critical thinking (e.g., Paul & Elder, 2000) attribute statements made during learning as answers to questions, even though questions are not explicitly asked. If questions are so crucial to doing the epistemic work of learning, then the virtual absence of student questions from the classroom is a matter for concern. Our central contention is that the lack of effective classificatory frameworks for questions contributes to the impoverishment of classroom discourse. A schema that classifies questions in terms of their epistemic function is a vital tool for highlighting the importance of questions in the classroom. Furthermore, developing a language for talking about the purpose and goal of questions can help teachers to enhance the questioning in their own classroom to support student knowledge construction and contribute to developing our understanding of what makes a question fit for purpose – in short, a better question.

## Acknowledgments

The research reported here was supported by the National Science Foundation, through Grant #1546804 for collaborative research with Lawrence Hall, UCB. The opinions expressed are those of the authors and do not represent views of the National Science Foundation.

## References

Anderson, L. W., Krathwohl, D. R., Airasian, P. W., et al. (eds.). (2001). *A taxonomy for learning, teaching, and assessing* (abridged ed.). New York: Addison Wesley Longman.

Bloom, B. (1956). *Taxonomy of educational objectives* (1st ed.). New York: Longman, Green, and Co.

Bowker, G. C., and Leigh Star, S. (1999). *Sorting things out: Classification and its consequences*. Cambridge, MA: MIT Press.

Cazden, C. B. (2001). *Classroom discourse: The language of teaching and Learning* (2nd ed.). Portsmouth, NH: Heinemann.

Chin, C., and Osborne, J. F. (2008). Students' questions: A potential resource for teaching and learning science. *Studies in Science Education, 44*, 1–39. https://doi.org/10.1080/03057260701828101

Chin, C., and Osborne, J. F. (2010). Supporting argumentation through students' questions: Case ctudies in science classrooms. *Journal of the Learning Sciences, 19*, 230–84. https://doi.org/10.1080/10508400903530036

Chouinard, M. (2007). Children's questions: A mechanism for cognitive development. *Monographs of the Society for Research in Child Development, 72,* vii–ix, 1–129.

Claxton, G. (1988). *Live and learn: An introduction to the psychology of growth and change in everyday life.* Milton Keynes: Open University Press.

Crombie, A. C. (1994). *Styles of scientific thinking in the European tradition: The history of argument and explanation especially in the mathematical and biomedical sciences and arts* (vol. 1). London: Duckworth.

Cuccio-Schirripa, S., and Steiner, H. E. (2000). Enhancement and analysis of science question level for middle school students. *Journal of Research in Science Teaching, 37,* 210–24. https://doi.org/10.1002/(SICI) 1098–2736(200002)37:2<210::aid-tea7>3.0.CO;2–I

Dalton, J. (1985). *Adventures in thinking: Creative & co-operative talk in small groups.* Melbourne: Thomas Nelson.

de Jesus, H. P., Teixeira-Dias, J. J. C., and Watts, M. (2003). Questions of chemistry. *International Journal of Science Education, 25,* 1015–34. https://doi:10.1080/09500690305022

Dillon, J. T. (2004). *Questioning and teaching: A manual of practice.* Eugene, OR: Wipf and Stock Publishers.

Edwards, D., and Mercer, N. (1987). *Common knowledge: The development of understanding in the classroom.* London: Methuen. https://doi.org/10.4324/9780203095287

Ericsson, K. A., Krampe, R. T., and Tesch-Römer, C. (1993). The role of deliberate practice in the acquisition of expert performance. *Psychological Review, 100,* 363–406. https://doi.org/363. 10.1037/0033-295X.100.3.363

Fenclova, J. (1978). How does a teacher of physics ask questions? *Mathematics and Physics at School, 2,* 134–37. https://doi.org/10.3102/00028312031001104

Feynman, R. P. (1999). *The pleasure of finding things out.* New York: Basic Books.

Fillmore, L. W., and Snow, C. E. (2002). What teachers need to know about language. In C. T. Adger, C. E. Snow, and D. Christian (eds.), *What teachers need to know about language* (pp. 7–54). Washington, DC: Center for Applied Linguistics and Delta Systems.

Gawande, A. (2007). On washing hands. In *Better: A surgeon's notes on performance* (pp. 13–28). New York: Henry Holt.

Good, T. L., Slavings, R. L., Harel, K. H., and Emerson, H. (1987). Student passivity: A study of question asking in K-12 classrooms. *Sociology of Education, 60,* 181–99. http://dx.doi.org/10.2307/2112275

Graesser, A. C., and Person, N. K. (1994). Question asking during tutoring. *American Educational Research Journal, 31,* 104–37. https://doi.org/10.3102/00028312031001104

Graesser, A. C., Baggett, W., and Williams, K. (1996). Question-driven explanatory reasoning. *Applied Cognitive Psychology, 10,* 17–31. https://doi.org/10.1002/(SICI)1099–0720(199611)10:7<7::aid-acp435>3.0.CO;2-7

Harré, R. (1984). *The philosophies of science: An introductory survey* (2nd ed.). Oxford: Oxford University Press.

King, A. (1990). Enhancing peer interaction and learning in the classroom through reciprocal interaction. *American Education Research Journal, 27,* 664–87. https://doi.org/10.3102/00028312027004664

(1992). Comparison of self-questioning, summarising and notetaking: Review as strategies for learning from lectures. *American Educational Research Journal, 29,* 303–23. https://doi.org/10.3102/00028312029002303

Kintsch, W. (1998). *Comprehension: A paradigm for cognition.* Cambridge: Cambridge University Press.

Lemke, J. (1990). *Talking science: Language, learning and values.* Norwood, NJ: Ablex Publishing.

MacWhinney, B., and Snow, C. (1985). The child language data exchange system. *Journal of Child Language, 12,* 271–95.

Michaels, S., O'Connor, C., and Resnick, L. (2008). Deliberative discourse idealized and realized: Accountable talk in the classroom and in civic life. *Studies in the Philosophy of Education, 27,* 283–97. https://doi.org/10.1007/s11217-007-9071-1

Millar, R., and Osborne, J. F. (eds.). (1998). *Beyond 2000: Science education for the future.* London: King's College London.

Montgomery, S. L. (1996). *The scientific voice.* New York: Guilford Press.

National Research Council (2012). *A framework for K-12 science education: Practices, crosscutting concepts, and core ideas* (N. A. Press Ed.). Washington, DC: Committee on a Conceptual Framework for New K-12 Science Education Standards. Board on Science Education, Division of Behavioral and Social Sciences and Education.

Newton, P., Driver, R., and Osborne, J. F. (1999). The place of argumentation in the pedagogy of school science. *International Journal of Science Education, 21,* 553–76. https://doi.org/10.1080/095006999290570

Norris, S. P. (1997). Intellectual independence for nonscientists and other content-transcendent goals of science education. *Science Education, 81,* 239–58. https://doi.org/10.1002/(SICI)1098-237X(199704)81:2<239::aid-sce7>3.0.CO;2-G

Ogborn, J., Kress, G. R., Martins, I., and McGillicuddy, K. (1996). *Explaining science in the classroom.* Buckingham: Open University Press.

Osborne, J. F. (2011). Science teaching methods: A rationale for practices. *School Science Review, 93*(343), 93–103.

Osborne, J. F., Simon, S., and Collins, S. (2003). Attitudes towards science: A review of the literature and its implications. *International Journal of Science Education, 25,* 1049–79. https://doi.org/10.1080/0950069032000032199

Paul, R. W., and Elder, L. (2000). *Critical thinking: Basic theory and instructional structures.* Dillon Beach, CA: Foundation for Critical Thinking.

Resnick, L., Michaels, S., and O'Connor, C. (2010). How (well-structured) talk builds the mind. In J. Sternberg (ed.), *From genes to context: New discoveries about learning from educational research and their applications* (pp. 163–94). New York: Springer.

Rogers, E. M. (ed.) (1948). *Science courses in general education.* Dubuque, IA: W. C. Brown Co.

Rowe, M. B. (1974). Wait-time and rewards as instructional variables, their influence on language, logic and fate control: Part one – wait-time. *Journal of Research in Science Teaching*, *11*, 81–94. https://doi.org/10.1002/tea .3660110202

Ryan, T. (1990). *Thinkers keys*. Retrieved from Queensland, Australia: www .thinkerskeys.com/

Schauble, L. (1996). The development of scientific reasoning in knowledge-rich contexts. *Developmental Psychology*, *32*, 102–19. http://dx.doi.org/10.1037/0 012–1649.32.1.102

Shepardson, D. P., and Pizzini, E. L. (1991). Questioning levels of junior high school science textbooks and their implications for learning textual information. *Science Education*, *75*, 673–82. https://doi.org/10.1002/sce .3730750607

Snow, C. (2010). Academic language and the challenge of reading for learning about science. *Science*, *328*, 450–2. https://doi.org/10.1126/science.1182597

Sutton, C. (1996). Beliefs about science and beliefs about language. *International Journal of Science Education*, *18*, 1–18. https://doi.org/10.1080 /0950069960180101

Thagard, P. (2008). Explanatory coherence. In J. E. Adler and L. J. Rips (eds.), *Reasoning* (pp. 471–513). Cambridge: Cambridge University Press.

Tizard, B., Hughes, M., Carmichael, H., and Pinkerton, G. (1983). Children's questions and adults' answers. *Journal of Child Psychology and Psychiatry*, *24*, 269–81. https://doi:10.1111/j.1469-7610.1983.tb00575.x

Tobin, K. (1987). The role of wait time in higher cognitive level learning. *Review of Educational Research*, *57*, 69–95. https://doi.org/10.3102 /00346543057001069

Watts, M., Gould, G., and Alsop, S. (1997). Questions of understanding: Categorising pupils' questions in science. *School Science Review*, *79*, 57–63.

Wells, G. (2007). Semiotic mediation, dialogue and the construction of knowledge. *Human Development*, *50*, 244–74. https://doi.org/10.1159 /000106414

# 15  The Questioning Child
## A Path Forward

*Samuel Ronfard, Lucas Payne Butler, Kathleen H. Corriveau*

In this volume, we have brought together leading researchers in psychology and education with the goal of generating an overview of key issues pertaining to the role of questioning in development, to assess where the field stands in terms of investigating these issues, and to chart a path forward for this research in the coming years. In our introduction, we outlined three broad questions of interest to researchers and educators:

1. *Where do questions come from, and how do children engage in questioning across development?*
2. *To what extent is questioning universal, and in what ways is it socialized?*
3. *What role does question-asking play in learning more broadly, in both formal and informal environments?*

   In this concluding chapter we revisit these three key questions, weaving together the contributors' insights before laying out a roadmap to highlight promising avenues of focus for future researchers in the field.

### Where Do Questions Come From, and How Do Children Engage in Questioning across Development?

This two-part question can be broken up into three separable questions: (1) Where does the capacity to ask questions come from? (2) How are questions generated? (3) What does question-asking look like across development? We discuss each of these in turn below.

#### Where Does the Capacity to Ask Questions Come From?

As Carruthers (Chapter 2) points out, theoretical discussion of curiosity, as well as our intuitive notions of curiosity, either explicitly or at least implicitly incorporate metacognition into the concept. We are curious and ask questions when we *don't know* something and *want to know* more about it. Carruthers proposes an alternative view, in which curiosity is rooted in a non-metacognitive, affective state or attitude, one most likely evolutionarily sculpted to motivate inquiry-driven behaviors that enable an organism to acquire relevant information. One advantage of this proposal is that it allows for the existence of curiosity-driven behaviors across species while acknowledging that such behaviors can also be triggered by metacognitive processes as these processes develop and as individuals acquire greater control over these exploratory behaviors.

This proposal is generally consistent with the ones put forth by Harris (Chapter 3) and Wellman (Chapter 4). Although on Carruthers' argument, metacognition is not necessary even for behaviors that may appear to require it (at least prior to age two), Harris argues that metacognition, specifically an awareness of uncertainty, is a core driver of early questioning behaviors. He does agree with Carruthers' proposal that toddlers' early questioning may well be more akin to an affective response to unusual or unexpected stimuli or events particularly in the first year. However, Harris diverges from Carruthers' proposal by arguing that children's questions quickly become shaped by metacognitive processes during the second year. In making this argument, Harris points to empirical work documenting children's early sensitivity to speaker accuracy as early as twelve months (Begus & Southgate, 2012; Kovács et al., 2014), children's greater retention of information provided following points as early as sixteen months (Begus et al., 2014; Lucca & Wilbourn, 2016), as well as children's developing capacity to make requests for clarifications during conversations between fourteen and twenty months (Gallagher, 1981; Ninio & Snow, 1996).

The proposal put forth by Wellman (Chapter 4), namely, that from the outset children seek to learn and understand via their questions, may help resolve this tension. Wellman's account does not require metacognition at the outset but allows for a potentially increasing role of metacognition over the course of development. Indeed, metacognition appears to play an increasing role in children's questions as children transition from infancy into toddlerhood. For example, children begin to use questions to resolve communicative breakdowns (Wellman et al., 2017) by age two, around the same time as they begin to seek explanations in conversation (Chouinard, 2007). The co-occurrence of these two types of questioning is revealing for two reasons. First, in order for children to learn from the explanations they are given they need to monitor the responses they receive. Second, requests for explanations and request for clarifications work together to help children steer conversations in ways that support their ability to acquire information from other people. This dual role of question-asking as a social learning strategy and as a strategy for managing interactions deserve more research. Specifically, we need to know more about how children learn to deploy these two types of questions during conversations to manage interactions in ways that allow them to obtain the information they want or need. By focusing on conversation as the focus of inquiry rather than on individual questions, we will be better positioned to explain how children's questions shape their cognitive development.

In sum, our contributors agree that metacognition may not be a necessary component of the question-asking process early in ontogeny, and Carruthers' proposed affective questioning attitudes seem like a likely candidate for a developmental starting point. The contributors also agree that metacognition plays a role in the questioning process later in development. However, they differ on a key open question, namely, when and how metacognition becomes incorporated into the questioning process. As Carruthers notes, some (but not all) of the results highlighted by Harris can be interpreted without appealing to metacognition. This suggests the need for additional research.

One way forward may be for researchers to carefully break down the process of questioning into broad components, and then ask when in development and in what ways metacognition plays a role for each of these constituent components. For example, Ronfard and colleagues (2018) suggest that the questioning process can be separated into four components: question initiation, question formulation, question expression, and following-up on one's question based on the response received (see also Mills and Sands, Chapter 8). This separation into components may be a critical piece of the puzzle, because the role of metacognition and its incorporation into the questioning process is likely to differ across components. Whether or not future research takes this approach, we believe it will be best served not by asking "*when* does metacognition drive infants and toddlers' information-seeking questions?" but rather by asking three related questions: "under what circumstances and in what ways does metacognition influence infants and toddlers' search for information?"; "how does this change over development?"; and "how is this developmental sequence shaped by variations in the conversational environments children are exposed to?"

Indeed, we urge researchers to carefully consider the relations between questioning attitudes such as curiosity, pointing, and question-asking. These relations may be key to the development of questioning in conversation in early development. Specifically, an important issue here is understanding how children learn that pointing reliably elicits information from a caregiver and, in turn, how they develop the expectation that they will receive a response – an expectation that boosts their retention of the to-be-provided information (Lucca & Wilbourn, 2016). Currently, the strongest hypothesis for this development is that children learn to use pointing to request information through interactions with their caregivers (Lucca & Wilbourn, 2016; Begus & Southgate, 2018). Indeed, caregivers in Japan and the United States interpret children's points as request for information (Kishimoto et al., 2007; Wu & Gros-Louis, 2014). Additional studies using longitudinal designs are needed to explore the relation between parental responsiveness to infant pointing and the development of infant's questioning behaviors – not only their expectation for information but also their sensitivity to speaker accuracy. Such research will eventually need to be followed up with intervention research to provide causal evidence that caregiver–child interactions (which are culturally influenced and thus vary widely) are indeed a key mechanism supporting observed developments in children's question-asking behaviors. If communicative interactions are shown to play such an important role in the development of question-asking in infancy, then we would expect large differences in the onset of this type of question-asking given the wide range of communicative practices across the globe. This would support the claim of Callanan, Solis, Castañeda, and Jipson (Chapter 5) and Gauvain and Munroe (Chapter 10) that questioning is a cultural practice acquired over time as children interact with others in culturally determined ways.

Children's questions can either spark or extend conversations. They are signposts that shape how conversations unfold and thus what is learned. For the most part, research on question-asking has focused on individual questions and sometimes on sequences within a conversation, for example whether and how children follow up explanatory and nonexplanatory responses (Chouinard, 2007; Frazier et al., 2016; Kurkul & Corriveau, 2017). Research will benefit from taking a step back to investigate how children learn to combine requests for both explanation and clarification in order to steer conversational exchanges in ways that scaffold their learning as well as the ways in which the ability to steer an exchange is – or is not – supported by the surrounding conversational environment and cultural practices.

### How Are Questions Generated?

This is an important question for both psychologists and educators. Unfortunately, we know little about this process (Coenen et al., 2018; Ronfard et al., 2018). Surveying the chapters in this volume, a distinction can be made between contexts in which children possess an accurate and relatively complete understanding of the search space and can use questions to identify an answer to their query, as contrasted with contexts in which there is no clear answer and children lack a representation of the search space. The former is typically assessed using 20-questions type paradigms where children have been given a set of items and have to identify the target. While this setup may seem artificial, there are many real-world cases where search unfolds in much this way. Consider for example a mechanic trying to diagnose a problem with a car. The mechanic has a good sense of the possible problems and through a series of questions can identify the root cause of the mechanical failure. This kind of search process is also present in other diagnostic searches – for example a doctor's search for what ails a patient or a teacher's search for why a student has a misconception. Jones, Swaboda, and Ruggeri (Chapter 7) review research that demonstrates surprising strengths in children's ability to engage in this type of search, as well as rapid developments. Importantly, they note that the efficiency of search (for children and adults), that is, how much uncertainty is reduced by each question, depends on the questioner's prior knowledge, biases, and expectations, as well as on specific task characteristics. This is because the value of search strategies like hypothesis-scanning questions or constraint-seeking questions depend on one's knowledge of or expectations about the likelihood of various hypotheses in the search space. If all hypotheses are equally likely then it is better to try to reduce the number of hypotheses by seeking to rule out as many as possible using a constraint-seeking approach. In contrast, if one hypothesis seems particularly likely then it makes more sense to focus on that hypothesis and take a hypothesis-scanning approach. This ability to engage in ecological learning, that is, the ability to flexibly adapt search strategies based on task characteristics, is also present early in development and develops rapidly between the preschool and elementary years. This line of work is particularly promising, as it may help provide a rich understanding of children's abilities to adapt their search based on the context and the task. Moreover, the paradigms and analytic tools developed in this line of inquiry, such as the formal quantification of information gain (Jones, Swaboda, and Ruggeri, Chapter 7), provide a solid foundation for better understanding exactly how and to what extent prior knowledge, biases, and expectations shape search and how this affects learning. Thus far, we know that these variables matter for how children search for information, but have yet to fully understand and quantify their impact more broadly. Indeed, it will likely be easier to measure the impact of children's prior knowledge and cognitive abilities on this type of search than on more open-ended questioning tasks. For example, the more controlled setting of 20-questions type games seems ideal to better understand how different parts of the questioning process (representing the search space, identifying relevant dimensions of that space, updating the representation of the search space following answers) call upon different facets of executive functions skills – working memory, cognitive flexibility, inhibition (see Jones and colleagues, Chapter 7, for other next steps). Of course, these processes may be different when children do not have a representation of the search space but understanding how they search when they do have such a representation will provide us with theoretical and analytical tools to gain that knowledge.

As noted, there are many cases where children do not have an accurate representation of the search space. Indeed, children's questions are diagnostic both of what they know *and* of what they don't know (Neale, Morano, Verdine, Golinkoff, and Hirsh-Pasek, Chapter 9) and are frequently used by caregivers, teachers, and researchers to better understand how children think about a particular domain of inquiry. Research investigating these types of questions suggests that children's concepts and intuitive theories influence the questions that children generate. For example, children's concepts of animals and artifacts shape the kind of information they seek when encountering novel exemplars of each kind (Greif et al., 2006) and children's questions are increasingly concerned with the mind as their Theory of Mind (ToM) is developing (Chouinard, 2007; but see Gauvain et al., 2013). In addition to these data, work by Chouinard (2007), Frazier, Gelman, and Wellman (2009, 2016), and Kurkul and Corriveau (2017) reveals that when children do not receive an informative response to their questions, they often follow up by either asking their question again or coming up with their own explanation. These data come exclusively from children growing up in the United States. Nevertheless, they suggest that when children ask a question, they are likely to have some expectation about what would count as an answer. Whether they voice such opinions, however, may differ by culture. Indeed, Kurkul and Corriveau (2017) report that children from families with lower socioeconomic status tend to provide their own explanations less often than peers from more advantaged backgrounds (see also Gauvain & Munroe, Chapter 10).

In sum, research on children's use of questions when they possess and do not possess (complete) information about the search space has uncovered suggestive evidence that the question-generation process is complex and influenced by multiple factors. However, our understanding of this process remains limited. Indeed, as Coenen and colleagues (2018) have pointed out in their review of research on inquiry in children and adults, there is still much we do not know (see also Ronfard et al., 2018). Specifically, we need more clarity on how prior knowledge and cognitive biases shape the question-generation process and the processing of responses to these questions. Answering this question is critical to understanding how question-asking helps children restructure their representation of a domain. That is, the role of question-asking for cognitive development.

### What Does Question-Asking Look Like across Development?

In Table 15.1, we provide a non-exhaustive and partial review of the developmental results discussed in this volume from birth to adolescence. A full review of existing research on question-asking across childhood is beyond the scope of this chapter, but see Ronfard et al. (2018) for a recent review. While perusing this table, three limitations must be kept in mind. First, almost all of the data we possess on question-asking have been collected in WEIRD countries (Henrich et al., 2010; Nielsen et al., 2017). Second, most developmental studies on question-asking that have been conducted in laboratory settings (and some that have drawn on recorded conversations between caregivers and their parents) have used cross-sectional rather than longitudinal designs. Thus, although we have a general idea of age-related differences, we do not have much data on how the performance of individual children changes over time. Finally, much of the data that has been collected has revealed large individual differences in children's performance at every age that has been tested. Many authors in this volume have speculated about the source of these individual differences but little research has been conducted on them. We urge future research to consider exploring the important factors resulting in these within-culture individual differences, and suggest that this might be an important way forward. At the moment, there is a lot of variability in the development of question-asking that we cannot account for.

## To What Extent Is Questioning Universal, and in What Ways Is It Socialized?

This is a key question raised by Callanan, Solis, Castañeda, and Jipson (Chapter 5) and by Gauvain and Munroe (Chapter 10). Both challenge us to make a distinction between taking an inquisitive stance (questioning with a big Q) and question-asking per se. Taking an inquisitive stance is likely a human universal (see also Carruthers, Chapter 2) but the way in which this stance is expressed both verbally and nonverbally is likely to differ across cultures as children are socialized into the cultural practices of their communities. As both sets of authors remind us, there are a myriad of ways in which children can acquire information from others, only one of which is explicit questions. Thus, a greater understanding of how *and* why children's reliance on these different methods of knowledge

Table 15.1 *A non-exhaustive review of the developmental results discussed in this volume*

| | |
|---|---|
| 1 years old | Children are sensitive to speaker accuracy (Begus & Southgate, 2012; Kovács et al., 2014), they show greater retention of information provided following their points (Begus et al., 2014; Lucca & Wilbourn, 2016), and they begin asking for clarifications during conversations (Gallagher, 1981; Ninio & Snow, 1996). |
| 2 years old <br> 3 years old | US children from middle-class homes increasingly ask for explanations and not just facts (Callanan & Oakes, 1992; Hickling & Wellman, 2001; Chouinard, 2007) and have begun to master the syntax of wh-questions (Bloom et al., 1982). They also use questions to repair communicative breakdowns (Wellman et al., 2017). |
| 4 years old | Children generate predominantly informative as opposed to redundant or uninformative questions, rely predominantly on hypothesis-scanning approach on 20-questions type paradigms (Legare et al., 2013), monitor the responses they obtain to their question and follow up by providing their own explanation or by repeating their question (Chouinard, 2007; Frazier et al., 2016; Kurkul & Corriveau, 2017). They prefer and remember satisfying explanations (Frazier et al., 2016) and can engage in extended bouts of questioning on a single topic with a responsive caregiver ("Passages of intellectual search," Tizard & Hughes, 1984). |
| 5 years old | Children can select the most informative question – the question that generates the greatest reduction in uncertainty – when given information about the likelihood of possible hypotheses (Ruggeri et al., 2017). However, overconfidence in their own knowledge and abilities sometimes leads children to attempt to guess answers rather than asking a question of a knowledgeable source when they are given the option (Robinson et al., 2011; Aguiar et al., 2012). Children are increasingly able to coordinate what to ask and whom to ask when asking questions (Mills et al., 2010; Mills et al., 2011; Mills & Landrum, 2016). |
| 6 to <br> 11 years old | Transition to relying predominantly on a constraint-seeking approach on 20-questions type paradigms (Ruggeri & Feufel, 2015; Ruggeri & Lombrozo, 2015) and increasing metacognitive awareness of using this strategy (Mosher & Hornsby, 1966). Relative to adults, children this age still ask many redundant questions – questions that provide information they already obtained (Ruggeri et al., 2016). However, even at this age, children demonstrate "ecological learning." They adjust their questioning strategy to match the probability distribution of hypotheses on the task they are asked to complete (Ruggeri & Lombrozo, 2015). |
| Adolescence | Questioning continues to develop in adolescence and adulthood where it is increasingly deployed to support argumentation. Through sustained practice, authentic learning opportunities, and scaffolding by teachers, adolescents can learn to use evidence (and to seek it) not only to support their own claims but also to weaken the claims of others (see Kuhn, Modrek, & Sandoval, Chapter 12). |

acquisition differs across cultures is needed. Notably, this does not mean that research cannot or should not focus on the benefits that might accrue from asking questions. However, before these benefits can be claimed to be both related and unique to asking questions (i.e., that they can only be obtained through question-asking, rather than through other behaviors, including some behaviors that are noncommunicative) much more extensive comparative research needs to be conducted. In what follows, we briefly echo some of the important points made by both chapters before outlining some next steps towards better understanding the socialization of question-asking.

By encouraging us to think of questions as a cultural practice, Callanan, Solis, Castañeda, and Jipson (Chapter 5) remind us to beware of inferring that an absence of question-asking in a cultural group necessarily entails an absence of support for thinking or learning in that group. Their chapter highlights the need for not only greater cultural diversity in research on big-Q questioning but also greater methodological diversity in research on question-asking specifically. Indeed, in order to better understand *how* cultural repertoires of practices (Gutiérrez & Rogoff, 2003) shape the development of question-asking specifically and questioning more broadly, we need to collect data at home and in the lab using methods that are likely to highlight nuanced cultural variability in children's use of questions to gather information. This includes collecting data across multiple settings (e.g., peer-dominated activities, caregiver-dominated activities, conversations about academic vs. nonacademic topics, during dinnertime and bath time as well as during less reflective times of the day), using multiple methods (e.g., observation, semi-structured experimental tasks, parent reports through diary entries). In addition to increasing the diversity of the methods we use to collect data on how children ask questions, more information is needed about what explains variation in the conversational environments that caregivers create for their children (both within and across cultures) and how this variation is tied to children's use of questions to obtain information.

In their chapter, Gauvain and Munroe (Chapter 10) provide researchers with theoretical and methodological tools for thinking more deeply about the socialization of question-asking. Specifically, they point to sociocultural approaches to development and theories of language socialization. These approaches are consistent with many of the findings reported in this volume which suggest an important role for communicative interactions (which are shaped by culture) in the development of question-asking: learning to expect information in response to one's points (Lucca, Chapter 6); caregivers' use of questions and its implications for children's language development (Zambrana, Hermansen, & Rowe, Chapter 11); learning from questions and by asking questions in the classroom (Kuhn, Modrek, & Sandoval, Chapter 12).

One challenge to increasing our understanding of the socialization of asking questions is that the absence of questions does not necessarily imply that questions are not being generated, only that they are not being asked of the interlocutors. Indeed, as research reviewed by Gauvain and Munroe (Chapter 10) and Callanan and colleagues (Chapter 5) demonstrates, there are many cases across cultures in which certain questions are not allowed to be asked: for example when asking a question would challenge authority or if the topic of the question is taboo. An additional challenge is that there appears to be multiple paths through which culture might influence question-asking. A greater under-standing of the effect of culture on question-asking requires targeted research on these various pathways. Below, we discuss some of these nonexclusive pathways but note that there are likely to be other ways as well.

First, cultural practices may directly shape the development of children's question-asking. Early infant–caregiver interactions are known to differ greatly across cultures. If, as we suspect, variability in such interactions accounts for unique variation in the early development of questioning – for example, by helping children develop an understanding of the information-eliciting function of points – then we would expect differences across cultures in the onset of the particular developmental milestones associated with questioning, as described in the previous section.

Second, as discussed above, cultural practices might shape children's willingness to ask questions and of whom they ask those questions. Under this proposal, children across and within cultures may not necessarily differ in the number of questions they generate but rather in whether they express these questions to familiar and unfamiliar adults. For example, children may prefer to seek out peers rather than adults if they have a question in mind because asking an adult may be culturally unaccep-table or taboo given the topic of the question.

Third, cultural differences in what is talked about with children may shape what children know about a topic (their prior knowledge) and thus shape the kinds of questions they ask about such topics (e.g., parent–child conversations about death or sex, Davies & Robinson, 2010; Rosengren et al., 2014). Under this proposal, differences across groups of children reflect differences in prior knowledge rather than reduced interest. This is because knowing more about a topic makes one less confident in one's knowledge (Kruger & Dunning, 1999) and perhaps more likely to seek out information. In addition, individuals who know more generate more precise questions (Graesser & Olde, 2003). Thus, group differences in the prior knowledge available to children could lead to differences in the number and type of questions children ask.

Fourth, being questioned about their own knowledge, being asked follow-up questions about their explanations, and being asked to clarify what they mean may lead children to internalize question-asking as a form of self-monitoring, improve their comprehension, and indeed their propensity to detect inconsistencies in their knowledge thereby increasing the frequency with which they ask questions (see King, 1990, 1992; Rosenshine et al., 1996). Some experimental research appears to be consistent with this hypothesis: having been asked to explain their prediction, children engaged in more sophisticated causal reasoning, than when they were just asked to describe an interaction (Legare & Lombrozo, 2014). Notably, as mentioned above, all of the research to date exploring the impact of question-asking and explanations has focused on cross-sectional data, and to understand the long-term impact of being encultured in an environment which supports question-asking and explanations more longitudinal data is needed.

Fifth, caregivers' conversational style – how often they ask questions and the type of questions they ask – may signal a distinctive stance toward the exchange of ideas via conversation and about how knowledge is structured and thus may influence children's epistemological development (Ronfard et al., 2017). Similarly, a caregiver's willingness to engage in explanations – and the type of explanations they give – may also signal to their child the likelihood that the caregiver will be a useful source of information in the future. Some research has speculated on this relation (Kurkul & Corriveau, 2017), but as Callanan and colleagues note, longitudinal data is needed to support this hypothesis.

In sum, we agree with Callanan et al. (Chapter 5) and Gauvain and Munroe (Chapter 10) that questioning is a cultural practice and that its absence in some cultures or its lower frequency does not imply a lack of thinking or learning. More research is needed to better understand variability in the impact of exposure to questions as well the relation between question-asking, how children learn, and how they think about the learning process. There are multiple ways in which culture may influence children's question-asking practices. Some of the pathways are likely to have minor influences on children's learning while others may be more consequential.

### What Role Does Question-Asking Play in Learning More Broadly, in Both Formal and Informal Environments?

The contributors to this volume reveal that question-asking shapes learning in at least two ways. Children's questions shape their interactions with others and thus what they learn. Adults' questions also shape what children learn. We therefore review each question in turn: (1) What role do children's questions play in learning? (2) What role do questions *to* children play in learning?

### *What Role Do Children's Questions Play in Learning?*

Conversations are a powerful means of gathering information. Children's questions support learning because they help generate and direct pedagogical exchanges. As Baldwin and Moses (1996) put it, questions "allow children to gather just the information they want, on just the topic that interests them, at just the time they require it" (Baldwin & Moses, 1996, p. 1934). More specifically, questions allow children to obtain explanations and to clarify what others are telling them (Harris, Chapter 3; Wellman, Chapter 4). Moreover, even when children fail to obtain an explanation, they may still learn by formulating their own. This is because the process of explaining itself can generate learning (see Walker & Nyhout, Chapter 13; Wellman, Chapter 4). However, the beneficial impacts of asking questions on learning are not yet fully understood. This is a ripe area for future research and Wellman (Chapter 4) outlines three nonexclusive hypotheses for why questions may be so effective at scaffolding learning that we hope will be explored in future research: (1) children's questions are (often) focused on topics that children are intrinsically motivated to learn about; (2) children's questions are triggered by uncertainty and novelty and thus push children to learn about things they don't already know; and (3) children's questions may (sometimes) force them to process information more deeply because it requires them to think through what they already know. As Wellman (Chapter 4) points out such research will benefit from comparing and contrasting the effect of questions on learning with the effects of explaining and predicting.

### *What Role Do Questions to Children Play in Learning?*

Questioning is a powerful teaching strategy. Indeed, using questions to teach has been a mainstay of Western philosophy for millennia. Within that context, questions have been used by adults to foster reasoning and comprehension. This volume's contributors provide strong evidence for the benefits of this pedagogical approach. Specifically, the chapters by Zambrana and colleagues (Chapter 11) and Walker and Nyhout (Chapter 13) raise two issues that cognitive developmental scientists and educators will find interesting: (1) How do questions to children scaffold learning? (2) What are the limits of questioning as an instructional strategy?

### Benefits and Drawbacks of Caregiver Questions

How do questions scaffold learning? According to Zambrana and colleagues (Chapter 11) and Walker and Nyhout (Chapter 13), the short answer is that adults' questions to children catalyze children's learning because they oblige children to speak more and to think more deeply. Specifically, adults' questions to children provide opportunities for children to practice their developing language skills and focus their attention on hypotheses they may not have considered on their own. However, in doing so, adults' questions may also lead children astray suggesting that adults' knowledge of a domain is likely to determine whether their questions have a positive impact on children's construction of new knowledge – a point we discuss in more length later.

Zambrana and colleagues (Chapter 11) draw on a longitudinal dataset of parent–child interactions at one, two, and three years old and show that parents' questions evolve alongside their children's linguistic abilities. As children age, parents ask fewer direct questions, more indirect questions, and increase the linguistic complexity of the questions they ask. Their analyses show that the kinds of questions children ask are related to their task performance (completing the task). Thus, parents are adjusting the kinds of questions they are asking, not only based on their children's general linguistic abilities, but also on their child's ability to complete the task at hand. This is an important point because as Zambrana and colleagues remind us, when parents use questions, they are seeking to fulfill multiple agendas – in this case, further strengthening their children's language abilities and helping their child solve a task. Importantly, Zambrana and colleagues also find that only parents' wh-questions at age two predict their child's language abilities two years later when children are four years old. This finding, which is consistent with prior work, implies that not all questions are equally effective in supporting children's language development. Wh-questions are particularly powerful because they challenge children to move beyond a simple yes/no response and produce a response that is more varied.

Walker and Nyhout (Chapter 13) provide further evidence of the power of wh-questions. They review the benefits and potential pitfalls of three question prompts: requests for explanations (Why?), requests for additional explanations (Why else?), and counterfactuals (What if?). As Walker and Nyhout note, each question type has benefits and pitfalls. However, when used in combination, the different question prompts can mitigate the drawback of each question type. For example, using a request for additional explanations (Why else?) following an initial request may lead children to consider more complex hypotheses than those prompted by the initial (Why?) question, which may lead them to focus on one possibility. An interesting question for future research is whether adults have an implicit understanding of the power of these prompts. Do they use them in sequences to guide children's thinking? Do they appropriately ask for additional explanations and counterfactuals?

Implicit in both authors' discussion is that for questions to be effective – for questions to perform as intended – the person asking the questions and taking on the pedagogical role must be knowledgeable and judicious in how they deploy questions. Do children take into account the knowledge of the questioner when responding to queries directed at them? Recent evidence suggest that they do (Yu et al., 2018). In other words, pedagogical questions such as those used in direct instruction may guide children's thinking about a domain based on children's reasoning about the knowledge and intentions of their informant (Shafto et al., 2014).

### Supporting Inquiry in the Classroom: Challenges and Opportunities

In their two chapters, Kuhn, Modrek, and Sandoval (Chapter 12) and Osborne and Reigh (Chapter 14) review the current state of question-asking in the classroom and find it mostly unchanged relative to past work. Teachers, rather than students, ask many questions. This is detrimental to the development of children's inquiry skills. They suggest ways in which teachers can create environments where questions could be used to support student learning.

Kuhn, Modrek, and Sandoval (Chapter 12) focus on older children and adolescents – an age group typically ignored when discussing inquiry in childhood. As they point out, younger children are often described as incredibly curious, whereas older children are not. Kuhn et al. suggest that this is partly because older children's educational environments do not provide many opportunities for expression of curiosity, nor develop "mature" inquiry skills that would prepare them for the modern workforce. They argue that teachers might best develop and support student inquiry skills both through modeling the types of inquiry behavior they aspire to see in their students and through actively creating learning experiences in the classroom that allow for the acquisition of these skills. Drawing on experimental work, they argue for learning environments that pose children "true" questions. That is, teachers should create environments that pose a problem and then provide students with the means to answer them – a suggestion that echoes Carruthers' (Chapter 2). In such environments, the role of the teacher is to ask the appropriate question to initiate the process for students (see Osborne and Reigh (Chapter 14) and Walker and Nyhout (Chapter 13) for how different question prompts might achieve this goal) and to use questions to help students to collaboratively weigh and discuss solutions. This latter point connects to Gauvain and Munroe's (Chapter 10) argument that learning to question involves mastering the pragmatics involved in asking questions in the cultural environment, which occurs as one is socialized into culturally influenced pattern of interactions – in this case questioning as a component of complex argumentation.

In their chapter, Osborne and Reigh (Chapter 14) agree with Kuhn and colleagues' (Chapter 12) assessments and solutions. However, they argue that teachers' ability to modify their practice and deploy questions to support learning, rather than for rhetorical reasons, is currently hindered by the lack of a clear and agreed upon classification scheme for teachers' questions. By making categories of questions explicit, teachers can reflect on the types of questions they employ to achieve particular pedagogical goals. Osborne and Reigh note that previous attempts at categorizing questions are not helpful for teachers partly because the categories generated by previous schemes do not clearly classify all questions, nor are they clearly aligned with the pedagogical goals of science classrooms. Thus, the lack of a clear classification system makes it difficult for teachers to critically think about the *type* of question they need to achieve a particular instructional goal. Osborne and Reigh's new scheme is aligned with instructional goals in the science classroom and categorizes questions into three groups: ontic question are about how to describe and categorize phenomena; causal questions are about understanding why things happen; epistemic questions are about understanding how we know and what constitutes good evidence for a claim. They demonstrate the usefulness of this scheme with their analyses of elementary teachers' questions, which show that teachers ask many ontic questions and very few questions about how and why a claim is made. Increasing the frequency of these questions early in children's schooling may pay important dividends in the later years when children are asked to reason and argue about evidence in more sophisticated ways (Kuhn, Modrek, & Sandoval, Chapter 12). Importantly, the goal is not just to help teachers recognize the kinds of questions they ask but also to enhance the questions asked by students. This suggests an interesting next step for research: When might it be useful to not only share the classification scheme with teachers but also with their students? Indeed, it might be helpful to teach students about the three types of questions that Osborne and Reigh have identified and to teach students when and how to deploy them during inquiry. Such knowledge about knowledge may be particularly helpful when children (and adults) need to engage in sustained reflective inquiry.

In sum, asking children questions is a powerful learning strategy that shapes children's language and cognitive development. Wh-questions seem particularly effective in shaping development. These questions help children develop their linguistic skills by encouraging them to talk more and to practice using more complex linguistic forms in their responses. Wh-questions also support children's cognitive development by pushing them to think more deeply about the domain of inquiry. However, for adults' wh-questions to drive learning forward, the questions must be asked by a knowledgeable and helpful adult who will not guide children to consider inaccurate or unlikely hypotheses. Moreover, as Kuhn and colleagues demonstrate, developing complex inquiry and argumentative skills requires a setting that incorporates multiple components: motivation – knowing you can do it but also having the freedom to do it on your own; pragmatic development – knowing how to engage in extensive back and forth that builds on the claims made by other participants; and conceptual development – understanding the link between inquiry, evidence, and argumentation, an understanding that is fostered as one is held accountable to these standards of evidence in extended conversations.

## Conclusions

This volume's contributors have provided insights into the origin of question-asking, its development, and potential sources of individual differences. They have also highlighted that there is much we do not know about questions and their impacts on learning. Nevertheless, there seems to be agreement that learning to ask questions happens over time as one is socialized into this practice. More research is needed to understand how this socialization process takes place and how culture shapes it. Are there unique cognitive benefits to asking questions or are the benefits that exist simply reflective of the fact that questions like other forms of active learning benefit from a high level of motivation, agency, and deeper processing? In addition to helping answer this question as well as others, we hope that this book will help build bridges between the various disciplines interested in the development of children's question-asking. In sum, we hope that this volume, like all good questions, generates interactions, explanations, and more questions!

# References

Aguiar, N. R., Stoess, C. J., and Taylor, M. (2012). The development of children's ability to fill the gaps in their knowledge by consulting experts. *Child Development*, *83*, 1368–81. https://doi:10.1037/t30548-000

Baldwin, D. A., and Moses, L. J. (1996). The ontogeny of social information gathering. *Child Development*, *67*, 1915–39. https://doi:10.2307/1131601

Begus, K., and Southgate, V. (2012). Infant pointing serves an interrogative function. *Developmental Science*, *15*, 611–17. https://doi:10.1111/j.1467-7687.2012.01160.x

(2018). Curious learners: How infants' motivation to learn shapes and is shaped by infants' interactions with the social world. In M. M. Saylor and P. A. Ganea (eds.), *Active learning from infancy to childhood* (pp. 13–37). https://doi:10.1007/978-3-319-77182-3_2

Begus, K., Gliga, T., and Southgate, V. (2014). Infants learn what they want to learn: Responding to infant pointing leads to superior learning. *PLOS ONE*, *9*, e108817. https://doi:10.1371/journal.pone.0108817

Bloom, L., Merkin, S., and Wootten, J. (1982). "Wh"-questions: Linguistic factors that contribute to the sequence of acquisition. *Child Development*, *53*, 1084–92. https://doi:10.2307/1129150

Callanan, M. A., and Oakes, L. M. (1992). Preschoolers' questions and parents' explanations: Causal thinking in everyday activity. *Cognitive Development*, *7*, 213–33. https://doi:10.1016/0885-2014(92)90012-G

Chouinard, M. (2007). Children's questions: A mechanism for cognitive development. *Monographs of the Society for Research in Child Development*, *72*, vii–ix, 1–129.

Coenen, A., Nelson, J. D., and Gureckis, T. M. (2018). Asking the right questions about the psychology of human inquiry: Nine open challenges. *Psychonomic Bulletin & Review*. Advance online publication. https://doi:10.31234/osf.io/h457v

Davies, C., and Robinson, K. (2010). Hatching babies and stork deliveries: Risk and regulation in the construction of children's sexual knowledge. *Contemporary Issues in Early Childhood*, *11*, 249–62. https://doi:10.2304/ciec.2010.11.3.249

Frazier, B. N., Gelman, S. A., and Wellman, H. M. (2009). Preschoolers' search for explanatory information within adult-child conversation. *Child Development*, *80*, 1592–611. https://doi:10.1111/j.1467-8624.2009.01356.x

(2016). Young children prefer and remember satisfying explanations. *Journal of Cognition and Development*, *17*, 718–36. https://doi:10.1080/15248372.2015.1098649

Gallagher, T. M. (1981). Contingent query sequences within adult–child discourse. *Journal of Child Language*, *8*, 51–62. https://doi:10.1017/s0305000900003007

Gauvain, M., Munroe, R. L., and Beebe, H. (2013). Children's questions in cross-cultural perspective. *Journal of Cross-Cultural Psychology*, *44*, 1148–65. https://doi:10.1177/0022022113485430

Graesser, A. C., and Olde, B. A. (2003). How does one know whether a person understands a device? The quality of the questions the person asks when the device breaks down. *Journal of Educational Psychology, 95,* 524–36. https://doi:10.1037/0022-0663.95.3.524

Greif, M. L., Kemler Nelson, D. G., Keil, F. C., and Gutierrez, F. (2006). What do children want to know about animals and artifacts? Domain-specific requests for information. *Psychological Science, 17,* 455–9. https://doi:10.1111/j.1467-9280.2006.01727.x

Gutiérrez, K. D., and Rogoff, B. (2003). Cultural ways of learning: Individual traits or repertoires of practice. *Educational Researcher, 32,* 19–25. https://doi:10.3102/0013189x032005019

Henrich, J., Heine, S. J., and Norenzayan, A. (2010). The weirdest people in the world? *Behavioral and Brain Sciences, 33,* 61–83. https://doi:10.2139/ssrn.1601785

Hickling, A. K., and Wellman, H. M. (2001). The emergence of children's causal explanations and theories: Evidence from everyday conversation. *Developmental Psychology, 37,* 668–83. https://doi:10.1037//0012-1649.37.5.668

King, A. (1990). Enhancing peer interaction and learning in the classroom through reciprocal questioning. *American Educational Research Journal, 27,* 664–87. https://doi:10.3102/00028312027004664

  (1992). Comparison of self-questioning, summarizing, and notetaking-review as strategies for learning from lectures. *American Educational Research Journal, 29,* 303–23. https://doi:10.3102/00028312029002303

Kishimoto, T., Shizawa, Y., Yasuda, J., Hinobayashi, T., and Minami, T. (2007). Do pointing gestures by infants provoke comments from adults? *Infant Behavior and Development, 30,* 562–67. https://doi:10.1016/j.infbeh.2007.04.001

Kovács, Á. M., Tauzin, T., Téglás, E., Gergely, G., and Csibra, G. (2014). Pointing as epistemic request: 12-month-olds point to receive new information. *Infancy, 19,* 543–57. https://doi:10.1111/infa.12060

Kruger, J., and Dunning, D. (1999). Unskilled and unaware of it: How difficulties in recognizing one's own incompetence lead to inflated self-assessments. *Journal of Personality and Social Psychology, 77,* 1121–34. https://doi:10.1037//0022-3514.77.6.1121

Kurkul, K. E., and Corriveau, K. H. (2017). question, explanation, follow-up: A mechanism for learning from others? *Child Development, 89,* 280–94. https://doi:10.1111/cdev.12726

Legare, C. H., and Lombrozo, T. (2014). Selective effects of explanation on learning during early childhood. *Journal of Experimental Child Psychology, 126,* 198–212. https://doi:10.1016/j.jecp.2014.03.001

Legare, C. H., Mills, C. M., Souza, A. L., Plummer, L. E., and Yasskin, R. (2013). The use of questions as problem-solving strategies during early childhood. *Journal of Experimental Child Psychology, 114,* 63–76. https://doi:10.1016/j.jecp.2012.07.002

Lucca, K., and Wilbourn, M. P. (2016). Communicating to learn: Infants' pointing gestures result in optimal learning. *Child Development*, *89*, 941–60. https://doi:10.1111/cdev.12707

Mills, C. M., and Landrum, A. R. (2016). Learning who knows what: Children adjust their inquiry to gather information from others. *Frontiers in Psychology*, *7*. https://doi:10.3389/fpsyg.2016.00951

Mills, C. M., Legare, C. H., Bills, M., and Mejias, C. (2010). Preschoolers use questions as a tool to acquire knowledge from different sources. *Journal of Cognition and Development*, *11*, 533–60. https://doi:10.1080/15248372 .2010.516419

Mills, C. M., Legare, C. H., Grant, M. G., and Landrum, A. R. (2011). Determining who to question, what to ask, and how much information to ask for: The development of inquiry in young children. *Journal of Experimental Child Psychology*, *110*, 539–60. https://doi:10.1016/j.jecp.2011.06.003

Mosher, F. A., and Hornsby, J. R. (1966). On asking questions. In J. S. Bruner, R. R. Olver, T. M. Greenfield, J. R. Hornsby, H. J. Kenney, and M. Maccoby (eds.). *Studies in cognitive growth* (pp.86–102). New York: Wiley.

Ninio, A. and Snow, C. E. (1996). *Pragmatic development*. Boulder, CO: Westview Press.

Nielsen, M., Haun, D., Kärtner, J., and Legare, C. H. (2017). The persistent sampling bias in developmental psychology: A call to action. *Journal of Experimental Child Psychology*, *162*, 31–8. https://doi:10.1016/j .jecp.2017.04.017

Robinson, E. J., Butterfill, S. A., and Nurmsoo, E. (2011). Gaining knowledge via other minds: Children's flexible trust in others as sources of information. *British Journal of Developmental Psychology*, *29*, 961–80. https://doi:10.1111/ j.2044-835x.2011.02036.x

Ronfard, S., Bartz, D., Cheng, L., Chen, X., and Harris, P. L. (2017). Children's developing ideas about knowledge and its acquisition. *Advances in Child Development and Behavior*. Advance online publication. https://doi:10.1016 /bs.acdb.2017.10.005

Ronfard, S., Zambrana, I. M., Hermansen, T. K., and Kelemen, D. (2018). Question-asking in childhood: A review of the literature and a framework for understanding its development. *Developmental Review*, *49*, 101–20. https:// doi:10.1016/j.dr.2018.05.002

Rosengren, K. S., Miller, P. J., Gutiérrez, I. T., et al. (2014). Children's understanding of death: Toward a contextualized and integrated account. *Monographs of the Society for Research in Child Development*, *79*, 1–141.

Rosenshine, B., Meister, C., and Chapman, S. (1996). Teaching students to generate questions: A review of the intervention studies. *Review of Educational Research*, *66*, 181–221. https://doi:10.3102/00346543066002181

Ruggeri, A., and Feufel, M. A. (2015). How basic-level objects facilitate question-asking in a categorization task. *Frontiers in Psychology*, *6*. https://doi:10 .3389/fpsyg.2015.00918

Ruggeri, A., and Lombrozo, T. (2015). Children adapt their questions to achieve efficient search. *Cognition, 143*, 203–16. https://doi:10.1016/j.cognition.2015.07.004

Ruggeri, A., Lombrozo, T., Griffiths, T. L., and Xu, F. (2016). Sources of developmental change in the efficiency of information search. *Developmental Psychology, 52*, 2159–73. https://doi:10.1037/dev0000240

Ruggeri, A., Sim, Z. L., and Xu, F. (2017). "Why is Toma late to school again?" Preschoolers identify the most informative questions. *Developmental Psychology, 53*, 1620–32. https://doi:10.1037/dev0000340

Shafto, P., Goodman, N. D., and Griffiths, T. L. (2014). A rational account of pedagogical reasoning: Teaching by, and learning from, examples. *Cognitive Psychology, 71*, 55–89. https://doi:10.1016/j.cogpsych.2013.12.004

Tizard, B., and Hughes, M. (1984). *Young children learning*. London: Fontana.

Wellman, H. M., Song, J. H., and Peskin-Shepherd, H. (2017). Children's early awareness of comprehension as evident in their spontaneous corrections of speech errors. *Child Development, 90*, 196–209. https://doi:10.1111/cdev.12862

Wu, Z., and Gros-Louis, J. (2014). Infants' prelinguistic communicative acts and maternal responses: Relations to linguistic development. *First Language, 34*, 72–90. https://doi:10.1177/0142723714521925

Yu, Y., Landrum, A. R., Bonawitz, E., and Shafto, P. (2018). Questioning supports effective transmission of knowledge and increased exploratory learning in pre-kindergarten children. *Developmental Science*. Advance online publication. https://doi:10.1111/desc.12696

# Index

active helping, of infants and toddlers, 10
active learning
    of children, 89
    of infants, 89, 93–94
    performance, working memory and,
        131–132
    through question-asking, 123–124
adaptiveness, 23–24
    ecological learning and, 126–128
    question-asking efficiency and, 130, 136
    social, physical environment connection
        and, 183
adolescents
    argument skills support by, 239
    inquiry learning studies of, 236–237
    questions from, 232
adults
    comprehension and repair signals for, 44
    constraint-seeking questions of, 128
    conversational glitch and clarifying ques-
        tions, 46
    expectancy violations of, 92
    infants learning environments and, 93–95
    pointing not universal in, 106
    questions posing and response by, 3
    reliable information for infants by, 94
affective attitudes, 2–3
    of anger, 13
    basic, 7
    of curiosity, 13
    of fear, 13
affective mental states, 42
American Samoa, 193–194
anger
    as affective attitude, 13
    motivation and, 13
animals, 306
    curiosity and, 8, 14–15
    knowledge, children concept
        development of, 167–170
    metacognitive awareness of, 17
    motivation and, 7–8

    as natural kind, 167
    relevant knowledge in domain of,
        167, 168
    reward-based learning and, 14–15
anticipatory looking, of infants and
    toddlers, 10
appraisal mechanisms
    emotions and, 23–24
    relevance and, 23
arguments
    dialogic engagement for skills in,
        240–241
    education environment fostering of, 4
    evidence and, 239
    inquiry and learning in, 238–241
    Q&A format in, 239–240
    skills, adolescent development of, 239
asymmetrical knowledge, caregiver and,
    40–41
attention
    information gain through selective, 90–91
    joint-attention behaviors, 13–14
attentional scaffolding, 66
attentional search, 7
authority relations, 200
automation, in education, 233
auxiliary questions, 219, 227
awareness. *See also* metacognitive awareness
    of belief and ignorance, 15–16, 39

basic affective attitudes, 7
behavior, observation of own, 9
Behavior Outlook Norwegian
    Developmental Study (BONDS), 217
belief, 24. *See also* false belief
    children awareness of, 15–16, 39
    empty belief files and, 11, 12
    I think statements and, 18
    ignorance awareness and, 15
    metacognitive awareness and, 16
    motivation and, 7–8, 13
    negative question-answering and, 19–20